Introduction to Decision Analysis

Third Edition

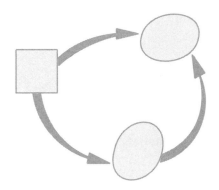

Introduction to Decision Analysis

Third Edition

A Practitioner's Guide to Improving Decision Quality

David C. Skinner

Probabilistic Publishing

Editor: Paul Wicker
Layout: Dave and Debbie Charlesworth
Graphics: Dave Charlesworth

Edition History:

First Edition, First printing: April 1995
First Edition, Second printing: June 1996
Second Edition, First printing: April 1999
Second Edition, Second printing: February 2001
Third Edition, First printing: January 2009
Third Edition, Second printing: July 2009

The cases and examples presented in this book are purely fictional. Any resemblance to actual people or companies is purely coincidental.

This book was written, edited, and formatted using Apple MacIntosh computers. The copy was originally produced using Microsoft Word; pages were composed with Adobe Framemaker, and cover and graphics were produced using Adobe Illustrator.

DATA® and/or TreeAge Pro® screen shots used with permission from TreeAge Software. DATA® and TreeAge Pro® are registered trademarks of TreeAge Software. Excerpts from the book "A Quest for Certainty" used with permission from SilverWare Software Company. Microsoft® is a registered trademark of Microsoft Corporation. Windows® and Excel® are trademarks of Microsoft Corporation. Lotus 1-2-3® is a registered trademark of Lotus Development Corporation. Apple and Macintosh are registered trademarks of Apple Computer Company.

Contact Information:

Probabilistic Publishing, 1702 Hodge Lake Ln, Sugar Land, TX 77478.
FL number: 352-338-1789   TX number: 281-277-4006
e-mail: dave@decisions-books.com or charledl@aol.com
www.decisions-books.com

Written, designed and printed in the United States of America.
Library of Congress Catalog Card Number: 2009922860
ISBN (13-digit): 978-0-9647938-6-6, ISBN (10-digit): 0-9647938-6-5

To my Grandfather C.M. Keathly, for giving me the understanding of value,

To all who struggle with making difficult decisions, and

To my wife, Kristen Hopper, for her consistent encouragement and inspiration.

Preface to the Second Edition

This book will introduce you to a new way of thinking. When making difficult decisions in a complex and uncertain environment, it is essential to identify important characteristics and uncertainties affecting the problem so you can develop a clear and compelling course of action. This book shows you how to correctly structure a problem, understand the inputs and outputs of evaluation, and gain insight into the appropriate course of action.

The idea for this book came when I was teaching a group of executives in 1992. They asked what book I would recommend for them to use as a reference on the decision analysis process. While there are many good books on decision analysis, most focus on theoretical and mathematical aspects of decision analysis – not decision consulting. I decided to write a book that would incorporate enough of the theoretical and mathematical aspects to provide a good understanding of decision analysis – but from a consultant's viewpoint.

My goal in writing this book was to develop a format that could be used for corporate training as well as for final year undergraduates or beginning graduate students in management. We present the most recent decision analysis techniques at a level understandable by anyone with a background in simple mathematics.

This book will help you start to learn decision analysis. I always give my students this caveat: don't try to tackle your hardest problem first. Start with a simple problem that is not convoluted. Use the process to solve the problem in detail. By solving simple problems first, you will gain a better and more solid understanding of decision analysis.

Since the first edition of this book was published, decision analysis has become more widespread in the corporate landscape. Much of this increased acceptance has come from companies like General Motors, Conoco, and Chevron. However, I am beginning to see two forms of decision analysis emerge – the technical and the cultural. From the early examples (like oil wildcatting) to more recent applications (like information technology), decision analysis has been considered by many to be another technical analysis. While no one would dispute the valuable insights and the value of the information which can only come from decision analysis, the cultural aspects have for the most part been ignored. What is encouraging now is to see companies embrace decision analysis as the standard way to make decisions! By making decision analysis a company practice, many of the myths and baggage that have accompanied it are now disappearing. Organizations are moving from command and control cultures to distributed decision making. These companies are seeing tremendous results – for example, Conoco saw $1 billion in value created using "DA" in 1996![1]

I believe this is still the only book written by a practitioner for a practitioner. What this means to you is that the book presents and discusses concepts using real world business cases. The book will take you step by step through the decision analysis process. I have filled the book with helpful tips and tools, and I have included stories of what has worked well and what has not.

---

[1] Decision Analysis Affinity Group (DAAG) conference, 1998

Acknowledgments from the Second Edition

This book could not have happened without the help, inspiration, and dedication of many people. I would like to first thank my wife, Kristen, for enduring the many late nights and weekends it took to write this book, and my students, who through curiosity and desire have fine tuned the material presented in this book. I also must thank my clients for providing me with interesting and challenging projects which often tested my knowledge and opened new avenues of thinking; to them I owe a sincere thanks. I also want to acknowledge the many contributions and comments given by friends and colleagues – Frank Rodd, Lisa Eisele, Léonard Bertrand, and David and Debbie Charlesworth.

Thanks to Ken Grech and Dan Ash for their comments on the manuscript and to Sally Grech for her encouragement with the project. Thanks to John Lynn for his excellent comments on the manuscript.

Of course, this book would not be possible if it were not for the many great minds that have contributed to the science and laid the foundation for the methodology presented in this book. In particular, I owe a sincere thanks to Ron Howard for influencing my thinking on this subject more than any other person.

David C. Skinner
January, 1999

Perspectives for the Third Edition

Since the Second Edition was published in 1999, the world has changed considerably but decision analysis continues to provide huge benefits for many companies who are using it. Some companies who had early success with decision analysis have back-tracked and have had corresponding degradation of financial performance. For many companies, however, decision analysis has been integrated into the normal business processes and has become a way of conducting business every day.

When Dave Charlesworth and I first discussed the idea of a decision analysis ("DA") book written from the viewpoint of a DA practitioner, we thought the book would be successful. However, we could not have predicted that several thousand copies would be sold over the next 10 years. More gratifying even than the sales is that I have observed that many of the books are on people's bookshelves and are well-worn, with yellow "sticky" notes hanging out the side! The book was designed to be a useful reference, and it has been fulfilling that purpose.

The second edition was not designed with academic usage in mind, however, several professors have used it successfully for executive MBA programs. Their feedback has been incorporated into this edition.

I'm very grateful to my clients, DSI colleagues, the DA community, and my friends and family for the encouragement and support that they have provided since the Second Edition was published ten years ago. I'd also like to thank Paul Wicker for his thorough and professional editing and Dave and Debbie Charlesworth for their consistent support with the publication. If you have comments, please e-mail me at dcskinner@decisionstrategies.com.

David C. Skinner
January, 2009

Comments and Reviews from the Second Edition

"Don't make another decision until you read this book!" ---Ken Grech, Integration and Test Department Manager for Lockheed-Martin, Management and Data Systems.

"This book will revolutionize your thinking." ---JT Lewellen, VP Marketing, Turn-Key Specialists, Inc.

"Written in the same style as the 'For Dummies' series, this book is for anyone who wants to start using decision analysis techniques right away!" ---James Mitchell, Leader, Decision Processes, Trans-Canada Pipelines, Ltd.

"Very readable...an excellent way to get started in decision analysis." ---Robert L. Cook, Technology Manager, Americas, Engineering Polymers, DuPont Co.

"Fabulous book! Practical approach to decision analysis that anyone can understand." ---Ellen Coopersmith, Director of Decision and Risk Analysis, Conoco, Inc.

"David's book is one of my best "working" books. I regularly use it to help my company come to closure on complex decisions. David has used his significant industry experience to develop a decision analysis methodology that is clear, that is absent of jargon, and that works even for new DA practitioners." --- Donald Zmick, Senior Analyst, Murphy Oil Corporation

"One of the best books on the market, for this topic! David's broad experience and ease of explanation contributes to this being a top choice as a teaching reference. 'Introduction to Decision Analysis' contains the appropriate level of detail for those interested in going beyond the basics, while being easily understandable for those that are just learning about decision management. Over 200 copies of this book reside on the bookshelves of individuals within our company...and I would venture that none of them are collecting dust!" ---Dewey McLemore, ChevronTexaco

"David offers us an accessible yet amazingly complete and practical book on decision-making. The presentation is very clear and understandable. The contents are relevant to real business situations. The examples are easy to translate to your real life. This is your first introduction and permanent reference to decision analysis. A bible for decision analysts as well as decision makers." ---Marc Desomer, Novartis

Publisher's Note

We are very pleased to be able to offer a Third Edition of David Skinner's classic book, *Introduction to Decision Analysis*. This edition has been several years in the making – Paul Wicker, David Skinner, and Probabilistic Publishing started working on this edition over three years ago. We very much appreciate Paul's steady and consistent editorial work and patience working on the project.

We appreciate the many comments and suggestions we received on the Second Edition. John Lynn from DuPont was especially thorough and constructive with his comments.

Thank you Mike and Debbie Stallsworth for your work proofing the final text.

I am grateful to the "old guard" DSI consultants (and former consultants) who have done so much to advance DA in practice and practical application and who regularly used the Second Edition as part of their tool kit (and who have been so much fun to work with) [in random order, and please forgive me if I have left anybody out]: Nick Martino, Alexa Bargmann, James Mitchell, Bob deWolff, Rob Brown, Mike Stallsworth, Stefan Choquette, Joel Busby, Bill Haskett, OJ Sanchez, Pat Leach, Paul Wicker, Lisa Eisele, Kevin Carpenter, Lisa Carpenter, Yemo Fashola, Eric Johnson, Jerry Lieberman, Michael Morgan, Steve Anderson, Fred Krumm, Sean Hester, and last but not least the guy who taught me more about decision analysis than anyone else (and very patiently I must add), Gary Bush.

And thank you DAAG "tribal elders" and speakers. It has been very rewarding to be able to attend DAAG conferences and talk with so many DA professionals through the years.

Most of all, I'm very appreciative of David Skinner's vision and his initial suggestion that Debbie and I start our publishing business. It was David's vision to make available resources for those who desire to learn to become DA practitioners and his hard work and persistence through the years that have enabled this work to be presented.

And thank you (once again) Tom Sciance for getting us interested in decision analysis in the first place!

If you do find any potential questions or if you have comments about the book, please send me an e-mail at dave@decisions-books.com or charledl@aol.com. Also, please check our web site, www.decisions-books.com, as we'll post items of interest to the decision analysis community from time to time.

Dave Charlesworth
January, 2009
Sugar Land, TX

Table of Contents

1

Introduction

The significant problems we face cannot be solved at the same level of thinking we were at when we created them.

–Albert Einstein

Decisions are the foundations of our lives, both professionally and personally. Some decisions are good, some are brilliant, and some are pure disasters. Decisions are made consciously and unconsciously, emotionally and analytically, but as a whole they provide the means by which we meet the challenges of life. In fact, you can trace all of your accomplishments and failures back to the decisions you have made. Each day you make hundreds of decisions that impact your life, but most are simple and the choice is obvious. You are hungry, so you decide to eat. The car is running low on gas, so you find a gas station and fill up (although many people make this decision harder by searching endlessly for the cheapest gas). However, most of the tough decisions you face are not simple but are complex and full of uncertainty. These decisions do not have easy choices and the outcomes often affect more than just you. Making the best decisions possible in these cases is critical to meeting your personal and professional goals and the goals of the companies and organizations for which you work.

1.1 My Most Difficult Decision

Let me tell you about the hardest decision I have ever made. In September of 1998, I was working on an oil joint venture project in Venezuela when I received a phone call from a good friend that my wife (31 years old and an aerobics instructor in very good physical condition) was in the hospital. My friend had no other information beyond the hospital phone number. I can tell you that this is the worst kind of phone call to receive!

I quickly called the hospital, and after several minutes of arguing with the front desk, I was put through to my wife's doctor in the Emergency Room. The doctor informed me that my wife was having a massive stroke and that her prospects were not good. I asked about her immediate condition and what course of treatment they were proposing. He informed me that the MRI scan indicated about 40% of the right side of her brain was affected by the stroke and she was completely paralyzed on her left side.

In the background, I could hear my wife arguing with the nurses and pleading with them to let her go home. I spoke with her for a few minutes to calm her down, and then the doctors and I began discussing the few treatment options available. They told me that given the amount of the brain affected, they did not know if she would live through the night. Often in these cases, the brain swells uncontrollably, crushes the brain stem (which controls all the involuntary functions), and you die. This is what would have happened without some sort of intervention.

As luck (providence?) would have it, my wife was brought to a teaching hospital with a world famous stroke team that was trying a new experimental therapy. In this new therapy, they cool the body down to put it into a hypothermic state. They hoped that this would give the body time to adjust to the trauma and help prevent further brain swelling. I asked about the success rate for this treatment, and the answer was not compelling. The doctor said, "She will be the fourth person in the world to receive this treatment protocol." When prompted about the other three patients, he replied that two had died from complications and one was severely paralyzed. This was not what I wanted to hear! I must admit that by now the shock was starting to set in and I was not doing well.

The other available treatment was to perform a craniotomy where they remove a portion of the skullcap to allow the brain to expand outside the skull. This did not sound like a great alternative either! At this point, I was shocked, confused, and concerned about my wife's treatment options. Adding to the anxiety of the moment was the fact that the treatment decision had to be made immediately. Time was of the essence.

A difficult decision...

I began to interview the doctor about the two treatment options. I needed more information about the probability of success, further complications, and the likely resulting quality of life. From experience, I knew that doctors are not always good at representing the probability of success for treatments so I began exploring the factors that contributed to the deaths and paralysis of the other three patients. I discovered that two of the patients had died from pneumonia as a complication from the hypothermic state. All three of the previous patients were considerably older than my wife and had other health problems. My wife was in extremely good health and actually had the stroke while teaching an aerobics class. The doctor did not feel that the other patients were a good indicator of my wife's situation.

Even though my wife was in good health, there was still a reasonable chance that this treatment would not work and could create additional life threatening complications. As I worked through these assessments with the doctor, I was able to construct a decision tree of the options (Figure 1.1) and develop an understanding of the various associated outcomes. Then I assessed the probability of occurrence for each of the outcomes and made my decision. The analysis showed a greater chance for a high quality of life coming from the hypothermic treatment. That is what I chose. Without the structured approach to decision making and the careful consideration of the various options and outcomes, I would not have had clarity of action and would probably have chosen the craniotomy treatment.

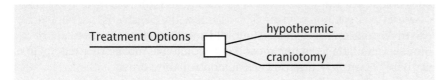

Figure 1.1 Experimental Treatment Options

It is now ten years later and I am happy to tell you that she is doing very well and has a good quality of life. The doctors are absolutely amazed at her progress and abilities and have begun having her speak at various stroke and heart association programs. And, in October 2004, my wife and I had our first child, Makenzie Elizabeth.

I tell this story to illustrate that decision making is crucial to everyone's life and well-being, but rarely is decision making discussed or taught. Most people just assume that decision making is a learned or inherited skill. But anyone's abilities can be improved by using a structured approach to thinking about difficult problems and developing clear and compelling courses of action. It is also important to understand that this process can work for personal as well as business decisions, and it can be done quickly with the right amount of knowledge and insight. As you read through this book, think of situations where using a structured approach would have helped you better understand and choose the right decision option.

1.2 Making Tough Decisions is Not Easy

In making tough decisions do you find that you are uncomfortable with the choices, the outcomes, and the consequences? Often people deal with these difficult decisions by procrastinating or over analyzing the situation in the hopes that the right choice will reveal itself or the decision will go away or be made for you. Others make quick intuitive decisions that lack clarity of understanding and consistency of thought. With either approach the results are often dependent upon luck, and the outcomes are usually less than desired.

Decision making is a uniquely human skill that has been in evidence since the beginning of time. Just read through the Bible, and you will come across great stories of decisions that have changed the world. There are now even management books based on the Bible (*Jesus CEO* and *The Leadership Wisdom of Jesus*), which apply biblical approaches and parables to today's business problems.

Making decisions: a uniquely human skill

While decision making is uniquely human, we must be able to learn how to improve our skills as we all have many important and tough decisions facing us each day. But few of us ever receive any kind of training or education in this important skill. Most people are even unaware of how they make decisions. This leaves us to learn from experience, which is often costly and usually ineffective in dealing with rare and complex decisions. How often do you buy a new house, deal with life or death treatment options, change careers, or start a new business?

Along with the decisions we make are traps into which we can fall. There is a great book written by Edward Russo and Paul Schoemaker called *Decision Traps*.[1] In this book, the authors present several decades of research that shows that most decision makers make the same kinds of errors. These errors include:

Common "Decision Traps" from Russo and Schoemaker

- not understanding the crux of the issue,
- solving the wrong problem,
- being unduly influenced by others,
- having overconfidence in their own judgments,
- relying too heavily on rules of thumb,
- thinking they can keep everything straight in their heads,
- having a group failure,
- not keeping track of decisions or failing to use the information from past decisions, and
- failing to audit the decision process.

I can tell you that I was keenly aware of these traps when dealing with the doctors working on my wife. I wanted to make sure that they were not being overconfident in their own abilities and that they were not unduly influencing me with their frame of reference for treatment options.

The track record of unstructured decision making

How would you rate your own decision track record? How many decisions have you made that worked out as planned or even stayed in place for a reasonable period of time?

In a recent study done by Paul Nutt at the London Business School, he found that fewer than 40% of business decisions made without a structured collaborative decision process are successful (his criterion for success was the decision stayed in place for at least two years).[2]

In addition, a survey by the American Management Association also found that most business people only make the right decision about 50% of the time. So what does this empirical evidence tell us? We have considerable room for improvement and there is a better way to make decisions.

Separate the Decision from the Decision Process

We all make many different decisions each day; some are tough, others are not. In each case we use a process for making the decision, but not always the same process. This is what usually impedes learning from mis-

---

[1] Edward Russo and Paul Schoemaker, *Decision Traps – The Ten Barriers to Brilliant Decision-Making & How to Overcome Them*, Simon & Schuster, 1989.

[2] Paul Nutt, London Business School, Business Strategy Review 1997, Volume 8, Issue 4, pages 44-52.

takes and successes. While there may not be any similarities in the circumstances of the decisions you make, there should be a consistency in how you decide. However, this does not mean that every decision requires the same level of thought or analytical rigor.

An effective decision process should provide the decision maker with the ability to:

- Identify the real problem,
- Clearly understand the goals and objectives,
- Develop unique and compelling alternatives,
- Discover what is important,
- Adequately deal with uncertainty and ambiguity,
- Make appropriate trade-offs of risk and value, and
- Provide the clarity to act with confidence.

Characteristics of an effective decision-making process

Each of the characteristics described above is necessary for making simple decisions to complicated strategic decisions. What tends to vary from decision to decision is the time and effort required to satisfy each characteristic. Each time you apply the process, you will become better at understanding the level of effort required and you will become more efficient in its use.

This book provides a proven, structured process for making both simple and complex decisions. The process is called decision analysis, and it can help you understand how to decide while not telling you what to decide. This is an important concept that should not go unnoticed. While decision theory was a somewhat abstract mathematical discipline used to arrive at an optimal decision, it has evolved into a set of frameworks for thinking that enables different perspectives on the problem to be brought together and new insights to be developed.[3]

Advantages of a structured process

The decision analysis process augments your current way of thinking by providing a structured approach that does not ignore your intuition, hunches, or gut feelings. In contrast, decision analysis actually provides a means of incorporating your subjective feelings and beliefs into the analysis so that both the tangible and intangible benefits can be analyzed. The process accomplishes this by breaking down the problem into a set of smaller problems which can be handled more efficiently and effectively. After resolving these smaller problems using both objective and subjective information, the process provides a structured means of recombining the various smaller problems into a coherent and compelling course of action. Decision analysis is a "prescriptive approach designed for normally intelligent people who want to think hard and systematically about some important real problems."[4] This does not mean that tough decisions will now be

---

[3] L. D. Phillips, Decision analysis in the 1990's, in A. Shahini and R Stainton *Tutorial Papers in Operational Research 1989*, Operations Research Society.

[4] R. Keeney and H. Raiffa, *Decisions with Multiple Objectives*, Wiley, 1976.

easy. Tough decisions are tough because of the complexity and consequences involved, but the complexity can be managed in a way that provides clear and compelling action.

Making Decisions Using Subjective Judgment

Decision analysis, in contrast with other analytical processes, does not disregard the need for information and subjective data from experts. While many processes will only work with large sets of historical data, decision analysis can easily provide the necessary insights for clear and compelling action when information is sketchy or non-existent.

This is because decision analysis actually requires using subjective inputs from subject matter experts to be effective. This reliance on subjective data usually creates intense debates between those with a frequentist

Egghead Software – Snatching Defeat from the Jaws of Victory

Egghead Software was founded 1984 on the premise of selling software in its stores. Here is the chronology of events surrounding the company's rise and fall:

- 1991: Egghead Software was a regional retailer with six store locations.
- 1996: Egghead began selling software online. At the time, it did not expect the Internet sales to cannibalize sales at its retail sites.
- 1997: Feeling the competition from companies such as Dell and Gateway, Egghead continued to withdraw from the retail market and push further into the e-commerce. Egghead added "virtual salespeople" and other features to its website to attempt to bolster activity. Egghead improved its balance sheet for the first quarter of 1997 and reported a loss of "only" $3.7 million versus much higher losses in the same period of 1996. Egghead attributed the improvement from cost savings from store closings.
- 1998: Egghead was down to only 80 stores when they made the strategic decision to withdraw completely from the "bricks and mortar" market and closed all of the remaining locations.
- 1999: Egghead changed its name to Egghead.com and merged with e-auction site Onsale. The new company offered new and surplus computer products, consumer electronics, sporting goods, and vacation packages as well as close-out and surplus goods through online auctions. The company predicted a 45 to 50 percent increase in revenue in 2000 and profitability by the year 2002. Both companies felt that competition with Amazon.com was a major factor that precipitated the merger.
- 2000: Fourth quarter sales were down 40 percent from fourth quarter sales in 1999.
- 2001: In August, Egghead.com filed for Chapter 11 bankruptcy. In November, Amazon.com purchased the online assets of Egghead.com for $6.1 million.

At its zenith, Egghead had revenues of over $700 million per year and over 280 locations.

1. Does it appear that Egghead made poor decisions or was Egghead the victim of bad outcomes?

2. What hybrid alternatives could Egghead have tried instead of the "all or nothing" e-commerce strategy?

point of view and those with a Bayesian point of view. I will discuss this in more detail in Chapter 8. But as decision making is a human science and not a mere calculation as many would like, we must use our judgment, as imperfect as it may be, to help us make the best decision possible.

Much research has been done over the past several decades on the validity and usefulness of subjective judgments. This work has focused on the various biases and heuristics that come into play as people are asked to provide assessments of future events. I will discuss these biases in more detail in Chapter 10. By understanding these biases and working to overcome and counteract them, decision making can be dramatically improved as well as decision maker confidence in the outcomes.

1.3 What is Decision Analysis?

The term decision analysis was coined by Stanford professor Ronald A. Howard some thirty years ago in a paper titled "Decision Analysis: Applied Decision Theory." You may also see references in the literature to the term "decision and risk analysis," which has the same meaning as decision analysis in this book. While the term decision analysis has been applied to both normative and descriptive processes, this book will emphasize the normative process.

*Decision analysis is divided into two distinct disciplines: normative theory and descriptive theory. **Normative theory** describes how people should make decisions, while **descriptive theory** tries to explain how people actually make decisions.*

Normative and descriptive theory

Decision analysis is more than a tool—it is a methodology. It provides a means for dialog between the decision maker and the project team. This dialog brings uncertainties, concerns, expectations, assumptions and meanings into the open to be clarified. Without this clarity and a means to obtain it, any analysis is left to the supposition and predisposition of its interpreters. This dialog also ensures the right problem gets solved. One of the most common mistakes is working on the wrong problem. While this may seem difficult to believe, without clarity of the decision problem, many teams answer the wrong question for the decision maker.

Decision analysis adds clarity

***Decision analysis** is a methodology and set of probabilistic frameworks for facilitating high quality, logical discussions which illuminate difficult decisions and lead to clear and compelling action by the decision maker.*

Decision analysis defined

Decision analysis is an iterative process of gaining insight and promoting creative alternatives to help decision makers make better decisions (See Figure 1.2). This iterative process involves uncovering key factors or uncertainties that affect the situation and understanding how they affect the situation. Decision analysis allows you to concentrate on what is important rather than refining what is already known and to know when to stop analyzing and make the decision. To that end, decision analysis uses

*Figure 1.2
Decision
Analysis
Process*

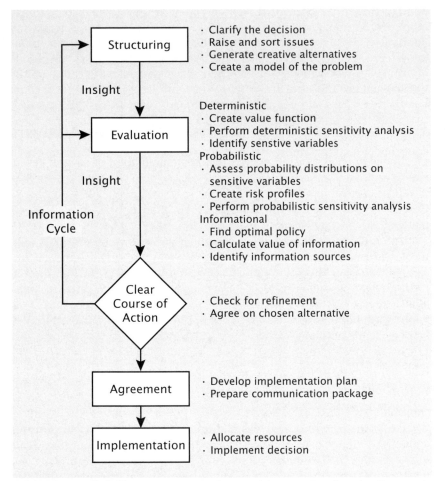

subjective probability assessments from subject matter (content) experts to obtain the likelihood of future events. This information is integrated with the decision maker's preferences and values to form a basis for the course of action.

*Decision
analysis as
integration*
　　　Decision analysis logically integrates what you value, what you can do, and what you know into a decision model (a representation) that accurately and concisely portrays the real problem. Once this model has been created, it can be evaluated to provide the decision maker with:

- A sensitivity analysis showing which uncertainties are key to the decision and how much they can change the overall value.
- The expected value (probability weighted average) of each alternative as well as a complete risk profile of the alternatives.
- The value of gathering additional information to reduce the uncertainty about various outcomes.
- A graphical model of the problem, which facilitates communication with all interested parties.
- The optimal policy for the decision, which indicates the best course of action if the decision must be made now.

Is Decision Analysis is a New Method of Cost-Benefit Analysis?

Decision analysis is not cost-benefit analysis. Cost-benefit analysis is focused on the willingness to pay, whereas decision analysis is focused on the value of the alternative course of action.

1.4 The Origins of Decision Analysis

Decision analysis is, in many ways, the culmination of several centuries of probability theory development. During the 1700's, two scientists developed probability theory with the objective of proving the existence of God. Reverend Thomas Bayes (an English Presbyterian minister, mathematician, and a Royal Fellow) and Abraham de Moivre (a French-born mathematician and Royal Fellow) both pursued the mathematical proof of the existence of God.

De Moivre in his book The Doctrine of Chances published in 1718 put forth the relative frequency concept of probability. Simply stated, the probability (p) approaches a specified value as the number of trials (n) approaches infinity. This is often referred to as the empirical approach to probability since it is based on data accumulated from a number of trials. The problem with De Moivre's method is the use of infinite trials to determine a probability. Bayes took a different approach.

Frequency approach to statistics

Bayes stated the problem as: *Given the number of times in which an unknown event has happened and failed, the probability of its happening in a single trial lies somewhere between any two degrees of probability that can be named.* Bayes' reasoning led to: "If nothing is known concerning an event but that it has happened r times and failed q times in $r + q$ or n trials, and from hence I guess the probability of it happening in a single trial lies between $r/n+z$ and $r/n-z$."[5] What Bayes did was to reverse the traditional flow of thought. Instead of considering the result from a given state, he thought about what state would cause a given result. Bayes' argument was that regulations in nature, not irregularities of chance, caused the concurrence of order. Bayes' work provides the basis for determining the value of information, which will be discussed in Chapter 11.

Bayesian approach to statistics

About the same time, Daniel Bernoulli (a Swiss mathematician who also developed the foundation work of fluid mechanics) developed the idea that when making a decision you should incorporate the likelihood of the possible outcomes and be able to state the relative desirability of those outcomes. Bernoulli's work helped to lay the groundwork for how decisions could be analyzed.

Bernoulli's approach

---

[5] Thomas Bayes, "An Essay Towards Solving a Problem in the Doctrine of Chances." *Philosophical Transactions of the Royal Society* 53 (1763): 370–418.

Rational decision making expanded

John von Neumann and Oscar Morgenstern published *Theory of Games and Economic Behavior* in 1947. They explained through axioms that people will choose bets which maximize expected interval-scale utility. This theory showed how a rational person making decisions involving uncertainty should use utility rather than a willingness to pay. Use of a utility function rather than willingness to pay is a major distinction between decision analysis and cost-benefit analysis.

Modern decision analysis

Modern decision analysis was developed during the late 1950's, partly due to the work of Robert Schlaifer at Harvard. Howard Raiffa published *Decision Analysis* in 1968, which established decision analysis as a methodology with real applications. Ron Howard and Jim Matheson started the Decision Analysis Group at the Stanford Research Institute in 1965. This group worked on many interesting public and private problems, including the decision to seed hurricanes, power generation problems, and the Mars probe.

1.5 Why Use Decision Analysis?

The most logical answer to this question would be to consistently make good decisions. So, what is a good decision?

What is a good decision?

If you think back to when you were a child, how were your decisions judged? You were probably judged like most of us were – by your outcomes. How do you judge decisions today? In my courses, I always begin by asking the participants to write down what they think is a sure sign of a good decision. I receive responses like:

- Everyone agrees with it.
- I had a good outcome.
- It met my risk tolerance.
- I was sure about the outcome.
- That's how we have always done it.

Every decision we make involves some level of uncertainty, complexity, and ambiguity about the future outcome. Because of these influences on our outcomes, there is no direct link between a good decision and a good outcome.

Consider the situation of purchasing lottery tickets. Do you think purchasing a lottery ticket is a good decision? I think most of us would agree that, from an investment standpoint, purchasing a lottery ticket is not a good decision. But what if you win? Was it a good decision? The answer is still no – it was a lucky outcome.

We all prefer a lucky or good outcome to a good decision. However, we need a process that is more consistent than luck in making difficult decisions! By carefully understanding the problem, its potential outcomes, and the likelihood of those outcomes, we can choose the best course of action and lessen the chances of having an outcome that surprises us or that we dislike.

*A **good decision** is one that is logically consistent with our state of information and incorporates the possible alternatives with their associated probabilities and potential outcomes in accordance with our risk attitude.*

A "good decision" defined

Decision analysis provides the means to make informed rather than purely intuitive or "gut level" decisions. A person wanting more and more data to make a decision does *not* characterize an informed decision. An informed decision is one made with the knowledge of what is and *is not* important as well as an awareness of the consequences of that decision.

Albert Einstein said, "The significant problems we face cannot be solved at the same level of thinking we were at when we created them." Decision analysis does not take the place of judgment by the decision maker, but it does provide a *higher level of thinking* that allows for a better understanding of the decision. This does not mean that decision analysis will change your luck. Nothing can accomplish that task, but the correct application of decision analysis will allow you to assess the potential outcomes and consequences of any decision you make – helping you avoid surprises.

1.6 Applying Decision Analysis

Decision analysis can be applied to any decision that you make, but it is most beneficial to those decisions you deem significant and or difficult. Consider the decisions an executive of a major corporation must make. During his/her career, an executive will make decisions about new products and services, company or business unit restructuring, litigation, and many other situations that could affect hundreds or thousands of people. These decisions can greatly benefit from a structured and logical process like decision analysis.

I continue to be amazed at the number of companies now applying decision analysis. Since the publishing of the second edition, I have seen decision analysis become widely applied in various industries and government agencies for making all types of decisions. Oil companies such as ExxonMobil, Chevron, ConocoPhillips and others use it to determine leasing strategies, to evaluate acquisitions and divestitures, and to make general drilling decisions. Due to the very expensive and highly uncertain activities that create value for the pharmaceutical industry, they are also very active in applying decision analysis. A new drug can cost one billion dollars to develop! At other large companies like General Motors, Kodak, Boeing, Johnson & Johnson, Novartis, Eli Lilly, Delta, AT&T, and Exxon Chemical, decision analysis is being used to determine new product launches, to forecast sales, and to evaluate new ventures.

Many companies use decision analysis

Decision analysis provides a method for incorporating uncertainty explicitly and quantitatively into the decision problem. Therefore, any problem that has a level of uncertainty that obscures the best course of action or could cause you to change your decision is an obvious candidate.

*Figure 1.3
Decision
Analysis Flow
Diagram*

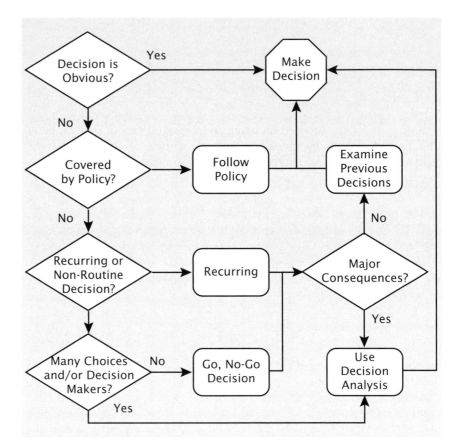

While most other analyses either completely ignore or put aside uncertainty until after the decision is made, decision analysis helps the decision maker to understand the state of knowledge in which the decision is being made, and helps him or her to work with limited information. The decision maker is then appropriately apprised of the situation and can choose the best course of action.

Besides uncertainty in a decision, there is also complexity. Complexity creates different problems than uncertainty as it can cloud immediate decisions with future decisions. Complexity can cause the decision maker to focus on the wrong problem or decision. Decision analysis helps to structure the complexity in a way that brings clarity to the problem.

There are situations where decision analysis may not be needed. I do not prescribe decision analysis as a hammer and every problem its nail. You should use your judgment and apply the process only when it will add value. A flow diagram that can be used as a practical guide for determining when to use decision analysis is presented in Figure 1.3.

1.7 The General Decision Analysis Process

There are several processes that are associated with decision analysis, and most that are based on the normative approach have a similar structure. While most of this book will focus on what I call the "general" decision analysis process, parts will be devoted to the process known as Integrated Decision Management® (IDM). IDM is different from the general process as it is focused on being an integrated part of the company's culture and, as such, becomes a "management" process. In my experience with client companies, I have found that too often the word "analysis" implies a one-off tool or box to check before getting approval. If decision analysis is to ever become truly useful in organizations, it needs to be the standard way of doing business, not a one-time activity.

For most of the published decision analysis processes, there is a common framework of:

A "generic" decision analysis process

- ■ identify the decision,
- ■ clarify the objectives,
- ■ create alternatives,
- ■ evaluate those alternatives,
- ■ choose the best alternative, and then
- ■ implement the alternative (see Figure 1.2).

By beginning with the decision to be analyzed, the decision maker must be able to clearly articulate to the project team both the situation and the particular question to be answered. This is not always easy for the decision maker and usually requires some facilitation by the decision analyst to clarify the real problem, not just the symptoms. Often teams work on solving the wrong problem simply because the decision maker could not clearly describe his or her question.

Once the decision has been clarified, the decision maker must also clearly communicate the objectives of the decision:

Understanding the objectives of the decision

- ■ Why are we doing this?
- ■ What do we expect to gain from it?
- ■ How will we know if we are successful?
- ■ What metrics will indicate we are on the right path?
- ■ And most importantly, what objective criteria will be used to trade-off one alternative against another? This must be answered before any evaluation work is performed so that you can minimize the analysis rework and keep an objective view of the alternatives.

For this part of the process, I like to use a purpose map or objectives hierarchy, which is based on work done by Ralph Keeney.[6] I think it is a good method to clearly identify the values and goals to be accomplished and to determine how those goals can be traded off among the various alterna-

---

[6] Ralph Keeney, *Value Focused Thinking: A Path to Creative Decision-making*, Harvard University Press, 1992.

tives. Keeney actually advocates doing this before trying to identify the real decision to be made. He believes that it is better to spend time understanding your goals before searching for decision alternatives to meet those goals.

Alternatives

The next step is to apply a creative approach to developing unique alternatives to evaluate. There are some common tools like strategy tables and brainstorming that people use to elicit decision options. The key is to develop a few clearly different alternatives that can be evaluated in a quantitative manner. I usually prefer teams to develop three or four good alternative strategies to take back to the decision maker for review. If you develop more, it often becomes confusing or the alternatives tend to be variations on a theme rather than unique.

Evaluation

In the evaluation step, models are developed which capture the essence of the problem and facilitate a dialog of the problem between the decision maker and project team. These models are commonly developed using influence diagrams and decision trees. These tools provide a means of both communication and analysis. During this stage, data is gathered from experts, and the likelihood of occurrence or probabilities is assessed. It is the gathering of these subjective judgments that sets decision analysis apart from most other analyses or decision making processes. Also during this stage, there are several tools such as sensitivity analysis, value of information, and sensitivity to probability that may be required to produce the insights needed to make a clear choice.

Once the evaluation step has been completed, the decision maker must determine the alternative that best meets his or her risk tolerance and the goals and objectives set forth in the beginning of the process. This again allows the decision maker to interject his or her preference into the process and to make a choice that best meets the decision maker's needs. If there is no rework to be done or additional choices to be evaluated, the decision should be made and implemented.

1.8 Understanding Some Basic Terminology

Before continuing, we need to establish clarity on the terms and concepts that will be developed in the following chapters. We will begin with the seven most common terms: decision, uncertainty, outcome, value, decision maker, probability and risk.

The following is my definition of a decision:

Decision defined

*A **decision** is a conscious course of action and allocation of resources to achieve a stated set of objectives.*

Consider the definition of a decision for a moment. Conscious means that you are thinking about what you are doing – you are acting deliberately. This is in contrast to involuntary actions, such as breathing.

Uncertainty defined

*An **uncertainty** is simply something that is unknown or not perfectly known.*

If someone asked you who would be the next Governor of Texas, you would be uncertain. This is an example of something that is *unknown*. If you were asked to name in order all of the previous Governors of Texas, unless you happen to be an expert on Texas history, you would again be uncertain. This second example is a case of not having perfect knowledge. The difference is that an unknown cannot be known until the event happens, while something that is not perfectly known can become known if the right information source can be found and if you can afford the cost of obtaining the information. This distinction causes much of the difficulty in making important decisions.

*An **outcome** is what actually happens—the result.*

Outcome defined

Outcomes are dependent upon the alternative chosen by the decision maker and result from that choice and the uncertainties impacting it. While decision analysis can help you make the best choice, it cannot guarantee a good outcome – no methodology or process can. Potential outcomes or possibilities are also sometimes referred to as outcomes.

*A **value** is something the decision maker wants and can trade-off.*

Value and value measure defined

*A **value measure** is how the decision maker compares values and can be anything that allows the decision maker to objectively evaluate one alternative versus another.*

As such, value measures should not be subjective in terms of criteria. This means you should use a formula or exacting method such as net present value rather than a measure that is open to interpretation.

A key factor in any decision is the decision maker (DM).

*A **decision maker** is anyone with the authority to allocate the necessary resources for the decision being made.*

Decision maker defined

You are the decision maker when deciding how to allocate your time at the office or at home. However, for many decisions, someone else is the decision maker, and identifying the correct decision maker is extremely important to ensure commitment to the chosen course of action. The decision maker must be involved to provide preferences and to establish the decision criteria. Without this input, it is easy to work on the wrong problem or develop a recommendation that is not compelling.

An important concept in decision analysis is probability. Probability is used as both a language with which to have a meaningful dialog and as a means to quantify our beliefs about uncertainty.

***Probability** is a subjective judgment about the likelihood of uncertain future events.*

Probability defined

You may be familiar with the terms *objective* and *subjective probability*. In this context, I am using the term subjective to represent beliefs, knowledge, data, and experience. By using subjective probability, we are able to quantify rare events and factors often considered intangible.

Objective and subjective probability

The term *risk* has often been used to only deal with the actual loss of something, usually money, but it could also be life, health, or happiness.

Risk   **Risk** *in decision analysis is used to describe both the likelihood that an event occurs and the consequences of the event.*

Both the likelihood and the consequences are important because you may have a very unlikely event with severe consequences or a likely event with not as dire consequences. These can be equal from an expected value perspective. If the decision maker is unaware of the seriousness of the consequences or the likelihood of occurrence, he or she cannot make an informed judgment or preference.

1.9 Overview of this Book

This book is structured to help you understand both the analytical and facilitation aspects of decision analysis. In chapters 2 through 5, I discuss the key principles of decision analysis, such as decision criteria, financial analysis, the principles of decision quality, and how to develop an appropriate decision frame. These concepts and principles are the building blocks of decision analysis and should be thoroughly understood before continuing.

Chapters 6 through 9 cover how to model and simulate decisions. Topics include building influence diagrams and decision trees, raising issues and creating a decision hierarchy, and developing creative alternatives by using strategy tables.

In chapter 10 through 13, you will learn how to analyze the decision models built in previous chapters. This includes how to conduct sensitivity analyses, generate risk profiles, and calculate the value of information.

The last chapters of the book focus on applying decision analysis. Topics include building project teams and decision boards, maintaining decision quality, portfolio analysis and management, and what to do for your first project.

1.10 Summary and Interpretation

Decision analysis is a powerful methodology based on hundreds of years of thought and several decades of application. The methodology provides a means to identify, characterize, and evaluate decisions involving uncertainty. While decision analysis can be used to solve any problem, it is most beneficial for significant or tough decisions.

We all want to make good decisions, regardless of the severity of the consequences. However, we can have a bad outcome from a good decision, and vice versa. By using the decision analysis process you will improve your ability to identify and create good opportunities.

1.11 Key Concepts

good decisions

good decision maker

normative

descriptive

outcomes

lucky outcomes

decision analysis cycle

applying decision analysis

probability

using intuition

uncertainty

1.12 Study Questions

1. Explain the difference between normative and descriptive decision analysis.

2. What is your definition of decision analysis?

3. Why should you use decision analysis?

4. What is a good decision?

5. Where can decision analysis be applied?

6. What is a bad decision?

7. Explain how you can have a good outcome from a bad decision.

8. What are some of the most common traps that decision makers and teams fall into when trying to solve a problem or make a decision?

9. What should an effective decision-making process be able to provide to the decision maker?

10. Define "risk" as it is used in decision analysis.

11. What issues can complexity bring to the problem solving process?

1.13 References and Further Reading

Bell, D.E., H. Raiffa, and A Tversky, editors. *Decision Making: Descriptive, Normative, and Prescriptive Interactions.* Cambridge, England: Cambridge University Press, 1988.

Howard, Ronald A. "Decision Analysis: Practice and Promise." Management Science 34 (6 1988): 679-695.

Huber, G.P. *Managerial Decision Making,* Glenview, IL:Scott, Foresman, 1980.

Raiffa, Howard. *Decision Analysis.* Reading, MA: Addison Wesley, 1968.

Schlaifer, Robert. *Analysis of Decisions Under Uncertainty.* New York: McGraw-Hill, 1969.

1.14 Guide to Action

Keep the following guidelines in mind when using decision analysis:

1. Decision analysis is designed to provide insight into the best course of action given the opportunities and the decision maker's preferences.

2. Decision analysis is not designed to give "the" answer.

3. Formal decision analysis can be used on any problem, but is most beneficial for problems that involve high degrees of uncertainty or ambiguity or in situations where the outcomes are significant.

4. Decision analysis is not designed to take the place of intuition, but it is a structured process to be used with intuition to ensure that the decision has been thoroughly thought through and framed properly.

1.15 Case for Analysis: "Dual Careers"

Jack is the R&D manager for a large manufacturing company. His wife Jill is an assistant vice-president for a regional bank. Jill has just been offered a promotion to full vice-president, but she would have to move to a city over 500 miles away. There is not a position available for Jack in that city with his current employer and Jack would have difficulty finding employment in his current field, as their new city has few manufacturing firms.

However, Jack has been considering going into the consulting business as an R&D consultant. Jack believes he has the credibility and the contacts to make the business successful, but he is unsure of the timing. In addition, Jack and Jill have two children Rick and Jane. Rick is about to enter college while Jane is still in high school. Jane does not want to leave her friends and move to a different city.

- ■ What should this family do and how should they structure their problem?

- ■ Which decision should be addressed first?

2

Decision Making in a Complex World

If you know the enemy and know yourself, you need not fear the result of a hundred battles. If you know yourself but not the enemy, for every victory you will also suffer a defeat. If you know neither the enemy nor yourself, you will succumb in every battle.

– Sun Tzu

Decisions today are probably more complex and difficult than at any time in the past. The technology revolution has united the globe in a way that was never before possible. People from across continents are communicating with each other instantly – exchanging information and ideas with the speed of a keystroke on a computer. For example, the manuscript for this book was sent in minutes over the Internet to reviewers across the country.

While these new technological tools are improving communication and collaboration, they are also creating problems for organizations as data and information are being accumulated at an unprecedented rate. Managers, executives, and even factory workers are facing information overload. This information exchange is increasing the uncertainty and ambiguity organizations face when making decisions. As a result, decisions are becoming even more complex than in the past.

In this chapter, I will discuss what makes decisions difficult, how to include considerations concerning "real world" decisions, and how you can develop a cogent and compelling course of action by using decision analysis.

2.1 Why are Decisions Difficult?

As individuals, we make decisions in different ways depending upon the situation. This is both natural and appropriate. For instance, you might use intuition to decide what movie to see on a Friday night. But choosing between building a new production facility and leasing industrial park space should involve more formal and structured analysis. There are similarities between the two situations. In both, you have:

- some *desired outcome* (see a good movie, choose the best location),
- some *level of information* which is currently available (friends' comments, average cost to build versus lease costs), and
- some *new information for which you would have to expend resources to acquire* (newspaper movie reviews, detailed plant designs).

Consequences and frequency

However, there are two dramatic differences between these two decisions:

- the *consequences* of making a poor decision, and
- the *frequency* with which you make similar decisions.

If you make a poor choice in movie selection, the cost of the ticket and the time involved are all you lose. You might make this type of decision every Friday night. However, if you make a poor choice for the new production facility, many jobs could be at risk and the financial health of the company could be disrupted. It is unlikely that you would make a decision of this importance every week! The potential results of this kind of decision are likely to create anxiety once you begin to understand what is at stake.

The Traditional Business Decision Process

Figure 2.1 shows the traditional process most organizations use to make decisions. It involves someone in authority first stating a problem to be solved or a project to be evaluated. Then a person or a team goes away,

Figure 2.1 Traditional Decision Process

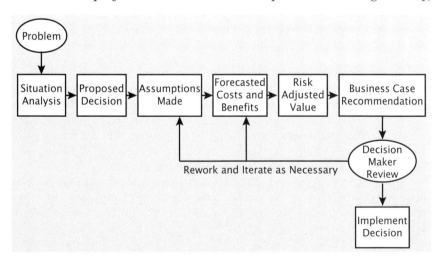

gathers data, picks an alternative, performs an evaluation, and presents the recommendation back to the decision maker. If the results of the analysis agree with the decision maker's beliefs and preferences, the recommendation is approved and funded. If the recommendation does not match the decision maker's beliefs or preferences, the team is asked to rework the evaluation. This cycle might be repeated several times as the decision maker may not agree with the person's analysis (or the team's analysis) of the situation, the proposed decision, the assumptions, or the analysis which led to the business case recommendation.

We call this an advocacy-based approach because it is like a lawyer presenting his case to a judge. In this case, the judge is the decision maker and he or she must try to uncover the truth about the situation before making a decision.

Over the years, I have participated in meetings where the decision maker is trying to determine funding levels for various projects or opportunities. These meetings become more of a sales opportunity than a dialog to uncover the highest value alternative for the organization.

Consider the following dialog between a decision maker and a project manager at a funding committee meeting:

PROJECT MANAGER: Thank you for taking time to meet with us. I know you will agree that this project is vital to the financial well being of the company and will allow us to gain at least an 18 month lead on the competition.

Example: traditional decision process

DECISION MAKER: Well...I will withhold my judgement of that until I see the results of the evaluation.

PROJECT MANAGER: That is your prerogative, but I know that when you see the results you will be ready to fund this project today.

DECISION MAKER: Possibly, but there are other projects I will need to consider before making my decision.

PROJECT MANAGER: As you can see from this business assessment, the market for this product is enormous. If we only get 20% of the market, our revenues will double next year.

DECISION MAKER: What will it take to achieve the 20% market penetration?

PROJECT MANAGER: I feel that we can deliver that target with a few additions to our sales staff and a $5 million advertising campaign.

DECISION MAKER: Who was consulted about this business assessment and target market projections?

PROJECT MANAGER: My staff developed these projections with the help of the company's marketing department.

DECISION MAKER: Will the marketing department stand behind these projections?

PROJECT MANAGER: I feel confident that they will.

DECISION MAKER: Well, what is the bottom line financial impact to the company?

PROJECT MANAGER: This project will have an NPV of $65 million and an IRR of 30%.

DECISION MAKER: What discount rate did you use?

PROJECT MANAGER: 12%

DECISION MAKER: I want to see the evaluation run at 18% given the risk of this project.

PROJECT MANAGER: I don't see how this project is any more risky than others we are considering.

DECISION MAKER: I feel that some of the inputs may be optimistic and I want to see the impact of a higher discount rate. I do not feel comfortable making a decision based on these numbers. I would also like to see the value if we only penetrate the market 10%.

This is an example of the project manager trying to persuade the decision maker to fund his project. A similar dialog could have occurred where the decision maker had already made the decision to fund a project but needed an evaluation to justify the funding. In this case, the team is often asked to make several iterations of the evaluation until the number presented matches the decision maker's belief of value.

The problem with advocacy decision making is that the real value and where it comes from is usually never understood. So why do companies use this method? Why are decision makers often skeptical of the projects presented to them for funding? What can be done to eliminate this lack of trust?

Inquiry-Based Decision Making

The traditional business decision process can never overcome the inherent problems it creates because it is based on one person or group advocating one position over another person or group. To eliminate (or at least minimize) this problem, the decision maker and those helping to evaluate the problem must work together. The goal of this collaboration should be to find the best choice based on insights gained through an inquiry process rather than trying to justify an initial choice or position.

Understanding the value proposition

Following an inquiry-based process requires keeping an open mind and developing alternatives and options which maximize the value to the organization. In an inquiry process, the decision maker must validate and accept key process outputs before moving to the next phase in the process. By doing so, the whole team (decision maker and analysis team) develops a shared understanding of the problem and is able to explore where and why value is created in the various alternatives. When it is time to make the decision, there is no advocating of a position – the whole team understands the value proposition and is ready and excited to pursue the chosen course of action.

One of the comments I regularly hear is that the decision maker is much more comfortable with the risk associated with a particular course of action. This comes from being involved in the process and understanding how the conclusions were determined. In addition, the decision maker is able to state his preferences and criteria for making the decision up front before working on the problem.

When Intuition is Not Sufficient

We all make decisions differently – that is the freewill that humans enjoy. If we all performed like a computer program where decisions and actions were known and standardized, we would not need a structured decision process. However, there are cultural, intellectual, and religious beliefs which are part of our decision making systems and which change the way we look at alternatives.

While everyone has different mental frameworks of how they process information and make choices, there are two kids of decision making used by the vast majority of people: *intuitive* and *analytical.* Intuitive decision making can range from emotional to judgmental, but these decisions are made without the use of formal analysis. Analytical decisions can range from simple problem solving to more sophisticated options theory.

Intuitive and analytical decision making

Both intuitive and analytical methods are valid for certain circumstances. For instance, when driving home from work you do not need a formal analysis to help you determine the best route given traffic conditions. You make the choice intuitively. However, a large trucking company may use sophisticated route planning systems to make the same decision. To decide between two alternatives that could impact the future success of your company, a more analytical process is often called for. We all use intuition as a means of helping us sort alternatives and make choices concerning many things that affect our lives and work. Intuition is a judgement or belief of what to do based on a mental model that integrates and assimilates information in a manner that we can understand. Intuition allows us to use past experience to make decisions quickly and with some level of confidence.

Since everyone processes information in different ways, intuition is difficult (if not impossible) to audit for completeness and quality of thought. Each person may have a different set of information and assumptions. While you may believe that a person made a poor decision or you may not understand how the person came to a conclusion, the decision may be very clear in that person's mind. Because of this inability to audit the decision, it is often difficult for people who are affected by the decision to commit to it – unless it is clearly the only decision that could be made. In addition, many of the decisions we make using intuition are short-term and have limited consequences.

However, organizations today face a myriad of problems from internal dysfunction to global competition. Decisions associated with these problems are long-term and have far reaching effects that are difficult to comprehend in an intuitive manner. These decisions need a systematic and in-depth evaluation before the final choice is made. Building a new plant, expanding into new markets, downsizing the organization, and building a new product pipeline are all long-term decisions which can significantly impact the organization. How many of these decisions are made in your organization by intuition?

Consider making personal decisions with long-term consequences like changing careers, choosing a college or degree, buying a car or house, or investing for retirement. How many of these decisions do you make by intuition only? The bottom line is that we all do some form or level of analysis to determine possible outcomes and how much we like those outcomes. This does not mean that intuition is not important or can be discarded. Intuition can provide a powerful framework for comparing a systematic analysis with your "gut" understanding.

Consider the case of allocating resources (money and people) among research projects. I am using the term research loosely to mean both basic research (which will lead to new products) and follow-on research for product improvements. How should you allocate your scarce resources? Do you allocate resources to product improvements, which will provide a quicker payback and provide short-term cash flow, or should you allocate more resources to basic research, which will ensure long-term success by keeping the product pipeline full?

Routine and Non-routine Decisions

One way of thinking about frequency and decision making was suggested by Herbert Simon, who distinguishes between two types of decisions – programmed and non-programmed.[1]

Coca-Cola – Good Outcome from an Interesting Decision

In the mid-1980's, the Coca-Cola Company decided to change formulas for its premier product, Coke. At that time, Coke was the market leader, but company executives were worried about losing market share to long-time rival Pepsi. As a result of this perceived threat, the Company developed a new formula dubbed "New Coke." After extensive market testing (which went well), new Coke was introduced and the old formula was withdrawn from the market.

Almost immediately customers began asking for the old formulation. Customers rebelled en masse and the original formulation was returned to the market. Normally, this would have been a marketing disaster. However, because of all of the publicity, Coke actually *gained* market share when the original formulation was brought back as "Coke Classic." The "New Coke" formula lasted for a few years after its introduction but eventually was withdrawn from the market due to lack of sales.

1. Did Coca-Cola management have their contingency ("Coke Classic") planned and ready before New Coke was introduced?

2. Or, did Coca-Cola quickly and effectively improvise under customer pressure?

3. Was the decision to introduce New Coke a good decision or was Coca-Cola lucky?

Programmed decisions involve situations which occur often and typically have a routine procedure that is used for solving them. Decisions are programmed to the extent that they are repetitive, and a definite procedure has been developed for handling them. Most organizations handle many programmed decisions in their daily operations. We usually call these decisions routine or operational to reflect their characteristics. These decisions should be made without unnecessarily expending organizational resources.

Programmed decisions (operational)

This does not mean these decisions are unimportant, but the level of understanding about the problem is generally great enough to solve the problem without significant resources or time. Often policies or standard operating procedures handle these decisions. However, even programmed or operational decisions can benefit from the logical structure of decision analysis – especially when setting up the procedures, programs, or systems that assist the decision making process.

Non-programmed decisions are usually single occurrence or non-routine events and are unstructured; there is no established procedure for handling the problem. Either the situation has not happened before in the same manner, or it is very complex and prior procedures (if they exist) must be modified or updated. These decisions are often called *strategic* and benefit the most from the decision analysis process. Distinctions between routine (operational) and non-routine (strategic) decisions are summarized in Figure 2.2.

Non-programmed decisions (strategic)

2.2 Consequences, Uncertainty, and Ambiguity

Studies have shown that, for the most part, we believe the world is more certain than it is. We all think we are right more times than we are. Managers or executive committees often believe that they know what the action or reaction of a competitor will be given a specific situation. How-

	Routine Decisions	Non-routine Decisions
Characteristics	Frequent, repetitive, lots of understanding about the key factors	Infrequent, unstructured, lots of uncertainty, ambiguity, and significant consequences
Solution	Policies and procedures, ignore uncertainty	Need creativity, ability to deal with limited information, incorporate uncertainty
Examples	Inventory control Promotions Purchasing	Constructing a new plant Introducing a new product line Strategy development

Figure 2.2 Routine and Non-routine Decisions

---

[1] Hogarth, Robin, *Judgment and Choice*, 2nd Edition, Wiley (1987).

ever, business textbooks and periodicals are full of examples where managers and executive committees were wrong and the competition zigged instead of zagged. The difficult or complex decisions we make usually involve three characteristics – *consequences, uncertainty,* and *ambiguity.*

Consequences

Consequences are the implications of what actually happens or the possible outcomes resulting from the decision. Consequences can be more than financial and can have effects beyond the decision under analysis. Most decisions involve consequences that are more than just financial. In these situations, the nonfinancial consequences should be evaluated and included in the analysis.

Uncertainty

Uncertainty is simply a lack of a clear understanding of the future. Uncertainty about an outcome can create anxiety or cause us to choose a less valuable but more certain outcome. Some people consider risk and uncertainty to be the same. However, I view uncertainty as the range of possible outcomes (consequences), and risk as the likelihood of the consequence occurring. In many decisions, these are the main components which make decisions difficult.

Ambiguity

The final component, **ambiguity**, is the lack of clear goals and objectives. Ambiguity is present in many decision situations when several decision makers or departments are involved. It is also present in organizations with weak or inexperienced management.

Figure 2.3
Routine and
Non-routine
Decisions

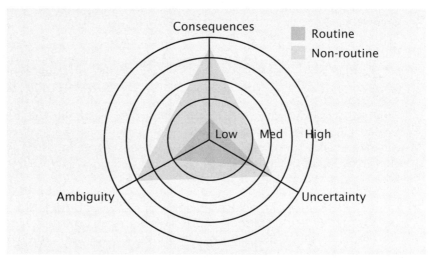

Having a high degree of any one of these three components or some combination of the three indicates that decision analysis is appropriate. Figure 2.3 illustrates the difference between an average routine decision and a non-routine decision.

The Simmstar case illustrates these concepts:

Simmstar Case

Chip West is the CEO of Simmstar, a small specialty computer chip manufacturing company located in Silicon Valley. The company makes video and memory chips for notebook computers. It recently unveiled a new 64 bit video chip that requires up to 20%

less power than the closest competitor's chip. Although this chip has very good performance metrics, computer makers are not buying the chip in large quantities because of its high cost, and the company can not produce the chip at a lower cost without an increased sales volume. The Director of Marketing is concerned that if the demand for the chip does not increase, the company will lose video chip market share to its rival, Megasimm.

A new opportunity has been presented to Simmstar by Notedesign, a major producer of notebook computers. Notedesign specializes in producing powerful high-end notebook computers for scientific computing. They contacted Simmstar about producing a 64 bit chip for their newest line of notebooks. If Simmstar can produce the chip in the needed quantities and is the lowest bidder, Notedesign would purchase a minimum of 25,000 units per month for the next three years. This would provide needed volume to expand production, decrease cost per unit, and help Simmstar to solidify its market share in the video chip market.

Notedesign also notified Simmstar that Megasimm has been given the same opportunity. However, neither company has yet produced a 64 bit chip with the specifications required by Notedesign. Because of the significance of this contract, Chip West called together a team made up of the CFO, Director of Manufacturing, and Director of Marketing to work through the decisions of whether to bid and, if so, at what price.

The Director of Manufacturing told the team he was certain the chip could be manufactured, but he was uncertain of the cost. The CFO asked him for an estimate of the cost and the Director of Manufacturing said between $30 and $40 per chip once the prototype has been developed. A prototype could be developed for about $250,000. The CFO quickly made a projection that if they could clear $10 per chip, the company would have a net cash stream of $3,000,000 per year. However, if they priced the chip at $30 and the costs were $40 per chip, the company would lose $3,000,000 per year, which could eventually bankrupt the company. The Director of Marketing quickly spoke up and said, "If we can become the market share leader, we won't go bankrupt." The CFO replied that profitability should be the main focus, not market share. At that point in the meeting Chip West stood up and said, "I think we should bid on this project. Work the numbers up for me by tomorrow."

■ How should Simmstar evaluate the uncertainty associated with the decision to bid?
■ Do you think the team is aligned with respect to the goals and objectives of the project?
■ What do you think the objective of the project should be?
■ Is the risk associated with this opportunity significant to the company?

Dealing with Uncertainty

While most of the decisions we make on a daily basis are routine, situations like Simmstar's opportunity do occur. However, any decision that involves future events has some uncertainty associated with it since we cannot predict the future perfectly. Depending upon the significance of the consequences, we typically deal with uncertainty by ignoring it, worrying about it, or trying to hedge against it.

Decision analysis methodology uses probability to manage uncertainty by incorporating it into the analysis rather than ignoring it. Decision analysis uses *subjective* probabilities or judgments gathered from content experts and *objective* data to evaluate the likelihood of some future event.

Decision trees provide a method of incorporating probability in a structured manner. The decision tree in Figure 2.4 illustrates how uncertainty can be structured to gain insight into the decision problem. The diagram uses squares to denote decisions, circles for uncertainties, and triangles for outcomes. This tree was created using the computer program TreeAge Pro®, available from TreeAge Software (www.treeage.com).

Figure 2.4
Simmstar
Decision Tree

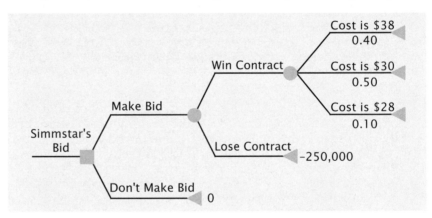

This diagram provides a logical method of incorporating the uncertain events which will influence the outcome that Simmstar could receive if the bid is pursued.

Using probability can cause some reluctance at first, since most people have never been taught how to incorporate uncertainty into their decisions. You have likely had many experiences of providing decision makers with deterministic outcomes or single point estimates, since they are most familiar with those forms of analysis. After reading this book, you should have a good understanding of probability and how to use it to make better decisions. Chapter 8 provides a thorough discussion of probability and how to incorporate it into decision problems.

Judging the Consequences

Again, consequences are the implications of what actually happens or the possible outcomes resulting from the decision. Both financial and non-financial consequences should be considered. As in the Simmstar case, there may be other consequences that could have positive or negative impacts on the potential outcomes. The obvious outcomes are $0 for not bidding and losing $250,000 for building a prototype and not winning the contract. The information shown in Figure 2.5 was provided by the Director of Manufacturing after consulting the engineering staff on the possible outcomes of building the chip.

This partial tree shows the expert judgment of the engineering staff. They believe that there is a 40% probability that the chip will cost $38 to produce, a 50% probability that it will cost $30, and only a 10% probability that it can be produced for $28. Most decisions (especially the difficult ones) have more than two possible outcomes and the consequences are often significant. In the Simmstar case, the difference in a few dollars per unit could be the difference between success and bankruptcy. It is this range in value that is important when judging the consequences associated with a decision.

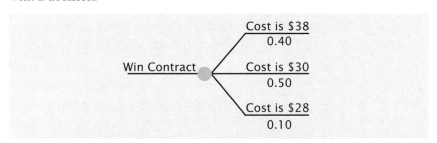

Figure 2.5 Video Chip Cost Assessment

As another example, consider the toss of a coin. You are given the opportunity to call either heads or tails. You can only do this once. If you call it correctly you win $10; if not you pay $3 (see Figure 2.6 for this decision tree). Would you take this deal? Why? How did you evaluate the consequences?

Coin toss example

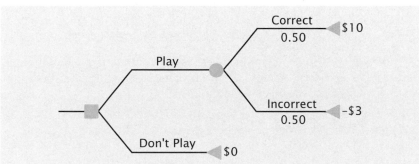

Figure 2.6 Coin Toss Decision Tree

A technique for incorporating uncertainty and its associated consequence is called **expected value**. I will discuss expected value in more detail in the next chapter.

Expected value

Expected value *is simply the sum of all the potential consequences multiplied by their associated probabilities.*

In the coin toss example, the expected value would be calculated as follows:

$$expected\ value = (0.50)(\$10) + (0.50)(-\$3) = \$5.00 - \$1.50 = \$3.50$$

Based on expected value, you should take this bet because you have the opportunity to make $3.50 on average. How many opportunities like this do you think you will be offered? Not many! In most cases, you will pay some entrance fee to play the game, or the probability of winning or consequences will not be as fair. What if the stakes were raised to $10,000 and $3,000? What would you do now? What if the stakes were raised even further to $1,000,000 and $300,000?

The effect of increasing consequences

In each of these cases the ratio is the same, but the consequences of an incorrect call increase dramatically! I expect that nearly everyone would accept the first deal. Think about the possible consequence of losing $3. Would this adversely affect your income? What about losing $300,000? By changing only the consequences of the decision, you have probably changed your decision from being willing to play to not playing (remember, you have only one chance to play).

This decision was relatively simple from the standpoint of outcomes – the consequences became increasingly more significant. If the number of outcomes increased from two to twenty, how would you handle the new situation?

2.3 A Scalable Process: Uncertainty and Ambiguity

Gary Bush of Decision Strategies, Inc. has developed a grid which illustrates the scalability of decision analysis as a function of ambiguity and uncertainty (see Figure 2.7).[2]

If both the goals and the "future" (i.e. the level of uncertainty) are relatively clear, a deterministic analysis may be all that is necessary to chose among alternatives.

If the level of uncertainty is relatively low (the future is quite clear) but ambiguity is high (goals are not clear or are conflicting), much insight can be gained from the first phases of the decision analysis process, which Gary refers to as "Discovery and Framing."

Discovery

Discovery includes appraising the overall situation, placing the decision maker's objectives into a hierarchy, and conducting an overall competitive analysis of the business situation.

Framing

Framing includes developing a decision hierarchy, strategy tables, and an influence diagram.

---

[2] Integrated Decision Management[TM] Workshop, Decision Strategies Inc., Figures 2.7 and 2.8 used with permission.

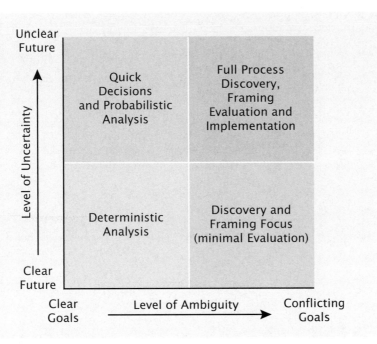

*Figure 2.7
Uncertainty
Versus
Ambiguity
Grid*

With some decisions, once the ambiguity is cleared away by proper discovery and framing, the course of action becomes obvious and the decision can be made. If the goals and objectives are clear but the future is highly uncertain, Gary recommends doing probabilistic analysis to compare opportunities. The probabilistic analysis can yield much insight as to which opportunities are prudent and which can be deleted. Note that if both ambiguity and complexity are high (and, as implied in Figure 2.3, the consequences are high), the full decision analysis process is appropriate.

Considering the x-axis (ambiguity) in Figure 2.7 from a facilitation standpoint, at the start of a project, teams range somewhere on a continuum from clarity and alignment all the way to open conflict. Therefore the facilitator needs to determine early in the framing part of the process whether clarification of goals is all that is needed (left part of Figure 2.7), versus progressing to the right, possibly all the way to conflict management (right side of Figure 2.7).

Gary Bush reports that as he has trained people in workshops and project teams, people ask, "How do you know what parts of the decision analysis process to emphasize?" or "How do you know what to do when from a facilitation standpoint?" Expanding Figure 2.7 to include some examples helps illustrate how to scale the tools to fit the situation (see Figure 2.8).

Consider the y-axis (uncertainty) in Figure 2.8. In a workshop, an experienced Russian frequentist statistician asked for examples of decision situations involving increasing level of uncertainty. Gary pointed out that descriptive statistics apply very well to decisions associated with airline safety – extensive statistical data exist.

*Practical
application of
the grid*

*Figure 2.8
Examples,
Uncertainty
Versus
Ambiguity
Grid*

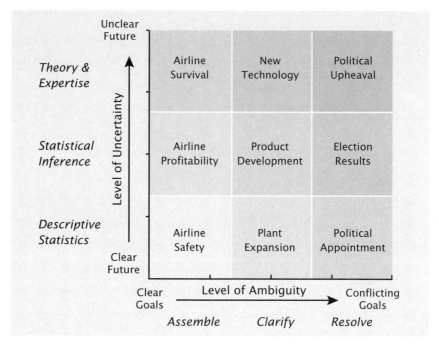

However, decision situations concerning airline profitability require statistical inference, and complete decision analysis tools and expertise would be required in highly competitive or unusual situations where survival of the airline might be at stake. The statistician was able to see the full continuum of decision situations and the bridge between a frequentist view to a Bayesian (inference) view. Developing a shared understanding of where the decision situation fits on the ambiguity / uncertainty grid helps the team understand the scope of the decision analysis problem and the work required to progress.

- A simple deterministic model and clear problem statement may be all that is required if the decision situation is in the lower left part of Figure 2.7 or Figure 2.8.

- Lower right part of Figure 2.7: focus on clarification and conflict resolution, i.e. get agreement on a *framework* and a *basis* for handling the situation before trying to solve the problem.

- Upper left part of Figure 2.7: quickly clarify the problem frame and focus on key assessments. Usually decision trees can help represent and gain insight into these types of situations.

Managing Complexity and Ambiguity

Difficult decisions often have many influences and variables that affect the decision. This often creates unnecessary complexity when thinking about decisions and building decision trees. This complexity can create a feeling of more uncertainty than is actually present.

Decision analysis manages complexity by focusing on what information is needed to develop an appropriate course of action. This helps to focus the project team and the analysis on those key issues. One tool which helps to define the various influences and uncertainties involved in choosing a course of action is the influence diagram.

Influence diagrams

The *influence diagram* is a tool for graphically depicting the decision problem. By using an influence diagram, you can show the relationships which are relevant to making the decision. Influence diagrams will be discussed in depth in Chapter 7. This diagram also acts as a communication device between the project team and the decision board. The influence diagram shown in Figure 2.9 is for the Simmstar Case Study.

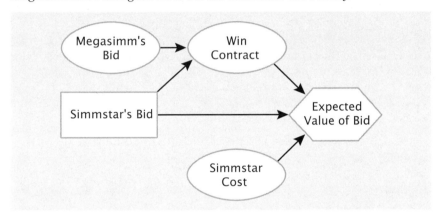

Figure 2.9 Simmstar Influence Diagram

Influence diagrams use a nomenclature similar to decision trees. Rectangles are used for decisions, ovals for uncertainties, and hexagons for the values or consequences. Influence diagrams are very powerful for showing an entire decision problem on a single sheet of paper. These diagrams are very useful for project teams and decision makers.

Note that the influence diagram also adds clarity to the decision, which makes it a useful tool to decrease ambiguity. Relationships between uncertainties, values, and decision points are clearly shown. This can be of great help to a group that is not clear on the objective or goal.

In the Simmstar case, the Director of Manufacturing and the Director of Marketing got together to discuss the bid price to give Notedesign. They both agreed that the price should be high enough to make a reasonable profit but not so high as to lose out to Megasimm. They were able to gather some industry intelligence which they felt indicated Megasimm would have to bid at least $38 to $40 per chip. Using this information and their own assessment of potential costs of manufacture, they came to agree on a price of $35 per chip. Their assessment was that, with a $35 bid, they had a 60% chance of winning the contract.

Simmstar case

Using this information, we can complete the decision tree (Figure 2.10) and evaluate it.

Figure 2.10
Simmstar
Completed
Decision Tree

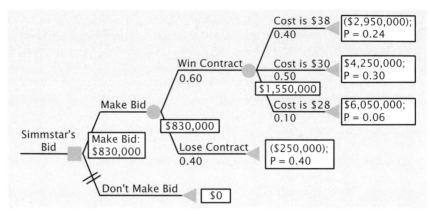

Making the bid is the preferred course of action, as the "make bid" alternative has an expected value of $830,000. Note that for each node of the tree, expected value is calculated by multiplying each possible outcome by its probability and adding these products together. For example, consider the expected value of the "make bid" node:

$$expected\ value = \$830,000 = (\$1,550,000)(60\%) + (-\$250,000)(40\%)$$

2.4 Real World Decisions

Most decisions we make are more difficult and complex than the coin toss and the Simmstar examples. Real world decisions often involve a high degree of ambiguity, conflicting goals due to multiple objectives, complex trade-offs, more than one decision maker, or several sequential decisions. It is these types of situations where decision analysis is most valuable. By carefully decomposing the problem into smaller more manageable problems and by focusing on what is truly important, we can develop clear objectives and defensible courses of action.

Multiple Objectives

We make decisions based on the belief that they will bring about some desired objective. Often there are multiple objectives that a decision maker is trying to fulfill. And these objectives may not all be financial in nature. Many times, especially in public decisions, the objectives are more social or political than financial; these nonfinancial objectives may be as or more important than the financial.

Nonfinancial
objectives

Examples of nonfinancial objectives include quality of life for employees, customer service, or a foreign government's perception of drilling competency in the case of oil and gas companies. When making an important decision, all of the objectives must be considered if the decision is to be defensible and compelling to the decision maker. Multiple objectives are very common when working with committees and other groups where dissimilar beliefs and opinions are common.

The influence diagram for such an example (a county commission considering building a new water treatment plant) is shown in Figure 2.11. If you have ever watched a commission meeting on television, you know that each commissioner has his or her own beliefs as to what is good for constituents. And often there is enormous disagreement as to the public value of a proposal. In these situations, having a logical discussion about the benefits and trade-offs of these objectives is necessary to develop a defensible course of action.

Figure 2.11
Treatment
Plant
Objectives

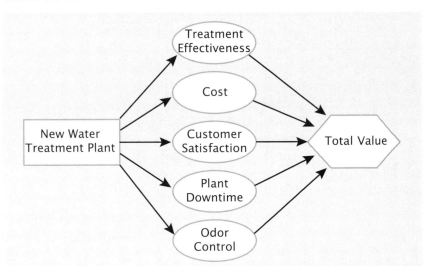

Making Trade-offs

Trading-off multiple objectives is often a difficult task, but one that must be done to develop a compelling course of action. For instance, in the water treatment plant situation, the people of the community may prefer higher cost for better odor control. Trade-offs are also common in purely financial situations. If you had an opportunity to take either (1) a guaranteed outcome of $1,000, or (2) a 50-50 gamble of either getting $2,000 or nothing, which would you choose? Your choice depends on your preferences toward risk and your belief about your probability of success. Other financial trade-offs could be between the present value of an opportunity and the time required to payback the original investment.

A helpful tool to use when multiple objectives are involved is the radar chart. Figure 2.12 shows a radar chart with two potential strategies. By ranking how each strategy compares against the established objectives, you can quickly and easily see potential trade-offs among the different objectives or strategies. While this tool is only quasi-quantitative, I have found it very beneficial in getting multiple decision makers to agree on the relative importance of the different objectives and in understanding how strategies compare against each other.

Figure 2.12
Treatment
Plant Multiple
Objectives
Radar Chart

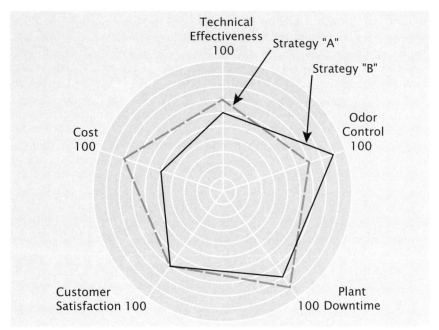

Multiple Decision Makers

Another common situation that arises in real world problems is that of multiple decision makers. In the past, most corporate decisions were made by a single decision maker. This person would weigh all the pros and cons of a situation and make a decision. However, in recent years, as organizations have evolved from hierarchical and dictatorial to more decentralized and empowering, the *single* decision maker has disappeared. What has reappeared are decision boards, committees, management review teams, and other groups which now serve in the role of a single decision maker. Many decisions are made by *consensus* between either a formal or an ad hoc group of managers and senior technical experts rather than by a single person deciding and then giving out orders.

This adds ambiguity to decision making since there may be two or more sets of preferences that need to be included in the analysis, where in the past there was only one. While most of the boards I have worked with are very constructive, it is still easier to deal with one person than several people when trying to get agreement on a course of action. The key to working with these boards is to have a board chairman or leader who can work to get consensus around issues, and who will maintain a focus on making a quality decision.

Identifying the Decision Maker

It is very important to identify the decision maker(s) before beginning an analysis. This may seem to be a simple task, but sometimes a person may believe that they are the decision maker when in fact they are not.

Consider a situation that happened to me several years ago. I was brought in to lead a team working on a complex R&D problem for the Vice-President of R&D at a major oil company. I questioned the Executive and was satisfied that he indeed was the decision maker and could provide the resources to implement the decision (a key distinction of a decision maker). The team worked to incorporate his preferences and uncertainties into the problem that he had defined.

When the project was ready for validation of the alternatives, the team was informed we would be presenting it to the technology committee. At that meeting, which was chaired by the Executive, we discovered that this committee was really the decision maker, not the Executive by himself. The Executive was able to allocate resources among projects, but the committee was the allocating body for new projects. This change in decision maker status was not a major setback, but it did create new preferences and a slightly different problem statement. Had this information not been made available until the end of the project, the recommended course of action would not have met the committee's objectives!

Sequential Decisions

One characteristic of real world problems is that many times they involve more than one decision, and not all of the decisions are made at the same time. For example, in R&D when developing a new product, after the initial idea you will make subsequent decisions about proceeding with a lab scale experiment, building a pilot plant, and then (if successful) commercializing the product.

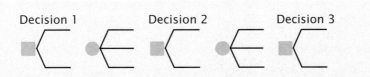

Figure 2.13
Sequential
Decisions

There are also situations where several sequential decisions must be evaluated at the same time so that the decision maker can decide on the first decision. For instance, consider building a new manufacturing plant. There are several decisions that may be involved – to build the plant or not, where to build it, what capacity to build, what products to produce, etc. When evaluating sequential decisions we need to know what the decisions are and in what sequence they must be made. Figure 2.13 illustrates sequential decisions. In addition to knowing the order of decisions, we also need to know what uncertainties will come before or after the decisions. This maintains a correct state of knowledge when making the first decision.

2.5 The Role of Decision Analysis

The real world decisions we face are usually difficult to intuitively evaluate and many involve conflicting goals and objectives. Decision analysis provides a method to decompose (i.e. break down) complex decisions into a set of smaller and simpler decisions, which can then be solved and integrated into a course of clear and compelling action. This can be referred to as the "divide and conquer" approach. This is a valuable aspect of decision analysis as the human mind has limited ability to process the large amounts of discontinuous information which is usually involved in large complex problems.

Use Decision Analysis to improve alignment

In addition, decision analysis provides a set of tools and processes which help facilitate a dialog with the decision maker about his or her own preferences and objectives. This information should be incorporated into the analysis but may not get incorporated in a typical business case evaluation. By incorporating these preferences and objectives, the level of communication is raised dramatically and the rationale used in the analysis can be easily traced. This provides the ability to discuss why a particular course of action might be preferred over another and what elements must exist for the course of action to succeed. All of this is predicated on the ability of the decision maker to clearly state his or her preferences. Again, the role of decision analysis is one of helping the decision maker to clarify and articulate these preferences and objectives so that a correct problem and problem frame can be analyzed.

Decision analysis does not take the place of intuition. It provides a formal structure so that greater insight into the problem can be gained. This insight comes in many forms – the influence diagrams and decision trees introduced in this chapter are very helpful in catalyzing new insight. Often you will be able to see new opportunities or create new alternatives as you gain insight.

2.6 Summary

Decision analysis is a methodology that helps a decision maker to think logically about complex and difficult problems. While good decisions do not guarantee good outcomes, we must make quality decisions to have the best chance of good outcomes. A good decision is made with a thorough understanding of the problem, careful thought about the consequences, and incorporation of probabilistic assessments with regard to the person's or organization's risk attitude.

Decision analysis can be applied to any decision, but is most useful for those with significant consequences or great complexity. Keep in mind while reading this book that all the concepts and principles can be applied to both personal and business decisions.

2.7 Key Concepts

routine decisions	non-routine decisions	difficult decisions
expected value	consequences	influence diagrams
ambiguity	multiple objectives	uncertainty
trade-offs	decision trees	sequential decisions
role of decision analysis	multiple decision makers	

2.8 Study Questions

1. Think about some decisions you have made recently. What type of decision making approach did you take to solve them? Did you use the same approach each time or did you use different approaches depending upon the complexity of each problem?

2. Consider the decision of raising the speed limit from 55 m.p.h. to 70 m.p.h. What issues does this raise and who is likely to make the decision?

3. What makes decision making difficult for you? What would you want in a decision making process to minimize these difficulties?

4. What is your definition of decision analysis?

5. Are good outcomes the direct result of good decisions? What are the differences between a good decision and a good outcome?

6. Do you currently face an important decision? If so, what uncertainties are you facing which make the decision difficult?

7. Give an example of a recent decision you made which involved a significant amount of uncertainty. Was the outcome lucky or unlucky?

8. Name two shortcomings of the traditional advocacy based decision making approach.

9. Can decision analysis be useful for making routine or programmed decisions?

10. What is the difference between risk and uncertainty?

11. Under what conditions of ambiguity and uncertainty would full decision analysis become the most appropriate course of action?

12. Influence diagrams can be used to add clarity to the decision process. How do these diagrams contribute to the process?

13. What change is occurring in organizations today with decision makers that adds complexity to the decision making process?

14. When is intuition appropriate to use in the decision making process?

2.9 References

Bayes, T. "An Essay toward Solving a Problem in the Doctrine of Chance." Philosophical Transactions of the Royal Society, 1763.

Bunn, D. *Applied Decision Analysis*. New York: McGraw-Hill, 1984.

Hogarth, R. *Judgment and Choice, 2nd ed.* New York: Wiley, 1987.

Howard, R. "Decision Analysis: Practice and Promise." *Management Science*, 34, 679-695, 1988.

Howard, R., and J. Matheson, editors., *Readings on the Principles and Applications of Decision Analysis*, 2 volumes, Menlo Park, CA: Strategic Decisions Group, 1984.

Raiffa, H. *Decision Analysis: Introductory Lectures on Choices under Uncertainty.* New York: McGraw-Hill, 1968.

Schlaifer, R. *Analysis of Decisions Under Uncertainty.* New York: McGraw-Hill, 1969.

von Winterfeldt, D., and W. Edwards. *Decision Analysis and Behavioral Research.* Cambridge: Cambridge University Press, 1986.

2.10 Case For Analysis: "Cancer Treatment"

Norman is a 42 year old businessman. He and his wife have two teenage children and live in the Midwest. He has recently been diagnosed with cancer. His cancer is a Ewing's type tumor that is difficult to treat. Without treatment, the doctors estimate that Norman will only have about six to twelve months to live.

Norman is concerned about both fighting the disease and his quality of life. Because of the location of the tumor in his right thigh, he has several treatment options. He could have surgery, chemotherapy, radiation, or some combination of the three.

■ How should Norman make this decision?

■ What information should be gathered before making the decision?

■ What are his options?

■ Draw the influence diagram for this decision situation.

3

Uncertainty and Making Choices

Our destiny changes with our thought; we shall become what we wish to become, do what we wish to do, when our habitual thought corresponds with our desire.

– Orison S. Marden

Nearly all important decisions, business or personal, are made under conditions of uncertainty. The decision maker must choose one course of action from all that are available to him or her. The difficulty is in understanding the consequences or outcomes of the different courses of action. Decision making under uncertainty implies that at least two outcomes exist for a chosen course of action.

Decision analysis provides a comprehensive means to evaluate and compare the degree of uncertainty associated with each course of action before committing to a particular one. In doing so, the decision maker should have a much clearer understanding of the value proposition and the risks involved with each course of action. This is in contrast to the more traditional approach to business decision making, which uses a forecast of future value based only on deterministic cash flows. This is also in contrast to making decisions using intuition.

Using Decision Analysis and uncertainty

This chapter covers the basic principles of evaluating complex and difficult decisions. I invite you to open your mind as you are reading this book and think about situations where you can begin using decision analysis both personally and professionally.

3.1 Decisions and Uncertainty

There are two distinct types of decisions – those with **certainty**, and those with **uncertainty**. The diagram below (Figure 3.1) illustrates this distinction.

Figure 3.1
Decisions and
Outcomes

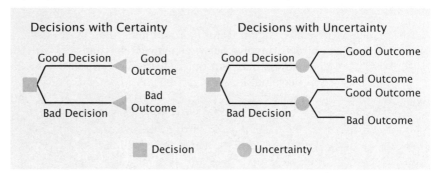

The distinction between decisions with certainty and those without is very important. How many decisions have you made in your life with complete certainty? **Certainty** means there is *zero* probability any other outcome other than the one you want will occur. In a decision with certainty, a good decision dictates a good outcome and a bad decision produces a bad outcome. Testing for decision quality in this situation is easy – examine the outcome. However, nearly all of the decisions we make *do not* involve certainty, but rather involve some degree of uncertainty. *It is this uncertainty in future outcomes that can produce a bad outcome from a good decision and vice versa.*

Sometimes we feel more comfortable with highly uncertain decisions that we make routinely than with less uncertain but infrequent decisions. For example, wildcat drilling for oil is a routine decision for most oil companies, but the chance of finding oil is only about 1 in 7. For the same company, a decision like building a new supertanker may have less uncertainty with regard to cost and profit but will be less comfortable to the decision maker.

Personal decisions can also be difficult due to uncertainty about future events. Consider a case study:

Case Study:
Saving for
College

A young married couple, Joe and Eileen, recently gave birth to a healthy baby girl named Sarah. Joe and Eileen begin talking about Sarah's future and about investing for her college education.

Joe states they should "wait until they have a nest egg built up" so they can put a reasonable amount of money into an investment.

Eileen, on the other hand, believes they should start putting money away for Sarah's education now. After several minutes of stating their positions to each other and several more minutes of arguing, it becomes apparent they are on opposite sides of the issue. This arguing goes on for several weeks with neither side making any headway – if anything, both now believe the other to be absolutely and completely wrong!

How can they find common ground, resolve their conflict, and solve the problem?

Personal decisions usually affect us at a deeper level than business decisions and can be as difficult, if not more difficult, than business decisions because they directly involve our well being. Many times (as with the case study), the distinctions between outcomes are small relative to the benefits of using the decision analysis process as a *method of working together* to reach an agreement that all parties feel good about. The decision analysis process can help you make decisions involving career choices, business start-ups, children's education, home and car purchases, and medical treatment choices. In these decisions, the uncertainty of the outcome is usually the key concern. While ambiguity can sometimes be a factor, it usually is not, because most people have clear personal goals and objectives.

Decision Analysis: a process for making personal decisions

In business decisions, however, ambiguity is very often a major factor and may outweigh the uncertainty involved. This is because business decisions usually involve more than one person's beliefs and perspectives about the problem or situation. Also, business decisions are made using different methods.

If an organization has a strong team culture, decisions may be made by group methods such as consensus or majority vote. In authoritarian organizations, decisions are made by the leader or executive with minimal input from the employees. In hierarchal organizations, decisions are delegated within authority limits. The method an organization chooses is often a product of the organization's culture and the particular industry. Given these differing methods, it is important to understand how to effectively evaluate and make decisions.

Organizational decision making

When We Are The Decision Makers

We all make decisions in different ways at different times. This is not only natural but also appropriate. Use the thinking style of decision analysis, but not the *formal* decision analysis process for every situation. For instance, when driving a car, if another driver suddenly pulls out in front of you, you don't pull out a pad and pencil and list your alternatives – you swerve to avoid an accident. We make emotional decisions when we become angry or frustrated, logical decisions when we have time to think, and intuitive decisions when we have a hunch. For very uncertain and ambiguous decisions, we should make informed decisions which draw on both logic and intuition. We need to use the appropriate decision response for each situation. A colleague of mine, Dave Charlesworth, and I developed what we call the decision response hierarchy. The decision response hierarchy (Figure 3.2) illustrates the different levels that we go through in making decisions.

*Figure 3.2
Decision
Response
Hierarchy*

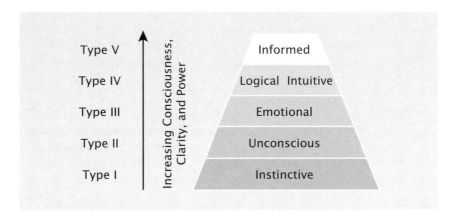

The **Instinctive (Type I)** response is the "fight or flight" response that is seen in animals and humans. Examples of this type of response would be jumping out of the way of an oncoming car or running out of a burning room. You instinctively react to the situation rather than consciously make a choice.

The **Unconscious (Type II)** response is a result of our learned behavior and is basically an automatic response. An example of this type might be putting on your car seatbelt. It is a decision you can consciously make but is usually a learned response.

The **Emotional (Type III)** response can be from any emotion. Many people are emotional decision makers and allow emotions to guide their decisions. Think about when you get angry. How does that anger cloud your decision making? Do you act as rationally and logically as if you were not angry? Emotions are useful but may cause us to make hasty decisions we later regret. I have witnessed many emotional decisions being made at auctions. It is always amazing to see people get caught up in the excitement and pay more for an item than they had planned and sometimes more than it is ever worth.

There are two related parts to the **Logical or Intuitive (Type IV)** response. Much has been written about the differences between the right side and the left side of our brain. For a right-handed person, the left side of the brain tends to process information in a logical linear manner, while the right side of the brain tends to process information instantly, holistically, and intuitively.[1] As an example, balancing your checkbook is a left-brain task while painting is a right-brain task. For left-handed people, the hemispheres may be reversed. With respect to decision response, Intuitive has to do with playing a hunch – an instantaneous feeling about the correct course of action. The Logical has to do with developing some line of logical reasoning to determine your course of action.

---

[1] This is not a new concept. The second scale of the Myers-Briggs Type Indicator [MBTI] ranks you as either "S" for "Sensing" or "N" for "iNtuitive." These correspond roughly to the "left brain" and "right brain" concepts

The highest level of decision response is called **Informed (Type V)**. This is when you use your intuition, experience, knowledge, data, and other information in a logically structured manner, incorporating probability and seeking the best course of action. Decision analysis is a process for making informed decisions. Informed decisions are based on opening your thinking processes and looking for the best alternative rather than trying to justify a position or belief.

An **informed decision** *uses a group of patterns of thinking (including probability) to develop a complete basis for and illumination of a conscious irrevocable allocation of resources, which ultimately leads to clear and compelling action.*

Informed decision defined

When We Advise The Decision Maker

The decision response hierarchy helps to describe the various levels used when we are the decision makers. But circumstances change dramatically when we are only advising or recommending a course of action to the decision maker. In these situations, biases, personal agendas and other factors often influence the situation and the decision maker. Most decision makers understand this and try to overcome these factors by making intuitive adjustments to the information or recommendation presented.

3.2 Measures of Merit

An inquiry-based process will eliminate many of the personal and organizational problems of an advocacy-based process, but the evaluation method used must also be valid. I use the term *measures of merit* (others use *profitability measures*) to translate things we value into quantifiable measures which provide comparability among alternatives. While there are many measures which a decision maker may choose, a good measure of merit should:

- Be able to provide a comparison of alternatives in a clear and unbiased manner,
- Incorporate the firm's cost of capital and risk,
- Provide an indication of whether a given alternative exceeds an economic hurdle and by how much,
- Indicate the size of the value proposition.

Measures of Merit: Characteristics

A common measure of merit used by many organizations and decision makers is the *payback* or *payout period*. This is the length of time needed for the accumulated net revenues to equal the investment. Many people like this measure because it is easy to calculate and understand. As an example, look at the cash flows in Table 3.1.

Payback or payout period

Many investments we make may require a reasonable amount of time before they payback the initial investment and create a net return for the company. This is why we need a measure of merit that incorporates timing

Table 3.1
Cash Flow Data

Year	Revenue	Expenditures	Net Cash Flow
1	-	150,000	(150,000)
2	25,000		25,000
3	50,000		50,000
4	50,000		50,000
5	75,000		75,000
6	75,000	100,000	(25,000)
7	75,000		75,000
8	100,000		100,000
9	100,000		100,000
10	100,000		100,000
Total	650,000	250,000	400,000

into the evaluation. By charting these cash flows in a cumulative manner, we quickly see that it takes a little less than four and a half years to pay-back the initial $150,000 investment (Figure 3.3).

Figure 3.3
Cumulative
Cash Flow

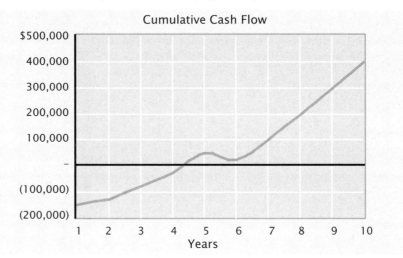

Projects which have a capital expenditure, or net investment, require that we consider the timing of the cash inflows and outflows. Here are a few principles to keep in mind:

Evaluation
principles

- Cash flows should *never* include sunk costs when evaluating a project.
- Cash flows should be measured on an after-tax basis.
- Cash flows should be on an incremental basis.
- Cash flows should include any ancillary effects from the project.

Net cash flow
(NCF)

The following formula is used for calculating **net cash flow** (NCF):

$$NCF = (\Delta R - \Delta O - \Delta D)(1 - t) + \Delta D$$

ΔR is the change in cash revenues between doing the project and not doing the project, ΔO is the change in operating costs, ΔD is the change in depreciation, and $(1 - t)$ is one minus the tax rate.

Although payback period is simple to use, it does not provide the decision maker with an understanding of the total profitability of the investment. For this reason, you should not use payback period as the only measure of merit in evaluating an alternative.

Another commonly used measure is **Return on Investment** or ROI. While the payback period does not reflect total profitability, return on investment does. Return on investment is simply the profit to investment ratio. Using the data from Table 3.1, the return on investment would be: *Return on Investment (ROI)*

> Net profit = Revenue ($650,000) – Investment ($250,000) = $400,000
> Return on Investment = $400,000 / $250,000 = 160% (over the life of the project)

Both payback and return on investment are frequently used by decision makers because they are simple to calculate and understand. If the measure is too hard to calculate or appears to come from a "black box," the decision maker will hesitate to use it because of its complexity. However, to truly understand and compare the risk and reward of various alternatives, the measure must be able to provide the decision maker with greater insights than how long it will take to pay back the investment. The measure must be able to help distinguish projects from a total value perspective over the life of the project. We often call this the time value of money effect.

3.3 Time Value of Money

The concept of "time value of money" is based on the relationship of cash flows and their timing to arrive at a single value that describes the value of all the cash flows today (present value, PV) or at some time in the future (future value, FV). Without a means to incorporate the time value of money, a project with a $1 million net cash flow today is worth the same as a project with a $1 million net cash flow in year five. We know the value of a dollar received today is worth more than a dollar received later than today, because you can reinvest today's dollar to create more value. Even if you do not have another project with which to reinvest those revenues, you can invest in securities or put the revenues in the bank for others to invest in projects. Since our focus is to make a decision today based on cash flows in the future, I will focus on present value. To arrive at present value, we discount the cash flows to account for when we receive them. There are two common measures used to discount cash flows – the internal rate of return and net present value.

Internal Rate of Return

The **Internal Rate of Return** (IRR), also known as profitability index (PI), is frequently used by organizations to evaluate the marginal efficiency of capital and prioritization of projects. *IRR is the discount interest rate at which the cash outflows and inflows equal each other at a particular point in time.* Calculating IRR is a trial and error process which begins by guessing an initial discount rate. This rate is then applied to the cash flows and discounted back to today. If the sum of the present values   *IRR defined*

Year	Revenue	Expenditures	Net Cash Flow	29%	Discounted Value
1	0	150,000	(150,000)	0.776	($116,453)
2	25,000		25,000	0.603	$15,068
3	50,000		50,000	0.468	$23,396
4	50,000		50,000	0.363	$18,164
5	75,000		75,000	0.282	$21,152
6	75,000	100,000	(25,000)	0.219	($5,474)
7	75,000		75,000	0.170	$12,749
8	100,000		100,000	0.132	$13,197
9	100,000		100,000	0.102	$10,246
10	100,000		100,000	0.080	$7,954
Total	650,000	250,000	400,000		0

of cash flow exceed the investment, the discount rate is too low. If the investment exceeds the cash flows, the discount rate is too high. When the present values equal the investment, you have found the IRR.

Table 3.2 shows that the internal rate of return for this project is 29% (28.81% rounded) using the data from Table 3.1 as a starting point. While IRR does discount the future cash flows and provides a measure to compare projects with different cash flow timing, it does not allow you to determine how much a project returns *over* the discount rate. For example, using the data from Table 3.1 and comparing it with another project in Table 3.3, you can see that both projects have the same IRR but very different net present values.

Year	Project 1 NCF	Project 2 NCF
1	(150,000)	(400,000)
2	25,000	(50,000)
3	50,000	(25,000)
4	50,000	(25,000)
5	75,000	175,000
6	(25,000)	225,000
7	75,000	275,000
8	100,000	250,000
9	100,000	1,000,000
10	100,000	1,000,000
Total	400,000	2,425,000
IRR	29%	29%
NPV @ 12%	$125,830	$690,557

Net Present Value

If you were presented with only the IRR information, how would you know which project provided more value to the organization? For this reason, I would not use IRR as the primary measure for evaluating projects or alternatives. A better measure is *Net Present Value* (NPV). NPV is commonly used because of its ability to discount present and future cash flows and to provide an understanding of the total value of a project.

Net present value is similar to IRR in that it uses a discount rate to convert a stream of future values to a single value today. However, NPV uses a management-specified discount rate which should represent the organization's rate at which it can reinvest future revenues. In doing so, this rate is much more realistic than many IRR's. For instance, in the previous example the discount rate is 29%. How many new investments can the organization make at those rates?

If the NPV of a project is zero, then the project has met its average opportunity rate and should be funded assuming that there are no better opportunities. NPV's greater than zero indicate the amount the organization will make over its reinvestment or average opportunity rate. This value can then be used to compare against other projects using the same factors. The formula for NPV is:

$$NPV = \frac{X_0}{(1+k)^0} + \frac{X_1}{(1+k)^1} + \frac{X_2}{(1+k)^2} + \ldots + \frac{X_n}{(1+k)^n}$$

Equation 3.1 Net Present Value

$$NPV = \sum_{t=0}^{n} \frac{NCF_t}{(1+k)^t}.$$

The letter n is the expected project life; k is the interest rate; and $\sum_{t=0}^{n} [NCF_t/(1+k)^t]$ is the arithmetic sum of the discounted net cash flows (X_t) for each year t over the life of the project (n years), or in other words, the present value of the net (annual) cash flows.

Using The Proper Discount Rate

It is important to choose an appropriate discount rate when calculating NPV. This can be a difficult task, but it is extremely important in making consistent evaluations. Part of the difficulty is that many people, even some analysts, do not understand discount rates and what they represent. As a consultant I often hear "Let's try 12% and see how the project looks. If it doesn't look right, we can try 8%." Arbitrarily choosing a number is not correct and can penalize or exaggerate the value of a project. Using the values from Table 3.1, I have constructed a comparison of using 8% and 12% discount rates on the same cash flows (see Table 3.4). The $400,000 in NCF is worth $188,325 today using an 8% discount rate and $125,825 using 12%. That is a $62,500 difference in value, which is almost 16% of the $400,000 NCF.

A common practice that I have seen in organizations that do not explicitly deal with risk is to consciously increase the discount rate to reflect risk, thereby creating a risk-adjusted discount rate. I have heard executives say they will increase the discount rate several points to account for the risk of the project. However, when applying a risk-adjusted discount rate you are combining the effects of both time and risk, which

Pitfalls of arbitrary discount rates

Table 3.4
Discounted
Cash Flow Data

Year	Net Cash Flow	8% Discount	Discounted Value	12% Discount	Discounted Value
1	(150,000)	0.926	(138,900)	0.893	(133,950)
2	25,000	0.857	21,425	0.797	19,925
3	50,000	0.794	39,700	0.712	35,600
4	50,000	0.735	36,750	0.636	31,800
5	75,000	0.681	51,075	0.567	42,525
6	(25,000)	0.630	(15,750)	0.507	(12,675)
7	75,000	0.583	43,725	0.452	33,900
8	100,000	0.540	54,000	0.404	40,400
9	100,000	0.500	50,000	0.361	36,100
10	100,000	0.463	46,300	0.322	32,200
Total	400,000		188,325		125,825

are not necessarily correlated. If there is no established relationship between time and risk, then why would you want to account for risk with a discount rate? I recommend using either your *true* cost of capital, also known as the *weighted average cost of capital* (what you would pay for internal use of the funds, which reflects your company's tax rate, cost of borrowing, proportion of equity financing, and stockholders' expected return on investment) or a risk-free discount rate – usually about 4%.

3.4 Dealing with Risk

Most people associate risk with uncertain choices. People often say that decisions are *risky*. But what do they mean by the term *risky*? Usually risk is the term we use to describe uncertainty about potential negative outcomes from a course of action. For example, you have just bought a new car and are evaluating insurance options. You can go with a low deductible ($100) which has a high premium ($600) or choose a high deductible ($1,000) with a low premium ($300). You believe the chances of having an accident before renewing the insurance is low (10%). With only $2,000 in the bank, what should you do? The decision tree shown in Figure 3.4 illustrates this decision.

Figure 3.4
Insurance
Decision Tree

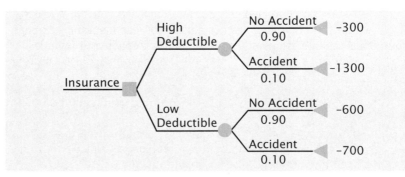

Risk seeking   Every risky situation has *at least* two approaches. You can take a *con-*
and risk   *servative* (risk averse) approach, wherein you take the alternative with the
aversion   highest probability of occurrence and/or the least amount of downside

potential. Or you can take the *risky* (risk seeking) approach, wherein you take the alternative with the greatest reward but usually not the highest probability of occurrence. In a risk seeking approach, you can end up in a worse financial situation than when you started. However, either approach can be used and may be appropriate given the situation and your **risk tolerance.**

Risk *is the product of a course of action or inaction taken under uncertainty to achieve a desired future outcome which poses the possibility of a loss, while* **risk tolerance** *describes your ability to handle the loss given your current situation.*

Risk and Risk Tolerance defined

In the car insurance example there are two alternatives – either a low or a high deductible. You can choose either alternative since you have enough money in the bank to cover the cost of insurance and the deductible. Which course of action should you pursue? What would be a good decision given a risk tolerance of $2,000? Can you really afford a situation where you could lose $1,000?

Decisions like buying insurance occur frequently, but how should we evaluate them to make the best decisions possible? What risk is appropriate to take? How do we know if we have made a good decision? To understand the answers to these questions, we must be able to quantitatively incorporate risk into the evaluation measure. This is the basis for a measure called **expected monetary value.**

Expected Monetary Value (EMV)

The measures of merit discussed so far (NPV, IRR, ROI, payback) do not include explicit statements about the risk or uncertainty associated with a given investment alternative. This is one reason risk-adjusted discount rates have been popular. However, good economic evaluations require identifying the sources of value, the values themselves, and the probabilities associated with obtaining those values. Using NPV to determine the discounted cash flow of a project is the first step in determining its value. We must also include the probability of success or, conversely, the risk of failure. Without including probability, we can only deal with projects where the outcomes are certain. In the car insurance example, the outcomes are uncertain and can significantly impact your finances.

In this example, the assessed probability of having an accident before renewing the insurance is only 10%. Using this probabilistic information, we can calculate the expected cost of an accident. In this case it would be $100 for the low premium (high deductible), and $10 for the high premium (low deductible). We calculate expected monetary value by multiplying the probability of having an accident times the deductible associated with each alternative and add the cost of the insurance to that value:

High deductible = (0.10) ($1,000) + $300 = $400
Low deductible = (0.10)($100) + $600 = $610

Deal or No Deal?

On December 12, 2005, NBC premiered a game show on American television – "Deal or No Deal" hosted by actor/comedian Howie Mandel. A form of the show had already been successful in other international markets and its success in the United States was almost immediate.

The premise of the show is simple. Dollar values between $0.01 and $1,000,000 (and higher for special shows) are randomly assigned to 26 sealed and numbered briefcases. The contestant starts the game by selecting one of the 26 briefcases to hold as their own.

In the first round, the contestant selects 6 of the remaining 25 to be opened. The dollar amounts in each of those briefcases are revealed (by attractive models) and those amounts are no longer "in play." A large scoreboard keeps track of the dollar values that are still within sealed briefcases. At the end of each round, a shadowy figure called the Banker makes an offer to the contestant to buy their briefcase and end the game. After the Banker makes the offer, Mandel asks the contestant, "Deal or No Deal?"

If the contestant selects "Deal," game play stops and he or she accepts the money and leaves. On a "No Deal" decision, the contestant must open more briefcases and receive a new offer from the Banker. The number of briefcases to be opened in each round follows this progression: 6, 5, 4, 3, 2, 1, 1, 1. If high value briefcases are opened, the likelihood of high value being in the contestant's briefcase goes down and so does the Banker's offer (and vice-versa).

As the play begins, the expected value of the game is the average of all 26 cases, or $131,477.50. The maximum expected value would result if only two briefcases were remaining containing the two highest amounts $750,000 and $1,000,000. The lowest expected value, $0.50, is on the other end of the spectrum.

Since this is a television show and not a pure experiment, the Banker's offers are designed to enhance the entertainment of the program. Early in the game, the offers are always a fraction of the expected value and this tends to encourage the contestant to continue playing.

As aptly stated on Wikipedia: "Deal or No Deal has attracted attention from mathematicians, statisticians, and economists as a natural decision-making experiment."[1] The show is an excellent study of expected value versus risk attitudes. The Banker's offer can be seen as a search for the Certain Equivalent discussed in Chapter 3. The show has inspired several research studies into decision making behavior and risk.

One research study done by Post, Van den Assem, Baltusssen, and Thaler[2] discovered that the risk attitude of the contestants, interpreted from their decision choices, was path dependent and could change as the game progressed. Specifically, they found that "Winners" or "Losers" (defined by opening low value or high value briefcases respectively) tended to be more resistant to make a "Deal" choice. Simply stated, both a large increase or decrease in the Banker's offer typically resulted in more risk seeking behavior.

1. Does the same type of behavior exhibit itself in business risk attitudes?

2. If your company has a series of bad outcomes or good outcomes, would that make the company more risk averse or more risk seeking?

3. How does this apply to your thinking about how you make personal decisions?

[1] Deal or No Deal/Deal or No Deal and scientific research. Retrieved January 26, 2009 from the English Wiki: http://en.wikipedia.org/wiki/Deal_or_no_deal.

[2] Thierry Post, Martijn J. Van den Assem, Guido Baltussen, and Richard H. Thaler: "Deal or No Deal? Decision Making under Risk in a Large-Payoff Game Show." American Economic Review, Vol. 98, No. 1, March 2008. Available at SSRN: http://ssrn.com/abstract=36508

By using this method, we are able to incorporate the risk of loss into the evaluation and make a logical, risk-based decision. In this case, the best course of action would be to take the high deductible. While your finances could be depleted by 50% if you had an accident, the probability is only 10% that it will happen. However, you must realize that *you either will or will not have an accident.* You cannot have 10% of an accident. It is like the saying that you can't be a "little bit pregnant." This often makes people uncomfortable in dealing with probabilities and risk.

Expected monetary value *is the average return we would expect to receive if we had many identical but uncorrelated opportunities. Expected value is calculated by multiplying each possible outcome (gain or loss) by its probability of occurring and then adding the products.*

Expected monetary value defined

It is important to understand that EMV represents a *probability weighted average value.* This implies that if you can repeat this opportunity many times, over time you will receive the average value. For example, suppose you are given an opportunity to call the toss of a coin. For a correct call you will receive $100, and for an incorrect call –$50 (See Figure 3.5).

Figure 3.5 Coin Toss

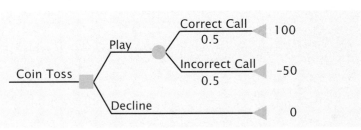

Assuming that the coin is fair (it does not favor one side over the other), the probability of calling the toss correctly is 50%. Using these values and probabilities, the expected monetary value of this deal is $25.

EMV= (0.50) x ($100) + (0.50) x (–$50) = $25

So, if you were given a single toss and a 50/50 chance of calling the toss correctly, would you will receive $25? The answer is no! Because your outcomes are either $100 or –$50, you cannot receive $25, it is impossible! Therefore, it is important to understand how EMV is calculated and how to interpret an expected monetary value. Let us examine what would happen if we had twenty trials or coin tosses.

As you can see from Table 3.5 and the cumulative graph in Figure 3.6, the average value per trial is about $25. The key to expected monetary value is to have more than one opportunity to play the game. If many opportunities are unlikely or if the risk is significant on any given trial, another method of evaluation may be needed to better account for the risk and uncertainty.

*Table 3.5
Coin Toss
Experiment*

Trial	Outcome	Gain or Loss	Cumulative Gain	Average Value per Trial
1	Heads	100	100	$100.00
2	Tails	-50	50	$25.00
3	Tails	-50	0	$-
4	Heads	100	100	$25.00
5	Heads	100	200	$40.00
6	Tails	-50	150	$25.00
7	Tails	-50	100	$14.29
8	Heads	100	200	$25.00
9	Tails	-50	150	$16.67
10	Heads	100	250	$25.00
11	Heads	100	350	$31.82
12	Tails	-50	300	$25.00
13	Tails	-50	250	$19.23
14	Heads	100	350	$25.00
15	Tails	-50	300	$20.00
16	Heads	100	400	$25.00
17	Tails	-50	350	$20.59
18	Heads	100	450	$25.00
19	Heads	100	550	$28.95
20	Heads	100	650	$32.50

*Figure 3.6
Cumulative
Average Coin
Toss Trials*

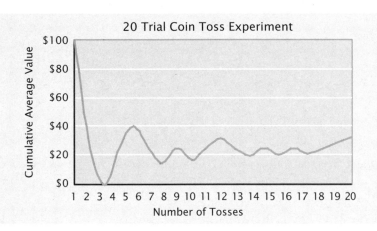

3.5 The Certain Equivalent

When the consequences of a course of action are not significant, using EMV is a good means to determine value. But as the consequences increase in significance, people become risk averse and assign a value less than the EMV to the project. In decision analysis, we have a method for determining the value of a project as risk increases – it is called the ***certain equivalent***.

Certain equivalent defined

*The **certain equivalent** (CE) is a single number that represents the value, which if offered for certain, would appear to the decision maker as an even exchange for an uncertain opportunity.*

The certain equivalent incorporates the risk associated with the project's probability distribution into the EMV of the project, providing a trade-off of uncertainty for certainty. The certain equivalent accounts for the risk of a project specifically by the use of a risk premium (risk pen-

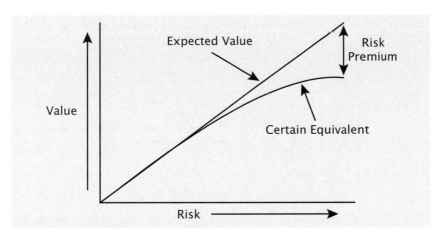

*Figure 3.7
Certain
Equivalent
and Expected
Monetary Value*

alty), determined by the risk tolerance of the individual or company. In contrast to the risk-adjusted discount rate, the certain equivalent provides a consistent approach to valuing projects.

Figure 3.7 illustrates how CE decreases relative to expected value as risk increases. The certain equivalent is an important valuation technique when dealing with strategic decisions which can impact the company or yourself. Mathematically, the certain equivalent equals the expected monetary value minus a risk premium. The certain equivalent can be calculated by approximation or by using a utility function. The utility function is the most accurate way of addressing the risk because it allows for curvature and scaling of the risk. Equation 3.2 is used to calculate the certain equivalent utility function:

$$U(X) = 1 - e^{(-X/R)},$$

Equation 3.2

where X is an outcome and R is the risk tolerance. R is assessed by the maximum you would pay for a 50/50 chance to win R or to lose 0.50 x R.

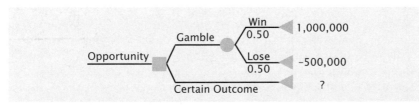

*Figure 3.8
Certain
Equivalent Tree*

Figure 3.8 is a decision tree representation of the certain equivalent measure. Depending upon the risk tolerance of the individual or organization, the value could be as high as $250,000 if no risk aversion is present. The graph in Figure 3.9 shows how the utility function U(X) changes with different levels of risk tolerance (R increasing from 1,000 to 10,000 to 100,000) and increasing values of X. Utility functions and their uses are discussed further in Chapter 11.

The certain equivalent is an important concept in dealing with high risk opportunities where your risk tolerance does not allow for an expected monetary value evaluation.

Figure 3.9
Certain
Equivalent
Utility
Function

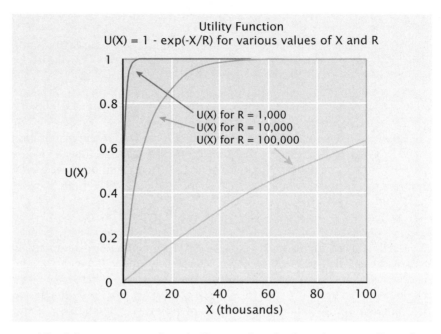

Economic
evaluations and
decision-
focused
evaluations

All of the measures of merit discussed so far have been predicated on good economic evaluations. The evaluations were logical, focused on what is important, followed general accounting and financial principles, and helped to provide meaningful insight into the appropriate course of action. There are a set of fundamental evaluation principles that are beneficial when performing decision-focused evaluations. Decision-focused evaluations are designed to provide insights into the appropriate course of action, which is different from an accounting model or evaluation which is focused on debits and credits.

3.6 Principles of Evaluations

Understanding the appropriate measure of merit is an important first step in performing a good decision-focused evaluation. But to make better decisions, evaluations must be decision focused, not accounting focused. A set of fundamental principles exists to guide us in evaluating decision alternatives. By applying these principles to your evaluations, you can minimize the confusion often created by traditional financial models.

Decision-Focused Economic Principles

■ Understand the whole value proposition.
■ Evaluations are between alternatives.
■ Only the differences are relevant.
■ Only the future is relevant.
■ The future is uncertain.
■ Timing is important.
■ Accounting is not decision making.

Understand the Whole Value Proposition

A common problem faced by teams is how to handle intangibles and synergistic values. There is a tendency to view projects as stand-alone or one-off situations. While many projects are stand-alone, a project team should not immediately assume this to be the case. It is important to understand the whole value proposition which includes understanding where value is created and where it may be destroyed.

I remember a situation with a large oil company where the exploration group wanted to swap some gas acreage for oil acreage. Based on the team's analysis, the plan appeared to add value to the company. However, the natural gas group had just signed a contract with another company to build a new gas processing plant. To make the plant economically viable to the company, it needed the gas acreage the exploration group was planning to swap.

Value proposition example

When evaluating alternatives, look for insight into where and why value is being created. Do not fall into the trap of quickly pursuing an initial alternative that meets the financial hurdles set by the decision maker. Instead, develop hybrid alternatives that maximize value creating activities. Seek to understand the different sources of value such as public image, consumer satisfaction, or product quality. Picking the "low hanging fruit" is easy! It takes time, commitment, and creativity to pick the tree clean.

Evaluations Are Between Alternatives

When evaluating a decision problem, we are evaluating alternative courses of action. If an alternative is not doable, then it is not an alternative and should not be considered. Sometimes we have problems where the alternative is either to do or not to do something. In this case we must decide between the following:

- What is the value if the proposed course of action is carried out?
- What is the value if the proposed course of action is not carried out?

If the economic consequences of (1) are better than the economic consequences of (2), then the proposal has economic merit in the sense that carrying it out is better than not. It is not the absolute value of the consequences but the difference between them that is significant.

Consider purchasing health insurance. You are a self-employed person and do not have health insurance. While you currently are in fair health, you anticipate having health problems in the future, given your age and family history. You estimate these problems could cost as much as $35,000 (this is based on a friend's experience). You can choose to not purchase health insurance and hope for the best, or you could purchase a policy for $7,000 per year with a $1000 deductible. In this case, purchasing insurance would appear to be a wise decision if you truly believe your health problems will materialize.

Example: multiple alternatives

What if another insurance company offered you a policy for $5,500 with a $500 deductible? Now the choice would be between no insurance and the $5,500 policy, as there would be no reason to consider the $7,000 policy. It is essential to understand that *no evaluation can identify the best course of action unless that alternative is included in the evaluation.*

Only the Differences are Relevant

When selecting from among alternative courses of action, it is only the differences that are relevant. In the previous example, the initial set of alternatives was between no insurance and a $7,000 policy. The differences between these two situations are very apparent and relevant. However, when the new policy for $5,500 was presented, the choice is really between this policy and no insurance, unless there were other differences in the two policies. For instance, if the $7,000 policy was underwritten by a AAA rated firm and the $5,500 policy by a BBB rated firm, the policy holder may question the reliability or customer service of the company underwriting the $5,500 policy. If the firm is not reputable, then the choice may again be between no insurance and the $7,000 policy. When evaluating alternatives, only the differences are relevant in making a decision.

Only the Future is Relevant

Since only the differences between alternatives are relevant, it follows that only future events are relevant. The past is common to all alternatives. The value of past transactions is important only if in some way it will affect future receipts and expenditures. For instance, the initial cost of an existing plant is irrelevant to the alternatives for expanding it. Likewise, an evaluation of whether to continue or stop a research program should not involve the amount of money already spent on the program (sunk cost). The decision should be based on how much more will be spent and the forecast of future benefits. Including sunk costs is a common failure mode for many teams and decision makers.

Sunk cost defined   **Sunk cost** *is a term used to describe money already spent on a project. Since it has already been spent, it is not relevant to the decision to be made about further spending.*

The Future is Uncertain

Evaluations involve subjective and uncertain assessments because they deal with future events. Issues like product sales forecasts, the actions of competitors, market growth rates and other future events are often very difficult to determine because of uncertainty. In dealing with the future, there is uncertainty as to *whether* events will occur and as to *when* events will occur. Assessments are therefore a matter of judgment. An analysis must be concerned not only with making assessments of future events, but also with the probability of those events occurring. Probability is the only way to correctly express our expectation of future events. I will discuss probability and how to obtain probabilistic assessments in depth in future chapters.

Timing is Important

The timing of events is as important as the cash flows in an evaluation. For instance, new products can gain a market share advantage by being first in the market. A good example is Pfizer's impotence pill Viagra®. It quickly captured the majority of the impotence market after introduction. In this case, being first to market was worth millions to Pfizer and definitely put the competitors at a disadvantage. Sometimes one event, like being first to market, can dramatically change the outcomes for all the participants in that industry or market. A manufacturing productivity improvement which could be made immediately might be more valuable than a step-change process improvement that would take more time to accomplish.

Because of the *time value of money*, we must understand and account for the timing of events and cash flows. Funds received today can be invested in other opportunities available to the company (or provided to the stockholders as dividends) to yield more revenue. This revenue can then be reinvested. Timing is very important!

Accounting is Not Decision Making

The purposes of accounting and decision making are different. Accounting involves past receipts and expenditures. It is not concerned with the alternatives of what could have happened – it is concerned with what actually happened. Decision making is concerned with the effect that different alternatives will make on the future economics of the company. While decision making and accounting have similarities, good accounting will never compensate for poor decision making.

We should not substitute accounting for decision making even though it is often easy to do. It is like trying to drive a car using only the rear view mirror. When the road is straight, there are not any problems, but with the first turn in the road, disaster strikes. Make sure that you know the appropriate use of both accounting and decision making.

Advanced Coatings Incorporated (ACI) is a large manufacturer of product coating and cleaning agents which are used in various industries. The company was founded in Philadelphia, Pennsylvania in 1922 by John Danbury. The company's first product was a brush-on waterproof coating for ship builders. Since then, the company has always been managed by a Danbury and currently is in the third generation with David Danbury, grandson of John Danbury. David became President and CEO four years ago and has since taken the company to its highest level of sales while at the same time increasing the debt load of the company by a factor of three.

Case Study: Advanced Coatings, Inc.

Once primarily a producer of spray-on coatings for the automotive industry, ACI has aggressively diversified through acquisition into cleaning agents that are used in automotive, semiconductor, molding and casting, and heavy equipment industries. David is responsible for ACI's entrance into the cleaning agent business. While this business has had tremendous success, it recently has come under intense pressure from competitors. David believes that the only way for the company to grow, both in earnings and market share, is to invest heavily in R&D for new products and to expand into new and untapped markets in the United States and overseas. ACI holds nearly 25% of the noncorrosive, spray-on coating market in the automobile industry.

Don Boldin is the research manager for the coatings group at ACI. Don brought a proposal to the review board for continuation of funding for a new spray-on rust inhibitor called "Norust." The product is a follow-on product for use in the automotive and marine industry. This project is in competition for funding with another new product being developed by the cleaning agents research group.

Table 3.6
"Norust" Project
Net Cash Flow

Year	1	2	3	4	5	6	7	8	9	10
Research Costs	-500	-500								
Development Costs			-1000	-500						
Capital Investment				-1000	-200					
Net Sales					500	1000	1500	2250	2500	2500
Depreciation				-100	-120	-120	-120	-120	-120	-120
Net Income	-500	-500	-1000	-1600	180	880	1380	2130	2380	2380
Taxes at 40%	-200	-200	-400	-640	72	352	552	852	952	952
Net Cash Flow	-300	-300	-600	-960	108	528	828	1278	1428	1428

Don told management, "You can't pull funding from this project because we have already spent over a million dollars on it." Don explained to the review board that it would take another $1 million to finish the research on this product. Once the research is concluded, the development costs for scaleup and manufacturing facilities could be as high as $3 million. Table 3.6 was presented to the review board for consideration of the Norust project.

What mistake did Don make when presenting his case to the review board?

He forgot about the principle of sunk cost. While his group may have spent $1 million on the project so far, that has no bearing on the future funding decision.

Calculate the net present value (NPV) and internal rate of return (IRR) for the Norust project.

If you were the decision maker, what information would you need to decide between funding Norust or the new cleaning agent? If both products pass the company's internal hurdle for capital projects, how should you determine which project to fund? How do you know that the alternatives considered and evaluated for the Norust project are the best?

In order to adequately define a decision, we must have a way to precisely define all the possibilities for that decision. We can do this by thinking in terms of distinctions.

3.7 Using Distinctions

To analyze decisions, we must have a precise and clear manner of defining the possible courses of action. One way of doing this is to use distinctions.

*A **distinction** is a distinguishing or differentiating aspect that is often provided by an expert. It provides clarity of dialog and a means to meaningfully separate one state or condition from another.*

Distinction defined

Distinctions allow us to speak clearly and carefully. Without distinctions we are unable to have clear dialog. Distinctions must be:

- clear,
- observable, and
- useful.

We can think of the simplest distinction as a binary event where there are only two states. A good example is the toss of a coin. There are two possibilities: either it will land heads up or tails up (while there is the possibility the coin could land on its edge, this event is relatively unlikely). This distinction of heads or tails is easy to understand since we are familiar with coins and tossing them. But what if we were going to talk about a more ambiguous distinction such as being an executive? How do you define the distinction of executive? Does this mean someone who has the title with the word executive in it, such as Chief Executive Officer (CEO)? Or could it be someone who is a supervisor of others? In that case, would a construction foreman qualify as an executive? This is why we need to speak clearly, and why we need distinctions.

Distinctions come in kinds and degrees. Consider the two distinctions of Teacher and Marital Status. Within each of these distinctions there are degrees. For instance, a teacher may teach math, science, or English. A person may be married, divorced, separated, widowed or single. These are all degrees of distinctions, and the different distinctions of teacher and marital status are kinds. The diagram shown in Figure 3.10 illustrates these properties. Distinctions provide the ability to have clarity in our discussions and to share knowledge.

Figure 3.10
Degrees and
Kinds of
Distinctions

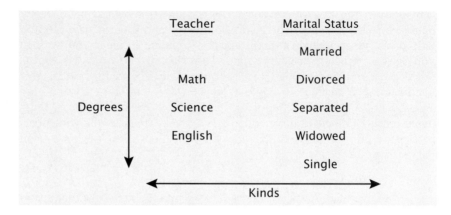

Consider the following case study of the uneducated criminal:

Case Study:
Uneducated
Criminal

John is a police officer with a large metropolitan police department. His wife Cathy is a school teacher at an urban high school. John and Cathy have a discussion one night about the number of high school students who are dropping out of school and the increasing number of them who are becoming criminals. John takes the firm position that anyone who breaks the law, regardless of the severity, is a criminal. Cathy, on the other hand, thinks only convicted criminals are really criminals (believing all people are innocent until proven guilty). Based on his experience as a police officer dealing with juvenile crime, John believes 90% of the students that drop out of high school become criminals. Cathy tells John that if he is correct, they should just put all the kids who drop out of school directly in jail. John hesitates for a moment and then agrees.

Why is having a clear definition important?

Without a clear definition, during a discussion it is easy for people to think they have agreement, when in fact they are in complete disagreement.

The Clarity Test

Our everyday language is filled with ambiguous terms and misleading information. To effectively communicate, we must have a test for clarity. To do this, we use a hypothetical being known as the Clairvoyant. The Clairvoyant is a truthful and all-knowing (imaginary) being (not the kind you find at carnivals). This being is able to tell you exactly (with certainty) any physically definable event that has occurred in the past or will occur in the future.

However, the Clairvoyant is unable to deal with ambiguous terms or make judgements and requires your questions to pass a clarity test. Another way to think of the Clairvoyant is as a database of information which requires the correct syntax before it will provide you with the information you want. You have passed the clarity test when the Clairvoyant can answer your question without using judgement or asking additional questions. Without clearly defined terminology and true understanding of the issues, assessments of uncertainty and analysis results can produce non-repeatable and possibly misleading conclusions.

For the case of the uneducated criminal, we will consider the following definition of a criminal to be sufficient for the clarity test: "A criminal is a person who has committed or been legally convicted of committing a penal crime." Using this distinction, we could say that the following possibilities are representative of Criminal – a person either is or is not a criminal.

3.8 Defining Possibilities

To use the distinctions we have created and the possibilities they provide, we must have a quantitative mechanism to compare and evaluate the possibilities. This mechanism is the possibility tree, and it is the first step in creating a decision model.

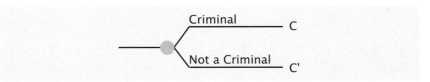

Figure 3.11
Criminal
Possibility
Tree

Figure 3.11 represents the possibilities for criminal (note that I will use C to represent "Criminal" and C' [*C* prime] to represent "Not a Criminal"). Constructing the tree in this manner provides a graphical representation of the distinction of Criminal. We could create other degrees of possibilities for the distinction Criminal such as Felony Criminal or Misdemeanor Criminal. However, for this example Criminal and Not a Criminal are sufficient. Using the definition of a Criminal, we could ask any person if they are a Criminal, and they could fit into one of the two possibilities we have created.

From the Case Study, the other distinction we can create is "High School Dropout." For this distinction we will use the following definition of a high school dropout. A "High School Dropout" is a person who withdraws or leaves high school before graduation and does not return to school to obtain an equivalency certificate. We could further define high school as to number of years attended and so on until we have a very clear definition of high school dropout. The possibility tree for this distinction would look like the one below in Figure 3.12.

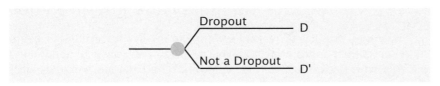

Figure 3.12
Dropout
Possibility
Tree

We will use D to represent "Dropout" and D' to represent "Not a Drop-out." Using this distinction, it would be possible to ask a person if they are or are not a "High School Dropout." From the Case Study, John is concerned with the number of high school dropouts who are becoming criminals. By building a possibility tree, we can examine the combined possibilities of being a Criminal and a High School Dropout. The tree (Figure 3.13) shows the possible combinations of these two distinctions. Notice that each path through the tree has a distinct elemental (i.e. unique) or joint possibility. These are labeled with the corresponding distinction possibilities, such as Criminal, Not a Dropout is CD'. Elemental possibilities are important in describing all the possible combinations of distinctions. Since only one elemental possibility will occur, we call this being **mutually exclusive**, and since one of the elemental possibilities *has* to occur we call this being **collectively exhaustive**.

Mutually exclusive and collectively exhaustive

Figure 3.13 Criminal and Dropout Possibility Tree

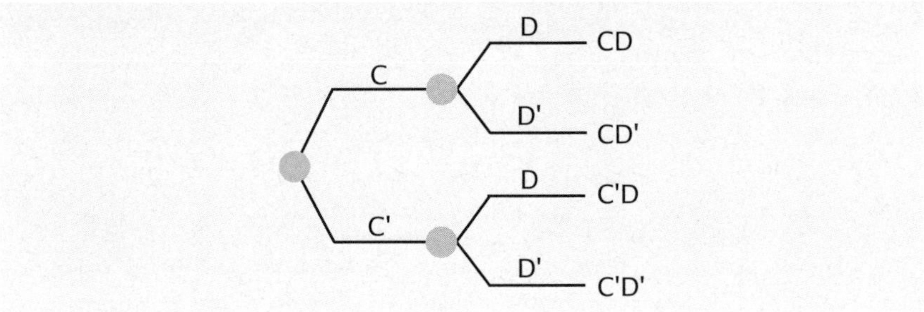

The ordering of the distinctions is not important. We could have just as easily put Dropout first and Criminal second. What is important is to include all distinctions which are relevant.

Creating trees in spreadsheets

Software is available for creating these trees in either a stand-alone program or as an add-in for Microsoft Excel®. Create this tree in either Microsoft Excel® or Lotus 1-2-3®, using cells to represent the distinctions and elemental possibilities. A shareware Excel add-in called Tree-Plan® is available at:

http://www.decisiontoolworks.com/.

TreeAge Pro®

The trees in this book were created using TreeAge Pro® by TreeAge (and then turned into Encapsulated PostScript files using Adobe Illustrator®). For information about TreeAge Pro see:

http://www.treeage.com/.

3.9 Summary and Interpretation

Nearly all important decisions we make involve uncertainty. Dealing with uncertainty appropriately is what decision analysis is all about. How we deal with uncertainty may depend upon the situation. Personal decisions usually have a more profound effect on us than do business decisions and therefore are sometimes the most difficult to make. In addition, the analysis we perform and the actions we may take will be different if we are the decision maker or are an advisor.

Many organizations follow the traditional advocacy-based approach to making business decisions because it has been ingrained in the organization, and it allows people to maintain hidden agendas and other issues. But in doing so, the decision maker and others become skeptical of analysis results and thereby develop their own offsetting assumptions and analysis interpretations. All of this usually results in reworking the original analysis and costing additional time and money. By using the inquiry approach, organizations can gain a much better understanding of the problem and commitment to the analysis results. However, all evaluations and analyses should be based on some basic financial principles with a focus on developing insights and making decisions.

An alternative to advocacy

We discussed the fundamental principles of economic evaluations and how to use measures of merit to value a project. With respect to decisions involving uncertainty, we know that accounting and decision making are different and that we should never include sunk costs in future decisions. Since risk and time are not necessarily connected, we should use a measure that accounts for both separately and that measure is the certain equivalent.

Finally, the Clairvoyant provides a means to have clarity in our discussions through the use of the clarity test. By using this test and creating distinctions, we can clearly understand the possibilities available to us through our decisions.

3.10 Key Concepts

uncertainty	certainty
decision response hierarchy	informed decisions
traditional decision process	advocacy based decisions
inquiry based decisions	measures of merit
net cash flow	return on investment
time value of money	internal rate of return
net present value	discount rates
risk	risk tolerance
expected monetary value	certain equivalent
evaluation principles	sunk cost
distinctions	mutually exclusive
collectively exhaustive	possibility trees

3.11 Study Questions

1. Give some examples of distinctions that you would use to describe yourself.

2. Describe a situation you currently face that involves significant uncertainty. Will you know the outcome of the uncertainty before or after the decision is made? How will you make the decision?

3. Give your definition of the clarity test.

4. Write your definition of a doctor and then draw a possibility tree with the possible outcomes.

5. Explain the fallacy of sunk cost.

6. Why is accounting a poor way to make uncertain decisions?

7. What characteristics should a measure of merit have and why?

8. Why is the time value of money important in making decisions?

9. Describe what an appropriate discount factor is and how it should be determined.

10. Write a short definition of net present value, expected monetary value, and certain equivalent.

11. When is net present value a sufficient measure for determining the acceptance or rejection of a project?

12. Why should you not use a risk-adjusted discount rate?

13. Organizations make decisions in different ways. Name three and evaluate how your company fits into these categories.

14. Name the seven basic decision focused economic principles for evaluations.

3.12 References and Further Reading

Bell, D.E., H. Raiffa, and A Tversky, eds. *Decision Making: Descriptive, Normative, and Prescriptive Interactions*. Cambridge, England: Cambridge University Press, 1988.

Hogarth, Robin. *Judgement and Choice*. New York: Wiley, 1987.

Howard, R. A. and J. E. Matheson, ed. *The Principles and Applications of Decision Analysis. Vol. 2*. Palo Alto: Strategic Decisions Group, 1984.

Moyer, R., J. McGuigan, and W. Kretlow. *Contemporary Financial Management. 4th ed.*, St. Paul,MN: West Publishing Company, 1990.

Raiffa, H. *Decision Analysis*. Reading, MA: Addison Wesley, 1968.

Skinner, David C. "Risk Based Decision Making: a Decision Analysis View-point." American Petroleum Institute Safety and Fire Protection Conference in San Antonio, TX, American Petroleum Institute, 47-57, 1994.

3.13 Guide to Action

Keep the following guidelines in mind when performing evaluations:

1. All decisions involve actions and events in the future and thus have uncertain outcomes.

2. Make sure you understand your role as either the decision maker or advisor to the decision maker.

3. Use the appropriate level of analysis given the decision situation.

4. Determine the most appropriate measure of merit or decision criteria for the analysis.

5. Don't include sunk costs in the evaluation. Money already spent is not relevant to future expenditures unless there is some salvage value or future offsetting costs.

6. Use probability as a means to incorporate and deal with uncertain events.

7. Use distinctions to speak clearly about possible courses of action and the resulting outcomes.

3.14 Case for Analysis: "Lease versus Buy"

You and your spouse have decided that it is time to buy a new car. You have decided on the specific make and model of the car. However, the saleswoman has offered a special lease rate. You can get a new car loan rate for 8%, which would make the monthly loan payment $445, or you can lease the car for $295. With the loan, you have to make a $1500 down payment. However, with the lease, there is no down payment.

- What measure(s) of merit should you use to use to evaluate your two alternatives?

- Draw an influence diagram for this decision.

- Which is the better deal?

- How could the saleswoman use the Decision Response Hierarchy (Figure 3.2) for the benefit of her employer, the automobile dealership? How could she use it to your benefit?

4

Making Compelling Decisions

I think there is only one quality worse than hardness of heart, and that is softness of head.

—Theodore Roosevelt

Have you ever wondered why some decisions get implemented and others do not? Have you made decisions or worked on projects that did not get implemented as planned? There can be many reasons why this happens:

- The decision maker may not have been involved.
- The risk was too high for the decision maker or the organization.
- Those charged with implementation were not committed to the course of action.
- Appropriate resources were not allocated.
- There was no shared understanding of the decision situation.
- The analysis had biased inputs or was biased in and of itself.

Why decisions (and projects) fail

Usually, the common cause is that the recommended course of action was not *compelling* enough to cause either the decision maker to approve it or the organization to support it. Developing compelling decisions is what decision analysis is all about!

Decisions made by large corporations differ from personal decisions in that several parties are usually involved, rather than just one or two people. The three functions involved are those who analyze the decision, those who make the decision, and those who implement the decision. Developing a compelling course of action is critical to gain commitment from all parties and ensure the decision is implemented as intended.

The project team is responsible for developing creative alternatives and evaluating them using the decision maker's preferences and unbiased information. From my experience, having the decision maker play an inte-

Decision maker involvement in the process

gral role in the project is the best way to make sure that the decision is compelling. Having frequent reviews with the decision maker to gather feedback and insights will facilitate the creation of hybrid alternatives that better match the decision maker's objectives. By involving the decision maker throughout the process, half of the implementation battle is already won. In addition to involving the decision maker, you should involve key implementation personnel in the later stages of the process.

Involve those who implement

I have seen many projects where a decision was made and then "tossed over the fence" for someone to implement. What usually happens is the people charged with implementing the project don't agree with the decision because they were not involved in its making. So the decision is reworked, costing the organization additional time and money. And if those people don't involve the next layer down, the decision may get reworked again and again. In the end, this situation could be avoided by involving implementation personnel in the decision making process and developing a course of action that is understandable and supported by all.

Defensible and compelling

A good test of whether a decision is compelling or not is its defensibility. Defensible means that the analysis is well grounded in facts and good judgment – not opinions and personal agendas. If you have done a good job of uncovering the key uncertainties, incorporating the decision maker's preferences, understanding the problem situation, and if you have performed a technically competent analysis, the course of action should be defensible as well as compelling.

I have a friend who was an analyst for a large corporation. He had been working on a strategy reassessment with a well known consulting firm. This consulting firm was not known for its analytical ability, but more for its creative thinking. They had been working on this project for several months when, a day before the presentation to the executive committee,

OPEC – A Delicate Balancing Act

The eleven member nations of the Organization of the Petroleum Exporting Countries (OPEC) state as one of their primary missions "to achieve stable oil prices, which are fair and reasonable for oil producers and consumers."

Whenever crude oil prices (and subsequently fuel prices) increase, OPEC is typically blamed. This organization loosely controls the flow and production of crude oil for export and the resultant pricing. While the member nations can disagree or even violate the recommendations of OPEC, in the long run, they participate in its forums and acknowledge its influence.

OPEC is constantly balancing production with crude oil pricing. When crude oil is in short supply, the price naturally increases and vice versa.

1. What goals and objectives would each member nation have in this decision making process?

2. What happens when the price of crude goes too high?

3. How do countries such as the United States protect themselves against higher crude pricing?

4. Are there benefits to high prices for the importing countries?

the team was asked to produce a cumulative distribution of NPV. While this would not have been a problem for a decision analysis project, it was a problem for a team that had not prepared for this type of analytical feedback. Since the team lacked the time and information to generate this insight, the consultant drew a cumulative curve in a drawing package, inserted some numbers he thought would look credible, and presented it the next day to the executives. Unfortunately for the company, the executives believed the curve to be credible and did not investigate the validity of the information presented. However, if they had probed the information presented, they would have found no factual basis and hopefully would have fired the consultant.

You may question the competence of that management team, but consider a more normal situation where your recommendation is questioned by the decision maker and others:

- How defensible is your recommendation?
- Are the facts representative of your situation?
- Are your conclusions logical and well documented?
- Are your analysis results technically competent?
- And above all, does your recommendation pass a reasonableness test?
- Would you invest your own money in this project based on the information presented? If so, then you probably have a defensible recommendation. If not, what is missing or what logic is violated that would cause you to answer no?

Questions to ask: defensible and credible

One last test of defensibility is to think of a person sitting at the back of the room during your presentation. All through the presentation this person does not appear to be interested or even paying attention. As you make your recommendation the person says, "Did you consider_____?" or "I do not see how you got to this conclusion." If you cannot answer the person with facts and confidence, then there is a good chance the decision maker will have doubts about the quality of the analysis and will not be willing to commit to the recommended decision. Many times this happens because the project team is too myopic about the problem and did not look beyond the problem boundaries to make sure the chosen course of action was appropriate, compelling, and defensible.

This chapter focuses on developing high-quality decisions which are both compelling and defensible. I will begin by describing the elements of any decision, and then describe what is necessary to make high-quality decisions. We will develop the mechanistic part of decision analysis later in the book, but it is important to understand the quality of thought being applied to decisions before we consider the mechanics.

4.1 The Decision Elements

All decisions we make involve choosing between one alternative or another. How do you make those decisions? How do you know you are making the right decision? We would all like to have a means by which we could guarantee good outcomes, but because of chance we cannot. The best you can do is to integrate in a logical manner:

Elements of a high-quality, rational decision

- what you want,
- what you know, and
- what you can do.

These are three basic elements of any decision and all three are needed to make a high-quality, rational decision. Decision analysis provides the means to integrate your alternatives (what you can do) with your information (what you know) and your preferences and values (what you want) into a logical, defensible, and compelling course of action. This is known as a ***decision model*** (Figure 4.1).

This structured and logical model can provide the insight necessary to make an informed decision and reduce the level of surprises that often comes from inadequate analyses.

Figure 4.1 Decision Model

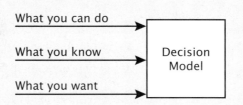

Understanding Preferences - What You Want

You must be able to define what you want or value. The easiest is money, but maybe you prefer something else over money such as safety, time, or control. This is your decision criteria, or the means by which you compare one alternative to another in a consistent manner. Whatever you define as the decision criteria must allow you to differentiate in a quantitative manner one alternative from the next. Without a means to reliably distinguish one alternative from another, you will not be able to choose the best alternative. We discussed the principle of decision criteria (measures of merit) in Chapter 3; here begin thinking about how you normally make decisions and what you use to value alternatives.

I frequently use a tool called the "Objectives Hierarchy" to help understand a decision maker's preferences and decision criteria. This tool also helps to develop alternatives that match the decision maker's values.

Objective defined

*An **objective** is simply the statement of a desired achievement. Objectives often state a preferred direction such as maximize or minimize.*

Many people have used this type of a process to gain insight into the values and objectives that influence a person to choose a particular course of action. Ralph Keeney's book, Value-Focused Thinking, provides a very good discussion of how to develop a hierarchy of objectives. Ralph uses the terms *fundamental* and *means objectives* to describe a contextual setting where the fundamental objective is an essential reason for interest in the situation, and the means objectives are the means to achieving the fundamental objectives.[1]

I have used the terms Primary, First order, and Second order objectives in describing objectives elicited from the decision maker. A Primary objective is the essence of the opportunity or what you want to accomplish. First order objectives are the main reasons for initiating some action, and Second order objectives provide resources or facilitate the Primary objective. Regardless of what terms you use, eliciting a decision maker's preferences, values, and objectives is critical for developing a compelling course of action.

The real situation outlined in the case study below illustrates how to develop a compelling and defensible decision.

A manufacturing executive of a chemical company once called me in to review a processing upgrade project that his staff had been working on for several months. This chemical plant had been very profitable for many years, but recently new competitors had entered the market and operating margins had been reduced. These new competitors had newer plants and processing technology which gave them a cost of manufacturing advantage. The executive knew that it was critical to increase margins if the plant was to remain viable. He was also concerned about the ramifications to his career if the plant were to continue to lose margin and market share to its competitors.

The executive was struggling with the decision of what technology to use for the plant upgrade. He believed that there were only two options available to him. He could install new equipment based on a proven technology that had not been used before in this application, or he could invest in a promising but completely unproven new technology. The new technology provided the opportunity to gain significant margin strength over the competitors but was very risky since it was unproven. The old technology, while never used in this application, was thought to provide competitive margins. Both options required capital investments of about $20 million and similar operating staff. An investment of this size was significant for the executive but was made routinely by the company.

I began interviewing the executive by asking about his preferences for this decision. He replied that he preferred a certain moderate success over the opportunity for a huge return or a significant loss. He believed if the project had a bad outcome (a

---

[1] R. L. Keeney, *Value-Focused Thinking*, Harvard University Press, 1992.

significant financial loss), he would be blamed for a bad decision and that would be detrimental to his career. He further felt certain that investing in the old technology would result in a success, even though this was a new and different application of the old technology.

Figure 4.2 provides a decision tree representation of the executive's initial alternatives.

Figure 4.2
Upgrade Case
Decision Tree

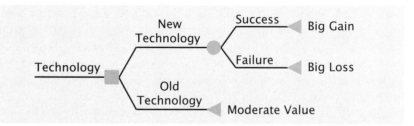

While he thought that the new technology could give the company a significant competitive advantage, the potential downside if unsuccessful was more risk than the executive wanted to accept. This discussion was very valuable in understanding the executive's preferences for risk taking, but it did not clarify the objectives he wanted to achieve.

Following the preferences discussion, we began examining his objectives for this project. We determined that the primary objective was to have a profitable plant with high-margins. To accomplish this objective, the plant needed to have process reliability, low costs, and a successful technology application. These are the first order objectives which the executive believed would achieve the primary objective. In addition to these objectives, there are some second order objectives which will further impact the primary objective. These include technology longevity, capital investment efficiency, and a long-term material supply contract (See Figure 4.3).

Figure 4.3
Objectives
Hierarchy

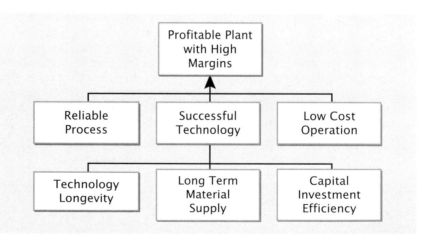

Incorporating Information - What You Know

When you make a decision, the focus is usually on what you know. You can always search for more data in the hopes that it will tell you what to do, but when should you stop gathering data and decide? Additionally, a common belief is that as you gather more data, you can refine the data set to eliminate uncertainty.

I wish it were true that data could be refined to the point that uncertainty is completely eliminated, but it can not! Your comfort level is increased through over-analyzing the data, but the underlying uncertainty is still there. Underestimating the "true" range of uncertainty in a problem can cause significant and sometimes catastrophic consequences. I would much rather have someone tell me the true uncertainty than show me a manipulated data set which obscures the uncertainty.

Attempting to eliminate uncertainty

A strategy project I participated in several years ago illustrates this point. The project team kept trying to refine the decision analysis to match the company's forecasted budget. In the end, it came close to the forecast, but there were so many manipulations of data that the insight into the problem had disappeared. I call this a perversion of decision analysis.[2] If you are not going to use the insights gained from decision analysis, then don't start the analysis.

What we know is important. It is the basis for thinking about and understanding the problem. Often we have all the information that is necessary to make a decision, but the information is not in a usable form. What we need is a framework to structure the information in a manner that allows for consistent evaluation. One of the most powerful tools available to the decision analyst for identifying and discussing uncertain information is the influence diagram.

Ron Howard has called influence diagrams "...the greatest advance I have seen in the communication, elicitation and detailed representation of human knowledge..."[3] Influence diagrams provide a tool to bridge the gap between a person's mental model of the problem and a graphical representation of the problem which can be communicated to all parties. By using an influence diagram, we can represent information and its relationship to the decision(s) under consideration.

We return to the case of the plant upgrade:

In discussing the uncertainties surrounding the technology to implement, the executive believed the key uncertainties were probability of technical success, cost of installation, reliability of the production system, and operating costs. The influence diagram (Figure 4.4) represents the decision problem from the executive's perspective.

Plant Upgrade Case Study continues

[2] D. C. Skinner, "Decision Analysis: Implication of Implementation in Large Corporations," *Decision Analysis for Utility Planning and Management in New Orleans*, EPRI, 1994.

[3] Ronald Howard, "Decision Analysis: Practice and Promise," *Management Science*, 34:6, 679-695, 1998.

Figure 4.4
Influence
Diagram

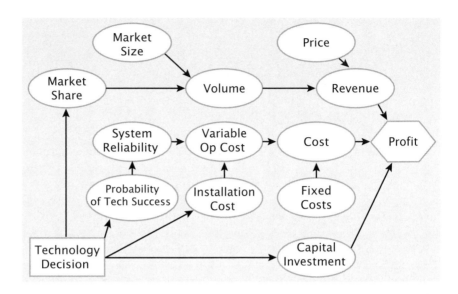

*Influence
diagram as a
framework for
adding clarity*

Let me illustrate the power of this tool with another example. I worked with a senior executive on a financial investment decision that he and his staff had been analyzing for some time. The analysis had been based on a few scenarios and some deterministic outcomes. However, the executive was having difficulty understanding the complexity of several dependent and uncertain variables. The executive had all the necessary information but lacked a framework for putting the information into a usable format. We spent about an hour over lunch discussing this problem. I was amazed at the level and detail of information he could recite from memory, and even more so, at his confidence level in the reliability of the information. At the end of lunch, I handed him a napkin I had been taking notes on. His eyes lit up and immediately he knew the answer to his problem. I had drawn him an influence diagram of the problem. This one graphic was able to structure the information in a manner that allowed the executive to think clearly about the problem and to understand the appropriate course of action. You will learn more about how to construct influence diagrams in Chapter 7.

Be careful not to focus on refining what you already know, but look for what you don't know to help you to understand the appropriate course of action.

Developing Alternatives - What You Can Do

What are your alternatives or options? Without alternatives, decision making is very easy as there is no decision to make. It is often the lack of significantly different alternatives that prevents us from attaining the best solution. How do you currently develop alternatives? Are the alternatives you develop significantly different, or do you find that you end with the same set of alternatives with which you started? The latter is characteristically true of many people. We often quickly develop a short list of alterna-

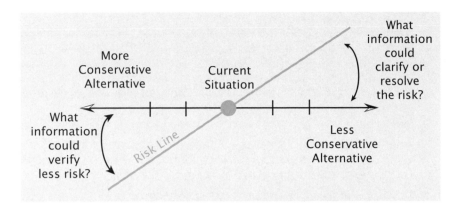

*Figure 4.5
Option Bar*

tives and stop, believing we have captured all the relevant or useful alternatives. But how can you pick the best alternative if it is not among the set of alternatives that you evaluate? There are many tools and processes which can help in developing creative alternatives or strategies.

A common tool used by decision analysts is the strategy table (see Figure 6.3, Chapter 6, for an example of a strategy table). This tool places the strategic decisions to be made at the top of columns in a table, then the team brainstorms possible decision options for each column. After developing these options, the team develops strategy themes which tie the various decision options together into a coherent strategy. *Strategy tables*

However, there are situations where there is only one decision to be made, and in those situations strategy tables may not be appropriate. I have developed a tool called the Option Bar for developing alternatives when only one decision is involved. The option bar shows a continuum of options from minimum through to maximum risk (Figure 4.5).

Here is an example of use of the Option Bar in the plant upgrade case:

> With the understanding that had come from the influence diagram, we began to discuss other alternatives or options that might be available. While it was apparent that only two alternatives were being considered, I reminded the executive that the best alternative might lie outside of his initial set of alternatives. I asked him if he had considered other possible alternatives, such as a combination of the two technologies. He replied that he had not considered other options but would be very interested in developing better alternatives than those already known. I suggested that we use the option bar to create some new and different options. The basic idea behind this tool is to stretch a person's thinking about a particular situation and the alternatives that may exist. *Plant upgrade case continues*

> We began by discussing the current situation. I asked the executive to think of a situation that was twice as conservative as the current situation. He replied that they could purchase a proven technology from a third party or possibly even a competitor in a different region. I then asked him what alternative would be twice as conservative as purchasing from a third party. He replied that

using the old technology would probably be that alternative. I then asked what alternative might be twice as risky as the current situation. He thought for a moment and replied, "Use the new technology." We then discussed that alternative for a few minutes, after which he said there could be an alternative which incorporates parts of the old technology with parts of the new to create a less risky process. Using this information, I plotted his responses on the option bar.

After the discovery of these new options, I suggested that we have a meeting with the project team to further discuss the alternatives and develop an information gathering and evaluation plan.

We met with the project team the following day to discuss the new options and to gather information that could further define the risk of each option. The project team was excited about the prospect of new alternatives and had actually considered using a mix of the old and new technology. But because of the executive's belief that only two alternatives were viable, the team did not pursue any other alternatives. (This is a common mistake many teams make.) During that meeting, we were able to design an information gathering path forward and a timeline for deliverables.

The effect of time and delay

One alternative that often escapes our thinking is time. What would be the consequences of delaying a decision for some amount of time – a day, a week, a month, a year? Delay may not always be appropriate, e.g. you would not delay surgery if you had acute appendicitis where a delay could result in death. But time is an important option that is often overlooked. More time may allow you to gather additional information, resources, or perform a more complete evaluation (I will discuss developing options in the next chapter). We must be able to find and develop creative alternatives if we are to choose the best course of action for a given situation.

By understanding the three elements of a decision, we are able to develop compelling and defensible decisions. You have done the best analysis possible if you have logically incorporated all three and have developed a full range of creative alternatives.

Plant upgrade case concluded

From the analysis of these new alternatives, the team was able to determine that the best course of action was to use a combination of processes from both the old and the new technology. All of this information had been available to the decision maker and the project team, but because of the decision maker's bias toward a certain result, these alternatives were never explored.

Using the three elements will help you to understand the basics of a high-quality decision, but developing a decision quality culture or process requires a more thorough understanding.

Making Quality Decisions

Analog with statistical process control

Decision quality means using a logical, systematic process that provides identification and improvement of key attributes of a decision, leading to clear and compelling action by the decision maker. We need to be able to test for quality before the decision is made rather than the typical approach which inspects the outcome after the decision is made. In many ways this is like statistical process control (SPC) used by manufacturers to control the quality of products and correct problems before the product reaches the customer.

Quality is important in every decision we make, but even more so for those decisions which are strategic in nature – that is, decisions which have a long time horizon or take the company in a new direction. These decisions set the direction of the company and often determine the policy for other decisions. It is imperative that there is quality both in the process and the content, as the "inspection of the outcome" approach to strategic decision making can devastate the company in the long-term.

4.2 Why We Have Difficulty Achieving High-Quality Decisions

Decisions made by individuals and by organizations are often inconsistent from a quality perspective. While everyone and every company can point to at least one decision they feel was of high quality, how many can say that they consistently make good, informed choices? We sometimes fall into the trap of solving symptoms and not the real problem. Other times we only focus on one parameter of the decision, usually costs. Also, as in the previous case study, alternatives are never developed or considered because of a preconceived belief or preference.

There are many traps that can influence our decision quality. However, there are seven specific quality traps that I see time and time again:

- lack of creative and significantly different alternatives,
- refinement of unimportant details,
- inability to deal with competing objectives,
- solving the wrong problem,
- not involving the *real* decision makers,
- wrong level of detail in the analysis, and
- lack of credibility in the information content.

Seven decision quality traps

Each of these traps is important enough to merit some elaboration.

Lack Of Creative and Significantly Different Alternatives

Everyone has a set of obvious alternatives when they begin thinking about a problem. In the previous case study, the decision maker was sure that he had to choose between the old and a new technology. If you end up with the same set of alternatives you began with, have you really found the best alternative? Finding these significantly different alternatives is usually the greatest source of value. Many companies, such as General Motors, have shown that creation of a hybrid strategy or alternative is often a great source of value in the decision analysis process.[4] These hybrids are the result of incorporating the best of several strategies or alternatives into a single alternative. This hybrid is usually several times the value of the original alternatives.

Refinement of Unimportant Details

Analysis
paralysis

Many analyses focus on refining details which turn out to be unimportant. While having "good" data is important, it is easy to fall into the trap of "analysis paralysis" or over-analyzing alternatives. We may feel more comfortable when information has been refined, but believing the information is of higher quality and the uncertainty has either been eliminated or reduced is almost always an incorrect assumption.

Several years ago, I was working on a strategic plan for a business unit of a large products company. The team had been working on the plan for about two months and was confused and frustrated with the enormous amount of information that had been gathered. I was called in by the project leader to help the team sort through the information and to build a course of action that would maximize value to the company. As I began to review the information already gathered, it was apparent they were constantly working to refine all of the information they had collected – not determining which information was valuable and focusing on developing a clear course of action. Within two weeks, we developed a clear and compelling strategy which the business unit quickly adopted.

During those meetings, I learned that the team was trying to refine the information to match a previously announced long-range plan. The long-range plan was not based on the same set of information being used to build this strategic plan, so the plans could never match exactly. We must not get caught in the trap of refining data to feel better or to meet some preconceived value, but we should look at the project to find out what we need to know to proceed with a clear course of action.

Inability to Deal with Competing Objectives

Life is full of competing objectives – as a decision analyst or a decision maker, you must be able to deal with these often difficult situations. Make sure the decision is based on value and not emotion and that you understand the risks and can accept them. The decision maker in the plant upgrade case was unwilling to accept the perceived higher risk of implementing the new technology because he did not want to tarnish his career. This is a very real case of competing objectives between a decision maker's preferences and the company's situation. The key is to focus on maximizing value to the company and to help the decision maker understand how that translates to him or her.

---

[4] M. Kusnic, "Lessons Learned from the GM Experience," presentation, October 1995.

This reminds me of a computing project where the head of information systems was lobbying for a new super-computer, but the head of the client department was advocating going to a third party for support. For three months, a team made up of representatives from both groups tried to develop a compelling case for either alternative. However, the two alternatives were very close in value, and because of this, neither side believed the other. The objective of information systems was to keep their people employed and to maintain ownership of the computing center, but the objective of the client organization was to lower overhead costs.

Competing objectives example

I reconciled the two sides in a half day meeting where both of the decision makers and their team members took part in an on-line decision analysis. We used NPV as the decision criteria and made a ground rule that the alternative with the highest value would be chosen. Then with the help of another decision analyst, we got concurrence from both decision makers as to the model being used and the inputs. While I was facilitating the meeting, the other analyst was entering ranges into the model. At the end of the meeting we were able to give each participant a copy of the model, the inputs used, and the final output. The next day both decision makers announced the decision to their organizations and began implementation.

We were able to accomplish this only by maintaining a focus on value to the company and working through the issues of each decision maker in a logical and objective manner.

Solving the Wrong Problem

It probably seems very unlikely you would solve the wrong problem – however, this is one of the most common mistakes, especially among new or infrequent users of decision analysis. We often refer to this as an error of the third kind after Type I and Type II errors in statistics[5] where incorrect conclusions are drawn. This error can occur if the decision maker cannot articulate the problem, has identified only a symptom, or the problem has changed during the analysis. The key to avoiding this error is to maintain interaction with the decision maker, validate the problem frame, and monitor the business situation for changes.

"Type III" errors

Not Involving the Real Decision Maker

Teams can sometimes make the mistake of not involving the real decision maker. This can happen if the project champion assumes the role of the decision maker but does not have the complete authority to allocate resources. If you cannot involve the real decision maker, I recommend waiting until the decision maker can be involved. You need the preferences and values of the decision maker if the analysis is to be compelling to the decision maker. If the decision maker is not willing to be involved,

---

[5] A *Type I error* occurs if the null hypothesis is rejected when it is true. A *Type II error* occurs if the null hypothesis is not rejected when it is false (Mansfield, "Statistics for Business and Economics," page 305).

this is a good indication that the analysis is not important and any recommendation the team makes probably has a low probability of being implemented.

I encountered this particular problem when I was working for the technology manager of an oil and gas company. He was in charge of a joint venture to develop a new crude oil refining process. However, the real decision maker was not the technology manager but the vice president of refining. The technology manager asked me to evaluate whether the company should continue funding this program, as it was progressing from the lab scale to the pilot plant scale. The technology manager informed the vice president of the plan to use decision analysis to evaluate whether to proceed with funding but received no real response or feedback from the vice president.

The project took about a month to complete and involved experts from both companies participating in the joint venture. The team had periodic reviews with the technology manager, but the vice president would never attend – usually saying he was too busy and to continue without him. I knew this was not a good sign but assumed the technology manager was keeping him informed.

The vice president was furious when we made the recommendation to stop funding the project. He claimed the model or the data used must be wrong. He could not understand why he should change his mind and not fund the next level of the project. Having not been involved in the process, he had no value for it. Therefore he did not change his mind and continued funding the project.

As a final comment, the project was not successful and failed in the areas the analysis had previously identified, costing the company over $5 million. Not involving the real decision maker can cause significant problems, and usually the analysis will not be believed or implemented.

Wrong Level of Detail

I have seen this trap happen many times. Usually the project starts with a narrow view and then encounters what I like to call "scope creep." This is where the problem starts small and then keeps expanding until the boundaries are too large for the team to manage. The wrong level of detail is usually the result of poor problem framing. The purpose of decision analysis is to produce insight and promote creativity to help decision makers make better decisions.[6] The problem with many analyses is that too many issues are included which mask the insights, providing no value to either the team or the decision maker. Complex problems can benefit greatly from the use of a simple model with only a few uncertainties. My rule is to keep it as simple as possible. There will always be people who want to dive into the detail and create huge descriptive models. **Only do the level of analysis necessary to achieve clarity of action!**

---

[6] R. L. Keeney, "Decision Analysis: an Overview," *Operations Research*, 30, 803-838, 1982.

Lack of Credibility in the Information Content

The most compelling reason to have quality in the decision making process is GIGO (garbage in, garbage out). Information reliability is critical for developing a compelling course of action. Notice that I said reliability, not accuracy. I often say that you can accurately calculate the wrong number. The key is to develop a credible and reliable range. I have found that most people can tell if an analysis does not "feel" right, even if they cannot articulate the specific problem. Holding peer reviews and other types of validation techniques will usually solve this problem.

Beware of GIGO...

4.3 How Do You Achieve Decision Quality?

Even though there are many traps that teams and decision makers can fall into, achieving decision quality can be accomplished. By using decision analysis, you are incorporating quality into the decision by thoroughly examining the problem and evaluating the alternatives. Below are ten principles of good decision making which if followed, will ensure quality in your decisions.

The Ten Principles of Good Decision Making

1. Use a value creation lens for developing and evaluating opportunities.

2. Clearly establish objectives and trade-offs.

3. Discover and frame the real problem.

4. Understand the business situation.

5. Develop creative and unique alternatives.

6. Identify experts and gather meaningful and reliable information.

7. Embrace uncertainty as the catalyst of future performance.

8. Avoid "analysis paralysis" situations.

9. Use systemic thinking to connect current to future situations.

10. Use dialog to foster learning and clarity of action.

These ten principles provide the overall framework for making good decisions, but we must also have constructive interaction between the project team and the decision maker(s). We accomplish this by establishing interaction points during the decision analysis process that act somewhat like quality stage-gates. Both the project team and the decision maker or Leadership Review Board must agree that each stage of the process has been completed before continuing on to the next stage. In Figure 4.6, I have identified these interaction points and the responsibilities of each team. These interactions *must* occur if you are to achieve clarity of – and commitment to – action.

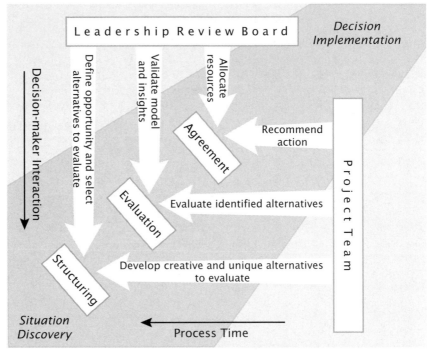

Figure 4.6
Key Interaction
Points

Leadership
review board
defined

*A **leadership review board** (also known as a decision board) is the team authorized to allocate the necessary resources for a specific course of action. The board is usually made up of the person requesting the analysis and several others who can provide valuable insights into the problem.*

As you can see in Figure 4.6, the leadership review board's responsibilities are to define the problem and validate the problem frame, to validate the information content and evaluation results, and most importantly to allocate resources so that the recommendation can be implemented. The project team must take the problem defined by the leadership review board and develop an appropriate project frame and alternatives. After a review and validation by the leadership review board, the team evaluates the selected alternatives and recommends a course of action.

Implementing
the solution:
RACI chart

It is also important that the project team integrate with the implementation team so that the right solution is actually implemented. At least one member of the project team needs to be on the implementation team. This provides the continuity of thought necessary to efficiently implement the solution.

A tool that I find useful in setting expectations and responsibilities when going through the decision quality process is the "RACI" chart. RACI stands for Responsibility, Accountability, Consulted, and Informed. In other words, Who is the Doer? Who is accountable for the decision? Who must provide input or resources to the decision or activity? and Whom must you inform about the decision or activity? This chart clearly details the involvement of each party in the process. It also helps in determining time commitments and the roles of each person. Figure 4.7 is an example of a RACI chart. Your roles and responsibilities may change depending upon the situation.

To create a RACI chart:

1. Create a chart with five columns. The column on the left, labeled Activity, should be the widest. Make four other columns to the right of it. Label them R, A, C, and I.

2. In the Activity column, write each activity or decision that you need to keep track of.

3. In the RACI columns, write the names or initials of all those who are responsible and accountable, as well as those who must provide input or resources, and who must be informed.

Activity	Responsbility	Accountability	Consultation	Information
Define Opportunity	DM	DM	ORG	ORG
Frame the Opportunity	PT	LRB	ORG	ORG
Assess the Business Situation	TM	PT	ORG	ORG
Develop Alternatives	PT	LRB	LRB, ORG	ORG
Select Alterntives to Evaluate	LRB	LRB	IMP	ORG
Evaluate Alternatives	PT	LRB	ORG	ORG
Choose Preferred Alternative	DM	LRB	IMP	ORG
Implement Alternative	IMP	DM	PT	ORG

Key: DM=Decision Maker, PT=Project Team, TM=Team Member, ORG=Organization
IMP=Implementation Team, LRB=Leadership Review Board

Figure 4.7 Example RACI Chart

4.4 The Ten Principles Of Good Decision Making

Use a Value Creation Lens

If we are to achieve quality we must focus on value. This means that you cannot focus only on one side of the equation. With many re-engineering efforts today, the key factor is cost. But if you do not include revenue effects, your analysis will be flawed. The goal of any business enterprise should be shareholder (or owner) wealth maximization.

Clearly Establish Objectives and Trade-offs

We must have clear objectives and trade-offs if we are to avoid making decisions that achieve something that we don't want. While this may seem like an obvious starting point, I have seen analyses begin framing without a clear understanding of what the decision maker wants to accomplish. If this understanding cannot be achieved, then it is very unlikely the analysis will yield any beneficial results. Establishing these clear objectives and trade-offs can only be accomplished through interactions with the decision maker. You must understand the decision maker's preferences if you are to develop a compelling recommendation and achieve commitment to action.

Use a radar chart to compare trade-offs

An interesting tool that is good for discussing these trade-offs and for measuring decision quality is the *radar chart*, sometimes referred to as a spider diagram (refer back to Figure 2.12). A radar chart allows you to include all the decision maker's preferences and then to evaluate them against each other.

Discover and Frame the Real Problem

It is relatively easy for an inexperienced person to frame the wrong problem; sometimes even an experienced analyst will frame the wrong problem. This is why the decision quality interaction steps are so necessary – you want to know early in the project if you are working on the right problem. Framing the wrong problem usually occurs because the decision maker did not clearly articulate the problem to you or you misinterpreted the problem. This can also happen if you are not viewing the problem from the right perspective. If you frame a senior executive's problem from a lower-level manager's perspective instead of the senior executive's, you may end up with a completely different solution which the executive cannot either understand or accept.

Understand the Business Situation

To frame a problem correctly, you must have the right perspective, and to have the right perspective, you must understand the business situation and the external factors influencing the problem. Without the right perspective, especially with strategic decisions, it is like seeing the trees but not the forest. In some cases, I have seen teams that see only tree bark. If you do not have a good understanding of the external forces which are affecting your problem, then take the time to investigate before you begin framing the problem. It is very important to have the right perspective and understand the influencing factors so that when you frame the problem, you can start at the right level of detail.

Develop Creative and Unique Alternatives

This principle is probably the most important after having a correct problem frame. I see many teams spend weeks working on a problem and end up with the same set of solutions they had when they started. I push people to think creatively and develop alternatives that push the envelope. One way of doing this is to ask each person on the team to write down their set of alternatives and put them away. The team now has to find a new set of alternatives. After creating this new set, they reconsider their first set of alternatives and try to find a hybrid that is made up of the best of the various alternatives.

After developing a set of creative alternatives, we must examine feasibility. If the creative alternatives are not feasible, then they are not really alternatives. However, we must be careful when talking about feasibility. Some responses I get include "we don't do things that way," "our management will never buy that," or "we don't have the authority to do that." These responses indicate states of will and empowerment rather than actual feasibility. Make sure an alternative's lack of feasibility is more than perception before discarding it.

A tool that I use for understanding the creativity of the alternatives developed is the alternatives map, sometimes called a s*trategy map*. This tool also uses the radar chart as a display graphic to clarify what options have really been considered.

Strategy map

Identify Experts and Gather Meaningful and Reliable Information

With any analysis, a typical response you will hear from someone on the team is "garbage-in, garbage-out," and this is very true. One reason many projects or solutions are never implemented is because of the lack of credible information. For this reason you must seek out and find credible, reliable expert information. While there are some situations where a team may have all the information, most require the subjective opinions and information from an expert. The key to finding true experts is to test for information depth and breadth and test ability to make powerful distinctions.

*A **distinction** is an insightful piece of information that only someone with expert knowledge could provide.*

Distinction defined

For example, if I were interviewing a refinery engineer about corrosion problems and the person could not describe how the refinery's crude slate affected corrosion, then I would know to look for a new expert. A true expert will be able to make powerful distinctions which provide both insight into the information we seek and an understanding of how it fits into the problem. If the identified expert cannot provide these powerful distinctions, then you need to find another expert. A true expert will also admit when you reach the limit of his or her knowledge.

In conjunction with finding and using expert assessment, you must gather information that is going to be useful to the analysis. Most analyses are a refinement of information already known. Capital budgets, operating expenses, and cash projections often require refining information already available or included in the analysis. You should update information as new information becomes available, but you should not believe that the current data set will provide all the insight needed. You must find new information that will give you the insight needed for the appropriate course of action. Don't just gather information that you know how to get – gather information that is necessary for decision quality.

This reminds me of a situation where a team had spent several days analyzing test market data which they knew was not of high quality because of serious flaws in both content and gathering technique. They thought some insight would come from the analysis, but no new insights were gained and actually the data proved to be completely useless because it was not important to the decision. Find out what information is needed to make the decision and gather it from a reliable source.

Embrace Uncertainty as the Catalyst of Future Performance

Uncertainty is a fact of life and business. Unfortunately most people tend to ignore uncertainty rather than deal with it, much less use it to their advantage. But uncertainty can be a competitive advantage for those firms who understand it and manage it better than their competitors. Every analysis we make involves some level of uncertainty and requires us to make some assumptions about the risk of the venture. The key is whether you are making explicit assumptions using probability or making uninformed guesses.

By embracing uncertainty as a fact of making decisions, we can eliminate many surprises or bad outcomes. We can also use uncertainty as a catalyst for future performance by educating organizations in dealing with uncertainty; they can then use it to their advantage in negotiations, product development, and joint ventures.

Avoid "Analysis Paralysis" Situations

It is easy to fall into the "analysis paralysis" trap. Since everyone would like to lower risk and narrow the boundaries of uncertainty, we often think that more analysis is the answer. In some ways this goes back to the theory of knowledge; what we perceive does not change the object of perception.

Analysis paralysis example situation   Think about this example. You are the analyst on a new product development project. You have some preliminary estimates about the costs involved (the typical plus or minus fifty percent estimates), and you have some market projections of similar reliability. You have been asked to prepare a series of analyses and get both the costs and market projections down to plus or minus ten percent before the project will be approved. While you may be able to get firm quotes from vendors on cost items, will further refinement of the data really change (much less lower) the riskiness of the project?

This is an easy trap for decision makers because they expect people to give them good concrete answers. By forcing extra analysis to get to these "good" numbers, we are often spending time and effort that is not required to make the decision, and we may make the wrong decision because of overconfidence in the degree of certainty. To overcome this we must educate ourselves and the decision makers as to what is an appropriate level of analysis for making decisions.

Use Systemic Thinking to Connect Current and Future Situations

Systemic thinking is concerned with the key interrelationships of variables that influence behavior or systems over time. Why is this important? All decisions you make today involve some action to be taken in the future. We cannot make a decision today that controls an event in the past. Therefore every decision we make is influenced by variables in the future, and not understanding these influences can have serious consequences.

For example, if you are an airline and you drop the ticket price significantly to gain market share in a certain market, what do you think other airlines in that market will do? They will usually match your price or offer an even lower fare. Will you really gain market share in the end? What if your cost structure is higher than your competitor's? Who will win the fare war?

We must have a good understanding of the structures that are present today and how they will change in the future. Many companies use scenario planning to help understand possible future situations and then develop plans for those situations. Systemic thinking goes beyond that to understand how your decisions today can influence those future scenarios. Make sure you don't fall into the trap of underestimating future responses or changes in underlying systems. Have a monitoring plan with contingent actions in place for when things change (remember the Coca-Cola case in Chapter 1!).

Scenario planning and systemic thinking

Use Dialog to Foster Learning and Commitment to the Recommendation

Dialog is critical to any project regardless of financial significance or level within the organization. But dialog should be meaningful and focused on generating insights that will illuminate the appropriate course of action. The more understanding that is created and shared, the more commitment to the course of action will be gained. Without commitment to action, there is no real decision. All the other principles build commitment to action, but without it, the other principles lose their value. Commitment to action links the decision with its execution.

To achieve this commitment to action, you must engage and involve the right people during the process. Waiting to involve them in the end almost always fails. Commitment to action is somewhat the cumulative effect of all the other principles – if you do them correctly, you should have commitment at the end. Remember that the product of your analysis is a clear and compelling recommendation, not the analysis itself.

4.5 How Do You Measure Decision Quality?

So far we have discussed what is necessary to have quality in a decision. But how do you measure it, and why would you want to measure it? Decision quality can be measured qualitatively by the team as it progresses from one phase to the next. It is a powerful tool and helps the team understand what additional work should be performed or why they should move on to the next phase. I have a template that I use to help guide the discussion, which is the important part of this assessment. The template is designed to help the team focus on what they have done and what they can do better as the project progresses. Again, this is a means of developing a compelling and defensible course of action.

In Figure 4.8 you can see the areas to concentrate on are developing unique alternatives and avoiding analysis paralysis. Provided with this kind of quick and visual feedback, the team can adjust focus and work to bring the quality of these elements to a higher standard. This does not mean every element must be high for the analysis to be of highest quality, but if the elements were all low, then the product of the analysis would probably not be a clear and compelling course of action. From my experience, any total score of less than 30 usually does not result in a successfully implemented course of action.

4.6 Summary and Interpretation

Attaining decision quality should be the goal of any analysis. Without decision quality, an analysis is no better than a quick intuitive judgement made with limited and often inaccurate information. The ten principles of good decision-making provide a framework for making quality decisions under uncertainty.

Figure 4.8   Example Project Quality Assessment

No: explain why.	During this project have you:	Yes: explain how.	Rank*	
	1. Used a value lens to focus on creating value?	*Not designed as a cost study.*	3	
	2. Established clear objectives and trade-offs?	*DM's preference is to maximize NPV and minimize risk.*	4	
	3. Discovered and framed the real problem?	*DM, LRB agree to problem as framed & validated w/stakeholders.*	5	
	4. Developed business situation understanding?	*Performed exhaustive business & industry assessment.*	5	Structuring Total
DM wanted to evaluate 2 options.	5. Developed creative and unique alternatives?		1	18
	6. Identified experts; gathered meaningful info?	*Brought in external expert*	3	
	7. Embraced uncertainty rather than ignore it?	*Used probabilistic assessments.*	3	Evaluation Total
DM insisted running multiple scenarios.	8. Avoided analysis paralysis?		1	7
	9. Used systemic thinking to promote insight?	*Developed multiple scenarios; possible competitor responses.*	3	Agreement Total
	10. Used dialog to foster learning and commitment?	*Involved DM and others in project.*	4	7
		Total Score (50 possible)		32

*Rank your confidence in each principle from 1 to 5 (1=lowest, 3=avg, 5=highest).

One of the most critical factors in achieving decision quality is to have decision maker interaction from the beginning. Without the decision maker's commitment to the process and the encoding of his/her preferences and uncertainties, the course of action is usually not implemented.

Decision quality should be assessed as a team progresses from one phase to the next. This provides valuable insight to the project team on principles which may have been overlooked or may hinder implementation.

4.7 Key Concepts

What you can do   RACI chart
What you know   creative alternatives
What you want   distinctions
"Analysis Paralysis"   Decision Quality
systemic thinking   Decision Quality Assessment
GIGO   value creation lens
primary, first order, second order objectives

4.8 Study Questions

1. Describe decision quality in your own words.

2. What is meant by commitment to action?

3. Do you have difficulty making quality decisions? If so, why?

4. Why is framing the *right* problem so important?

5. Describe a RACI chart.

6. Why are creative alternatives so important?

7. Explain how a radar chart can be used to communicate decision quality.

8. Think of a recent difficult situation and, using the ten principles, rate yourself on a radar chart.

9. Give an example of analysis paralysis.

10. Have you encountered the GIGO syndrome? If so, what did you do to correct it?

11. Explain why the decision quality process is important.

12. Why should experts be able to make powerful distinctions?

13. If your decision analysis team becomes overwhelmed with the shear volume of data collected, what can you do to still move the process forward?

14. What are three benefits to having the real decision maker involved in the decision analysis project?

15. Why is it important to consider the effects of time and/or delay on the decision?

4.9 References and Further Reading

Howard, R. A. and J. E. Matheson, ed. *The Principles and Applications of Decision Analysis*. Vol. 2. Palo Alto: Strategic Decisions Group, 1984.

McNamee, P. and J. Celona. *Decision Analysis with Supertree*. 2nd ed., San Francisco, CA: The Scientific Press, 1990.

Skinner, David C. "Decision Analysis: Implementation and Implications for a Large Corporation." In *Decision Analysis for Utility Planning and Management in New Orleans*, EPRI 1994.

4.10 Guide to Action

Keep the following guidelines in mind when performing evaluations:

1. Be sure to involve all stakeholders in the decision making process. Don't "toss it over the fence" for someone else to implement. Involve the decision maker.

2. Categorize what you can do, what you know, and what you want.

3. Help the decision maker categorize and define what he or she values.

4. Use influence diagrams as a powerful tool to organize and communicate information about the decision.

5. Use the "option bar" to help generate creative alternatives.

6. Beware of "analysis paralysis."

7. Use the RACI chart to set expectations and responsibilities.

8. Use the ten principles of good decision making as a checklist for the quality of thinking being applied to the decision. The Project Quality Assessment is a good tool to facilitate this process.

9. Use distinctions to test an expert's knowledge.

4.11 Case for Analysis: "Dual Careers, Part 2"

Consider once again the case of Jack and Jill from earlier chapters – Jack and Jill have career decisions to make. Jill has just been offered a promotion, but she would have to move to a city over 500 miles away. There is not a position available for Jack in that city with his current employer, and Jack would have difficulty finding employment in his current field, as their new city has few manufacturing firms. And, as noted in Chapter 1, Jack and Jill have two children – Rick is about to enter college while Jane is still in high school.

Use the Project Quality Assessment chart below.

- In the "No" column on the left-hand side of the chart, brainstorm potential ways in which Jack and Jill could fail to achieve a decision of high quality.
- In the "Yes" column on the right-hand side of the chart, brainstorm the kinds of things Jack and Jill would be doing to insure that they do achieve a high quality decision.
- Think through as many items as you can for each of the ten aspects of decision quality.
- Think through for a personal or work decision of your own – what are potential pitfalls relative to decision quality? What can you do to make sure that you achieve a decision of high quality?

Project Quality Assessment

No: explain why.	During this project have you:	Yes: explain how.	Rank*	
	1. Used a value lens to focus on creating value?			
	2. Established clear objectives and trade-offs?			
	3. Discovered and framed the real problem?			
	4. Developed business situation understanding?			Structuring Total
	5. Developed creative and unique alternatives?			
	6. Identified experts; gathered meaningful info?			
	7. Embraced uncertainty rather than ignore it?			Evaluation Total
	8. Avoided analysis paralysis?			
	9. Used systemic thinking to promote insight?			Agreement Total
	10. Used dialog to foster learning and commitment?			
		Total Score (50 possible)		

*Rank your confidence in each principle from 1 to 5 (1=lowest, 3=avg, 5=highest).

5

The Scalable Decision Process

If history repeats itself, and the unexpected always happens, how incapable must Man be of learning from experience!
— George Bernard Shaw

The chapters so far have been focused on providing an understanding of what decisions are, why they are difficult, and how to make compelling and high-quality decisions. This chapter begins the discussion of the decision analysis process and the tools and techniques used to evaluate difficult decisions. This chapter is short and to the point. You will learn more about the specific tools and processes in future chapters. The goal of this chapter is for you to quickly understand the ten step process and how it can help you make difficult decisions.

I use the term **Scalable Decision Process** or **SDP** to emphasize the importance of fitting the decision analysis toolkit to the decision situation which you are facing, and describe a larger scope than what is usually considered traditional decision analysis. Most textbooks focus only on the evaluation techniques and ignore facilitating the process and implementing the decision. The goal of this chapter is to quickly convey the different phases and steps in the Scalable Decision Process.

5.1 Is SDP Different than Traditional Decision Analysis?

The term decision analysis has often been associated with decision trees, utility theory, and even Monte Carlo simulation. But these are more tools of the trade than a process for gaining clarity of action, and these tools are designed to deal with uncertainty not ambiguity. SDP uses the same tools, techniques, and frameworks as traditional decision analysis,

Figure 5.1 The Scalable Decision Process

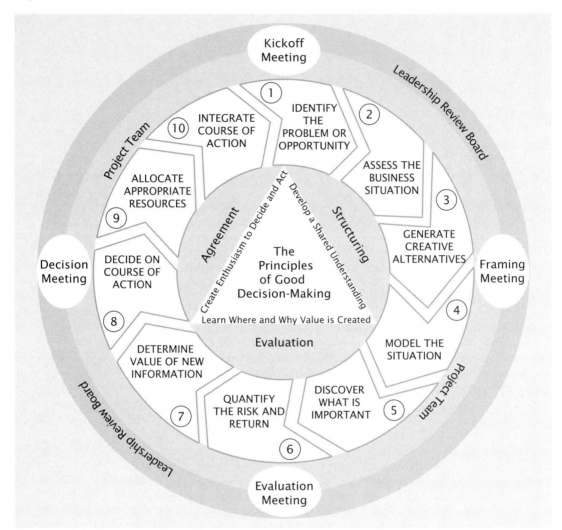

but it is different in that it is a process designed to handle *both* uncertainty and ambiguity. This more complete process is accomplished by integrating best practices from project management, business process design, meeting facilitation, and learning systems into the decision analysis frameworks. The detailed process in this book is based on insights gained by working on hundreds of projects of various sizes in many different industries.

Beyond large projects   Another difference (more philosophical than actual) is the belief by many people, including some consultants, that decision analysis can only be applied to large projects. I am often asked about the organizational level at which to apply decision analysis. I am also asked, "What is the minimum dollar amount or project size?" My reply is always the same: "It depends!" These questions are usually asked because of a perception that this process takes a lot of time and money to deliver a quality product. This is not true!

Decision analysis is as much, if not more, of a way of thinking and dialoguing than a formal process with many steps. This is why I call the process *scalable*. It can be scaled back for small projects which can be completed in few hours. A medium-sized project might be completed in a few days. Or, it can be applied in a very formal way for large multi-billion dollar projects which may take several months to complete. This process is valuable for decisions ranging from strategic to operational. *The key is to only use the tools and processes needed to gain clarity of action.* When you are finished with this book, I hope that you will understand this distinction and apply it to all difficult decisions that you make.

The Scalable Decision Process includes ten steps and 90 different activities for developing a high-quality analysis and successful implementation of the decision. Each step adds to the development of a shared understanding, to the learning of where and why value is created, and to the enthusiasm to decide and act. While all 90 activities may be needed for a large strategy project with many competing goals and values, only a few activities may be required for a simple project analysis. That is the power of using a scalable process – you can match the scope of the process to the needs of the problem. The thought of 90 activities may seem formidable, but think of this tool as a *checklist* to be sure that you have applied the appropriate level of work and quality of thinking to your problem.

Use the process as a checklist

SDP is based on the principles of good decision making and uses a ten step process which incorporates three frameworks – Structuring, Evaluation, and Agreement. These three frameworks provide the necessary structure to develop and evaluate a logical and compelling course of action. As each framework builds upon the insights of the previous, the clarity of the decision and the commitment to action increases. Figure 5.1 shows the ten steps in the process. The following biotech case study illustrates the various steps in the process.

Structuring, evaluation, and agreement

BioAgra is a start-up firm focused on developing disease resistant genetically engineered crops. The company has been in business for five years and has gained recognition in recent months for breakthroughs in disease resistant varieties of corn. The company was founded by a leading biochemist, Frederick Beushaw. Many other leading geneticists and biologists have joined the company. In addition, the company has gone through three rounds of venture capital funding and has liquid assets of $58 million.

Case Study: BioAgra

Currently the company is facing a product development decision for its new corn variety C12-X4. This new corn variety has a gene inserted from the common soil bacterium Bacillus thuringiensis or Bt. Using this gene, the corn is able to fend off the dreaded corn borer, which costs farmers more than $1 billion per year in destroyed crops. Initial testing by BioAgra indicates that their corn has higher yields and better resistance than anything now on the market.

Three large companies have broad patent coverage use of Bt. However, over the past year a series of patent applications reflecting a novel extension of the technology (beyond the scope of previous coverage) have been granted to BioAgra. The three large companies have not challenged the new patents, but BioAgra has not yet attempted to market a product.

A large agricultural products company (one of the three large companies now dominating the business) interested in purchasing the new corn seed has approached BioAgra. The company wants to purchase all rights for manufacturing and distribution of C12-X4. If BioAgra sells C12-X4 rights to this larger company, it could pursue other research and it would have tangible sales that would improve chances for future venture capital funding or an initial public offering. However, BioAgra would lose opportunities to license the product to other companies. What should BioAgra do?

5.2 Structuring Phase

The ***Structuring*** phase contains four steps for proper identification and framing of the problem. During this phase, the goal is to develop a shared understanding of the decision problem and a set of credible alternatives to evaluate. This involves defining the real problem, understanding and quantifying the factors affecting it, and developing alternative strategies to deal with the situation. In addition, in this phase we are developing the framework for the quantitative decision model which we use to evaluate the various alternatives in the next phase.

Identify the Problem or Opportunity

Step One:
Identify the
problem

The **first** step is to identify the problem. This means understanding the decision problem from the perspective of the decision maker. This perspective is critical for developing an analysis which meets the decision maker's needs. Without this perspective, many teams find that their recommendation is not well received or compelling and usually is not implemented.

One means of identifying problems is by establishing goals and then measuring the gap between actual and forecasted. Goals can be useful and are necessary for any organization to maintain effectiveness. However, sometimes goals can cause us to mistake a symptom for a problem. For instance, consider a company who is losing market share to its competitor. The competitor has a less expensive product, and so immediately it may be assumed the problem is the price of the product. The company reduces the price of the product hoping to regain market share, but market share still continues to fall. The real problem, it turns out, was not the price, but a quality problem in the manufacturing line.

Huber described this as identifying symptoms as problems.[1] Huber also defined two other situations which create difficulties identifying the real problems: defining the problem in terms of solutions and perceptual problems. Defining the problem in terms of a solution is like jumping to a conclusion before the true problem is known. I have seen this situation many times, and it is common after a good problem framing session. Many people think since the problem frame is well understood, the solution should be intuitively obvious.

Symptoms versus problems

Perceptual problems result from an individual's desire to either protect you from negative information or to defend a position. In doing so, the individual may distort or completely ignore the negative information, thus making it difficult to uncover the true problem. Perceptual problems become increasingly apparent in highly ambiguous situations. These are the typical "turf" battles that are commonly waged in many organizations. Decision analysis provides a means to deal with these perceptual problems in an open and objective manner. Once these perceptions are understood, they can be addressed in a manner that provides for input from everyone and develops commitment to the recommendation. Without this understanding, people may agree to the recommendation during the analysis, but when it is time to implement, the recommendation is changed or issues surface which delay the implementation.

When identifying problems, there are three broad categories which adequately describe most of the situations you will encounter – routine, non-routine, and opportunity (refer back to Figure 1.3). The majority of the problems you will encounter are routine and can easily be solved using intuition, procedures, previous experience, or a structured decision process depending upon the level of uncertainty and ambiguity involved. Non-routine problems are often of a strategic nature and should be handled using a structured and logical decision process like decision analysis. Both routine and non-routine problems are usually easy to find because they quickly become apparent to management, although sometimes not until the crisis stage. However, opportunity problems are often never discovered– they slip by inattentive managers and disappear or (even worse) are discovered by competitors. You should be continually looking for these opportunities and seize the most attractive of them. The situation analysis in the next step is useful in uncovering these opportunities.

Routine, non-routine, and opportunity problems

Tom Johnson is the CEO for BioAgra and has described the business opportunity to the team. Tom explained to the team his decision criteria and preferences for the evaluation. Among those criteria are net present value and an acceptable level of risk. Tom is concerned that selling out too early could hurt the company's future cash flow, but he is also interested in the public relations benefits from selling a product this early in the development cycle.

BioAgra Case Study continues

---

[1] George Huber, *Managerial Decision Making*, Foresman, 1980.

You are a member of the project team which must evaluate the possible options available to the company and make a recommendation to the board of directors in two weeks.

Tom and his team have agreed that this is a non-routine decision. Their statement of the problem is, "What strategy can BioAgra pursue to maximize Expected Monetary Value (EMV) from commercialization of the C12-X4 product?"

Assess the Business Situation

Step Two: Assess the business situation

The **second** step involves assessing the business situation. This step is crucial to forming a complete basis of the problem. Situation analysis can take on many forms from industry intelligence to benchmarking to competitor analysis. Figure 5.2 is a template for the basic components of a situation analysis.

Figure 5.2 Business Assessment Template

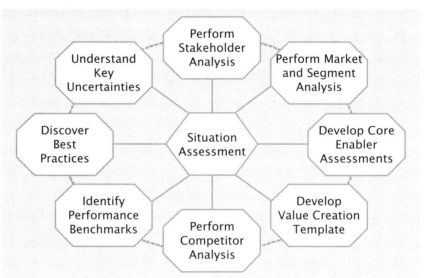

You should determine the depth and breadth of the assessment based on the importance of the problem and the general understanding of the factors affecting your business situation analysis provides the team with an understanding of the current business environment and the business' strategic position within the environment. The business assessment:

Business assessment objectives

- identifies trends for the industry, customers, and competitors,
- includes a cost analysis and an organization capability assessment,
- integrates both external and internal analyses into an overall understanding of the sources of competitive advantage, and
- provides an understanding of the dynamics of the current competitive system as a guide in anticipating the future.

Using this information, the project team is able to develop more credible and actionable alternatives. This information also helps to orient the team as to the validity of internal information assessments and the sources of external corroborative information. Without a good business assessment, many teams find themselves in endless iterations and rework before the decision maker will decide on a course of action.

The BioAgra team performed a competitor analysis to identify key industry players and their strategies with respect to acquisitions, marketing, and product development. From this information, the team was able to identify one other credible and potential buyer of C12-X4. The team was also able to better quantify the potential impact of the product in the marketplace and to identify several key issues that may impact the analysis. Graphs showing information gathered in the business assessment are shown in Figure 5.3.

BioAgra Case continues: competitor analysis

Figure 5.3 BioAgra Case Business Assessment

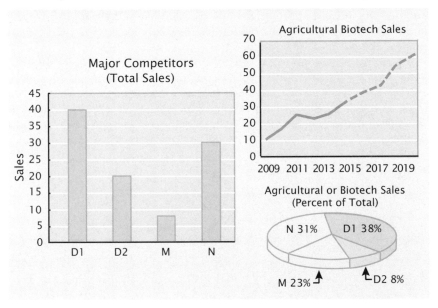

Generate Creative Alternatives

The **third** step is generating creative and significantly different alternatives. It is just as important for the group to be creative as it is for the alternatives to be significantly different. Many teams develop a long list of possible alternatives, but only two or three are truly different; the rest are minor variations from the core set. Do not spend too much time trying to develop *all* the possible alternatives the decision maker may want to see. Develop a small list of very different alternatives and then let the decision maker develop the incremental or hybrid strategies from those few. The lack of significantly different and creative alternatives is a common problem for many organizations. There are several tools which I will discuss in the next chapter to help teams think creatively and develop very different alternatives.

Step Three: Generate alternatives

BioAgra Case: alternatives

The BioAgra team spent about a day and a half developing possible alternatives which would fit with the preferences expressed by the decision maker. The team ended up with three possible solutions:

1. Sell all the production and distribution rights to the buyer (also known as the "cash out" strategy).

2. Partner with a production and distribution company and finish the development internally

3. License the technology to several companies.

Model the Situation

Step Four: Build a decision model

Finally, the **fourth** step is to build a decision model of the problem or opportunity. The model should be at a level of detail that provides clarity and insights into the appropriate course of action but does not involve the detail of a financial budgeting model. There are two basic types of decision models: the *decision diagram* and the *quantitative model*.

A decision diagram is a means of conveying the essence of the problem to others in logical and understandable manner. Influence diagrams and decision trees are usually used to perform this function. While these tools can also be used for the quantitative model, many times a spreadsheet is all that is needed. Figure 5.4 is an influence diagram of the BioAgra decision.

Figure 5.4 Influence Diagram

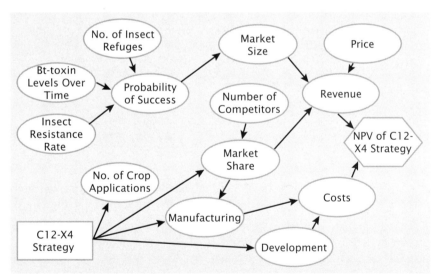

Decision models versus accounting and budgeting

A quantitative decision model should be designed to achieve clarity of action, *not* accounting accuracy. While this does not mean the model should use improper accounting rules or techniques, the detail needed and the information content is quite different from a budgeting model. For instance, in a decision model you use one depreciation rate for all capital even though in reality the accountants may use four different rates. The true test here is understanding the difference between accuracy and relevance. If the depreciation rate is a major factor in the analysis and could change the decision, then it would be appropriate to include all four rates in the decision model. However, if having all four rates in the model only changes the NPV from say $50MM to $51MM and your economic hurdle is $30MM, then this added NPV is not going to change the decision, only the forecasted economics. Do not fall into the trap of analysis paralysis and lose sight of the difference between relevance and accounting accuracy.

From the business assessment, the team was able to determine that the probability of success in a particular application had a tremendous impact on the future finances of the company. They also determined that the probability of success had three main components – insect resistance rate, number of refuges per application, and Bt toxin levels over time. Insect resistance is the ability of an insect to become immune to the genetic toxins of the plant. The number of refuges per application refers to the number of nonresistant insects allowed to feed on non-genetically engineered plants, and the Bt toxin level over time reflects the potency of the plants in the various seasons. These three components determine the efficacy rate of the genetic crops over time against certain insects. This is important because if the insects become resistant quickly, the engineered plants will be no more effective than non-engineered plants.

Constructing the BioAgra Case influence diagram

Using this information, the team was able to construct the influence diagram in Figure 5.4. This decision model was then tested with the decision maker for completeness. (For this example the model has been simplified for illustration purposes. Normally the model would further decompose costs and revenue streams.) The team then identified information sources and experts to interview so that the model could be evaluated. After gathering ranges on the uncertain variables, the team was ready to begin evaluating each alternative.

5.3 Evaluation Phase

The *Evaluation* phase deals with the analysis of the alternatives generated in the structuring phase and learning where and why value is created. It is important to have an understanding of both where and why value is being created so that hybrid alternatives which maximize value can be created. Of the three phases, the evaluation phase is the most mechanical and can be accomplished with specialized decision analysis software or spreadsheets.

Discover What is Important

Step **five** involves using deterministic sensitivity analysis to discover the most important variables in the problem. Once these have been identified, the model can often be simplified, thereby clarifying the course of action further. Many uncertainties which are initially considered the most

Step Five: Discover important variables

important, in the end, may turn out to be relatively unimportant. For example, when building a production line for a new product, capital cost usually will be at the top of most people's lists. But market share more often turns out to be the most important variable. This situation happens many times because people have been trained over time to focus on costs rather than revenue.

Performing a sensitivity analysis can be accomplished with either specialized software like TreeAge Pro® from Treeage software or by using either Lotus® or Excel® spreadsheets. The idea behind the sensitivity analysis is to vary each variable from its low to high value and examine its impact on the value of the alternative. It is that simple! This analysis can be performed in a short amount of time and sometimes provides all the information necessary for clarity of action. It is important that all parties involved in the analysis understand which variables are important and what can be done to mitigate the downside effects. We will discuss using spreadsheets and other software in more detail in Chapter 7.

BioAgra Case: gathering assessments and developing the sensitivity analysis

Using the decision model from Figure 5.4, the team gathered the necessary data for a deterministic sensitivity evaluation. By doing so, the team gathered ranges for each of the uncertainties identified in the influence diagram for each alternative. These ranges should be in the form of a three point estimate using a low, base, and high value. This information is then entered into the decision model and a base case number is generated. Up to this point, the process was similar to what the team had done in past analyses. However, the team was now focused on developing insights into the problem rather than just generating numbers to present to the decision maker. Figure 5.5 is a tornado diagram showing the most important variables given this problem's understanding and information.

Figure 5.5 "Partner" Alternative Tornado Diagram

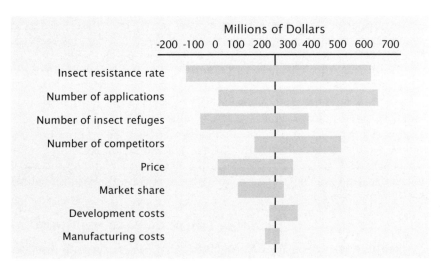

Quantify Risk and Return

In step **six**, we need to understand the risk and return trade-off and make sure that the appropriate risk attitude is applied to the problem. Choosing the highest net present value alternative is not always the most appropriate choice for an organization. Consider a start-up company which has two alternatives and only $5 million in liquid assets. One alternative has an expected value of $25 million and the other an expected value of $20 million. Based on expected values only, you would choose the $25 million alternative. However, risk must be taken into account. The $25 million alternative has the following distribution: 50% at -$10MM, 20% at $0MM, and 30% at $100MM. Should a firm with only $5MM be risking its future on the reasonable probability of losing $10MM? In contrast, the $20 million alternative had a distribution of: 20% at $100MM, and 80% at $0MM. While it is more likely the company will only cover its cost of capital, it has the opportunity for a large return without the downside of the first alternative.

Step Six: Quantify risk and return

The three alternatives were evaluated by the BioAgra project team. From this evaluation, the most aggressive and risky alternative is for BioAgra to finish development of the new seed and then pursue a production and distribution partner (See Figure 5.6). This alternative has a downside of up to $20 million due to some development and production issues still unresolved. Also, the burden for the development costs is with BioAgra and not a third party.

BioAgra Case: evaluating the alternatives

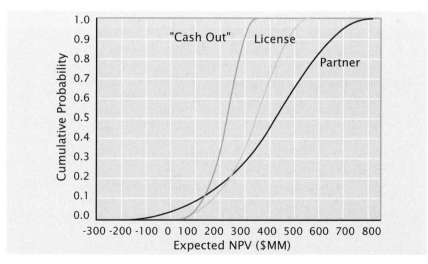

Figure 5.6 Cumulative Probability Graph of Case Study Alternatives

The least risky is the "cash out" option because it has a guaranteed purchase price and future royalties based on sales. The third option (license the technology to several companies) has the opportunity to provide both greater and lesser returns than the "cash out" alternative but does not have the downside risk of "partner."

If a recommendation is to be compelling, it must fit within a decision maker's risk tolerance. Many times a decision may be analyzed and recommended based on one risk attitude, only to find that the decision maker's risk attitude has changed, and he or she is not willing to commit the resources necessary for implementation. We must ensure that the recommendation fits the decision maker's risk tolerance.

BioAgra Case: risk mitigation

The project team presented the evaluation of the alternatives to the CEO and asked for feedback. Tom thanked the team for their hard work and began probing the analysis. His main concern was what could be done to mitigate the downside risk if the company wanted to pursue the Partner strategy. The team said they would do further analysis to provide insight into the possibility of mitigating the downside risk. When asked specifically what level of risk would be acceptable, Tom replied, "Well the less risk the better, but I would seriously consider an option with a downside risk of less than $50 million."

Determine the Value of New Information

Step Seven: Explore value of information

Step **seven** explores the value of the alternatives with current and possible new information for determining the best course of action. The decision maker, when making a decision, is committing to a course of action designed to bring about some specific objective. But decision making is a dynamic process and not just the act of choosing an alternative. Often specific new information about key uncertainties will change the decision. If this is the case, then this new information has a value which can be calculated prior to making the decision. We call this the *value of perfect and imperfect information*. Perfect information implies that there is no chance the information will be incorrect, while imperfect information is associated with high-quality but not perfect information. In most cases, we cannot purchase perfect information, but we can purchase imperfect information and can calculate its value.

Perfect and imperfect information

BioAgra Case: value of information

In the BioAgra Case Study, the key uncertainties influencing value were the insect resistance rate and the number of applications for the new seed. We can calculate the value of resolving both of these uncertainties before making a decision. The value of new information, whether perfect or imperfect, is the difference between the expected value with the new information and the value without the new information.

- Value with new information $590 million
- Value without new information $380 million
- Value of perfect information $210 million (partner alternative)

The team reported back to the CEO this new insight and was asked to develop alternatives which could provide the needed information. The team returned with a list of alternatives, however none of the alternatives could provide reliable information before the decision needed to be made.

5.4 Agreement Phase

The ***Agreement*** phase is the final framework designed to bring together all the parts of the analysis in a coherent and compelling form that will lead to immediate action by the decision maker. This phase is also involved with ensuring that implementation of the decision will proceed as intended.

Decide on the Course of Action

Step **eight** is the last appraisal of the analysis and should be focused on any refinements which could change the recommended course of action. The test for the robustness of any course of action, regardless of how it looks on paper, is found in the behavior and responsiveness of the people involved with the decision. If you are appraising the course of action– and have involved the decision maker(s) and the team members–

Step Eight: Refine course of action

Amazon.com – Mega Revenues - Micro Initial Profits

In the spring of 1994, Jeff Bezos "came across a startling statistic that worldwide web usage was growing at a rate of 2300% per year." This was the clarion call that led Mr. Bezos to quit his job and start Amazon.com. The company was started in his garage in a Seattle suburb with Mr. Bezos driving the packages to the post office himself. Amazon.com expanded quickly and today is the world's leading online shopping service with $14.8 billion in revenues.[1] With unlimited virtual shelf space, Amazon.com markets an ever-expanding product offering.

From the Amazon.com website: "Amazon.com is the place to find and discover anything you want to buy online. We're very proud that millions of people in more than 220 countries have made us the leading online shopping site. We have Earth's Biggest Selection™ of products, including free electronic greeting cards, online auctions, and millions of books, CDs, videos, DVDs, toys and games, electronics, kitchenware, computers and more."

With revenues of $5.26 billion in 2003, the company posted its first ever profit of $35 million or $0.08 per share. In 2007, the company made $476 million profit (corresponding to $1.12 per share) on $14.8 billion of revenue.

1. What preferences or values do you think Mr. Bezos uses to guide decision making?

2. Based on these numbers, would you consider the financial performance of the company to be a successful outcome?

3. Did Amazon.com reinvest too much in growth?

[1] For the year ending 12/31/2007; source: www.wsj.com

and the course of action is not compelling, you may have solved the wrong problem. If you have, then look to re-frame the decision rather than push to make a decision that is not supported.

The BioAgra team developed a communication and information package to present to the board of directors. At the meeting, the team explained the analysis process and the key variables which influence the value of the product decision. The team further explained the risks involved with each alternative and how the value could be enhanced by gaining new information. The team recommended pursuing the licensing strategy as it had the best risk/return ratio and did not have a negative downside.

The board of directors unanimously approved the recommendation and chartered a team to develop and pursue a licensing strategy. The board also chartered a team to develop a plan for acquiring information about the key uncertainties to minimize the risk of this strategy and future products.

Allocate the Appropriate Resources

In step **nine**, the decision board agrees on the proposed course of action and begins to develop a list of resources necessary to implement the decision. Because most situations involve people, you must ensure that the course of action is fully supported by the necessary personnel. Additional teams may need to be chartered to address specific uncertainties or issues which surfaced in the analysis. The worst mistake a decision maker can make is to assume that once the decision is made it will automatically happen as planned!

Implement the Course of Action

Step **ten** involves the actual implementation of the course of action and the development of a communication package for the organization. A decision analysis is little more than a fancy report if not implemented, and it must be effectively implemented to achieve the desired objective for which it was designed. Many good analyses and decisions have been impaired by poor implementation, and for the most part, implementation is more important than the analysis. A good analysis will not make up for a poor implementation.

Each of these three phases, structuring, evaluation, and agreement, are unique and important to the decision analysis process. **When performing a decision analysis, if the answer becomes clear and compelling at any point in the process, you should stop and make the decision**. Remember, the purpose of the analysis is to gain insight into the proper course of action– not to do an analysis!

However, remember that there can be temptation to "short circuit" the process, which may result either missing the best alternative or difficulty during implementation.

5.5 Summary and Interpretation

By approaching important decisions systematically, we can pick the tools and processes necessary to gain clarity of action. The *Scalable Decision Process* integrates decision analysis with best practices from project management, business process design, meeting facilitation, and learning systems.

The structuring phase includes identifying the correct problem, assessing the business situation, generating truly creative alternatives, and developing a decision model. The objective of the business assessment is to map the competitive situation affecting the decision. Note that an influence diagram is an excellent tool for developing and communicating the decision model.

In the evaluation phase, we perform a deterministic sensitivity analysis to discover what is important relative to the decision; we then quantify risk and return, and finally determine the value of new information. Note that there are two kinds of new information– perfect and imperfect.

The agreement phase is the final phase. It includes making the decision, allocating appropriate resources, and implementing the course of action. Note that events are unlikely to proceed automatically just because a decision has been made; appropriate energy and attention must be applied for successful implementation.

5.6 Key Concepts

Scalable Decision Process (SDP)	creative alternatives
Structuring Phase	decision diagram
Evaluation Phase	quantitative model
Agreement Phase	sensitivity analysis
goals	tornado diagram
solutions versus problems	cumulative distribution
perceptual problems	value of perfect information
routine, non-routine opportunity	value of imperfect information
business assessment	resource allocation

5.7 Study Questions

1. Why is the 10-step decision process outlined in this chapter referred to as the *scalable* decision process?

2. What is the distinction between *uncertainty* and *ambiguity*?

3. What causes perceptual problems (in the context of problem or opportunity identification)?

4. What are the purposes of the business assessment?

5. What is likely to happen if the business assessment is not completed or is completed poorly?

6. What is the purpose of the *deterministic sensitivity analysis*?

7. What do we mean by *value of imperfect information*?

8. If you complete the entire process, but the course of action is not compelling, what does this mean and what should you do?

9. What should you do when the answer becomes clear and compelling?

10. Give an example of how you could mistake a symptom for a problem?

11. Name three broad categories of problems you will encounter and the SDP methods that are necessary for each category.

12. Instead of trying to develop all the possible alternatives in a decision analysis, what should the team focus on?

5.8 References and Further Reading

Doyle, Michael and Straus, David. *How to Make Meetings Work*. New York: Jove Publications, 1976.

Huber, George. *Managerial Decision Making*. Glenview, IL: Foresman, 1980.

Howard, Ronald A. and Matheson, James E. (editors). *Readings on the Principles and Applications of Decision Analysis*. Palo Alto, CA: Strategic Decisions Group, 1983, 1987, 1989.

5.9 Guide to Action

Keep the following guidelines in mind when performing evaluations:

1. Use the 10-step Scalable Decision Process as a guide for decision quality. Pick the tools you need to gain clarity of action.

2. When framing the problem, be sure not to mistake *symptoms* for *problems*. Do not define the problem in terms of solutions and be conscious of perceptual problems.

3. Opportunity problems are not discovered unless you are alert for them. Try to discover them before your competitors do!

4. A thorough business analysis will give you a complete picture of the competitive environment and where you are creating value. This will help prevent endless iterations and rework.

5. Be sure that your alternatives are truly creative and not just variations on the same basic theme.

6. Design the quantitative decision model to achieve clarity of action, not accounting accuracy.

7. Perform the deterministic sensitivity analysis to determine what is important.

8. Work with the decision maker to be sure that the recommendation fits with the decision maker's risk tolerance.

9. At the end of the process, if the course of action is not compelling, you probably need to re-frame the problem.

10. Implementation is *not* automatic!

11. If the answer becomes clear and compelling at any point in the process, you should stop and make the decision. However, beware of framing the problem in terms of solutions!

5.10 Case for Analysis: "Buy or Remodel?"

Mike and Sandy are a young couple. They purchased a two bedroom house in a well established neighborhood with a good school district four years ago. When they bought a house, they were planning to have one child, however, Sandy is now pregnant with twins. In addition, when they bought the house, Mike was working downtown, but now Mike in working at home and he needs an office.

As their current situation is no longer feasible, Mike and Sandy begin discussing their options. Because they really enjoy their neighborhood, Mike believes their best option is to renovate their house to add two bedrooms and an office. Sandy, on the other hand, is interested in buying a new house in a more prestigious neighborhood. Also, Sandy is concerned that if they put too much money into this house, they may not be able to get it back if they move at a later date. While they do not agree on the course of action, they do agree that both options are viable.

Both Mike and Sandy have a joint income of about $120,000 per year. They originally paid $55,000 for their 1200 square foot house, but now the house should be worth about $90,000 according to two different Realtors that Sandy contacted. In addition, the Realtors said that a four or five bedroom house in their neighborhood would be worth between $200,000 and $275,000, depending upon the condition and square footage. Mike made a quick estimate and determined they could add another 1800 sq.ft. based on zoning restrictions in the area. He also estimated that the renovation and addition would cost about $100 per square foot.

The Realtors also sent them a listing of new homes in the Afton Woods subdivision, the most affluent new neighborhood in their community. The least expensive home on the list was $350,000, and prices for some homes exceeded $1 million. It was now time for Mike and Sandy to begin thinking hard about their options and about their objectives.

Mike wants an office at home with enough space for his two computers. He also would like to have a short commute time to both the airport and the company headquarters. Finally, Mike wants a house payment that they can afford on one salary. Sandy wants new kitchen appliances and a play area for the children. They both want to minimize the disruption to their lives and are planning for the long term.

Write a statement or series of statements which identify the problem(s) and the opportunity Mike and Sandy face.

- How should Mike and Sandy structure their problem?

- What are Mike and Sandy s objectives?

- Develop a small list of significantly different and creative alternatives.

- What tools could Mike and Sandy use in the Evaluation phase of their problem?

6

Creating a Shared Understanding of the Problem

Some problems are so complex that you have to be highly intelligent and well informed just to be undecided about them.
– Laurence J. Peter

Structuring is the first phase of the decision analysis process. During this phase the team develops a shared understanding of the problem and the business situation. The structuring phase of the process is the most critical. Regardless of how good the rest of the analysis is, it can never make up for a bad problem frame. This chapter covers how to properly structure a problem for evaluation.

6.1 Framing the Problem

We often refer to the structuring phase as *"framing the problem."* Ron Howard once wrote "framing is uniquely human" because it is the phase of the process that cannot be duplicated by software or other means. Framing is also somewhat of an art, and as such, it takes time to develop the required facilitation and analytical skills.

An appropriate frame is developed when:

- the problem is *clearly understood* by all the process participants,
- the business situation has been assessed
- key insights and factors affecting the problem are understood, and
- creative and unique alternatives to the problem have been clearly identified.

Tests for an appropriate frame

The two key words are *clearly* and *understood*. It is amazing how many teams start to work on problems without first having a clear and shared understanding of the problem from the decision maker's perspective. Without this perspective, many teams find themselves in a continual re-examination of the problem and the results. It is also important to have the right people on the project team so that issues are raised and information is gathered in a timely manner.

6.2 The Participants in the Process

Part of the Structuring phase is determining who should be included in the project or decision team. Often this discussion is conducted before the kickoff meeting between the decision maker and project leader, but it can occur during the kickoff meeting. Building a good project team and leadership review board is important if the problem is to be framed with the proper perspectives. To ensure these perspectives are captured, the decision team (decision makers and project team members) will include four broad classifications of people: decision makers, project team members, decision analysis facilitators, and content experts.

Decision Maker

In Chapter 1, I defined a decision maker as *anyone with the authority to allocate the necessary resources for the decision being made.* It is important to understand *who* the real decision maker is and ensure that this person is involved in the project. I remember one project where a plant manager asked me to help solve a particular production problem. When I asked if he was the decision maker, he assured me he had full authority. However, the alternative chosen was beyond his funding authority and the initial frame had to be discarded.

Review Board role in decision quality

The decision maker or leadership review board (also know as a decision board) is responsible for the overall quality of the analysis by maintaining the problem's focus, removing organizational hurdles, setting policies, and guiding the analysis team. The leadership review board is responsible for determining the value measures or decision criteria and for expressing preferences about risk and outcomes. In the end, it is the leadership review board who will allocate the resources necessary for implementing the chosen course of action.

Project Team Members

The project team should include people who are knowledgeable about the problem or situation in question, but who are not so involved that they have a preconceived outcome or bias (to the extent possible). These team members are responsible for gathering specific data, performing some analyses that are within their expertise, attending project team meetings, and communicating team findings to the organization. The project team members should come from the different functions or groups within the organization that will be affected by this project.

Decision Analysis Facilitator

The decision analyst's or facilitator's role is to be the decision analysis process expert, not the content (information) expert. The decision analyst's role is to build the decision model, conduct expert interviews and gather unbiased assessments, evaluate the model, and communicate the results. If the project team does not have a decision facilitator, the analyst will also facilitate the project team meetings. The facilitator's role is to ensure the project team understands the decision to be solved and to organize and lead project meetings. For large projects, it is advisable to have an analyst and a decision facilitator on the project team.

Content Experts

The decision analysis process could not happen without the insight and expertise provided by the content (information) experts. These experts help the project team model the relationships between the decision problem elements, share knowledge about the key uncertainties and their relationships, and provide probability assessments in their area of expertise.

For personal or tactical decisions, you may find yourself in all four roles. However, you should recognize the *real* possibility of reaching a biased conclusion. If the decision is going to be overly biased, you may want to consider just going with your intuition or finding another person to review your analysis.

Building a Good Decision Team

As already mentioned, each person on the team has a specific role, but it is important to note some characteristics for developing an effective project team and leadership review board. For large projects, the project team will usually consist of 4 to 6 team members, a project leader, and a process analyst and facilitator. Small or operational projects may only involve one to two team members and a part-time process facilitator.

The team members should not be experts in the information content but should be able to characterize the situation to the identified experts. The key to any team is picking the best people for the particular project. Try to look for people with different perspectives, backgrounds, and disciplines – but who have the ability to work together effectively.

The leadership review board should be comprised of the project champion or decision maker and key peers who can provide additional information and valuable insights into the team's work product, recommendation, and project implementation. Often this board is comprised of only one person, the decision maker. However, if the decision must be made by more than one person, you should seek out board members who can compliment each other and who have similar authority levels. Most leadership review boards are purposeful and effective, but you should always have the project champion clarify the roles and responsibilities of each member and agree on how disagreement will be handled.

Review Board considerations

6.3 Developing an Appropriate Frame

There are three main steps to developing a problem frame:

1. Identify and clarify the problem to be solved.

2. Assess the business situation and raise issues which affect the problem.

3. Generate creative and feasible alternatives which are compelling to the decision maker.

These three steps are the most important in the project. If they are done well, your project will succeed.

Identifying and Clarifying the Problem

By far the most important step is to make sure you are solving the right problem. I cannot emphasize this point enough! If you do not identify the decision maker's true problem, you will be forever in the mode of reworking the analysis. Part of identifying the problem is also clarifying it. You must clarify the decision(s) to be made so a correct perspective and scope can be applied to the problem.

For example, a company may be losing market share to a new competitor with a lower price. The team quickly identifies price as the problem, but in reality the real problem is that the product has been experiencing quality problems which have led to the drop in market share.

Sometimes we begin solving a problem before it has been clearly defined. This usually leads to reworking the problem or issues associated with the problem. The following are items to consider when clearly defining a problem:

Elements of problem definition

- ■ Who is the decision maker?
- ■ Is this problem strategic or operational?
- ■ What level of management is involved?
- ■ Is the decision maker at the right organizational level for this problem?
- ■ What assumptions have been made?
- ■ Does this problem affect areas outside of the decision maker's control?
- ■ What assumptions are being taken as given (policy)?

These are important considerations for developing an appropriate frame. I have seen many projects proceed without a clearly defined problem only to end up with either a recommendation the decision maker will not implement or a poor solution that is implemented because of time constraints.

Building an objectives hierarchy is a good way to clearly identify the problem to be solved and determine the decision maker's preferences. Using the objectives hierarchy, a project team can clearly define the various first and second order objectives (See Chapter 3).

Assess the Business Situation

Once the team has clarity on the problem to be solved, it must begin gathering information about both the problem itself and the surrounding business situation. There is not a magic formula or trick to performing a business assessment – it is simply getting the issues that affect the problem out into the open and recorded. This assessment should look at both internal and external issues. Before gathering information, it is a good idea to have an issue raising session to develop a list of potential information to be gathered and its source.

*An **issue** is anything which concerns or influences the possibilities or probabilities of a project. Issues can be decisions, uncertainties, values, or objectives.*

Issue defined

There are many ways to raise issues. The method I think works the best is to give each team member a pad of sticky notes and ask them to write one issue per note. I usually give them about ten minutes to do this before comparing issues. While this does cause duplication of some issues, it also tends to surface many unique issues that might otherwise not have been brought up. For example:

Raising issues

- We should be the low-cost leader (Objective).
- I wish I knew what our competitor's response would be to our new pricing strategy (Uncertainty).
- What should our pricing strategy be (Decision)?

After comparing and combining issues, we need to sort them into decisions to be made, uncertainties, values, or objectives. The easiest way to sort them is to write on the note: **D** for decision, **U** for uncertainty, and **V** or **O** for values or objectives. Decisions are things under your control, uncertainties are things out of your control, and values and objectives are things you want.

Compiling issues

By sorting the issues before building a problem frame, you can quickly check to see if you have the right perspective. Are your issues more strategic or operational (tactical)? Can you see the forest *and* the trees? If not, maybe you should spend some more time raising issues. Once you feel comfortable with the set of issues and have sorted them as to their type, place the *decisions* into a decision hierarchy and make a "bucket list" for each of the uncertainties, values, and objectives.

Using these lists, develop an "information wish list" that the team can then prioritize. You can develop this wish list by completing the following statement, "If I knew _____ I would be able to _____." This will make the information actionable and hopefully lead to a more narrow search. In addition to this information list, there are several business assessment tasks that should be performed to ensure a thorough understanding of both the internal and external business drivers.

Information "Wish List"

As part of the internal assessment, the team should identify the stakeholders for the project and understand how they gain value from the project. In addition, the team needs to identify and understand the organization's current strategy and what is working and what is not working. As part of that understanding, the team will need to know what processes are facilitating or hampering the current strategy and how those will affect any new strategies or alternatives the team develops. Many times these show up in the decision hierarchy as policy decisions. The team should also perform some type of core enabler assessment. This may be an examination of core competencies or other enablers that allow the organization to compete.

The following checklist is a guide to activities which can prove useful as the team performs the business assessment:

Business assessment checklist

- Perform stakeholder analysis.
- Identify and understand current momentum.
- Perform market and segment analysis.
- Develop key processes and organizational map.
- Develop core enabler assessment.
- Develop value creation template.
- Perform competitor analysis.
- Identify performance benchmarks.
- Discover best practices.
- Develop performance gap analysis.

The team will be able to build a decision hierarchy using the information from the objectives hierarchy, the issue raising, and the business assessment.

Building a Decision Hierarchy

The decision hierarchy is a valuable tool for determining the level of the issues identified as decisions. Figure 6.1 illustrates the format for the decision hierarchy. The top decisions are *closed decisions* (sometimes called *policy decisions* or *givens*) and are set by executive management and external governing bodies. For example, OSHA and EPA requirements often determine policy around operating a business in a particular industry, while executive management decisions set the tone for the company's particular operations.

Closed decisions

Figure 6.1 Decision Hierarchy

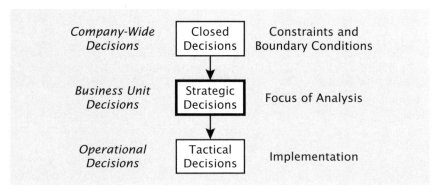

Examples of closed decisions for a company might be found in their mission statements – things like obeying the laws of the land, being a good corporate citizen, reducing emissions and waste, etc. Other policy decisions might include setting project economic hurdle rates (e.g., IRR must be greater than 15%), not operating or doing business in a specific country, only purchasing from the least expensive or preferred supplier, etc. Closed decisions are constraints on the decisions you can make at the strategy level.

Next is the strategy level, which is the focus of the analysis. This is where most of the issues which were identified as decisions should be if the problem is being considered at the right level (a good way to determine if you are seeing both the forest and the trees). These decisions should be the crux of the problem at hand. Things like building a new plant, expanding a production line, or buying out a competitor are strategic decisions for the organization. Most of the projects I have worked on have between one and ten strategic decisions. Since this is the focus of the analysis, these decisions must be framed properly. *Strategic decisions*

The next level is the tactical or operational level. These are the implementation items needed to make the strategic decisions happen, e.g., hiring a work force, opening a new office, putting in a computer network, buying a particular software package, etc. Be careful not to focus on these issues, as the strategic decisions will often dictate the implementation style and options. *Tactical decisions*

The "Swanson" Case Study illustrates developing an appropriate frame:

The Swanson Company is a small, privately held manufacturer of consumer health care products. The company has spent the last two years developing a new product, code named S234. The product, if successful, would be used as a key ingredient in cosmetic anti-wrinkle creams. It has advantages over other active ingredients used in these types of creams – it is not acid based, it is less expensive to manufacture than competing products, and it has a longer shelf-life. The R&D department believes the product has superior characteristics and therefore should have a large potential market. However, the Marketing department is unsure of the market size and S234's potential market penetration. Swanson has limited financial resources and is concerned about pursuing commercialization of the product if the market is not sufficient to make a reasonable profit. *Swanson "S234" Case Study framing*

John Anderson, the CEO, attended a conference where he learned about the benefits of decision analysis. He believes that decision analysis will help him make the right decision for S234. The following is a dialog between John and the decision consultant hired to help analyze the problem.

JOHN: I have not seen an application of the decision analysis process, but I feel that it might provide me with the guidance I need to make the right decision concerning S234. This is a difficult decision because last year the company had some financial setbacks which have caused us to increase our debt load beyond where I am comfortable. I do not want to borrow more money if this product doesn't deliver market share and profits.

CONSULTANT: I feel confident that decision analysis will help you choose the best course of action. Let's begin by clarifying the decision to be made.

JOHN: I want to know whether to commercialize S234 and if not, what should be done with the product?

CONSULTANT: Are you the final decision maker or should others be involved in making the final decision?

JOHN: I am the decision maker, but I would like Bill Peterson the CFO to be involved, as well as Kristen Harper, the director of marketing, and Jim McMillan, the director of R&D.

CONSULTANT: John, what criteria would you use to determine whether this product should be commercialized?

JOHN: I am familiar with NPV and prefer to use it over IRR.

CONSULTANT: Are there any other preferences you have for this product or how it will be evaluated?

JOHN: Because we are not in the financial condition we were several years ago, I would also consider myself risk averse if this project could cause severe financial problems for the company.

CONSULTANT: What is your definition of severe?

JOHN: If it could cause a loss greater than $1.5 million.

CONSULTANT: Are there any other requirements or considerations you have which concern this project?

JOHN: No.

CONSULTANT: Other than the three people you mentioned, who would you like to be involved on the project team?

JOHN: Greg Johnson, the manager of manufacturing, and David Stanley, the area representative for cosmetic intermediates.

CONSULTANT: Thank you for your time. The team will need periodic meetings with you to validate the decision model and the alternatives generated. Are you willing to spend the time necessary to ensure project clarity and quality?

JOHN: Yes. I am behind this process one hundred percent.

The project team met later that week and created the following list of issues and a decision hierarchy (see Figure 6.2).

"S234" Case Study issues and alternatives

Issues and alternatives list for project S234:

1. Should we commercialize S234?

2. If we don't commercialize, should we sell or license the technology?

3. Is the market for this product going to last or is it a fad?

4. How big is the market for S234?

5. How much market share will S234 capture given the current products already available?

6. Is S234 really a better product than competing products?

7. The CEO wants S234 to "bail" the company out of financial problems.

8. What will be our cost to manufacture?

9. How will we know if S234 is successful?

10. If S234 fails, what will be the consequences?

11. How much will we lose if we don't commercialize it?

12. How will our competitors react to this product?

13. What distribution system should we use to market the product?

14. Which manufacturing plant should produce S234 and how much will it cost to retool the line?

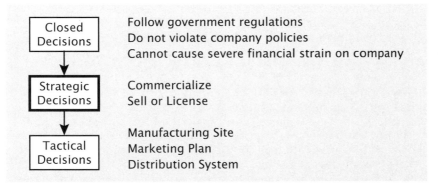

Figure 6.2 "S234" Decision Hierarchy

Closed Decisions	Follow government regulations Do not violate company policies Cannot cause severe financial strain on company
Strategic Decisions	Commercialize Sell or License
Tactical Decisions	Manufacturing Site Marketing Plan Distribution System

6.4 Creating Alternatives

Generating creative, unique, and feasible alternatives is an important part of the structuring phase. This step of the methodology requires the team to expand their boundaries and, as the cliche goes, to think out-of-the-box. I have seen projects where the teams did not actively search out new and innovative solutions but merely evaluated the same set of alternatives that was on everyone's mind. These alternatives are often not appealing to the decision maker; he or she has most likely already thought of them. When this happens, the team may be sent back to rework the problem.

An even worse situation happens when the alternative is accepted by the decision maker but the organization quickly dismisses the strategy or alternative as either no different or worse than their current path. Finding new or hybrid alternatives is what provides the real value to the project. While creativity is not something you can bottle or dispense with precision, there are ways to encourage teams to think creatively.

Take the time to encourage creative thinking

Begin by encouraging team members to be outspoken and "think out loud." Too many times I have seen team leaders focus only on the "time contract" or making sure the team is "on schedule." While maintaining a schedule is important, the *real reason for the team is to find the best alternative to the problem.* If the leader does not allow "thinking time" for the team members, then the set of alternatives will usually be rather narrow and not very creative. I try to develop agendas which are flexible and have time built into them for group discussion and what I call "guided wandering." I use the term *guided wandering* to reflect how a leader should act in a creativity session.

Guided wandering

Think of when you have taken a field trip. While the guide knows where you are going, he allows you to wander and explore along the way; this is how you learn. The same is true for a creativity leader. The leader should know where the group is going but should not stop the group from exploring.

Hypermarkets – We have Met the Enemy and He is Us!

In the 1990's, "Hypermarkets" (mass retailers - supermarkets, discount retailers, warehouse stores) in Europe began selling retail gasoline to their customers. Despite some initial disbelief from the major oil companies, the retailers' efforts have been quite successful. Today, over half the motor fuel purchased in France is sold through hypermarkets. The major oil companies continue to feel the squeeze on their margins and market share in the areas where hypermarkets expand.

Since the hypermarkets are not in the refinery business, where do they buy wholesale fuel for their stations? The answer - they buy fuel mostly from the major oil companies. They are also free to purchase fuel from any of the refineries, as they are not "branded" like the retail gasoline stations that must purchase from their brand refinery.

How does a major oil company sell wholesale fuel to their most aggressive competition? Most major oil companies have separate departments: one that handles sales through their branded stations and another that markets wholesale fuel - in this case to hypermarkets. Each department has its own set of objectives.

The major oil companies have watched their retail market shares decline in areas where the hypermarkets expand. The oil companies have devised a number of strategies to counter the decline in retail sales. Some strategies focus on cost reduction while others involve differentiation of the oil companies by the creation of a higher level of value proposition.

1. If you were put on the decision analysis team of a major oil company in France to deal with the market erosion, how would you frame the "problem" and how would you gather information?

2. Can you think of some creative (legal) alternatives for this problem?

Use the Explorer's Compass

Here is a simple suggestion that often helps one to think creatively. Begin by thinking of a map. Every map has many paths. These paths will lead to different destinations. Each destination has its pros and cons. By using what I call the "explorer's compass," you can map out the possibilities in all directions. Begin by building a simple matrix and determine two interesting characteristics you would like to map out. Then plot the alternatives you have in the matrix and develop new alternatives for the areas that are blank. This method often uncovers many "routes" which were thought to be impassable, but in reality may be better than the current path.

Think "Out-of-the-Box"

When you mention creativity to people, the common phrase I always hear is "out-of-the-box" thinking. How do you get teams to think out-of-the-box? A good method that I use to catalyze out-of-the-box thinking is to ask each team member to write down on a piece of paper all of the alternatives they think are possible. I then take these lists and deposit them in a shoebox in the middle of the conference table. At this point I tell the team that these alternatives are no longer available, and they must think of new alternatives which are not in the box. This tends to get the point across and usually sparks some lively and beneficial discussion. After about 10 to 20 minutes, I open the box and allow them to discuss the alternatives that were written. In the end, the team usually develops a creative "hybrid" alternative made up of the best parts of several alternatives.

Develop Model of Ideal Competitor

Another exercise that aids in expanding the collective mind of the project team is the concept of an ideal competitor. This exercise asks the project team to construct a competitor who has only the best characteristics. After doing this exercise, I like to ask why their organization has not tried to implement some of these qualities or abilities. This provides a good basis to start brainstorming possible alternatives.

Create a Strategy Table

Developing creative and coherent strategies that involve many decisions often confuses teams. Strategy tables provide a means to brainstorm decision alternatives and then visualize the set of decisions for each strategy. Strategy tables are also useful for presenting information to the decision makers. However, be careful not to overload a table with too many strategies (two to four strategies is best).

The following are step-by-step instructions for building a strategy table:

How to create a strategy table

Step 1   Explain why the team is performing this activity.

Step 2   Prepare templates or wall materials. You can use a PowerPoint template to make changes on-line using a computer. Or you can create a paper template using paper on a wall. Determine which method the team is more comfortable using.

Step 3   Transfer the focus decisions from the decision hierarchy to the strategy table (Figure 6.3). Place one decision in each column heading and arrange the decisions by grouping similar functions or putting them in sequence. If decisions are combined, break them into two or more separate and distinct decisions.

Figure 6.3
Decision
Hierarchy and
Strategy Table

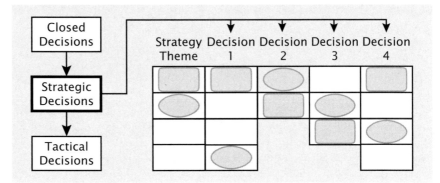

Step 4   Have the team discuss the meaning of each decision in the column headings and validate that the decision should be listed and has a clear and specific meaning. If a decision is tactical or contingent, list it on a separate sheet and remove it from the strategy table

Step 5   Give each team member a pad of sticky notes and ask them to brainstorm possible alternatives for each decision heading. It is a good idea to have team members work in groups of two to four depending upon the size of the team. Alternatives should be written one per note.

Step 6   Place the alternatives in the columns under the appropriate decision headings. Alternatives should be significantly different and range from incremental to radical in nature. The alternatives should also be mutually exclusive and collectively exhaustive. That is, you should not be able to choose more than one alternative for a strategy, and the alternatives listed should encompass all possible choices within the constraints of the problem.

Step 7   Develop strategy themes. A theme is a short phrase or set of words which communicates the essence of the strategy. The theme should convey the path developed through the strategy table. Brainstorming is a very useful process for developing these themes. Have team members work in groups or pairs to develop several themes.

Step 8 Develop initial strategy write-ups. Once the team has developed its set of themes, each team member should develop a write-up or rationale for each theme. The write-ups should be no more than two paragraphs and convey why the company would want to pursue this strategy.

Step 9 Review and prioritize strategy themes. Using the write-ups, each group should describe to the team their rationale for each theme. The team should then choose the compelling strategy themes for mapping through the table.

Step 10 Map out each strategy theme in the strategy table. Examine the strategy table for other compelling strategy hybrids that may have been missed earlier.

Develop Strategy Write-ups

Developing strategy tables helps to link each of the decision alternatives together into a coherent set of decisions. However, these tables do not adequately tell a complete story. Each of the decisions, and more importantly, the interactions and combination of decisions, must be fully illustrated in terms that the general organization will understand. By putting the strategy in a narrative form with the benefits and risks of each strategy theme, the organization can better understand the intricacies of each strategy.

Test Strategies for Creativity and Distinctiveness

Once the team has developed a set of strategies which they believe will accomplish the business goals, they need to test those strategies for both *creativity* and *distinctiveness*. Creativity has to do with how unique the strategy is to current momentum, while distinctiveness has to deal with how different each of the new strategies are from each other.

6.5 Preparing for Evaluation

Once the team has developed a creative set of alternatives and strategies, it is time to review these with the decision maker and the leadership review board. A decision review meeting is the primary means of interaction among the participants of a decision analysis project. The meeting participants should include the project team and team leader, decision review board members, and meeting facilitators. The project team members should all attend unless the team is larger than seven or eight. If the team is larger than eight, the team should agree as to who should attend and what information each member should present. These meetings are held at key interaction points during a project between the project team and the leadership review board (See Figure 6.4).

Decision review meetings

A decision review meeting is designed to provide the decision makers with insights into the decision problem. The insights provided should be based on the relevant knowledge and any analysis that has been performed up to that time. The meeting is also designed to get the decision maker's feedback on project direction and particular insights that the decision makers can provide. At this point in the process, the project team should receive feedback from the leadership review board on which alternatives the board would like to see evaluated and any new alternatives that were not considered. With this information, the team can then proceed to begin evaluating the selected alternatives.

Figure 6.4
Review Board
Interactions

Swanson Case
Study
continues

In the Swanson Case Study, the team developed a list of possible issues and alternatives including partnering with other companies and spinning the product off as a separate company. However, given Swanson's financial condition and the risk aversion of the CEO, these alternatives were not evaluated.

6.6 Summary

Properly structuring the problem is critical for good evaluation and alternative generation. Begin by clarifying the decision to be made and identifying and incorporating the decision maker's preferences and uncertainties. Raise and sort issues which are relevant to the decision problem and then develop a decision hierarchy showing policy, strategic, and tactical decisions. Model the problem using decision trees or influence diagrams and validate these models with the decision maker. Generate creative alternatives to the problem by using the explorer's compass and out-of-the-box thinking, and by modeling the ideal competitor.

6.7 Key Concepts

decision maker   bucket list
decision analysis facilitator   decision hierarchy
content expert   guided wandering
problem frame   explorer's compass
objectives hierarchy   strategy table
issue   strategy themes
business assessment

6.8 Study Questions

1. Why can't a good analysis compensate for a poor problem frame?

2. What may happen if you do not know who the real decision maker is?

3. What are the distinctions between *policy* and *strategy* decisions?

4. What are the distinctions between *strategic* and *tactical* decisions?

5. What is a *strategy theme*?

6. What types of content should a business assessment contain?

7. What are the distinctions between project team members and content experts?

8. Name two ways to inspire a team to think creatively and why is that important?

9. When should the project team meet with the leadership review board?

10. Why should the alternatives be mutually exclusive and collectively exhaustive?

6.9 References and Further Reading

Baird, Bruce F. *Introduction to Decision Analysis.* Belmont, CA: Wadsworth Publishing Company, 1978.

Clemen, Robert T. *Making Hard Decisions: An Introduction to Decision Analysis.* PWS-Kent, 1991.

Howard, Ron and James Matheson, editors. *Readings in Decision Analysis.* Second ed., Menlo Park: Stanford Research Institute, 1977.

McNamee, P. and J. Celona. *Decision Analysis with Supertree.* 2nd ed., San Francisco, CA: The Scientific Press, 1990.

Raiffa, Howard. *Decision Analysis.* Reading, MA: Addison Wesley, 1968.

6.10 Guide to Action

1. Be sure that the *problem frame* is clearly understood by all.

2. Make sure that a business assessment is performed and that the business situation is understood clearly by all team members and the decision maker.

3. Alternatives need to be really distinct and creative – not just variations on one theme.

4. Use the decision hierarchy as a means of communicating to the project team where the domain of their work should be. Make sure the team understands the distinctions between strategy and policy decisions.

5. Use tools to help the group develop truly creative alternatives.

6. Be sure to use appropriate reviews to keep alignment between the decision maker(s), the project team, and the implementation team.

6.11 Case for Analysis: "Sell or Pass On?"

Jim Smith is facing a difficult decision. Jim started a software business in his basement of five years ago. The business developed real estate software which allows buyers to view real estate over the Internet. The business has grown dramatically in these last five years and Jim has been approached to sell the business to a national real estate firm. The real estate firm has offered Jim $650,000 for the company. With this money Jim could retire, but his son has just begun working for the company and wants to buy it some day. However, his son cannot match the real estate firms offer at this point in time. Jim feels that the company can continue to grow and in the future may be worth as much as two and half million dollars.

- What measure(s) of value should Jim use for this decision?

- Identify constraints, strategic decisions, and deferrable decisions for this case.

- Develop creative alternatives for Jim's situation.

- Develop a strategy table for Jim – first, list the decisions across the top of the table.

- Second, list the alternatives under each decision.

- Then develop strategy themes and circle the appropriate decisions which correspond to the themes.

- Develop a "Strategy Write-up" for each theme.

7

Developing a Decision Model

The essence of knowledge is, having it, to apply it; not having it, to confess your ignorance.

– Confucius

Decision models are used to transition from the Structuring phase to the Evaluation phase of the decision analysis process. Decision models are necessary for quantitative evaluation of alternatives developed by the team. The issues generated during the business assessment and the decision hierarchy are important for laying the foundation for the decision model. The decision model provides a means to precisely define the relationships of decisions, uncertainties, and values. The decision model can be a simple spreadsheet or a complex influence diagram or decision tree. These models allow you to examine the decision and how the world interacts with it.

Decision models have two uses – *communication* and *evaluation*. The decision model is used as a communication tool in meetings with the decision maker to convey the essence of the problem and to gain further guidance and insight from the decision maker. In addition, the model is used to provide the proper setting and perspective when interviewing subject matter experts. The influence diagram is one of the most useful decision models. Often an influence diagram is developed early in the project, even before the business assessment, as a means to ensure that the team is working on the right problem.

A model as a communication tool

As an evaluation tool, the decision model is the quantitative engine which generates the insight used by the team to develop its recommendation. Usually the evaluation is conducted in stages which increase in complexity and thoroughness. The intent and design of the model change as complexity increases. The first model is designed for deterministic evaluations of different alternatives. A deterministic model is simply an eco-

A model as an evaluation tool

nomic calculation engine which relies on single number inputs and generates a single number output. You are probably familiar with these models as this is the type most organizations use for economic analyses. The second model contains probabilistic information on the important variables. It is used to compare alternatives and estimate the value of information and control.

7.1 Building Influence Diagrams

An ***influence diagram*** is a graphical tool used to capture the essence of a problem and to facilitate communication among multi-disciplined teams and the decision board. It provides clarity in identifying information sources and evaluating the decision problem. Influence diagrams use different shapes or nodes to represent the elements of a decision problem:

Elements of an Influence Diagram

- rectangles for decisions,
- ovals for uncertainties,
- hexagons or octagons for values, and
- double ovals indicate a deterministic or calculated uncertainty.

These elements are linked together with arcs (arrows) which indicate relevance. A node with an arc leaving it is called a *predecessor*, and a node with an arc entering it is called a *successor*. The absence of an arc often tells more than the existence of an arc, as it shows the *absence* of an influence relationship. We will begin with a decision problem which contains only one node of each element:

Going to the races

Bob is an avid horse racing fan. He is interested in playing the "pick six," where he must pick the winners of six consecutive races before any of the races start. If Bob picks all six winners he will win $50,000; if not he will lose $200. Bob has a system of picking horses based on the day of the week and has already determined his picks for today's races. What uncertainty affects Bob's decision to invest? Figure 7.1 is the influence diagram for Bob's decision.

Figure 7.1 Race Influence Diagram

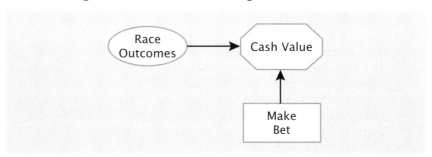

Bob's influence diagram is very simple, yet it communicates the decision problem he is facing. This influence diagram shows the uncertainty in the race outcomes or winners and Bob's decision to place the bet, both of which influence the cash value he would receive. Bob cannot control the

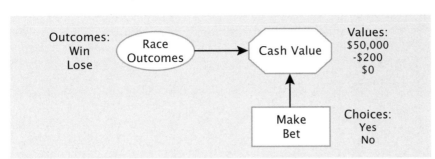

*Figure 7.2
Race Influence
Diagram with
Information*

outcome of the races. He can only control whether or not he places the pick six bet. Figure 7.2 is the same influence diagram as in 7.1 except it shows the information contained in each node.

Influence diagrams provide a concise and graphical means to communicate difficult problems. Figure 7.3 shows how this decision would be depicted by a decision tree and how it compares to an influence diagram. Decision trees are built from left to right, while influence diagrams are built from right to left.

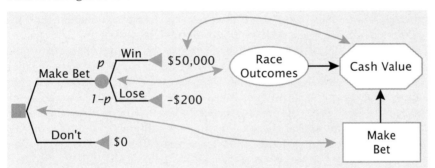

*Figure 7.3
Influence
Diagram and
Decision Tree*

This example shows that even simple decisions can be communicated effectively through the use of influence diagrams. Bob's next task is to gather information concerning the probability of correctly picking the winners of the six races.

Rules of Construction

Influence diagrams are a very clear and concise means of conveying the essence of any problem, but there are a few rules that must be followed for proper construction. The first and most important rule is that influence diagrams are not flow diagrams – an influence diagram cannot have feedback loops. There cannot be any path which allows you to go from A to B and then back to A. Paths are determined by the placement of arcs. An arc indicates the relevance of one node to another. Figure 7.4 shows the four basic relationships which can occur.

The first two diagrams in Figure 7.4 indicate a conditional situation, where B is conditional upon A. For example, in the first diagram if Decision A had two states – Yes and No – then Event B would have one set of outcomes for Yes and another for No. However the third and forth dia-

*No feedback
loops within
influence
diagrams*

Figure 7.4
Influence
Diagram
Relevance Arcs

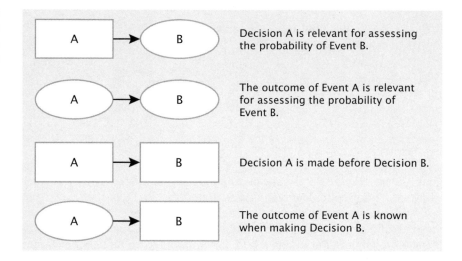

grams indicate a flow of information, that is, A is known or made before B. The placement of arcs is important both for showing relevance and information, and the lack of an arc often makes a stronger statement than the existence of one – because it explicitly shows irrelevance.

Build influence
diagrams from
right to left

Another rule is that influence diagrams are built from right to left beginning with what you value. This is in contrast to a decision tree which begins with the decision (Figure 7.3). Influence diagrams begin with the value measure and ask the question: what do you need to know to determine the value? For instance, to determine profit you need to know revenue and cost. You then continue decomposing the problem until you find an expert who can provide a proper assessment of the variable in question.

Swanson
"S234" Case
Study
continued

Continuing with the Swanson Case Study from Chapter 6: the consultant verified that John Anderson, the CEO, wanted to evaluate project S234 on the basis of net present value (NPV). He asked John what time horizon he thought was appropriate for this decision. John stated that he recently established a policy of using ten years as the commercial time horizon for all new products because of the intense competition in the industry and the number of new products developed each year. The consultant then asked if the company had a similar policy on the discount factor. John replied, "All new products use the company's cost of capital, which is currently 10%." In addition, John told the consultant to use 40% for the tax rate.

The project team met again to begin building an influence diagram of the decision problem. How would you structure the influence diagram to reflect the decision John Anderson was facing?

Begin with the value measure and decompose (Figure 7.5). What do we need to know to calculate NPV? Since NPV is the discounted stream of cash flows over time, you need to know the cash flows, the time horizon, and the discount rate. When building influence diagrams, the purpose is to communicate and evaluate the interactions of decisions, uncertainties, and values. Often there is information which can be taken as given, such as a company's discount rate or a decision maker's preference for a time horizon (i.e. how many years into the future to consider for the analysis).

*Figure 7.5
S234 Value
Node*

This information is best incorporated into the diagram by using a notation for communication only. When building the computer model these inputs would be incorporated into the functions they effect. As you can see from Figure 7.6, the determinants of value for project S234 are revenue and cost (the double circle means that the node will be calculated from other nodes).

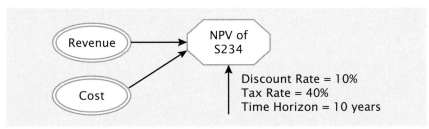

*Figure 7.6
S234 Value
Determinants*

Could an expert give you proper ranges of revenue and cost at this level of aggregation, or would he need to decompose the problem further?

The problem should be decomposed further to understand the influences affecting value. To further decompose the problem, begin with either revenue or cost and continue decomposing until you feel the uncertainties can be properly assessed by an expert. Figure 7.7 shows the revenue side decomposed to the level of detail necessary for proper assessment

The team discussed whether price should be an uncertainty, but decided to fix the price of S234 at $5 per pound because of three other competing products at that price range. Continuing with decomposing the cost side, we see that the two main uncertainties are Marketing and Manufacturing costs. These costs could have been further decomposed into fixed and variable costs. However, product S234 is a "drop-in" product for most of the manufacturing train and only requires an investment of $1,500,000 to add the finishing and packaging processes for S234. The company has a firm bid for purchasing and installing this equipment, so it is not necessary to include the cost as an uncertainty. If the expert was uncomfortable with this level of decomposition, he could further decompose the variables until he could give a proper assessment.

Decomposition

Figure 7.7
S234 Revenue
Determinants

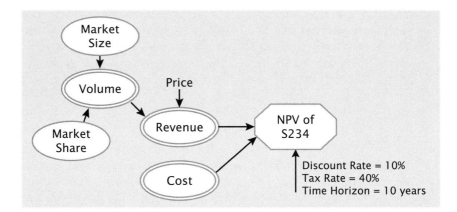

The last node included in the influence diagram is the decision node (Figure 7.8). At this time, the team has decided to only evaluate the "Launch" decision and will build separate influence diagrams for "Sell" and "License" after evaluating Launching the product.

Figure 7.8
S234 Completed
Influence
Diagram

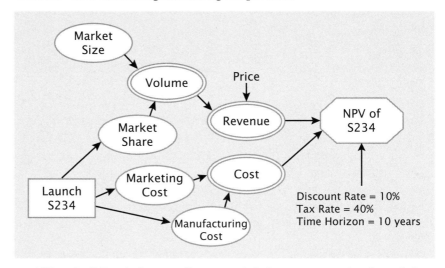

Practical
influence
diagram
considerations

When building influence diagrams, it is best to start simple and then add in complexity as it is necessary to correctly address the problem. Often I see teams try to build a very complex model which fully describes the problem situation. This usually results in a model which is so complicated the team is not sure it understands the results or how they were derived. A rule of thumb that I use is to make sure the diagram can fit on one 8 1/2 X 11 sheet of paper with a reasonable font size. By following this rule, you can build very good models that communicate the decision problem without information overload. I also find that by developing the diagrams in stages, you can better communicate the problem situation to the decision board.

One way of increasing the complexity is to build models in three stages – pilot, prototype, and production (Figure 7.9). The pilot model is very simple and quickly communicates the problem at a high level. The prototype model is more in-depth and begins to uncover many of the nuances of the problem. The production model is very in-depth and completely and accurately describes the problem situation. Many problems never need to go through all three stages, but if the problem is very complex, this provides a good method for adding in complexity.

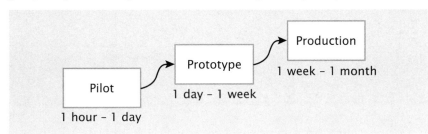

Figure 7.9 Model Progression

What is a Correct Influence Diagram?

Influence diagrams are similar to subjective probabilities in that there is no absolutely "correct" diagram – there can be many ways to show the relationships of decisions, uncertainties, and values. If the diagram accurately communicates the decision problem, then it can be considered complete and correct.

The project team validated the "Launch" model with the leadership review board. John was very pleased with the way the model captured the essence of the problem and asked the team to complete models for the "Sell" and "License" alternatives (See Figures 7.10 and 7.11).

S234 Alternatives

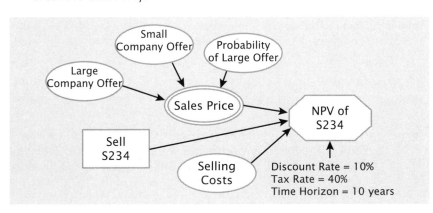

Figure 7.10 S234 "Sell" Alternative Influence Diagram

Figure 7.11
S234 "License"
Influence
Diagram

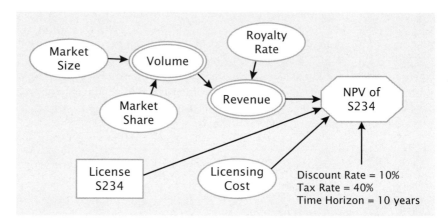

Step-by-Step Construction.

Influence diagrams are as much an art as a science. When facilitating teams, focus on developing a clear and meaningful diagram. Ask probing questions and make sure to *not* develop a flow diagram. Again, ***influence diagrams do not have feedback loops***.

Step **1**   Explain to the team why they are doing this activity and how it will be used in the future.

Step 2   Begin by considering the essence of the problem. Is it business development, marketing, R&D, exploration, etc.? This understanding will help in guiding development of the diagram.

Step 3   Put a value node with the decision criteria written in the center at the middle of the right side of the white board or flip chart. Most diagrams begin with NPV as the value node being influenced by Revenue, Costs, and Capital.

Step 4   Begin development by asking what piece(s) of information would most help in resolving the uncertainty or deterministic value.

Step 5   Choose one uncertainty emanating from the value node and develop it completely before beginning with the other nodes. Make sure nodes are clearly defined and specific.

Step 6   Review the uncertainties from the issue-raising list developed earlier. If there are uncertainties which are not in the influence diagram, determine which should and should not be included and why.

Step 7   Identify deterministic uncertainty nodes (those which are calculated). Designate these nodes by using a double oval. Can you write the formula that would calculate the value in the oval? If not, list the information that is missing and needed to complete the calculation.

Step 8   Identify information sources and write each source's name by the node it can resolve.

Step 9   Review the diagram for completeness and problem description accuracy.

Step 10   Develop an information gathering task list.

7.2 Decision Trees

Influence diagrams provide a concise method of graphically communicating the decision problem and are an excellent tool for discussions with management. However, much of the information for evaluation is hidden behind the nodes. Decision trees, on the other hand, provide a means to communicate all of the detailed information in a highly structured and logical manner.

Decision trees use nodes similar to those of the influence diagram – circles for uncertainties and squares for decisions. One advantage decision trees have over influence diagrams is the ability to indicate the sequence of decisions and uncertainties. Often the decision problems we face involve more than one decision and many times all the decisions cannot be made at the same time. Decision trees provide the ability to graphically display the timing of decisions. When building decision trees, you must ensure the correct sequence of decisions and uncertainties which will be resolved before making the next decision. While the order of uncertainties between decisions does not matter, the order of decisions is important. Figure 7.12 is the decision tree for the licensing decision in the Swanson case. There is only one decision and it is followed by four uncertainties which will affect the possible outcomes if the decision is to license.

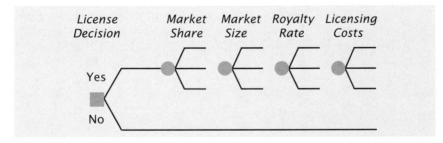

Figure 7.12
S234 License
Decision Tree

Rules of Construction

Decision trees have a few rules of construction to ensure a proper and complete tree is built. First, the decision tree starts with the decision node, rather than the value node as in the influence diagram. The decision node should have branches emanating from it which include all of the possible alternatives the decision maker could choose. However, the decision maker can only choose one path or alternative emanating from the decision node.

Mutually exclusive and collectively exhaustive outcomes

The next rule states that uncertain nodes should have branches that correspond to a set of **mutually exclusive** and **collectively exhaustive** outcomes. This means that when the uncertainty is resolved, *only one* of the outcomes can occur, and one of the outcomes *must* occur.

The third rule states that the decision tree must contain all possible paths available to the decision maker given the current state of information. This is the test for completeness of the tree – if a path the decision maker could take is not included in the tree, then it is not complete. However, some judgement is always used to eliminate paths or alternatives which are completely unfeasible or unreasonable.

Step-by-Step Construction

Decision trees are straightforward and logical in design. Here are the five steps for constructing decision trees:

Decision Tree Construction Steps

Step 1   Identify the decisions and uncertainties from the influence diagram.

Step 2   Construct a skeleton decision tree. Determine the chronological order of decisions and key uncertainties.

Step 3   Build the full tree by propagating the tree and connecting the branches.

Step 4   Add probabilities and outcomes to the tree diagram.

Step 5   Roll back the tree to calculate expected value.

Case Study: Offshore Oil

Offshore Oil and Gas is preparing to enter a bid round for oil and gas leases off the coast of Norway. The government of Norway is offering a select number of leases to six companies. These six companies were selected because of their exploration and production capabilities and environmental record. Of the six companies competing for leases, Offshore believes only one competitor, Royal Oil, will be a competitive threat on the four leases on which Offshore is bidding.

Figure 7.13 Offshore's Influence Diagram

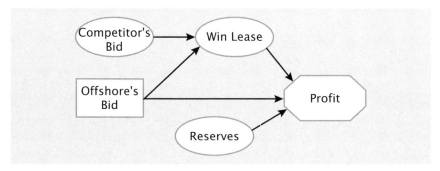

While Offshore does not know what Royal's bid will be, Offshore's exploration team has studied Royal's past bidding patterns and has developed some opinions. In addition, Offshore has developed the influence diagram shown in Figure 7.13. To convert the influence diagram into a decision tree, begin by developing a skeleton decision tree.

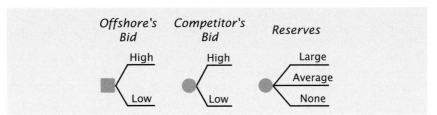

Figure 7.14 Offshore's Skeleton Tree

Using the information from the influence diagram, the team is able to develop a skeleton decision tree with three nodes (Figure 7.14). These are called skeleton decision trees because the branches are not connected to each node. Skeleton trees are a much better communication tool than a fully expanded tree unless you only have a few nodes like the Offshore case. Once the nodes have been properly ordered and labeled, the fully expanded tree can be developed. Figure 7.15 is the fully expanded decision tree.

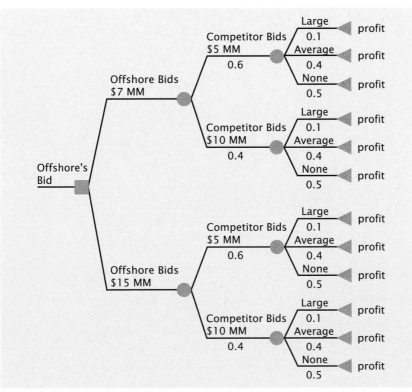

Figure 7.15 Offshore's Expanded Decision Tree

Offshore's exploration team has been working on determining the possible net asset value or profit potential of the leases, the probability that Royal Oil will bid on the leases, and the amount that Royal Oil might bid on the leases. This information will then be used to complete the decision tree.

Offshore's exploration team believes that Royal Oil's bids will be in the range of $5 million to $10 million per lease with a 60% chance of the $5 million bid and a 40% chance of the bid being $10 million.

The exploration team has also determined that the range of net asset value or profit could be $100 million if the reserves are large, $10 million if the reserves are just average, and a loss of the cost of the lease plus the cost of one exploration well of $8 million if no new reserves are located.

Offshore is positive that it can capture a single lease with a bid of $15MM. What should Offshore bid to maximize its expected profit?

Evaluating the Tree

In order to evaluate a decision tree, we need input on the probabilities of each branch emanating from an uncertainty. These probabilities reflect the likelihood of that branch and its associated outcomes happening. We can multiply the probabilities of a complete path through the tree to determine the overall probability that a particular path will occur. This also allows us to calculate the expected value of that path. The expected value is simply the value of that path times its probability of occurring. Expected value allows us to compare different paths through the tree (see Figure 7.16).

Figure 7.16
Offshore's
Evaluated
Decision Tree

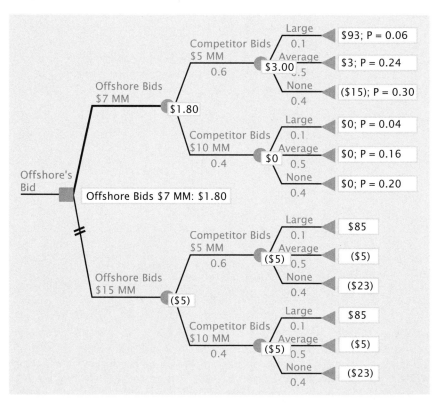

Martha Stewart – Decisions and Outcomes

In December of 2001, Martha Stewart was faced with a decision. She had received some financial information concerning ImClone, a company in which she owned 3,928 shares of stock valued at just over a quarter of a million dollars. Based on this new information, Martha decided to sell her stock. She netted $51,000 from the transaction. This was apparently a good decision.

However, the information acted upon by Martha was not public information and came from an insider at ImClone. That insider sold a large quantity of shares just before some bad news about ImClone became public. The stock then dropped dramatically. This triggered an SEC investigation. Caught up in the investigation, Martha was faced with a second decision: should she cover up her contacts and information?

On June 4, 2003, an indictment was opened against Martha Stewart. She was convicted on March 5, 2004. Since the indictment was made public, the following has occurred:

- Martha Stewart resigned from the board and as chief creative officer of the Martha Stewart Living Omnimedia, a company she founded.
- Viacom dropped the syndicated show "Martha Stewart Living."
- The New York Times renamed two columns to remove any reference to Stewart.
- Martha Stewart Living Omnimedia stock dropped appreciably in value (Martha Stewart is the largest shareholder) – reducing the company value by about $400 million.

1. Draw a decision tree that Martha could have used to make the two decisions above.

2. If Martha had stopped to perform this type of decision analysis, do you still think she would have made the same decisions?

Trees and influence diagrams are very effective tools for communicating the essence of problems ranging from simple to complex. Over the last decade, new and useful computer programs have made the application of these tools much easier.

7.3 Computer Modeling Programs

Decision analysis for simple problems can be performed using anything from the back of a napkin to sophisticated decision software. However, as problems become more complex, the need for computing speed increases. While simple problems with three uncertainties can be solved in a matter of minutes with a handheld calculator, a problem with eight uncertainties may take several hours. These complex problems with many uncertainties necessitate the use of some type of modeling software.

There are many good decision analysis programs on the market which can decrease the computational time needed for an analysis. However, there are no programs available which can replace the human ability to reason. This is an important point, as many people believe decision analysis is a "model" rather than a methodology or way of thinking. One program which I use and would highly recommend is TreeAge Pro®. This is a graphical tree program available from TreeAge Software. TreeAge Pro® is user friendly with point and click simplicity. The new version has included

Decision Analysis is not just the model

the ability to draw influence diagrams as well as perform Monte Carlo and Markov analyses. TreeAge Pro® is only available for Windows. The trees shown in this book were produced using TreeAge Pro® and modified via Adobe® Illustrator.

Another influence diagram and decision tree program is available from Syncopation – their program is called DPL and is suited for experienced analysts. DPL was originally developed by Applied Decision Analysis.

7.4 Summary

Decision models are necessary for quantitative evaluation of alternatives developed by the team. The decision model provides a means to precisely define the relationships of decisions, uncertainties, and values. Decision models should be developed with decision trees or influence diagrams and validated with the decision makers. Decision models have two uses - communication and evaluation.

Influence diagrams and decision trees provide both a graphical means of communicating the decision problem and a logical method of evaluating the alternatives. Remember that influence diagrams are not flow diagrams and cannot have feedback loops, and decision trees show the sequence of decisions and uncertainties but not relationships.

There are many computer modeling programs which can simplify the analytical task of calculation. These programs do not replace the thinking necessary to have good decision quality. Remember decision analysis is not about the model but creating insight so an appropriate course of action can be chosen.

7.5 Key Concepts

influence diagram	decision tree
predecessor	sequence of decisions
successor	mutually exclusive
relevance	collectively exhaustive
decomposition	computer model

7.6 Study Questions

1. How do you start building an influence diagram?

2. What is the significance of the arrows in an influence diagram?

3. Why do we say that no influence diagram is "absolutely correct?"

4. What advantages do decision trees have over influence diagrams?

5. What advantages do influence diagrams have over decision trees?

6. How do you start building a decision tree?

7. How do you evaluate a decision tree?

8. What is meant by "decomposing" an influence diagram and how do you know that the process is complete?

9. Name the three rules for constructing influence diagrams.

10. What is a skeleton decision tree and for what is it useful?

11. What are the three rules for constructing decision trees?

7.7 References and Further Reading

Baird, Bruce F. *Introduction to Decision Analysis.* Belmont, CA: Wadsworth Publishing Company, 1978.

Clemen, Robert T. *Making Hard Decisions: An Introduction to Decision Analysis.* PWS-Kent, 1991.

Howard, Ron and James Matheson, editors. *Readings in Decision Analysis.* Second ed., Menlo Park: Stanford Research Institute, 1977.

McNamee, P. and J. Celona. *Decision Analysis with Supertree.* 2nd ed., San Francisco, CA: The Scientific Press, 1990.

Raiffa, Howard. *Decision Analysis.* Reading, MA: Addison Wesley, 1968.

7.8 Guide to Action

1. Be sure that the problem is properly structured before starting to develop the decision model.

2. Use influence diagrams and decision trees to model the problem and validate these models with the decision maker.

3. Remember that both influence diagrams and decision trees have dual uses – communicating the problem and providing a logical method of evaluating the alternatives.

4. If your influence diagram has a feedback loop in it, the diagram is not correct.

5. Keep the model in perspective; modeling is a subset of decision analysis.

7.9 Case for Analysis: "Pension Investing"

Bill Webster is preparing to retire after working for 40 years. His company is giving him a lump sum pension. Bill is trying to decide how to invest his money.

At his current age of 65, Bill does not want to take too much risk, but he also wants a good return on investment. He has determined three different investment options – company stock, mutual funds, or certificates of deposit. Each of these investment options has different risks and returns.

- Develop an influence diagram for Bill's situation.

- Draw the decision tree for Bill.

- What do you think he should do?

- How did the events of the second half of 2008 affect your opinion about what Bill should do?

8

An Introduction to Probability

All business proceeds on beliefs, or judgements of probabilities, and not on certainties.

— *Charles Eliot*

As discussed in Chapter 3, nearly all of the important decisions we make involve some level of uncertainty; it is this uncertainty that often makes decisions difficult. How can we effectively deal with the uncertainty inherent in our decisions? We use the language of probability to explicitly express our views about the uncertainty of future outcomes or outcomes which have occurred but about which we are unsure of the outcome. Usually we express our views using ambiguous words such as "likely," "might," "probable," and "unlikely." However, these words do not convey a uniform meaning. The word "might" could mean a probability of 20% to one person and 80% to another.

Incorporation of probabilistic assessments is a cornerstone of decision analysis. It is probabilistic incorporation that elevates decision analysis above mere deterministic analysis and allows us to gain insight into the likelihood of future outcomes.

8.1 What is Probability?

Probability is simply the likelihood of an outcome occurring. However, there are two different approaches to obtaining probabilities—objective and subjective.

Most people are familiar with the more classical or **objective** approach to probability. This is where an outcome occurs X number of times out of Y possible events. The basic characteristic of objective probability is that if two people were given the same sets of data, they would come up with the same probabilities.

Subjective probability

Subjective probability differs in that two people could be given the same information and derive different probabilities. The subjective or Bayesian view of probability is based on your beliefs, knowledge, data, and experience.

In making decisions under uncertainty, we use probability both as a language to have an intelligent and useful dialog and as a means to quantify our beliefs. Quantitative statements about an uncertainty are given by numerical probabilities—decimal fractions from 0 to 1.0. The sum of probabilities concerning any opportunity must add up to 1.0. If an outcome is *certain* to occur, it has a probability of 1.0. As probabilities approach zero, their corresponding outcomes become increasingly less likely to occur, and any outcome which cannot occur has a probability of zero. Probability is the only clear way to state your beliefs about a future outcome.

Why Use Probabilities?

Pierre Simon de Laplace stated in *A Philosophical Essay on Probabilities* that probability is the "expression of man's ignorance" and that probability is relevant to "the most important questions of life" and not just to games of chance. Therefore, if probabilistic statements are important for decision making, why do people tend to use vague and ambiguous terms? I often hear people say, "Why do we need probabilities to express the likelihood of future outcomes?" This is usually followed by, "I know what I mean and I am sure other people understand me." Probabilities allow us to clearly and unambiguously describe uncertainty.

Three probability statements test

I often use the following test in my class. I make three statements and ask the students to quantify through probability their beliefs of certainty about each of the following statements. Try this test yourself:

Low   High

_____   I think it will happen.   _____

_____   There is a chance it will occur.   _____

_____   It probably will happen.   _____

I have found over the years that people with common educational backgrounds sometimes exhibit similar ranges, but I have never had a class with consistent answers. In general, those with mathematical or engineering backgrounds tend to give narrow ranges, while scientists and physicists tend to give ranges which are wider and often lower than those given by people with business backgrounds. However, all disciplines tend to give different ranges within the class participants. For instance, the statement "I think it will happen" is very broad and the distribution is often from 5% to 95%. Probabilistic statements eliminate the ambiguity of common everyday language and allow us to convey information that is relevant and in-line with the state of knowledge of the person making the statement.

While realizing the potential of using probabilistic statements, many people are often intimidated by their use. There is often an emotional block in accepting uncertainty because people feel a loss of control. However, by understanding uncertainty, you will gain greater control over your decisions. By explicitly recognizing uncertainty, you can avoid deluding yourself about the certainty of outcomes. The people who accept and understand uncertainty will be more successful in the long run.

Determination of probabilities is important for both business and personal decisions. For example, technical managers in research need to know the probability of the technical success of projects; manufacturers need to know the likelihood of flawed products; marketers need to know the probability of commercial success for products, etc. However, many feel that assessing their colleagues or others in a probabilistic manner is difficult and time consuming. We will discuss the techniques used to assess probabilities later in Chapter 10.

What is a Correct Probability?

One of the most often asked questions is, "What is the *correct* probability of an outcome occurring?" The answer is that *there is no one correct probability*, but a good probability assessment incorporates all relevant information into the state of knowledge.

So if there is no one correct probability, how can we assume the probabilities given are appropriate? Since probability is a statement of personal judgment and experience, we can audit and search for biases to determine if accurate and adequate information was provided and whether the person is competent to process the information. The probabilities that the person elicits are not a property of the outcome, but the person's interpretation of the likelihood of the outcome.

As an example, if you watch the evening weather report on several different television channels, you might see the following situation:

- Bill on Channel 4 says the chance of rain for tomorrow is 60%, while
- Mike on Channel 9 says the chance of rain is 70%, and
- John on Channel 6 says the chance of rain is 50%.

Probability example: weather forecasting

What if they are all certified meteorologists and have similar forecasting records? Which meteorologist is correct? All of them are correct, assuming that they have incorporated all available relevant information and are capable of processing that information in a consistent manner. But how can this be? Each person has their own means of processing data and interpreting results. While the probabilities given are different, if the same level of attention and quality has been given to each assessment, then they are all correct.

Probability *is a state of knowledge about the likelihood of an outcome based on your beliefs, data, knowledge, and experiences.*

Probability defined

First Movers - Observing Strategy Themes in the Market

Pfizer's impotence pill Viagra® was the first to market. The US Federal Drug Administration (FDA) approved the drug on March 27, 1998. Pfizer launched their marketing campaign in April and over $400 million dollars worth of product was sold in the first quarter.* The next competitor, Levitra®, was approved by the FDA in August of 2003. This was followed quickly by Cialis® November, 2003.

Being first to market gave Pfizer over five years of sales in a competitor free environment. This "innovator" type of strategy has other benefits such as setting market standards and pricing, establishing barriers to entry, and creating brand presence.

While Pfizer celebrated great success with Viagra, there are negative aspects to being first to market. Pfizer risked significant capital on research and development based on the belief that a market existed. Even when the product was ready, Pfizer had to educate the buyers in order to create the market from a zero base.

The risk of being the first to launch a new product into the market also has inherent risk of the unknown. What if the product does not perform as anticipated? What if the product has a hidden complication that causes problems or even death? Use a web search engine with the words "VIOXX" and "Merck" for a look at a pharmaceutical product with issues. The "fast followers" are typically able to learn from the mistakes and successes of the "innovators."

There are many classic strategy themes that can be observed in the market. Some examples include:

- Low Price Marketer – Wal-Mart
- Quality – Zenith – Mercedes – Rolex
- Fast Follower – BASF – Microsoft – Google
- Technology Leader (Innovator) – Pixar Animation Studios – Apple Computer
- Customer Zealot – Nordstrom

What strategy themes might be the driving forces behind the following advertising slogans?

- Burger King - "Have it your way."
- McDonalds - "You deserve a break today."
- Wendy's - "It's waaaay better than fast food.™ It's Wendy's.®"
- John Deere - "Nothing runs like a Deere."
- Oreck Vacuums - "Healthier, Easier, Smarter™"
- Magnavox - "Smart. Very Smart."
- Nike - "Just do it"
- Energizer - "Nothing outlasts the Energizer. It keeps Going and Going..."

* Alison Keith, "The Economics Of Viagra," Health Affairs, Volume 19, Number 2, March / April 2000, Page 148.

Events and Outcomes

Events and outcomes defined

When using probabilities to represent our beliefs of likelihood, we must be clear in our definitions of **events** and **outcomes**, as we will use these terms throughout the rest of the book. An *event* has one or more *outcomes*. *Outcomes* are what *can* happen.

As an example, if you were going to have heart surgery, the event would be the surgery and the outcomes could be:

- complete recovery, no side effects,
- partial recovery, some side effects, or
- death.

Objective Probability

Most people think they understand the concept of probability. This may come from participating in games of chance, watching weather reports, or giving odds on outcomes to coworkers. What are these statements of probability based upon?

Consider the coin toss. If you were to ask someone the probability of a coin landing either heads up or tails up, they would answer 50-50. But do they believe the coin will land heads up exactly 50 times out of 100 trials? No, we base this statement on the physical aspects (only two sides) of the coin and how it was tossed (with or without bias) in determining the 50-50 likelihood. We could have also based the probability on the actual number trials, which is the relative frequency of an outcome in a long sequence of events. This view is often called the empirical or objective approach to probability. However, it is the method of assigning the probabilities that is objective, not the actual values being assigned.

Consider the situation of buying a new car. We have all either experienced buying a defective product or know someone who has. Even though the car company offers a 3 year/ 30,000 mile warranty, we do not want to purchase a car with defects. If you had access to quality control information from the manufacturer which indicated the model you were going to purchase had a defect rate of 6 in 150,000, what is the probability you would purchase a defective car?

Probability example: defective automobile

$$P = \frac{Number\ of\ Outcomes\ X}{Number\ of\ Events\ Y} = \frac{6}{150000} = 0.00004$$

The probability of buying a defective car from this manufacturer is 0.00004, which would indicate there is only a slight chance you would end up purchasing a defective car.

How do you calculate probabilities of outcomes that have either never happened, are rare occurrences, or have occurred but you are unsure of the outcome? In these situations, you must use subjective probability. Consider the following statements:

- What is the probability that DuPont stock will be $60 per share on December 31, 2014?
- What is the probability that you will die in a car accident before you are 65 years old?
- What is the probability that you can name all the Presidents of the United States in order without making any mistakes?

In the first two examples, you do not know the outcome of the events. In the third example, the outcomes have occurred and the uncertainty you feel is about your state of knowledge, not the outcomes.

Subjective Probability

Subjective probabilities are statements of how likely we believe an outcome will occur in the future or has occurred in the past. This is a fairly simple concept, but one with which many are uncomfortable in giving assessments. This uncomfortable feeling often comes from our belief that there is one right number and we must strive to give that number. However, probabilistic statements reflect our degree of uncertainty; they are not single point estimates of certainty. We must be able to convey our beliefs about outcomes which will happen or have happened if we are to make good decisions involving uncertainty.

What if the car manufacturer in the previous example only produced six cars in the first month of operation. If the first and third cars were defective, does this mean 1/3 of all the cars to come off the line will be defective? Possibly, but most likely it means you do not have enough data to accurately portray the relative frequency of a product defect. As the production manager, would you only look at the initial data and stop production, or would you use your knowledge and experience with previous lines to conclude this is not a probable view of future production defects?

Most of the difficult decisions we make require subjective probability because many of these decisions are one-time or rare outcomes. Without subjective probability, these decisions could never be evaluated. Subjective probability is an expression of your state of knowledge, which is based on your beliefs, knowledge, data, and experience. Viewing probability as a state of knowledge allows for different people to have different probabilities based on the same information.

8.2   Probability Basics

Probability theory is very simple to understand because there are only three axioms that must be followed to ensure correct application. Probability theory does not involve difficult mathematical computation or understanding, however it is easy to get confused when thinking about probability.

The Three Axioms

1. Probabilities must be positive and between 0 and 1. I will denote outcomes by E and the probability of an outcome by $P(E)$.[1]

Equation 8.1 $0 \leq P(E) \leq 1$

---

[1] The letters E and F are used for outcomes of a *general* nature to express probability theory, e.g. to show the derivation of Bayes' rule. Other letters are used for *specific* examples, e.g. C for Criminal and D for Dropout in the "Case of the Uneducated Criminal" example. Equations of a general nature are numbered; equations relating to a specific case are not.

2. The sum of all probabilities of all possible outcomes must add up to 1. If a set of outcomes are mutually exclusive and collectively exhaustive, then one and only one of the possible outcomes must occur. Therefore, the total of all the probabilities must equal 1 (Equation 8.2):

$$P(E_1) + P(E_2) + \ldots + P(E_n) = 1$$ *Equation 8.2*

3. Probabilities are additive. If two outcomes are mutually exclusive, such as E_1 and E_2, then the probability that one or the other occurs is the sum of the individual probabilities.

$$P(E_1 \text{ or } E_2) = P(E_1) + P(E_2)$$ *Equation 8.3*

Mutually Exclusive and Collectively Exhaustive

When we talk about outcomes being mutually exclusive, we mean if one outcome occurs then none of the other outcomes can occur. This is mathematically illustrated by Equation 8.4:

$$E_1 \text{ and } E_2 = \emptyset$$ *Equation 8.4*

The symbol $\emptyset$ denotes a null set; E_1 and E_2 cannot both occur. This is like saying if you flip a coin, in one toss it cannot be both heads and tails.

Collectively exhaustive means that either E_1 or E_2 or both E_1 and E_2 must occur. Using the example from above, the coin must land on either heads or tails, thus the outcomes are a universal (Ω) or complete set. Therefore, we could write:

$$E_1 \text{ or } E_2 \text{ or } \ldots \text{ or } E_n = \Omega$$ *Equation 8.5*

The ability to define outcomes as mutually exclusive and collectively exhaustive is important if we are to understand outcomes and make the best decision. In order to define these outcomes appropriately, we need to decompose or subdivide the problem into finer and finer subsets.

Decomposition

Thinking about uncertainties is often a difficult task. Take, for example, the marketing success of a new product. For an expert to provide the probability of market success is a difficult task. The expert would have an easier task and would give a better assessment if the uncertainty was decomposed into other influencing uncertainties. By breaking market success into market share and market volume, the expert can better understand the problem. Decomposing the problem reduces the complexity and provides effective use of judgment. Also, by decomposing the problem into smaller more specific pieces, different experts with different knowledge can contribute to the analysis. Remember when performing an assessment to clearly define the variable to be assessed and only decompose the uncertainty to the point where someone can give a credible assessment.

8.3 Venn Diagrams

Venn diagrams provide a graphical representation of probability and are often useful in defining outcomes. Figure 8.1 is a Venn diagram of two mutually exclusive outcomes.

Figure 8.1
Venn Diagram
of Mutually
Exclusive
Outcomes

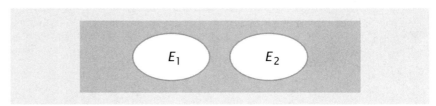

The two ovals inside the rectangle denoted E_1 and E_2 represent two possible outcomes. The shaded rectangle, including the two ovals, represents all the possible outcomes. An easy way of thinking about Venn diagrams is by considering a single point in the rectangle. If that point is in the oval E_1, the outcome E_1 does occur. If the point is outside of E_1, the outcome does not occur. Since both ovals E_1 and E_2 do not overlap or intersect at any point, they cannot both occur at the same time and are mutually exclusive.

Joint Outcomes

Continuing the
"Uneducated
Criminal"
example

In "The Uneducated Criminal" Case Study from Chapter 3, there are two sets of outcomes or distinctions: either the person is or is not a High School Dropout, and either the person is or is not a Criminal. We can use a Venn diagram to represent the four possibilities. In Figure 8.2, C represents the person is a Criminal, and C' the person is not a Criminal.

Figure 8.2 is an example of being collectively exhaustive. Notice the entire rectangle is represented by the two regions C and C'. Another term which is useful and which this diagram can represent is complements. In the Criminal example, C' is the outcome complementary to C, for whenever C' occurs, C cannot occur and vice versa.

Complementary
outcomes

Figure 8.2
Collectively
Exhaustive
Venn Diagram

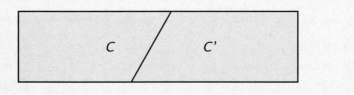

Rearranging Equation 8.2 expresses the general form of complementary outcomes:[2]

Equation 8.6

$$P(E_1) = 1 - [P(E_2) + \ldots + P(E_n)].$$

If outcome E only has two outcomes E_1 and E_2, Equation 8.6 becomes:

---

[2] Note that some authors use the notation of $\bar{E}$ ("E-bar" or "not E") as the outcome complementary to E. For specific examples, the (') prime symbol to show the complement, e.g. $P(C')$, is used.

$P(E_1) = 1 - P(E_2)$, or $P(E) = 1 - P(E')$.   *Equation 8.7*

We can further define the outcomes by adding the possibilities of being a High School Dropout. This is represented by Figure 8.3.

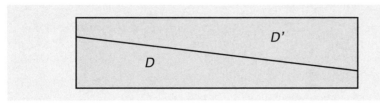

*Figure 8.3
Venn Diagram
for High School
Dropout*

In Figure 8.3, D represents the probability that the person is a high school dropout, and D' that the person is not a high school dropout. By examining the joint probabilities of the outcomes Criminal and High School Dropout, we can clearly understand the situation. Figure 8.4 illustrates the joint outcomes.

When defining outcomes in decision analysis, we need to be sure that they mutually exclusive and collectively exhaustive if we are to gain insight and clarity of action.

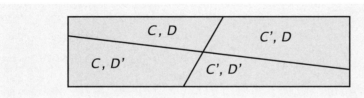

*Figure 8.4
Venn Diagram
of Joint
Outcomes*

8.4 States of Information

Having adequate information to know whether an outcome happened or did not happen makes probability assessments easy. But what happens when you do not have adequate information? You can still make a probability assessment, but it will be based on some incomplete state of knowledge — usually your current state. While we do this subconsciously every time we make probability assessments, we should clearly define the state of information we are using to make the assessments. We can define this state of information with the notation shown in Equation 8.8:

$P(E|\&)$.   *Equation 8.8*

E is the outcome being assigned the probability given our present state of information ($\&$). We use the vertical line to separate the outcome whose probability is required (left side of the line) from the state of knowledge or that which we know to have happened (right side of the line), and we use the parentheses to indicate that a probability assessment is being made.

Consider the set of outcomes of being a Criminal C and C'. If we say that P(C) is the probability of being a Criminal and that the probability is 0.05, we could write it as follows:

$$P(C|\&) = 0.05.$$

If later we find out that a recent government survey indicates one in forty people meet our definition of Criminal, then we should revise our probability given this new state of information. We can write this new state of information as follows:

$$P(C|\&_n) = 0.025.$$

Denoting $\&_n$ as the new state of information, we see that now our probability has changed to 0.025. This new state of information ($\&_n$) signifies the addition of the new information to our previous state of information. If we denote the government survey by G, we could write the following:

$$P(C|\&_n) = P(C|G, \&_n) = 0.025.$$

We must be able to clearly define the state of information for which the probability was assigned. Without this ability, probabilistic assessments can become very confusing and often misleading.

8.5 Probability Trees

While Venn diagrams are very useful in graphically representing outcomes, they become complex and confusing with all but the simplest of problems. For this reason, we use the probability tree. The probability tree allows for the graphical representation of many sets of outcomes through the use of nodes. We represent uncertainty nodes as circles with branches for each possible outcome. By constructing the tree out of the sets of outcomes, we can construct joint outcomes by following each path (left to right) through the tree.

Criminal example continues   Continuing with the case of The Uneducated Criminal from Chapter 3, we can construct a tree (Figure 8.5) using the probabilities of 0.025 for being a Criminal and 0.20 for being a High School Dropout as well as a Criminal.

Figure 8.5 Probability Tree for Criminal and Dropout

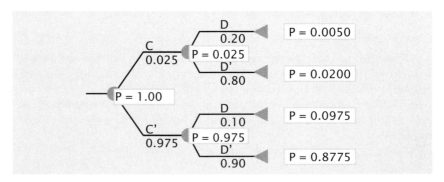

Figure 8.5 was developed using the program TreeAge Pro, available from TreeAge Software. The tree shows joint (elemental) probabilities of 0.005, 0.020, 0.0975, and 0.8775. From this we can see the joint probability that a person is a Criminal and a High School Dropout is only 0.005. Using the Law of Multiplication, we can write the joint probability as follows:

$$P(E,F \mid \&) = P(F|E,\&)\, P(E \mid \&),$$

Equation 8.9

or specifically for the Uneducated Criminal example:

$$P(C,D|\&) = P(D|C,\&)\, P(C|\&) = 0.005.$$

The ability to decompose problems into smaller sets of outcomes provides the means to adequately and systematically deal with the uncertainties influencing the problem.

From Figure 8.5, we can also calculate the marginal probabilities of the outcomes. Marginal probabilities are calculated by summing the probabilities at the margins of the rows and columns in a probability table or on the tree. Figure 8.6 illustrates how the marginals can be calculated using a spreadsheet.

	C	C'	Marginals
D	0.005	0.0975	0.1025
D'	0.020	0.8775	0.8975
Marginals	0.025	0.9750	

Figure 8.6 Probability Table for Criminal and Dropout

Notice that the marginals all sum to 1.0. This is from rule number two, the Law of Addition. We can calculate the marginals with equation 8.10:

$$P(E|\&) = \sum_{i=1}^{n} P(E, X_i|\&)$$

Equation 8.10

Let E be any outcome and X_i ($i = 1...n$) be a set of mutually exclusive and collectively exhaustive outcomes; F is any other outcome. We can now derive the marginal for E as shown in Equation 8.11.

$$P(E \mid \&) = P(F,E \mid \&) + P(F', E \mid \&)$$

Equation 8.11

For the Uneducated Criminal example,

$$P(C \mid \&) = P(C,D \mid \&) + P(C,D'|\&) = 0.005 + 0.020 = 0.025.$$

Conditional Probability

In most complex business and personal situations we do not have complete knowledge or information concerning the outcome of an event. By incorporating this partial knowledge we may gain insight into the problem and decide to revise our previous probabilities. Conditional probability refers to the modification of the probability of an outcome that precedes it. Using this conditional method, we can account for relationships between uncertain future outcomes and make appropriate decisions based on the probabilities of associated outcomes. We can write the following formula to describe conditional probability:

Equation 8.12

$$P(E|F,\&) = \frac{P(E, F | \&)}{P(F|\&)}$$

Let E be any outcome such that $P(E) > 0$, and F is any other outcome. If $P(E) = 0$, the conditional probability of F given E is undefined. Using this notation, we can determine the conditional probability of being a Criminal given that the person is a High School Dropout.

$$P(C|D,\&) = \frac{P(C, D | \&)}{P(D|\&)} = \frac{(0.005)}{(0.1025)} = 0.04888$$

Prior and posterior probabilities

When revising probabilities due to new states of information, we refer to the unconditional probability, $P(E|\&)$, as the **prior** and to the conditional probability, $P(E|F,\&)$, as the **posterior**.

It is important to note when constructing a Venn diagram for the conditional probability that knowing F has occurred changes the universal set of outcomes (Ω). Now the outcome must occur within the area defined by F, and E is replaced by (E,F). This is illustrated by Figure 8.7.

Figure 8.7 Venn Diagram of Conditional Probability

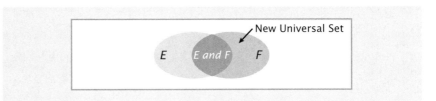

8.6 Reversing the Tree

The ability to relate posterior probabilities $P(E|F,\&)$ to prior probabilities $P(E|\&)$ through reversal of the conditional probabilities is of great importance to decision analysis. Bayes' Rule is derived by using conditional probability in terms of $P(E|F,\&)$ and $P(F|\&)$ using the Law of Addition (Equation 8.2) to calculate $P(F|\&)$ and using the Law of Multiplication (Equation 8.9) to calculate $P(E|F,\&)$. In this way, we can relate the joint and marginal probabilities to the conditional probabilities.

Bayes' rule is simply if n outcomes $E_1, E_2, \ldots E_n$ are mutually exclusive and collectively exhaustive and if F is any other outcome for which $P(F) > 0$, then the conditional probability of any outcome E_i given that outcome F has occurred is:

Equation 8.13

$$P(E_i,F|\&) = P(E_i|F,\&)\, P(F|\&) = P(F|E_i,\&)\, P(E_i|\&)$$

By using the Law of Multiplication and the Law of Addition we have:

$$P(E_i|F,\&) = \frac{P(F|E_i,\&)\,P(E_i,\&)}{P(F|E_1,\&)\,P(E_1,\&)+P(F|E_2,\&)\,P(E_2,\&)+\ldots+P(F|E_n,\&)\,P(E_n,\&)}$$

Equation 8.14

An easier way to understand this reversal of distinctions is to calculate it through the tree. Figure 8.8 is the original probability tree.

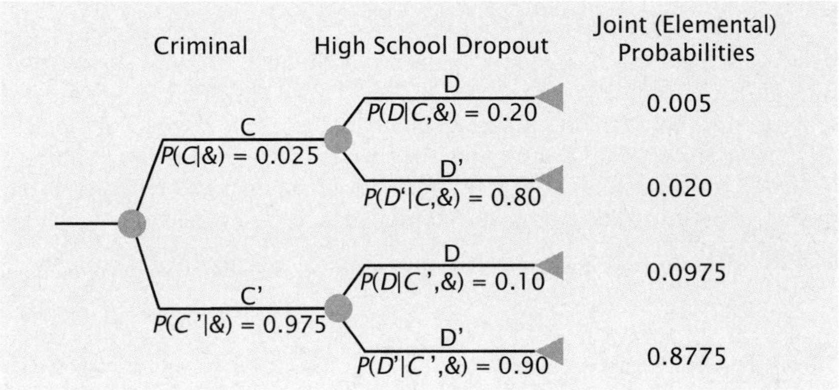

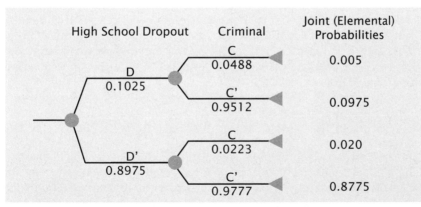

Figure 8.8 Original Probability Tree

We must maintain the same elemental probabilities when reversing the tree, since reversing the order of distinctions should not change these probabilities.

Figure 8.9 shows the reversed tree and the associated probabilities. We reconstruct the conditional probabilities by following the tree paths and maintaining probabilistic coherence. From the tree in Figure 8.8, we know the probability for the path Criminal was 0.025. We can see in Figure 8.9 the same probabilities exist except that the inner elemental probabilities have switched.

Figure 8.9 Reversed Probability Tree

In calculating the new conditional probabilities, we begin by summing the elemental probabilities for the branches of the distinction Criminal and allocate those to the distinction Dropout. This yields the probabilities of 0.1025 for Dropout and 0.8975 for Not a Dropout. The individual probabilities for the distinction Criminal are now simply the elemental probabilities divided by the probabilities for either D or D'. Therefore,

$$P(C|D,\&) = 0.005/0.1025 = 0.0488$$

and the complement must be

$$P(C'|D,\&) = 1 - P(C|D,\&) = 0.9512.$$

Further Insights from Reversing the Tree

From the original tree (Figure 8.8), we can see the majority of people are Not High School Dropouts and are Not Criminals as shown by the path C' and D', the probability of which is $P(C',D'|\&) = 0.8775$. By reversing the tree we can show the probabilities that must be assigned to the distinction High School Dropout (if you know the results of the distinction Criminal). You will notice that none of the information has changed but has simply been reconstructed in a manner that indicates the relevance of one distinction to another.

Relevance

If the two distinctions are not relevant to each other, we call these distinctions independent. That is, if the conditional probabilities are the same regardless of which conditioning distinction occurs then:

Equation 8.15 $$P(E|F,\&) = P(E|F',\&)$$

whereas if the two distinction are relevant, then:

Equation 8.16 $$P(E|F,\&) \neq P(E|F',\&)$$

Relevance is important in understanding the problem and how the uncertain outcomes interact.

From the reversed tree (Figure 8.9), we can see that if we know the person is a High School Dropout, then there is a 4.88% chance the person is a Criminal. This is very different than John's belief that all High School Dropouts are Criminals. From the original tree, we can see that if John apprehends a perpetrator in the act of a crime and that person is later convicted and becomes a "Criminal," there is a 20% chance the person is a High School Dropout.

8.7 Using and Understanding Distributions

Trees are very helpful in displaying information in a graphical manner, but often get confusing if they get too large. A more practical way to examine probability and its associated values is to use graphical probability distributions. To help understand the use and calculation of these distributions, we will continue with the ACI case study.

Don Boldin, the research manager for the coatings group at ACI, is interested in understanding the sales forecasts for project Norust that were made by the planning group. His understanding is that sales were based on market share and market size projections, and that the forecast he was given for project Norust was the base case estimate. Don recently attended a decision analysis course and would like to know what the probability tree looks like for sales of Norust, given market share and market size. In particular, he would like to know what the worst and best cases are and the associated probabilities.

Advanced Coatings (continued from Chapter 3)

The following tree (Figure 8.10) illustrates the market share and market size branches. This tree was created by the planning group using information provided by the marketing department. Marketing believes that, based on the test data, the market size for Norust will either be Average ($7–$10 million) or Huge ($15–$30 million) in the year of introduction, and has assigned probabilities for market size of 30% to being Huge and 70% to Average. The planning group then asked marketing, given that the market size will be Huge, what is the range of market share for Norust? Marketing responded that three possible outcomes would adequately and completely describe the market share–High, Base, and Low market share. Marketing assigned the probabilities of 10%, 70%, and 20% to High, Base, and Low, respectively. Marketing provided the same information concerning Average market size. The planning group then used this information in conjunction with price assumptions provided by marketing and calculated the resulting sales values shown at the end of the tree.

Would you feel comfortable presenting this tree to management?

Simple trees like Figure 8.10 can be presented to management, but trees with more than a few branches usually will confuse all but the most analytical managers.

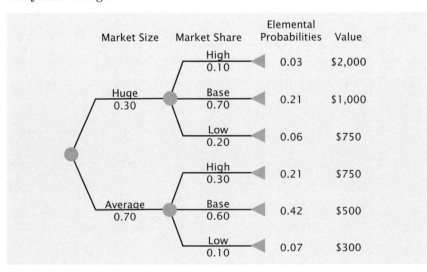

Figure 8.10 Probability Tree for Market Share and Market Size

We can show the same information contained in the tree using a graph, Figure 8.11, which is a density plot. Density plots or histograms allow you to directly graph values with their associated probabilities. Using Table 8.1, we can plot the values and probabilities from the tree in Figure 8.10.

Figure 8.11
Density Plot for
Market Share/
Market Size

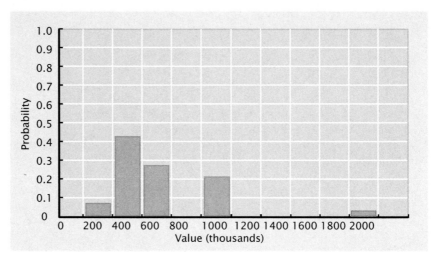

The density plot (Figure 8.11) graphically illustrates the likelihood of attaining the values specified in the tree. As you can see from the plot, the most likely value is between $400 and $600 and the next likely is between $600 and $800, with the least likely being $2,000. However, an even better way to show the relationship between probabilities and values is to use a cumulative distribution. The cumulative distribution shows the probability that the actual value is less than or equal to the value on the horizontal axis. Any point on this plot is read as less than or equal to value X at probability Y. For example in Figure 8.12, you could read point A as "there is a 97% chance of making $1000 or less."

Figure 8.12
Cumulative
Distribution
for Market
Share/ Market
Size

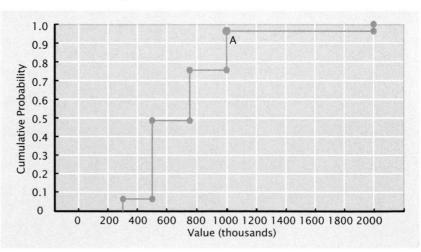

To build a cumulative distribution, begin by sorting the values from lowest to highest. Start the plot at the lowest value and draw a line from that value vertically until it intersects with the probability associated with that value. Then, draw a horizontal line from that intersection to the intersection of the next value. Again draw a vertical line until it meets the intersection of the sum of the first value probability and the second value probability. Continue this process until you have summed all the probabilities to 1. This process is performed easily by using a spreadsheet like Excel®.

Value	Probability	Cumulative Probability
300	0.07	0.07
500	0.42	0.49
750	0.27	0.76
1000	0.21	0.97
2000	0.03	1.00

Table 8.1
Probability
Table

Using the data from Table 8.1, recreate Figure 8.12 using Microsoft Excel®. Note the step change in values will require duplication of some data. What would be required to make this curve smooth?

Presenting graphics which are easy to understand and explain will help you to achieve commitment to action and will diminish the "black box" feeling that many decision makers have about decision analysis.

8.8 Summary and Interpretation

If we are to clearly speak about things which are not known for certain, then we must use the language of probability. Probability provides the ability to express our state of knowledge in a quantitative manner so we can incorporate uncertainty into the analysis.

Probability trees facilitate the assessment of states of knowledge and provide a structure to process this information. Reversing probability trees gives new insight into the problem by providing a different view of the relevance of distinctions to each other.

Probability distributions easily show the relationship between probability and value and are very useful in presentations to management. These distributions can be shown by density (histogram) or cumulatively.

Finally, without probability, an analysis can only be deterministic, which ignores uncertainty and allows for various interpretations.

8.9 Key Concepts

objective probability	decomposition
subjective probability	conditional probability
event	marginal probability
outcome	prior probability
three axioms of probability	posterior probability
mutually exclusive	density plot
collectively exhaustive	cumulative distribution
Venn diagram	

8.10 Study Questions

1. What is probability?

2. What are the two types of probability?

3. What is the correct probability of an outcome?

4. What are the three axioms of probability?

5. What is meant by the term decomposition?

6. Describe what a Venn diagram is used for.

7. What do we mean by marginal probabilities?

8. What do marginal probabilities always sum to?

9. What is conditional probability?

10. What do we mean by "reversing the tree?"

11. What is a cumulative distribution graph and how is one prepared?

12. Why is it important to define your current state of knowledge with your probability assessments?

13. What are probability trees and how do they differ from Venn diagrams?

14. What advantages to density plots and cumulative probability graphs have over probability trees?

8.11 References and Further Reading

Bayes, Thomas. "An Essay Towards Solving a Problem in the Doctrine of Chances." *Philosophical Transactions of Royal Society* 53 (1763): 370-418.

Bernoulli, Daniel. "Specimen theorial noval de mensura sortis." *Comentarii Academiae Scientiarum Imperiales Petropolitane* 5 (1738): 175-92.

Cyert, R. and M. DeGroot. *Bayesian Analysis and Uncertainty in Economic Theory.* Totowa, NJ: Rowman & Littlefield, 1987.

De Moivre, Abraham. *The Doctrine of Chances.* 3rd ed., London: 1756.

Earman, J. *Bayes or Bust?: A Critical Examination of Bayesian Confirmation Theory.* Cambridge: MIT Press, 1992.

Hymans, Saul H. *Probability Theory with Applications to Econometrics and Decision-Making.* Englewood Cliffs: Prentice-Hall, Inc., 1967.

LaPlace, P. S. *Essai Philosophique sur Les Probabilités.* Paris: 1816.

McNamee, P. and J. Celona. *Decision Analysis with Supertree.* 2nd ed., San Francisco, CA: The Scientific Press, 1990.

Olkin, Ingram, Leon J. Glesser, and Cyrus Derman. *Probability Models and Applications.* 2nd ed., Macmillian, 1994.

Spetzler, Carl S., ed. *Probability Encoding in Decision Analysis.* Vol. 2. Readings on the Principles and Applications of Decision Analysis. Menlo Park, CA: Strategic Decisions Group, 1972.

von Winterfeldt, D. and W. Edwards. *Decision Analysis and Behavioral Research.* Cambridge: Cambridge University Press, 1986.

8.12 Guide to Action

1. Use assessments of probability rather than words so that meaning can more precisely be communicated.

2. Recognize that there are appropriate probabilities but there is not a correct probability.

3. Use probability trees to communicate and solve problems.

4. Reverse the tree to gain insight as to relevance.

5. Use the cumulative distribution graph to convey probability information.

8.13 Case for Analysis: "The MBA Degree"

John has been working as an engineer year for the last five years. He has been thinking about going back to get a masters of business administration (MBA) degree. John believes that an MBA will help him advance faster up a technical ladder, and he also believes that this will make him competitive for other job opportunities within the company. John's wife supports him going back to school, but she is concerned about the time away from the family. She is also concerned about the cost of the degree and how much time John will have to spend away from work.

John has talked to his supervisor about going back to school and has his support. However, the company will not pay for this advanced degree, and John will have to use his vacation and sick leave for days away from work.

John has found an MBA program where he can get his degree in two years. The program has a good reputation and costs $35,000.00. The program offers courses on the weekends so that John would only have to take off one day every other week. John believes that if he gets this degree, he would see a promotion two years sooner than without it. John also believes that he would see an annual increase in his paycheck of about $5,000.

- What should John do?

- How would you value this situation?

- What is the expected value of the MBA?

- Draw a decision tree for this decision.

- How can good working knowledge of probability theory help John make an informed decision?

Using Simulation to Solve Decision Problems

The complexity of real-world problems can create an analytical nightmare when many uncertainties are involved. Consider a situation where you have a symmetrical tree with twenty uncertainties – even if you use a discrete approximation with only three values, the decision tree would have 3^{20} or 3,486,784,401 branches. If you wanted to use continuous distributions (rather than discrete), this would compound the problem even more.

Influence diagrams and skeleton decision trees can help by providing a graphical representation of the problem. But even these tools can become complex and confusing when many uncertain quantities must be used to find the probability distribution of expected value. However, one method which does work very well and which can handle the large amount of data is Monte Carlo simulation.

9.1 What is a Monte Carlo Simulation?

A Monte Carlo simulation is a process that generates random number inputs for uncertain values, which are then processed by a mathematical model, so that many scenarios can be evaluated. Results are plotted to provide a probability distribution of the output. The term Monte Carlo comes from the icon of all gambling, which is in fact what the process is – it performs many "gambles" over and over, relying on large numbers of trials to define the probability distribution.

9.2 Why Use Monte Carlo Simulation?

Monte Carlo simulation provides an easy way to deal with many uncertainties in a decision problem. Most problems you will face usually have only a few key uncertainties; these can readily be handled by decision trees or influence diagrams. However, some problems are too complex for decision trees or influence diagrams.

For example, Figure 9.1 shows a typical tornado diagram for a problem with seven uncertainties. The first three or four uncertainties provide the most variability in value. This is generally the case - even if there are ten or twenty uncertainties.

Figure 9.1
Typical
Tornado
Diagram

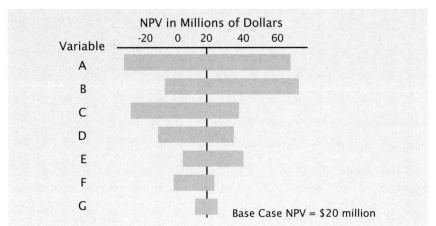

However, there are cases where many uncertainties may contribute relatively the same amount of uncertainty. Examples of these types of problems are safety and health decisions, major new product developments, and environmental decisions. Figure 9.2 illustrates an atypical tornado diagram.

Figure 9.2
Atypical
Tornado
Diagram

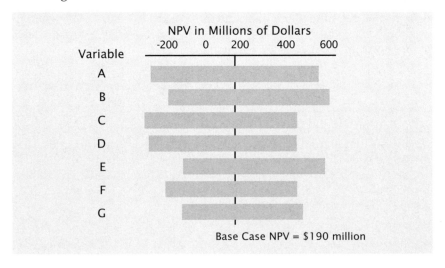

If the number of variables which are important to the decision are more than what a normal decision tree can handle (you would be building decision bushes), we can use Monte Carlo simulation to create a probability distribution of the value using the continuous distribution of each uncertainty.

9.3 Using Random Numbers to Simulate Reality

The power of Monte Carlo simulation relies on the ability to use random numbers to choose values from a distribution and calculate an output value for a particular model many times. Using random numbers to generate values eliminates the need to discretize a continuous distribution. It also allows you to use defined distributions such as normal, binomial, or Poisson. In some instances, this may save a tremendous amount of time by using previously generated data or known distributions.

*A **random number** can be any number (x) from a group of uniformly distributed numbers that falls within an established boundary, usually between 0 and 1. Uniformity is important, in that it means every number within the boundaries is possible and has an equal chance of being chosen.*

Random number defined

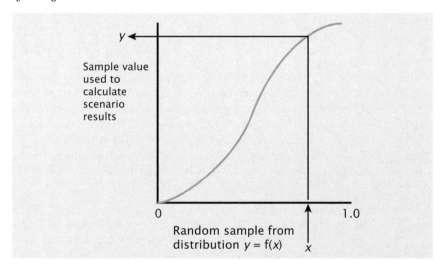

Figure 9.3 Random Sampling of a Distribution

Figure 9.3 illustrates how a random number (*x*) can be used to pick a value from a given cumulative distribution *f(x)*. The process is simple. First define the cumulative distribution $y = f(x)$. Then generate a random number (*x*) between 0 and 1. Find the value of *x* on the horizontal axis, follow it up until you reach the cumulative distribution, and then draw a line straight across to find the value *y*. Once this value has been chosen, it is input into the decision model and used to calculate an output value – usually expected value. While you can generate random numbers from tables, a much easier method is to use a computer spreadsheet such as Microsoft Excel®.

Y2K-razy

In 1999, the world faced a potential computer problem known with the shorthand name "Y2K." At the root of the issue was how computers stored dates. Most computers were designed to store the year with only two digits, i.e. "99" instead of "1999." When the year 2000 began, the computers would only see "00" and many were worried that computers would begin to malfunction.

The almost mystical significance of the Year 2000 coupled with a large dose of media hype fueled a drive by corporations and governments to resolve the problem before the end of the year 1999. Computer systems were upgraded at a frantic pace. The US Government spent over $8 billion and US Corporations poured more than $100 billion into fixes.

In retrospect, the danger associated with Y2K was likely exaggerated. The New Year arrived without a single major computer related problem. No planes fell from the sky and no power grids were disabled. Those who spent large sums of money on the problem heralded the "non-event" as evidence of a job well done. Bill Gates was quoted to say that Y2K fostered "a sense of team work". Countries that spent little to update their computers experienced a few minor problems.

1. If you were the IT Manager of a major corporation faced with the Y2K problem, what decision analysis tools would you find most useful in determining your course of action? Decision trees? Value of Information?

2. What decision analysis tools would assist in countering some of the media hype associated with these kinds of issues?

The Power of Spreadsheets

While there are commercial software packages dedicated to performing Monte Carlo simulation, you can also use the built-in random number functions in Excel®. These functions, like RAND( ) in Excel, return random numbers between 0 and 1 every time the spreadsheet is recalculated. By using these functions, you can create a new scenario each time the spreadsheet is recalculated. With the use of macros, you can automate the task to run hundreds or thousands of scenarios. Consider the following case study:

Case Study:
United Motors

United Motors wants to calculate the expected annual cost of fuel for its new car the Starfire. The project manager believes that four factors will influence the final cost of fuel - the price of gasoline, driving conditions, the car's fuel efficiency, and number of miles driven (See Table 9.1). The uncertainty "driving condition" subtracts from the car's fuel efficiency to account for suboptimal driving conditions, like extreme heat or cold.

Table 9.1
United Motors
Variable
Inputs

Variable	Units	Low	High
Gas Price	$ / Gallon	$2.50	$3.50
Driving Condition	Miles / Gallon	0	2
Fuel Efficiency	Miles / Gallon	15	30
Miles Driven / Year	Miles / Year	10,000	20,000

Using the information from the United Motors example, we can build a spreadsheet that will calculate an expected annual fuel cost. The basic spreadsheet would look like Figure 9.4. I have included the formulas for each of the functions at the top of the spreadsheet for easy reference. The formula for calculating the annual cost of fuel is:

(Miles driven / (Fuel efficiency – Driving condition)) x Gas price.

Recreate this spreadsheet using Excel®.

	A	B	C	D	E
1	Variable		Formula		
2	Gas price		y=RAND()+Base		
3	Base gas price		$2.50		
4	Driving condition		y=RAND()*2		
5	Fuel efficiency		y=15+RAND()*15		
6	Miles Driven/Year		y=10000+RAND()*(10000)		
7					
8				Miles	
9		Driving	Fuel	Driven	Annual
10	Gas Price	Condition	Efficiency	per Year	Cost
11	2.78	1.37	20.55	16,836	$2,444

Figure 9.4
United Motors
Spreadsheet

Generating Uniform Distributions

When the spreadsheet executes the RAND( ) function, it returns a value for x between 0 and 1. But what if we wanted the random value to be 0 to 2? We can do this by simply multiplying x by 2:

$$y = (x)(2)$$

By using the preceding formula you can alter the random number to fit the particular uniform distribution you need. The general formula for fitting the distribution to your particular needs is:

$$y = a + x(b - a)$$

Equation 9.1

By multiplying x times $(b - a)$, you can enlarge the range to fit within the parameters of a and b, and by adding a to the equation you set the base for the distribution. This method is easy to apply. The values in Figure 9.5 were calculated using these formulas.

Using a spreadsheet to calculate random numbers and the resulting values is an easy task when you are only running a few hundred scenarios. However, if you need to run many thousands of scenarios, it is often worth the time and effort to set up macros to make the process faster and more consistent. Figure 9.5 shows several scenarios and included is a simple macro (in column D) for running a hundred scenarios at a time. However, sometimes you may need to use discrete distributions in addition to continuous distributions.

Figure 9.5
United Motors
Spreadsheet

	A	B	C	D	E
1	Variable	Formula	Monte_Carlo (a)		
2	Gas price	y=RAND()+Base	SELECT("R8C2:R8C6")		
3	Base gas price	$2.50	FILL.AUTO("RC:R[100]C[4]",FALSE)		
4	Driving condition	y=RAND()*2	RETURN()		
5	Fuel efficiency	y=15+RAND()*15			
6	Miles Driven/Year	y=10000+RAND()*(10000)			
7					
8				Miles	
9		Driving	Fuel	Driven	Annual
10	Gas Price	Condition	Efficiency	per Year	Cost
11	2.78	1.37	20.55	16,836	$2,444
12	2.74	0.40	29.17	12,384	$1,179
13	2.62	0.91	20.17	17,902	$2,436
14	2.73	0.39	23.84	14,831	$1,727
15	2.65	0.87	24.64	10,359	$1,155
16	3.11	1.68	15.56	19,234	$4,314
17	2.86	1.58	19.23	12,843	$2,078
18	3.18	1.68	18.30	13,443	$2,569
19	2.90	0.46	18.45	13,566	$2,189
20	2.60	1.00	18.67	11,486	$1,692
21	3.12	0.81	22.02	13,789	$2,029
22	2.56	1.51	17.17	12,320	$2,018
23	3.49	1.77	21.70	14,543	$2,549
24	3.36	1.46	23.03	12,378	$1,929
25	3.42	1.98	22.22	13,140	$2,221
26	3.08	0.49	15.43	10,293	$2,124
27	3.25	1.55	24.12	14,951	$2,156

Using Discrete Distributions

You may have a situation where you need to apply a discrete distribution to solve a problem. This is easy to accomplish by dividing the uniform distribution of 0 to 1 into intervals which correspond to the discrete values you are wanting to model. For example, suppose you want to evaluate the even or odd number outcomes of a normal six sided die. If the die were to roll a 1, 3, or 5, you would receive $100, and if the roll was 2, 4, or 6, you would pay $25. Assuming that the die is not biased, the probability of rolling an odd number is the same as rolling an even number. Using this information, we need two intervals to evaluate this problem. We could construct the following formula:

$$\text{IF } (x \le 0.50, \text{"Even", IF } (x > 0.50, \text{"Odd",0)).}$$

Using Microsoft Excel®, the formula would be proceeded by an "=" sign and the "x" would be replaced with cell references. The "Even" and "Odd" results could then be converted into the dollar values, or you could use:

$$\text{IF } (x \le 0.50, 100, \text{IF } (x > 0.50, -25,0)), \text{ or, more simply:}$$

$$\text{IF } (x \le 0.50, 100, -25).$$

If you use more than a few discrete outcomes, nested IF statements become rather complex. A better way is to use lookup tables.

Lookup tables provide an easy way of using discrete information when there are many possible values. The lookup table contains the cumulative probabilities and their associated discrete values. The probabilities should be in the first column and the associated values aligned with the probabilities in the second column. The spreadsheet searches for the largest value in the first column that is still smaller than the generated random number (x). Once it finds that number, it reads the value in the second column and uses that number in the decision model. An example of a lookup table is shown in Figure 9.6.

	A	B	C	D	E
1	Probabilities	Discrete Values		Random Number	
2	0	15		0.05	
3	0.15	34			
4	0.28	58		Lookup Value	
5	0.65	92		15	
6	0.86	112			

Figure 9.6
Example
Lookup Table

9.4 Using the Results of a Monte Carlo

Once we have built a spreadsheet model of the uncertainties and run as many scenarios as necessary to generate an appropriate probability distribution, we need to analyze the data. Two easy to create and very informative graphs are the histogram and cumulative distribution.

The histogram is a useful graph because it shows the relative frequency of outcomes. This is beneficial if you want to see what outcomes occurred the most times in the simulation. To build a histogram, simply sort the outcomes from smallest to largest value and plot using a bar graph the number of times a value occurs in a given range, referred to as a "bin." The resulting "bins" are evenly spaced ranges across the x-axis.

Having calculated a hundred scenarios using the spreadsheet in Figure 9.5, we now can analyze the data. The project manager is interested in what range of fuel cost is most likely to occur. We can graphically show this information by using a histogram chart. A histogram breaks the data into intervals and then plots the number of times a value falls within that interval. Figure 9.7 shows a histogram using the data from the United Motors case. From this analysis we can see that the interval of $2,000 to $2,260 had the largest number of resulting values

In addition to the histogram, cumulative probability distributions help to show the risk profile of the outcomes. This allows the decision maker to better understand the range of possible outcomes and how likely they are to occur. Figure 9.8 is the cumulative distribution of the United Motors data.

United Motors
case continued

Figure 9.7
United Motors
Histogram

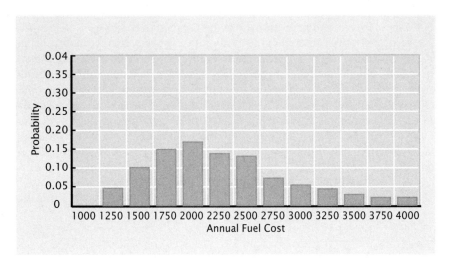

Cumulative distributions are also easy to create using a spreadsheet. Begin by sorting the data from lowest to highest. If you are only using 100 outcomes, like in this case, then each outcome represents an increment of 1%. However, if you are using more than 100 outcomes you will need to adjust the weight of each outcome by the number of outcomes, since you can not have a probability greater than 100%. Then you can generate a plot such as Figure 9.8.

Figure 9.8
United Motors
Cumulative
Probability
Graph

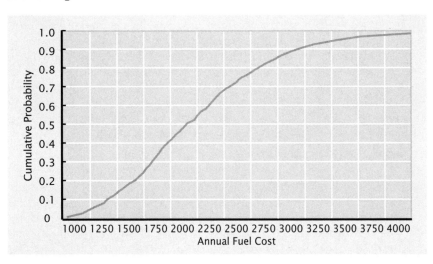

The goal of a Monte Carlo simulation is to allow you to generate many possible outcomes which can then be used to better understand the uncertainty surrounding the problem.

9.5 Commercial Software

While I have shown how to use ordinary spreadsheets to calculate Monte Carlo simulations, there are several commercial software packages available to run Monte Carlo analyses on either a Macintosh or Windows machine. The two most prominent packages are Crystal Ball® by Oracle and @Risk by Palisade. Both products have the ability to run large simulations very quickly and can display the results in many ways, including histograms and cumulative distributions.

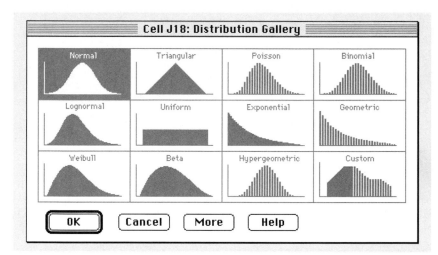

Figure 9.9 Screenshot of Crystal Ball® Distributions

These programs function as an "add-in" function to Microsoft Excel®. They include named functions such as normal, Poisson, exponential, beta, and triangular distributions. Figure 9.9 is a screen shot from Crystal Ball which shows the many different types of distributions that can be used. Using a commercial package like Crystal Ball makes performing Monte Carlo simulations quick and easy. You can find more information on Crystal Ball at Oracle's web site: www.Oracle.com/CrystalBall/Index.html.†

Case Study: ChemCorp

ChemCorp is a chemical manufacturing company located in the Northeast. The company has a manufacturing site that has been in operation since 1910. Over the years, due to poor environmental practices, the site has become contaminated with many hazardous chemicals. The standard practice of disposal from about 1920 to 1970 was to bury 55 gallon drums of waste on-site. Thousands of these drums are assumed to be buried at the plan.

The company has decided to remediate the site but is not sure whether to build an on-site incinerator or to contract with a waste disposal firm located 10 miles away. Since the cost of either alternative is dependent upon many factors, this problem may best be handled by a Monte Carlo simulation. The influence diagram (Figure 9.10) illustrates the uncertainties affecting the situation.

Figure 9.10
ChemCorp
Influence
Diagram

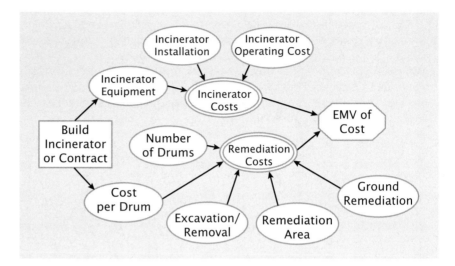

As you can see, there are many uncertainties that affect the decision of whether to build an incinerator or to contract with a waste management firm. The decision maker for this decision assembled a small project team to work on this problem. The team has since made some initial estimates of the costs involved with both alternatives. Table 9.2 lists the possible ranges for each uncertainty.

Table 9.2
ChemCorp
Uncertainty
Ranges

Variable	Units	Low	Base	High
Incinerator				
Equipment	Millions of $	2	4	5
Installation	Millions of $	3	4	6
Operating Cost	Millions of $	2	6	8
Remediation				
Cost per Drum				
< 100,000	Dollars/Drum		40	
< 600,000	Dollars/Drum		25	
<1,500,000	Dollars/Drum		15	
No. of Drums	Thousands	100	400	1200
Excavation Cost	Dollars/Drum	5	10	15
Remediation Cost	Square Yards	4,500	14,500	29,000
Ground				
Remediation Cost	Dollars/Yard	2	4	8

This information can be easily entered into Crystal Ball by using the graphical interface. Figure 9.11 is an example of how the equipment costs for the incinerator can be entered using a triangular distribution. The inputs needed for this distribution are minimum, maximum, and most likely values.

*Figure 9.11
Equipment
Cost Triangular
Distribution*

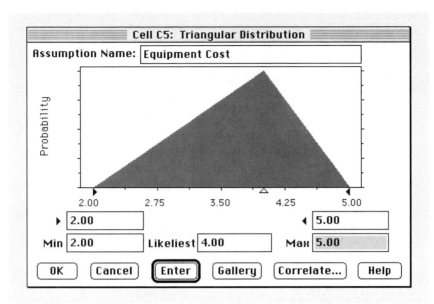

Using the input ranges shown in Table 9.2, we can build a spreadsheet model of the decision problem.

Figure 9.12 is the decision model for the ChemCorp decision. Crystal Ball uses the inputs entered into the program as the basis for randomly choosing values to substitute for the base values shown in the spreadsheet. It then substitutes these values and records the changes in outcomes. You can specify how many trials or scenarios you want Crystal Ball to run by using a pull down menu.

When the simulation is finished, Crystal Ball creates a very thorough and useful report which contains all the simulation statistics and graphically shows the uncertain cumulative distributions used and the resulting outcomes in either histogram or cumulative form. Figure 9.13 shows the outcomes from the ChemCorp decision to contract the waste disposal displayed in histogram form.

9.6 The Role of Monte Carlo

Monte Carlo analysis is not a substitute for decision analysis, but it can be very useful in building distributions of uncertain quantities. Simulation is a useful tool, as it is relatively easy to create and run the models, especially with specific software like Crystal Ball or @Risk. You can use simulations to develop risk profiles of multiple uncertain quantities which are then used as inputs to a decision analysis.

Figure 9.12
ChemCorp
Spreadsheet

	A	B	C	D	E
1	Business Model 1.0 - ChemCorp				
2					
3	Variable	Low	Base	High	Units
4	Incinerator				
5	Equipment	2	4	5	Millions of $
6	Installation	3	4	6	Millions of $
7	Operating Cost	2	6	8	Millions of $
8					
9	Remediation				
10	Cost per Drum				
11	≤ 100,000		40		Dollars/Drum
12	≤ 600,000		25		Dollars/Drum
13	≤ 1,500,000		15		Dollars/Drum
14	No. of Drums	100	400	1200	Thousands
15	Excavation Cost	5	10	15	Dollars/Drum
16	Remediation Area	4500	14500	29000	Sq. Yards
17	Ground Rem. Cost	2	4	8	Dollars/Yard
18					
19	Build Expected Cost	17.2464			
20	Incinerator Cost	14			
21	Drum Removal Cost	3.2			
22	Ground Remediation Cost	0.0464			
23					
24	Contract Expected Cost	15.558			
25	100,000≤ X	4			
26	100,000≤ X ≤600,000	7.5			
27	600,000≤ X ≤1,500,000	0			
28	Drum Removal Cost	4			
29	Ground Remediation Cost	0.058			

Figure 9.13
Histogram of
Contract
Expected Cost

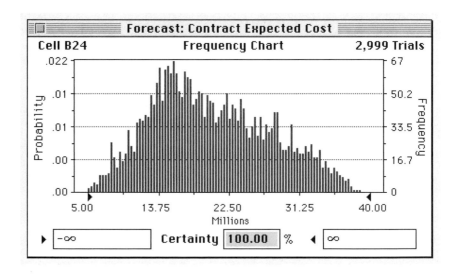

While simulation can be performed with much less difficulty using a specialized software package, ***this does not mean that the thought and model construction should be of any less rigor***. I have often seen analysts use these programs indiscriminately, not knowing really what the program is doing or how it arrived at the final distribution. Even more so, I see analysts who use incorrectly shaped distributions. These problems can lead to the "garbage in, garbage out" syndrome. A Monte Carlo simulation requires the same level of thought that is required of any decision model.

Table 9.3 shows a comparison of Monte Carlo and typical decision analysis tools.

Cautions concerning simulations

	Influence Diagrams	Decision Trees	Discrete Monte Carlo	Continuous Monte Carlo
Number of Uncertainties	Limited	Limited	Unlimited	Unlimited
Dependencies	Unlimited	Unlimited	Unlimited	Correlation Coefficients
Sampling	Controlled Discrete	Controlled Discrete	Uncontrolled Discrete	Uncontrolled Discrete
Secondary Decisions	Yes	Yes	No	No
Value of Information	Yes	Yes	No	Yes

Table 9.3 Comparison of Decision Analysis Tools

9.7 Summary and Interpretation

Monte Carlo simulation provides another approach to dealing with uncertain quantities. We can use this method to learn about the interactions of many uncertainties, which before may not have been possible using decision trees or influence diagrams. Monte Carlo simulation will in most cases require the use of a computer, although simple models can be run using tables or hand-held calculators.

While Monte Carlo simulation is easy to set up and run using a spreadsheet and/or specific software, the same amount of care must be taken as when building any decision model.

9.8 Key Concepts

Monte Carlo simulation
random numbers
discrete distributions
Crystal Ball
cumulative distribution curves

why use Monte Carlo
continuous distributions
histograms
@Risk

9.9 Study Questions

1. What is a Monte Carlo simulation?

2. Explain the term uniformly distributed.

3. What is a random number?

4. Describe the difference between using Monte Carlo simulation and using decision trees to find expected value.

5. What is a discrete distribution?

6. What is a continuous distribution?

7. Describe how to construct a histogram chart.

8. Why should you use Monte Carlo simulation?

9. Why is Monte Carlo analysis not a substitute for decision analysis?

10. How can you modify the random number to fit a particular uniform distribution?

11. If the results of a Monte Carlo simulation are plotted on a cumulative distribution graph, what information can be interpreted from the graph?

9.10 References and Further Reading

Clemen, Robert T. *Making Hard Decisions*. Belmont, CA: PWS-Kent, 1991.

Gregory, Geoffrey. *Decision Analysis*. New York: Plenum, 1988.

Law, A.M., and D. Kelton. *Simulation Modeling and Analysis*, 2nd ed. New York: McGraw-Hill, 1991.

9.11 Guide to Action

Keep the following guidelines in mind when using Monte Carlo:

1. Monte Carlo is a good technique for generating uncertainty ranges and distributions for highly uncertain events. However, Monte Carlo is not a substitute for careful evaluations.

2. Monte Carlo provides a quick and simple method to evaluate complex problems.

3. Do not use Monte Carlo as the only evaluation method when value of information is an important part of the decision.

4. There are several popular Monte Carlo packages available, or you can use the built-in random number generator in Excel®.

5. As with decision analysis, some training is necessary before using Monte Carlo analysis. This training should focus on understanding distributions and which distribution is appropriate for a given uncertainty.

9.12   Case for Analysis: "Changing Jobs"

Dan and Diana currently enjoy living in a small town, where there is one major employer. Dan works for this employer, an oil company, as an engineer. During the past few years the company has gone through several layoffs and Dan fears that he will lose his job in the next round. Diana works for a local bank but does not make enough to support both of them if Dan lost his job.

Because of the fear of losing his job and growing dissatisfaction with his work environment, Dan is considering changing jobs and even changing careers. Dan has contacted a headhunter to help him search for a new job. After several weeks, the headhunter located two jobs for Dan. One job was in the oil industry working for another oil company. This company is very conservative and does not use layoffs as a way to manage cash flow. The other company is a ship building company, which needs Dan's specific skills as a metallurgical engineer. Both jobs are a considerable distance from where they currently live and would be even further away from both of their families. Both Dan and Diana are willing to move if they have to, but they are concerned about being able to sell their house. Because of the layoffs, the local real estate market is down and homes are generally taking up to nine months to sell. Additionally, the real estate markets in the two cities that Dan is considering are about 15-20% higher than where they currently live. Because of this, Dan is concerned about the down payment and mortgage costs for a new home.

Dan is also concerned about leaving a known organizational situation and moving into an unknown situation with either of the new jobs. Diana's manager at the bank told Diana that she thinks the economy is getting softer and that a recession of 1 to 3 years duration is likely. Diana believes that she could get a comparable position with a bank in either new job location.

Dan is currently making $65,000 per year. Dan estimates that he would have to make an additional $10,000 per year for the shipbuilding job and $15,000 more per year for the oil company job to maintain their standard of living.[1]

Both the oil company and the ship building company offered Dan a position with a starting salary of $70,000.

- ■   How should Dan and Diana evaluate this situation?

- ■   What uncertainties do you think are important to their decision?

- ■   What do you think Dan and Diana's objectives hierarchy would look like (draw their decision hierarchy)?

---

[1]   You can make the same comparison that Dan did by using www.home-fair.com/real-estate/city-profile.index.asp to compare living costs in different cities.

- What choices do they have?

- Draw an influence diagram for this situation.

- How could Dan and Diana use Monte Carlo simulation to assist them with their decision making process?

10

Using Uncertain Information and Judgment

To be absolutely certain about something, one must know everything or nothing about it.

— Olin Miller

We are all concerned with the future and how it will affect us. We make decisions every day when there is uncertainty about some set of future events. We may be concerned with the stock market and how it will impact our investment portfolios or retirement accounts. In business, we may be concerned with market penetration of a new product or the impact of a financial crisis on foreign markets. All of these involve decisions which involve uncertainty.

Uncertainty can come from not understanding how specific courses of action will affect the future or from having limited information about the courses of action themselves. The problem is, how do you effectively deal with future uncertain events? In the traditional business decision making approach, we would gather data to help us understand events that have already happened and then make some extrapolation about the future based on this data. However, unless the future is like the past, we may extrapolate some very poor conclusions. For example, during the oil crisis of the 1970's, most oil companies predicted that oil would reach $50 to $100 per barrel. However, as we now know, oil did not reach $100 per barrel until decades later.

To effectively deal with uncertainty, we must become comfortable with using limited information and with subjective assessments about the future. We need to understand what information is necessary to make a decision and what information would change our decision. This chapter illustrates how to uncover and effectively deal with uncertainty in the form of subjective ranges and probabilities.

10.1 Using Limited Information

Sir Francis Bacon said, "If we begin with certainties, we shall end in doubts; but if we begin with doubts, and are patient in them, we shall end in certainties."

Analysis paralysis

To deal effectively with the future, you must be able to use limited information to identify and select the best course of action. It is easy to fall into the trap of asking for more and more information, hoping that with each additional piece, the course of action will become obvious. However, usually what happens is that you become inundated with information and become so unclear about the problem that you are paralyzed ("analysis paralysis"). Only after careful thought and a clear understanding of the range of possibilities and their associated probabilities can we have a clear understanding of the future. Because almost all decisions, especially those involving the future, are based on limited information, we must understand both the *variability* and the *reliability* of our information.

Variability

We understand that events in the future cannot be known for certain until they happen. But, given a set of circumstances, we can develop a range of possibilities that describes what *could* happen. This is the variability of the information or the range of possibilities. To further define this variability, we can also assign probabilities to each of the possibilities to further describe our views as to the likelihood of each of the events. Understanding this range is important for determining the best course of action.

Reliability

While having a range of possibilities is necessary, these possibilities must be grounded in reality, that is, they must be *reliable*. The range should adequately reflect the uncertainty but not be so encompassing as to lose meaning and insight. This is why I use the term *reliable* rather than *accurate*. Accuracy implies precision, and precision is difficult if not impossible to forecast about the future. Think about experiences you may have had in forecasting the future price of a certain stock that you own. Have you been able to accurately predict the highs and lows of the stock as well as when they will occur? Reliable implies a reputable and informed source; if the source is not reliable, it will be difficult to gain commitment to action by either the decision maker or the organization.

10.2 Gathering Information

To use even limited information, you must gather it from some source. The key to gathering information is to first understand what information is relevant and needed to solve the problem. Next determine which experts should be assessed. This is not always an easy task, and you should not confine yourself to using only internal experts. Many times the best expert may be external to the organization - at a university or research institute. Once the experts have been chosen, they must be unbiased and then assessed. Uncovering biases is not a trivial task, but it *must* be done to ensure that reliable information is gathered.

What Information is Needed?

The first step is to determine what information should be gathered. This may seem obvious, but how many times have you or someone you know spent long hours gathering or refining information which later turned out to be unimportant? The influence diagram is very helpful in identifying what information should be gathered and what expert sources may have the necessary information. I often take a completed influence diagram and write the names of the experts and their areas of responsibility by each of the uncertainties to be assessed. This allows the team to keep track of who is being assessed and for what. It is also a quick and easy way to communicate the same information to the decision board. Figure 10.1 is an example of how to use this method for the Swanson case.

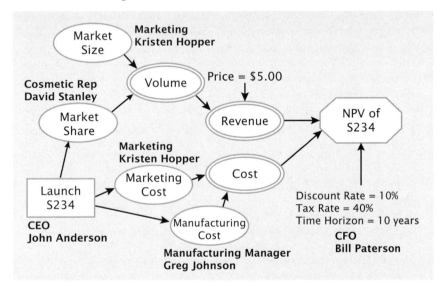

Figure 10.1 Information Sources for Swanson Case

Finding the Right Expert

As important as understanding what information to gather is knowing who to ask. An expert is like an onion in that he or she should have many layers of knowledge. As each layer of knowledge is peeled back, another layer should appear until you reach the core of knowledge. Once you have reached this core of knowledge, the expert should tell you that he or she has no more information to provide.

The expert should be able to make what we call powerful distinctions at each layer of knowledge. A ***powerful distinction*** clearly indicates the expert's grasp of the subject and distinguishes the expert from others with lesser knowledge. For example, a professional car mechanic will be able to describe the inner workings of an engine and the use of each engine part. This is in contrast to most of us who can only distinguish an air filter from the radiator. These powerful distinctions will also increase the

Powerful distinctions

shared knowledge of the subject for the team. As more and more of these distinctions are revealed, the project team becomes more informed and better able to gain insight from the analysis.

Finding the right expert

To make these distinctions, we must have the right expert. Often the right expert may not be found in your organization. If this is the case, you have two choices. You can gather information from the best available internal experts and seek external experts later if the information value warrants it, or you can go to external experts first. I have seen both situations. Some companies will only use internally generated information because of cost or confidentiality, while others will only believe information if it is obtained from a third party! The key is to understand the organizational culture and decision maker preferences.

Use a step-wise approach to gathering information

In general, I recommend using a two-step process that follows the idea of developing increasingly complex models. Begin by developing quick but adequate ranges for each uncertainty using the experts you have available. Then, by performing sensitivity analysis, you can determine which uncertainties are critical to the value and success of the project. If you believe the experts you assessed were not sufficiently knowledgeable or the uncertainty is pivotal to the decision, then you should consider finding a second expert assessment to validate the original.

When Experts Don't Agree

One problem with expert assessments is that they are subjective and depend upon the expert's knowledge, data, and previous experiences. Often you will find two qualified experts with completely different opinions. When this happens, you must carefully explore the knowledge and assumptions each expert is relying upon. Usually there is some missing piece of information or assumption that is causing the discrepancy. If the two cannot be reconciled and the information is critical to the evaluation, a peer review or a third expert may be necessary to bring consensus to the assessed range. If the information is not critical, use both experts' extremes and combine into a single range.

10.3 Uncovering and Dealing with Biases

An expert provides his or her beliefs in the form of a quantitative answer – both values and probabilities. To ensure that the expert is providing a unbiased perspective and assessment, you must search for and counteract cognitive and motivational biases.

Bias defined

Bias *is a conscious or subconscious discrepancy between the expert's response and an accurate description of his or her underlying knowledge.*

Motivational Bias

Motivational biases are caused by personal interests which can conflict with proper evaluation of the project, such as:

- I won't have a job if this project fails.
- I can do anything given enough time and money.
- I am an expert; why should I be uncertain?

Motivational biases are usually easy to identify and almost as easy to correct. Begin by educating the expert about the assessment process and by telling the individual you are not trying to extract a promise, only an honest assessment. Then try assessing something the expert has no personal interest in, such as the time of sunrise or sunset. This will provide both you and the expert with a practice run before starting the actual assessment and will allow the expert to become comfortable with the process.

Cognitive Biases

Cognitive biases are introduced by the way the expert processes information and are more difficult to detect and correct. There are six general cognitive biases that can affect an expert's assessment. These are:

- anchoring
- availability
- coherence
- overconfidence
- representativeness, and
- sampling.

Anchoring is a bias towards a starting value and occurs when you let the expert give you their best estimate first. Anchoring is also probably the most prevalent cognitive bias you will encounter. To avoid this bias always begin by assessing either the worst outcome (p10 value) or the best (p90 value). Also test for symmetry – is the expert's range only plus or minus some percent from their best guess? If so, make sure they really believe that it is a credible and reliable range.

Anchoring bias

The **availability** bias causes an over estimation of the probability of occurrence due to recent events. An example would be assessing the probability of an airplane crash. The expert may really believe it is 1 in 10 million. But if there was a recent crash, especially one that affected the expert in some way, this recent information will change the expert's assessment. In this case, the expert may give an assessed probability that is considerably higher, like 1 in 100 thousand. While the expert is incorporating the new information into the probability assessment, he or she is assuming that a recent crash indicates a higher probability of occurrence. This bias can be counteracted by asking the expert what the probability would have been prior to the recent event, then exploring whether the recent event really should alter the probability of occurrence.

Availability bias

FORD PINTO – When Economic Analysis is Not Enough

In the 1960's, American automakers began to feel the competitive pressure from German and Japanese companies. The need for a smaller car to compete with these inexpensive imports was recognized. The President of Ford, Lee Iacocca, set into place a very aggressive plan to launch a new vehicle – the Ford Pinto. It normally took three and one half years to produce a new automobile, but the Pinto began rolling off the assembly line in a record 25 months.

Before production began, a major design flaw was discovered in the Pinto's fuel system, but Ford decided to move forward with the vehicle launch based on the following economic analysis.

- **CAVEAT EMPTOR SCENARIO:** Based on estimates of car sales and crash statistics, Ford's believed that the unsafe tanks would result in 2,100 burned vehicles every year. These accidents would in turn cause 180 burn deaths and 180 serious burn injuries. Using cost figures of $200,000 per death, $67,000 per injury, and $700 per vehicle, Ford calculated a total cost of $49.5 million.
- **NON-EXPLODING SCENARIO:** The cost for fixing the design flaw was approximately $11 per Pinto. Ford estimated sales of the Pinto to be 11 million vehicles. At $11 per car, the cost to fix the Pinto was $121 million, more than double the potential cost to compensate burn victims.

Lee Iacocca was known for saying, "Safety doesn't sell." Ford launched the Pinto in 1971. Ford ceased production of the ill-fated Pinto in late 1980 after:

- 1978: A California jury awarded the largest personal injury judgment to date with an astounding sum of $128 million in damages to victims of 53 Pinto crashes.
- 1978: Ford recalls 1.5 million Pintos.
- 1979: In the landmark case of State of Indiana v. Ford Motor Company, Ford became the first American corporation to be indicted of criminal homicide. They were later acquitted of reckless homicide, but the damage to Ford's reputation was irreparable. Video of Pintos exploding during crash testing was particularly upsetting.

Ford's decision not to correct the design flaw led to many other lawsuits. Court costs, lawsuit settlements, the Pinto recall, and Ford's damaged reputation cost Ford many times the estimated $121 million that it would have cost to avoid this entire disaster.

1. Could this happen in today's business environment?

2. Could this calculation be done in your company?

3. How could correct application of decision analysis have prevented Ford's fiasco?

Coherence bias

Coherence is a bias that produces a higher probability of occurrence than is warranted due to an easy and plausible scenario. Consider the task of determining the price of oil at some time in the future. If a person could build a case about a war in the Persian Gulf area occurring at some time in the future, even though there is not information to suggest such an event, this could alter your assessment of the price of oil. Coherence is one of the most difficult biases to counteract but can be counteracted by examining why the event is so plausible.

The *overconfidence* bias usually results when an expert believes he or she knows everything about the subject in question. This bias will cause many surprises or unexpected outcomes if it is not carefully addressed. The best way to deal with this bias is to discuss many scenarios with the expert to reveal that their information and knowledge may not be as complete or certain as he or she thought.

Overconfidence bias

Representativeness results from an expert stereotyping events which are similar. This bias can be counteracted by pointing out the differences in the events.

Representativeness bias

The *sampling* bias is a result of having too much faith in certain information. Usually it is information which has either been refined or comes from a noted authority such as the U.S. Government. While the information may be accurate and of good quality, the expert may be placing too much faith in the information without knowing all the assumptions and manipulations that are present in the data. The expert should consider if the information fits his or her frame of reference and if he or she is comfortable with the way the information was gathered and formatted. If not, the information should not be used.

Sampling bias

10.4 Assessing Information

Having determined what information should be gathered, which experts should be assessed, and having searched for and corrected biases, the assessment of the information can begin. The formal process of assessing probability distributions is called **encoding**. Encoding information is not a difficult task, but it can be time consuming, especially if an expert is uncooperative or has many biases that need to be counteracted. When assessing the expert, explain the assumptions that have been made and ask for any assumptions he or she is making which could affect the assessed information. This will help you uncover biases and make sure the expert has the right perspective. Figure 10.2 illustrates the steps to take to successfully assess an expert.

Encoding expert assessments

Begin the assessment process by motivating the expert. It is important to establish a rapport with the expert so he or she becomes comfortable with the process. This will also allow you to search for motivational biases. During this step you should try to determine if the identified expert is the right expert for this assessment. You can do this by asking if the expert is comfortable providing the needed information or if they know someone else who would be more qualified.

Next describe the problem situation and define the variable or event to be assessed. You must make sure the event being defined can pass the clarity test. If the expert is comfortable with the level of decomposition, you can begin the interview; if not, work with the expert to decompose the event until he or she can give a reliable assessment.

Figure 10.2   Assessment Process

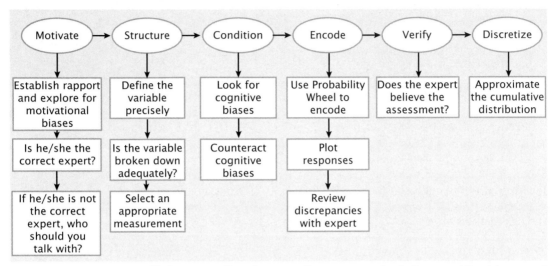

Before encoding the expert's responses, look for cognitive biases and counteract them so the assessment can be as reliable as possible. Look for statements like:

Cognitive bias:
example
statements

- We had the same thing happen last month.
- The data clearly indicates...
- I know this will definitely happen.
- I know the range is ± 10%.
- This information will not help make the decision.
- I know the answer to the problem.

These statements often indicate that a cognitive bias may be affecting the quality of the information being given.

Ways to encode
expert
judgment

There are several methods you can use to encode an expert's judgment. Some people use a probability wheel; others use a bag of balls. I have even seen a person use a stack of metal washers to encode a plant machinist's judgment. It should depend on what is most comfortable for the expert and the assessor. Whatever method is used, you should capture the expert's knowledge of the variable by plotting a cumulative probability distribution as in Figure 10.3.

Typically, several points on the distribution will be assessed by asking the expert questions which are not leading and are free from interpretation. Always begin with either the p10 or p90 value (never the p50 value), and ask questions in a manner that covers the entire curve but is not linear in thought, otherwise the expert could devise responses to some predetermined answer. When you are through with the interview, discuss discrepancies in the expert's responses and verify that the assessed distribution matches the expert's belief. If the responses plotted and the expert's belief do not match—reassess. Finally, discretize the curve into as few values as possible that will adequately describe the full distribution – usually three values often referred to as a 10–50–90 (or p10–p50–p90).

Figure 10.3   Encoding Form

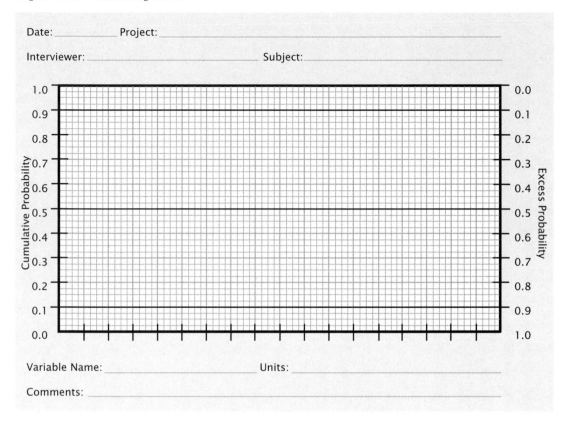

10.5 Using Probability as the Language of Uncertainty

In Chapter 8, we addressed the need for using probability to describe our belief in the likelihood of an event happening. When assessing an expert, you are obtaining information concerning both the value of the event and the probability of achieving that value. To quantify these values, we use a term called the 10-50-90.

The ***10-50-90 method*** uses three values to fully describe the entire range of possibilities or distribution (Figure 10.4 illustrates the idea of the 10-50-90). The ***10 value*** reflects a 1 in 10 chance the actual value could be that low or lower. The ***50 value*** is a value where the expert is indifferent between it being $1 higher or $1 lower – it is the expert's best estimate. The ***90 value*** is a 1 in 10 chance the actual value could be that high or higher. By using these three values, we can describe the entire probability distribution and simplify the calculations necessary for determining the best course of action.

You can obtain 10-50-90's indirectly from experts using tools such as a probability wheel or directly by simply stating the assumptions and assessing the values. Using the indirect method will require discretization so the three values can be incorporated into a decision tree or influence diagram calculation.

Figure 10.4
10-50-90
Distribution

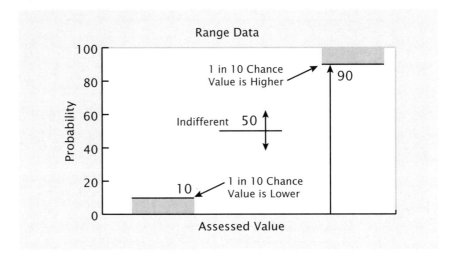

10.6 Discretizing the Information

The 10-50-90 values are not just points on a curve; they describe the areas above and below the curve. To discretize the assessed information, begin by fitting a curve to the assessed points on the graph, as in Figure 10.5. Then locate the 10-50-90 values. These values are assigned weights which describe the area of the curve. By applying weights to these three values, we can then easily solve for expected value.

Figure 10.5 shows the encoding form for the uncertainty "Royalties." Using this information, we can identify the 10-50-90 values and calculate the expected value of Royalties. From the graph we can see the 10-50-90's are $0.50, $1.00, and $1.50 respectively. By applying weights of 0.25, 0.50, and 0.25 to the values we can calculate an expected value of $1.00 as follows:

$$EV = (0.25)(0.50) + (0.50)(1.00) + (0.25)(1.50)$$
$$= \$0.125 + \$0.50 + \$0.375 = \$1.00.$$

The 10-50-90 weights of 0.25, 0.50, and 0.25 are based on the Gaussian quadrature method[1] and the McNamee-Celona[2] shortcut method. These weights work very well with Gaussian or normal distributions and are considered the standard weights for use with 10-50-90's. However, these weights can cause some problems with non-Gaussian distributions.

Figure 10.5 Swanson Case – Encoding Form for "Royalties" Uncertainty

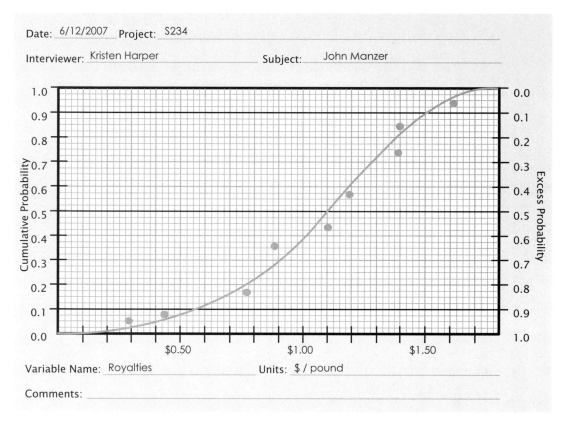

Another weighting method called the Extended Swanson-McGill[3] solves this problem by preserving the mean and variance and uses 0.30, 0.40, and 0.30 for the weights. The 30-40-30 weighting provides a more accurate mean for distributions with a lot of skewness than the 25-50-25 weighting.

We continue with the Swanson Case Study. The project team has just finished the assessments for the uncertainties identified in the influence diagrams for all three cases. Information was gathered from reliable company experts. The probability of a large price for selling S234 was assessed as a range because no one claimed to be an expert, and there was a large discrepancy from 0.6 to 0.25 in the assessments. Because of this, John Anderson wanted to

Swanson Case Study continues

[1] A. Miller and T. Rice, "Discrete Approximations of Probability Distributions," *Management Science* 29 (3 1983).

[2] P. McNamee and J. Celona, *Decision Analysis with Supertree, 2nd Edition*, The Scientific Press, 1990.

[3] D. Keefer, "Certainty Equivalents for Three-point Discrete Distribution Approximations," *Management Science* 40 (6 1994).

include both viewpoints in the initial evaluation to see if it would change the decision. While this is not a typical procedure, it does allow for sensitivity analysis of the uncertainty.

We can complete a decision tree by using the assessed values and applying the appropriate weights. Table 10.1 shows the assessed values for the Swanson Case Study.

Table 10.1 Assessed Values for S234 (License Case)

Variable	Units	10	50	90
Market Size	lbs	200,000	1,000,000	2,000,000
Market Share	%	0.15	0.20	0.25
Manufacturing Cost	$/lb	1.00	1.50	2.00
Marketing Cost	$/lb	0.50	0.75	1.00
License Market Size	lbs	500,000	1,000,000	2,000,000
License Market Share	%	0.25	0.30	0.35
Licensing Cost	$	200,000	250,000	300,000
Royalties	$/lb	0.50	1.00	1.50
Large Sales Price	$	6500,000	1,000,000	1,200,000
Small Sales Price	$	400,000	550,000	750,000
Probability of Large Price	%	0.25	0.45	0.60
Selling Cost	$	150,000	200,000	225,000

10.7 Summary and Interpretation

To choose the best course of action in difficult problems, you must be able to effectively deal with uncertainty. When using limited information, it is especially important to examine the variability and the reliability of the information. Because the future is uncertain, we need to use ranges and probabilities assessed from experts to gain insight into the appropriate decision. We can use the completed influence diagram as a road map for gathering the necessary information and to help clarify the situation when interviewing experts.

Finding the right expert is critical to gathering reliable information. Without reliable information, the analysis can become the "garbage-in, garbage-out" stereotype. Once the right expert is identified, you must search for biases and try to counteract these as much as possible.

10.8 Key Concepts

limited information	finding the right expert
gathering information	uncovering biases
anchoring	availability
coherence	overconfidence
representativeness	sampling
encoding judgement	10-50-90 method
discretizing a curve	

10.9 Study Questions

1. Why do we need to use limited information?

2. How do you determine what information is important or needed for the analysis?

3. What does uncertainty mean to you, and how do you typically deal with it?

4. Describe what is meant by the "right" expert.

5. What is a bias and how many kinds are there?

6. How do you counteract a motivational bias?

7. What are the six cognitive biases?

8. Why should you never begin an assessment with the expert's best guess?

9. In your own words, describe the overconfidence bias.

10. What are the six steps to assessing an expert?

11. Why is it important to understand the expert's assumptions?

12. What is a 10-50-90 distribution?

13. When discretizing a curve, how many points are needed to accurately describe it?

14. What do you consider yourself to be an expert at?

15. How do you know if you are an expert?

16. What area does the 10 value describe?

17. What weights should be applied to a 10-50-90 distribution and why?

18. What is the advantage of the Extended Swanson-McGill method over the McNamee-Celona method?

10.10 References and Further Reading

Keefer, D. "Certainty Equivalents for Three-Point Discrete Distribution Approximations." *Management Science* 40 (6 1994).

McNamee, P. and J. Celona. *Decision Analysis with Supertree.* 2nd ed., San Francisco, CA: The Scientific Press, 1990.

Miller, A. and T. Rice. "Discrete Approximations of Probability Distributions." *Management Science* 29 (3 1983): 352-362.

Reckhow, Kenneth H. "Importance of Scientific Uncertainty in Decision Making." *Environmental Management* 18 (2 1994): 161-166.

Tversky, Amos and Daniel Kahnemann, eds. *Judgement under Uncertainty: Heuristics and Biases.* Vol. 2. Readings on the Principles and Applications of Decision Analysis. Menlo Park, CA: Strategic Decisions Group, 1974.

10.11 Exercises

1. Assess a friend or family member using the probability encoding form in the Appendix.

2. Using the curve generated in Exercise 1, discretize the curve using the McNamee-Celona method.

3. Using the information in Exercise 2, calculate the expected value of the probability assessment. Does the expert feel comfortable with the assessment?

4. Give an example of a situation where you remember a cognitive bias affecting your ability to accurately describe the situation.

5. How many points should you assess when encoding a probability distribution? Give an example.

6. Describe how a 10-50-90 distribution captures the entire range of uncertainty and what probabilities should be attached to these values.

10.12 Guide to Action

Keep the following guidelines in mind when encoding expert judgment:

1. Understand the information needs before contacting and interviewing the subject matter experts.

2. Search for the best expert for the subject matter. Do not limit yourself to internal experts.

3. If an external expert will not be available in a timely manner or is too costly for the first pass evaluation, use an internal source and determine the significance of the information from the sensitivity analysis.

4. Use peer reviews as a means to audit internal and external information assessments.

5. Before encoding an expert's judgment, make sure that you have counteracted the expert's biases.

6. When plotting an expert's responses be sure to ask questions in a manner that does not allow the expert to anticipate the curve.

7. Always remember to tell the expert you are not trying to extract a promise but merely gather uncertain information.

10.13   Case for Analysis
"Cancer Treatment, Part 2"

Recall Norman's case from Chapter 2: Norman is a 42 year old businessman. He and his wife have two teenage children and live in the Midwest. He has recently been diagnosed with cancer. His cancer is a Ewing's type tumor that is difficult to treat. Without treatment, the doctors estimate that Norman will only have about six to twelve months to live.

Norman is concerned about both fighting the disease and his quality of life. Because of the location of the tumor in his right thigh he has several treatment options. He could have surgery, chemotherapy, radiation, or some combination of the three.

- What information does Norman need?

- How will he know if he has found the right expert?

- What kinds of biases could he encounter with his expert(s) and why?

- What can Norman do to counteract the potential biases?

11

Gaining Insight
Through Evaluation

The willingness to take risks is our grasp of faith.
— George E. Woodberry

In the first six chapters, we learned about processes and techniques which develop an appropriate problem frame and build the foundation for gaining insight into the problem. The following chapters formed the basis for understanding and developing good evaluations:

- Chapter 7 explained how to build decision models using influence diagrams and decision trees.
- Chapter 8 taught the basics of probability.
- Chapter 9 introduced the concept of Monte Carlo simulation as a means of evaluating highly uncertain events.
- Chapter 10 discussed assessing and encoding expert opinions.

In this chapter, we will focus on using techniques such as sensitivity analysis and value of information to illuminate insights that will provide the decision maker with a clear and compelling course of action.

In the traditional business decision process, a team would return a single number to the decision maker. The team might also provide some what-if analyses to convey other possible scenarios and outcomes. However, the focus of these analyses is on generating a number to prove or justify a course of action. Decision analysis, in contrast, is focused on generating insights and learning where and why value is created in each alternative. These insights are developed using a structured process that begins with a deterministic analysis and then incorporates probability to account for uncertainty and risk to finally reveal the most appropriate course of action.

Decision analysis should provide insights and understanding

Figure 11.1 Example of a Deterministic Model

	A	B	C	D	E	F	G	H	I	J	K
1	S234 Project Sheet - Launch										
2											
3	Variables		10	50	90						
4	Market Size	lbs	200,000	1,000,000	2,000,000						
5	Market Share	%	15%	20%	25%						
6	Mfg Costs	$/lb	$1.00	$1.50	$1.00						
7	Mkt Costs	$/lb	$0.50	$0.75	$1.00						
8	Survey										
9	Fixed										
10	Discount Rate	%	10%								
11	Setup Costs	$	1,500,000								
12	Tax Rate	%	40%								
13	S234 Price	$	$5.00								
14											
15	Year	1	2	3	4	5	6	7	8	9	10
16	Revenue	1,000,000	1,000,000	1,000,000	1,000,000	1,000,000	1,000,000	1,000,000	1,000,000	1,000,000	1,000,000
17	Setup Costs	(1,500,000)									
18	Variable Costs	(450,000)	(450,000)	(450,000)	(450,000)	(450,000)	(450,000)	(450,000)	(450,000)	(450,000)	(450,000)
19	Gross Profit	(950,000)	550,000	550,000	550,000	550,000	550,000	550,000	550,000	550,000	550,000
20											
21	Taxes	(380,000)	220,000	220,000	220,000	220,000	220,000	220,000	220,000	220,000	220,000
22											
23	Net Profit	(570,000)	330,000	330,000	330,000	330,000	330,000	330,000	330,000	330,000	330,000
24											
25	NPV	1,209,525									

11.1   Deterministic Sensitivity Analysis

In Chapter 7, we discussed how to build a spreadsheet deterministic model from an influence diagram. Spreadsheets are a powerful tool in the decision analyst's tool kit because they provide tremendous modeling flexibility and do not have the "black box" stigma of some specialized computer programs. Using the deterministic model, we can perform deterministic sensitivity analysis. Sensitivity analysis is focused on answering the question, "What is important in this decision?" This is probably the most important question to ask when making a decision. We can answer this question because decision analysis uses ranges of values and probability distributions assessed from experts.

These ranges describe the full range of uncertainty rather than hiding the uncertainty with a single point estimate. Sensitivity analysis provides the insight to focus on the key variables that could change the decision and that have the greatest impact on value. Variables which have little or no effect on the value measure can be set to their base or 50 value in the probabilistic phase of evaluation. This will allow the decision model to be simplified from an evaluation perspective. However, variables which do materially affect the value measure will be formally assessed and incorporated into the probabilistic phase of the analysis.

Use the following four steps to perform a deterministic sensitivity analysis:

Steps used to develop a deterministic sensitivity analysis

Step 1   Build a deterministic value model (like the one shown in Figure 11.1) which uses the variables identified in the influence diagram and calculates according to the decision criteria.

Step 2   Choose a low (10), base (50), and high (90) value for each variable.

Step 3   Setting all variables to their base value, calculate a nominal value for each alternative. This value is now the base value for the alternative and each swing value will be a delta from this value.

Step 4   Calculate the swing of each variable by changing the value each variable one at a time – using its high (90) and its low (10) while holding all other variables at their base (50) value. Record the changes in value. We will use these values when we build the tornado graph.

In the deterministic analysis, the alternative with the highest base value is considered the preferred alternative. Sensitivity analysis can provide more insight than the single base case number and can also reveal the dominance of one alternative over another.

Dominance

A dominated alternative is one that, regardless of the variable value, is always an inferior choice. For example, if at any variable setting, alternative A is always better than alternative B, then A dominates B. This is an important concept, as inferior courses of action can be dropped from further evaluation. Dominance can be detected using the output from the sensitivity analysis. However, a better method is to use a tornado diagram to graphically display the information.

Tornado Diagrams

A tornado diagram is a graphical tool designed to show the change in value created by swinging each variable from its low (10) to high (90) value. This diagram can show which variables are most important to the value of the project and the strategic decision(s). Tornado diagrams are created from the calculations performed in the sensitivity analysis and are plotted by following these four steps:

Step 1   Rank order the variables by their swing in project value, from largest to smallest.

Steps used to develop a tornado diagram

Step 2   Draw a horizontal line with a scale that is appropriate for the size of the swings in value.

Step 3   Draw a vertical line down from the horizontal line at the intersection of the nominal value.

Step 4   Draw horizontal bars for each uncertainty relative to their swings in value.

Figure 11.2 is the tornado diagram for the Swanson Company Case Study "launch" decision. From this tornado, we can see that Marketing Costs do not greatly affect the value of the decision. Using this information, we could then simplify the decision model by setting the Marketing Costs to the base value. We could also remove the Marketing Cost node from the influence diagram and show the costs as the base value.

Figure 11.2
Tornado
Diagram for
"Launch"
Decision

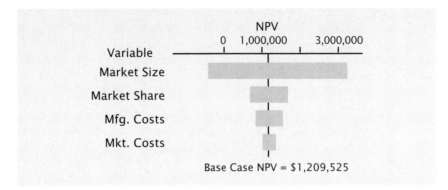

11.2 Probabilistic Evaluation

The next step in the evaluation phase of the process is to model and analyze the uncertainty surrounding the critical variables. These variables were identified using the deterministic sensitivity analysis in the previous step. The incorporation of probabilities provides the additional information necessary to determine the likelihood of ascertaining the outcomes we desire. By incorporating the full probability distributions of each critical variable into the analysis, we can appropriately deal with the risk of the project and the risk attitude of the decision maker.

Using Decision Trees

We used decision trees in Chapter 7 to model the decision problem and to determine the sequence of decisions and uncertainties. Decision trees are also a very useful evaluation tool, as they allow us to calculate the value and associated probability of every possible path through the tree. The tree at this point in the process will be "pruned" to only include the variables or uncertainties which impact the problem the most.

Figure 11.3 is the decision tree for the Swanson Company Case Study. By using decision trees, we can show the relationships between decisions, uncertainties, and values. As you can see in Figure 11.3, the first node is the decision node which has the three alternatives of *Launch*, *License*, or *Sell*. All of the other nodes are uncertain or chance nodes which have the discretized 10-50-90 distributions as inputs and the McNamee-Celona shortcut weights. For example, Market Size has inputs of 200,000 – 1,000,000 – 2,000,000, and weights of 0.25 – 0.50 – 0.25.

This allows us to **rollback** the tree and to calculate an expected monetary value for each of the alternatives. We use the term *rollback* because that is what you are doing when you calculate the values in the tree. You are rolling the numbers back to the decision to choose the best course of action. As you can see from Figure 11.3:

- *Launch* decision has the highest expected value at $1,310,910, followed by
- *License* at $1,135,180, and finally
- *Sell* at $320,450.

Swanson case expected values

While expected monetary value is a good measure for many decisions, it is usually beneficial to understand the risk profile or cumulative probability distribution of each alternative.

Creating Risk Profiles

Risk profiles (or cumulative probability distributions) show the entire range of values and their associated probabilities. This allows the decision maker to quickly view the upside and downside potential of each alternative and decide whether the risk is appropriate given the reward. Figure 11.4 shows the risk profiles for the *Launch, License,* and *Sell* alternatives. You can pick any point on the curve, and that point will represent the probability that the value you will receive will be equal to or less than the value at that point on the curve.

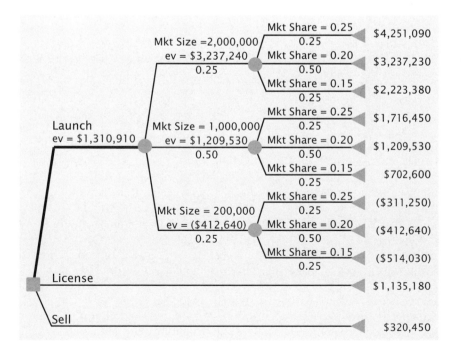

*Figure 11.3
Decision Tree
for S234*

For example, in Figure 11.4 there is a 30% chance of making an NPV of less than or equal to $649,140 in the launch strategy. The key to understanding and communicating the information provided by the risk profile is to emphasize the **less than** part of the statement. Decision makers often focus on a specific probability and a specific value – remember that the future is uncertain and so are project returns.

Figure 11.4
Cumulative
Probability
Distribution
for S234

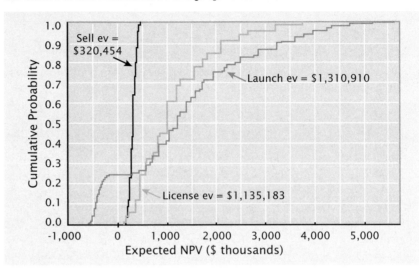

By placing several risk profiles together, as in Figure 11.4, it is easy to compare the different alternatives from both risk and reward standpoints. If the risk of loss, or downside potential, is not of concern, pick the alternative which is farthest to the right or has the highest expected monetary value. If risk of loss is a concern, a utility function may provide the additional insight necessary to make the decision. I will discuss utility functions later in this chapter.

Sensitivity to Probability

Since the risk profiles are created by using expert assessments of uncertainty, a question often asked by the decision maker is, "What if the subjective assessments and probabilities are not reliable?" This is a valid question, since we are basing the decision on the beliefs of an expert and not what many would consider hard data. To answer that question, we can perform a sensitivity analysis on the probabilities rather than the values. This analysis can help to identify issues to be refined and to understand the significance of conflicting expert opinions.

Sensitivity to probability is different than deterministic sensitivity. All of the variables are allowed to vary probabilistically rather than holding them constant at the 50 value. Each variable is then adjusted from an extremely low value to an extremely high value, and the changes in **optimal policy** are recorded. Figure 11.5 shows the sensitivity to probability for Market Size. Notice that unless the probability drops below 48%, the Launch alternative is always preferred.

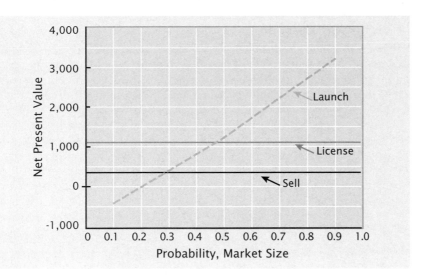

*Figure 11.5
Swanson Case:
Sensitivity to
Probability*

Finding the Optimal Decision

The optimal policy for a decision is the preferred course of action if the decision has to be made immediately. The key word here is immediate – if the decision can be postponed or additional analysis or information gathered, the optimal policy decision may be different. Using sensitivity to probability and sensitivity to risk tolerance can help identify the optimal policy, given the decision maker's preferences.

11.3 Value of Information

The uncertainty associated with a decision is usually the result of having to use limited information. Because gathering more information is typically an alternative to making an immediate decision, we often spend lots of time and money hiring consultants or others to gather and develop more information. What is it worth to gather this information? Will more information actually help you to make the decision, or will it only cloud the real issues? Decision analysis provides a means to calculate the value of gathering more information. This allows us to determine the benefits of the new information before spending the money and time to gather it.

Perfect Information

The value of perfect information provides a maximum amount you would pay to receive perfect information about the true outcome of some uncertain quantity or future event. While perfect information is rarely available, quantifying the value of this information provides the maximum value you would pay to know the information for certain.

"Clairvoyant"
(value of
information)

We often use the concept of a Clairvoyant as a means to think about perfect information. We use the premise of an all knowing and truthful being who we could ask any question and receive perfect information about any event to illustrate this concept. The key is, how much would we be willing to pay for this information and what would the Clairvoyant want for it?

Swanson case:
value of perfect
information
(VOPI)

John Anderson has been pleased with the progress of the team and the insights the analysis has produced so far. However, John is concerned about the uncertainty of the market size and is considering a proposal by Kristen Harper to do a market survey. Kristen is working to determine the size and cost of the survey, but the report will not be ready for another week. The decision analysis consultant has suggested calculating the value of information to determine if the market survey will provide the needed insight for a clear and compelling course of action.

The value of perfect information is calculated by taking the value of the project *with* perfect information and subtracting the value of the project *without* perfect information. The expected monetary value of project S234 with and without perfect information is shown in Figures 11.6 and 11.7, respectively. The expected monetary value with perfect information is $1,697,868 (multiply the probabilities of each branch of Figure 11.6 by their corresponding expected values and then add together). The expected monetary value without perfect information is $1,310,910. Therefore the value of perfect information is:

$$VOPI = \$1,697,868 - \$1,310,910$$
$$= \$386,958.$$

The simple way of calculating the value with perfect information is to put the uncertainty in question before the decision to be made. Since you will have perfect knowledge of this uncertainty before making the deci-

Figure 11.6
S234 Tree with
Perfect
Information

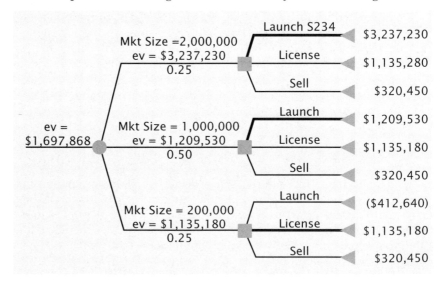

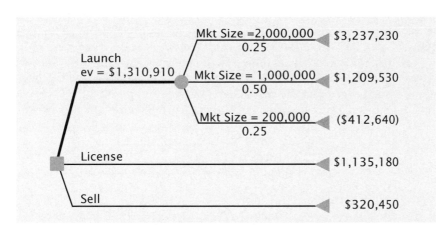

*Figure 11.7
S234 Tree
without Perfect
Information*

sion, this is an intuitive way to reassemble the decision tree. If a market survey with 100% accuracy could be devised, it would be worth $386,956. However, since perfect information is nearly impossible to find, we need to determine the value of imperfect information.

Imperfect Information

The value of imperfect information is much more useful than the value of perfect information since imperfect sources are often available. This value can be calculated by adding an uncertainty to the decision tree or influence diagram that represents the uncertainty in the accuracy of the information.

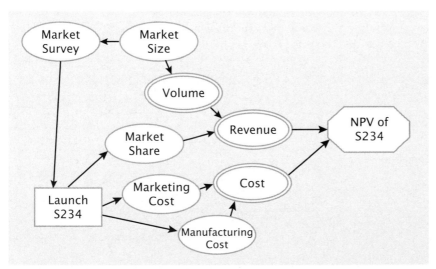

*Figure 11.8
Swanson Case
Influence
Diagram with
Market Survey*

Using the Swanson Case Study as an example, we could add a new node to the influence diagram called *Market Survey*. Figure 11.8 shows the new influence diagram. Notice that Market Size now influences Market Survey. This is to preserve the state of nature. If we had put Market Survey influencing Market Size, that would be like saying if you carry an umbrella it will cause it to rain, rather than you carry an umbrella because it might rain.

By placing the Market Survey node into the diagram, we can now assess the reliability of our estimate of Market Size, given that we have some assumption about the reliability of the survey. Figure 11.9 is a simplified decision tree showing only the Market Size and Market Survey nodes.

Figure 11.9
Nature's
Decision Tree

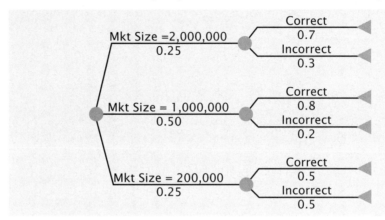

In order to calculate the value of imperfect information, we need to use Bayes' Rule to reverse the tree. Bayes' Rule simply states that we can place the indicator node (Market Survey) before the state of nature node (Market Size) and calculate the probability of the true state of nature given the indicator's result (See Chapter 8 for a discussion on Bayes' Rule). The procedure for applying Bayes' Rule is quite simple.

Begin by calculating the joint or elemental probabilities from nature's tree, also called the prior tree.

Figure 11.10
Reversed
Decision Tree

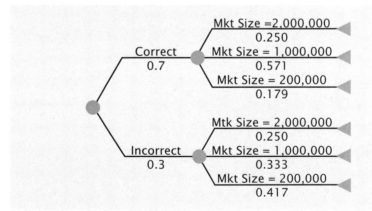

Then, reverse the order of the nodes (Figure 11.10) and transcribe the probabilities to their appropriate paths in the reversed tree (also known as the posterior tree).

Next, calculate the probabilities for the first node by adding the probabilities of all paths that pass through a specific branch. Then calculate the probabilities of the second node by dividing the joint probabilities at the end of the branch by the probability for the branch of the first node.

The team believed the Market Survey would be 70% accurate in detecting a 2 million pound market, 80% accurate with a 1 million pound market, and only 50% accurate with a 200 thousand pound market.

The new tree (Figure 11.11) reveals the value with imperfect information is worth $1,339,300. By subtracting the original EMV of $1,310,910 from this value, we get $28,390 for the value of imperfect information.

This indicates that *we should only invest in a market survey if we can get it for $28,390 or less*. Otherwise we should use the information we have and make the decision now.

11.4 Applying an Appropriate Risk Attitude

Risk means different things to different people. Some people think risk is the possibility of a big loss; others think it is just the unknown. In decision analysis, we use the term to mean uncertainty in future (generally financial) outcomes. Risk is a common factor when dealing with the future outcomes from a course of action.

How we choose to deal with risk can be very different depending on our personal or corporate risk tolerance. We can incorporate the decision maker's attitude towards risk into the decision analysis model by creating

Figure 11.11 Complete Reversed Decision Tree

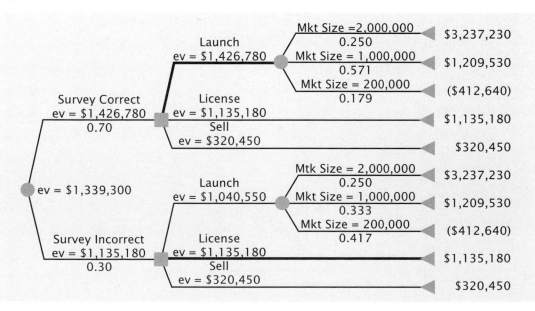

a utility function. By incorporating the risk tolerance into the model, we can develop a course of action that will be more compelling than a purely financial measure would be to the decision maker.

Assessing Risk Attitude

Risk averse, risk neutral, and risk seeking

Everyone has an attitude towards risk taking, and depending upon the situation, that attitude can change dramatically. There are three attitudes toward risk – *neutral, averse,* and *seeking.* In situations where the risk is below or meets your risk tolerance, you will be risk neutral. This means that you should make your decision based on the expected value of the decision. Usually we are expected value decision makers for decisions involving small amounts of money.

For example, if you were offered a 50-50 deal to win $10 or lose $5, you would probably take it based on an expected value of $2.50. However, as the stakes and risk increase, most individuals and companies become risk averse (See Figure 11.12). If the same 50-50 deal had outcomes of win $1,000,000 and lose $500,000, you would probably not be as quick to accept expected value as the decision criteria!

Risk aversion causes many companies to seek out partnerships and joint ventures for major investments. In the oil and gas business, it is common for several companies to own interests in an offshore field development. Any given company could probably afford the development, but they prefer to share the risk of the development with others.

Our personal decisions are also affected by risk. When you open a new brokerage account, you will be asked to fill out an account application. On that application, you will be given four investment preferences (Speculative, Growth, Income, and Conservative) and asked to list them in order of importance. While this is not as useful as a utility function, the brokerage is trying to understand your risk tolerance so that it can recommend suitable securities.

Figure 11.12
Risk Preference

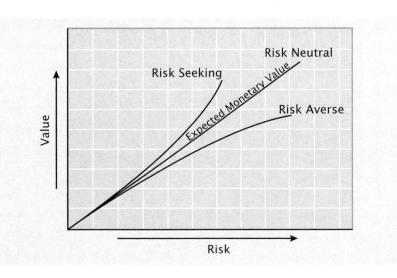

There are some people that actually find risk preferable and can be considered risk seeking. Often we characterize these people as gamblers because the risk of a venture is actually an added value to them. Either through enjoyment of the game or some other means, they view an opportunity with high risk as more valuable than the same opportunity with lower risk. I have not yet experienced a company with this attitude, but I have come across a few individuals in companies that have this attitude when dealing with the company's money. These are usually people in business development functions whose sole job is to develop opportunities. The problem is that often their performance metrics are based on activity and not value.

Risk seeking behavior

As an individual, your personal risk preference can be whatever you choose. However, for most corporate decisions, you should be risk neutral (expected value), unless the decision involves a large portion of the company's assets (rule of thumb is about 1/6th of net assets). Often individuals place their own personal risk attitude on corporate decisions. When this happens, the corporation may pass on opportunities that it should have taken. Consider the following example (Figure 11.13) of deciding whether to enter a market or license a product.

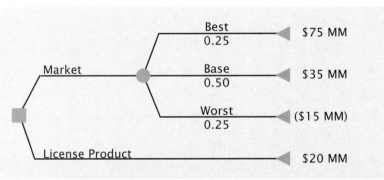

Figure 11.13 Market versus License Decision

You have just been promoted to product manager for a new corporate textiles division. You know that you will be judged by the outcomes of your decisions, not on the quality of the decisions. You must show positive cash flow from operations to keep this promotion. Your first day on the job, you are presented with a decision to either market a new fabric or license the weaving technology to another company. The associated values and probabilities of each alternative are shown in the decision tree (Figure 11.13).

Risk preference example

What should you do?

Based on an expected value of $32.5 million, the decision maker should choose to market the product (as this maximizes potential future value). However, since EMV is not always the most compelling criteria, the evaluation should include the decision maker's risk preference. If the decision maker is risk averse, a utility function could be constructed to account for the degree of risk aversion.

The decision is between commercializing the product for an uncertain amount or licensing the process for a guaranteed amount to another company. If the risk of commercializing the product is not significant to the company, you should commercialize it. This is because the expected monetary value of the Market alternative is $32.5 million. However, if the risk warrants taking the guaranteed amount for Licensing the product, make sure that you are using the company's risk attitude and not your own.

What is a Utility Function?

Utility functions are a means of describing how much a particular outcome is worth to you, given your particular financial status. The **utility function** measures worth by translating values into utiles or utility values. Utility values are determined by arbitrarily setting any two values based on outcomes and then determining the scale between them. Generally the scale is from zero to one, with zero being the least preferred and one being the most preferred value. Utility functions allow you to measure the decision maker's preference for any given quantity or value. The higher the preference for a value, the higher the utility of that value. The Consolidated Foods case illustrates how utility may provide a better measure of value and preference than expected value:

Utility function example: Consolidated Foods Case Study

Consolidated Foods is a national food distribution company. The company operates distribution warehouses in twelve states along the East Coast and throughout the Southwest. The company has been in business for over fifty years and has grown mainly through limited expansion. The company is family owned and recently the founder's son, Ben Stein, has become the CEO. Ben believes that the company must expand further and faster if it is going to be able to compete in the future.

Ben has hired an outside consulting firm to develop several strategies for him and the Board of Directors to consider. While Ben is aggressive and wants to expand the company's markets, the Board is more conservative and will not authorize faster expansion without a sound business case. The consulting firm, after careful evaluation, has returned to Ben and the Board with three possible strategies.

The first strategy is to "Maintain" the company's current position and focus. This strategy would not involve any new acquisitions or expansion of markets and has an expected value of $17 million over ten years. Ben characterized this strategy as the "die on the vine" strategy. However, the Board views this strategy as "prudent" and is inclined to keep things the same.

The next strategy presented is "Steady Growth," which is dependent upon the company making opportunistic acquisitions of competitors and continued expansion into new markets. This strategy has an expected value of $28 million over the same time period. Ben is interested in this strategy but believes there is more value to faster expansion.

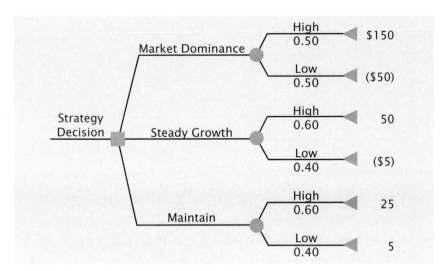

*Figure 11.14
Consolidated
Foods Case:
Strategy
Decision Tree*

The final strategy presented is the "Market Dominance" strategy, which as the name implies, is a strategy to control certain geographic regions in the United States. This strategy has an expected value of $50 million, but it also has a significant downside if it is not successful. Ben loves this strategy, but as you can expect, the Board hates it. In this situation, applying an appropriate risk profile or tolerance is very appropriate. Figure 11.14 is the decision tree for the three strategies (the outcomes have been simplified for illustrative purposes).

By multiplying each outcome by its associated probability, we can calculate the *expected monetary value* (EMV) of each alternative. As you can see, the highest outcome value is the high branch of the Market Dominance strategy. This outcome, if it happened, would be $150 million. However, there is only a 50% probability of this outcome occurring. Using this outcome and its associated probabilities, we can calculate an expected value of $75 million for this branch: $150 million X 50% = $75 Million.

After calculating the expected values for each branch, we can calculate the expected value of each alternative. Figure 11.15 shows the strategy tree "rolled back," and the preferred alternative is Market Dominance based on expected value.

However, given the Board's risk aversion, we need to apply an appropriate risk attitude to the valuation. We will do this by developing a utility function which describes the Board's preferences for value. In this case, we are going to directly assess the utility function (in Chapter 3, we discussed an exponential utility function; this function is easier to calculate).

*Figure 11.15
Strategy Tree
"Rolled Back"*

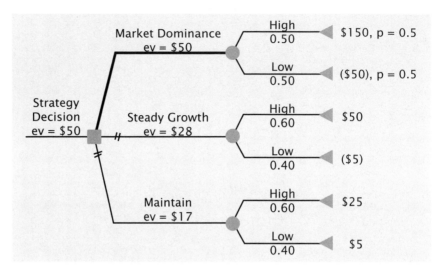

We write the utility of an outcome, x, as $u(x)$. Begin by setting the worst outcome of $u(-\$50\text{MM})$ to 0 and the best outcome of $u(\$150\text{MM})$ to 1. Next we need to gather at least one additional point to plot the curve.

*Figure 11.16
Market
versus
License
Decision*

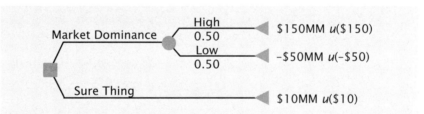

In this case, the consultants assessed the Board's indifference point. They found that the Board would be indifferent between receiving a guaranteed return of $10MM and the Market Dominance strategy (see Figure 11.16).

Using this information, we can now establish a utility function for the strategy decision maker's preference:

$$u(\$10\text{MM}) = (0.50 \text{ X } u(\$150\text{MM})) + (0.50 \text{ X } u(-\$50\text{MM}))$$
$$u(\$10\text{MM}) = (0.50 \text{ X } 1) + (0.50 \text{ X } 0)$$
$$u(\$10\text{MM}) = 0.50$$

Using this point, we can draw a curve which represents the entire function (Figure 11.17). By extracting utilities from the curve, we can then calculate the expected utility for each strategy (see below). This will allow us to evaluate each strategy consistently by accounting for the decision makers' preferences.

*Calculating
expected
utilities for
each strategy*

The expected utility for each outcome is calculated by multiplying each utility by its associated probability. The expected utility for the Steady Growth strategy with a High outcome is shown below:

Expected utility = $(0.69)(0.60) = 0.414$

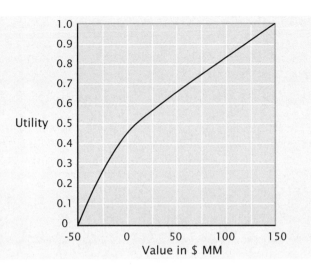

Figure 11.17 Consolidated Foods Case: Utility Function

The expected utility for each alternative is calculated by adding the High and Low expected utilities of each opportunity. Using this expected utility provides a valuable insight into the relative worth of each alternative. Table 11.1 shows a comparison of the alternatives with their respective EMV's and expected utilities.

Expected utility of Steady Growth = 0.414 + 0.192 = 0.606

Table 11.1 shows the Market Dominance is the best alternative using EMV as the criteria, but the Steady Growth alternative is a better alternative when accounting for the Board's aversion to risk.

Strategy	EMV	Utility
Market Dominance	$50	0.500
Steady Growth	$28	0.606
Maintain	$17	0.574

Table 11.1 Comparison of EMV to Expected Utility

As you can see from the comparison Table 11.1, while the Market Dominance strategy is the best EMV choice, it is the worse expected utility choice. The risk preference of the Board is so strong that, based on utility, the Maintain strategy is better than Dominance. This comparison also points out that there is a good choice for both the Board and Ben Stein in the Steady Growth strategy. By incorporating the risk attitude into the evaluation, the consultants were able to develop an alternative that would be supported by all parties.

We can develop utility functions by asking the decision maker a series of questions that elicit risk taking preferences for different gambles using certain equivalents or by using an exponential utility function.

If more is always better than less, why should I worry about utility?

In general, more of something we like is always better than less, but as we get more units, the value we place on each additional unit is usually less than the previous.

As additional utiles are received, there is often less satisfaction with each new utile. Think about having dinner at a nice restaurant. At first there is a lot of value for each dish served, but after five or six courses, each additional course brings less satisfaction. At some point, you cannot eat anymore and have reached maximum value (and you don't want to risk getting sick to your stomach).

Using the Exponential Utility Function

An alternative approach to assessing a utility function from the decision maker is to apply the exponential utility function. The exponential utility function uses the constant e (2.71828) to create a concave curve, which represents the decision maker's risk attitude. We will discuss more about the utility function after considering axioms of rational thought.

Axioms of Rational Thought

Decision analysis does not attempt to describe how decisions are actually made (descriptive) but rather expresses what is necessary for making a rational decision (normative). While this may be different from what is observed in real life, making decisions based on the axioms of rational thought is the only way to quantitatively and effectively evaluate decisions involving uncertainty. These axioms (self-evident truths) provide the basis for rational thought and have been accepted as being logically sound and well established. By using these axioms, we can describe a utility function which:

- has a higher utility for the outcomes you prefer,
- describes the weight of your preference for each possible outcome,
- can be described by one parameter – risk tolerance, and
- describes your attitude towards risk.

There are five axioms or rules, which if followed, allow the creation of a utility function describing your preference for taking risk. These axioms are logically sound and provide consistency for rational thinking. Without following these axioms, it is easy to become confused, or much worse, to be taken advantage of by unscrupulous people.

When writing the axioms in mathematical form we use the > to indicate a preference to, as in A > B, which states that A *is preferred to* B.

The probability axiom is fundamental to the application of probabilities in a consistent and logical manner. Simply stated:

Any sequence and number of opportunities can be reduced to a single opportunity.

This implies that the opportunities hold no value other than the outcomes for the decision maker. Figure 11.18 shows that the decision maker would be indifferent between either alternative, as the outcomes and their associated probabilities are the same for either alternative (the arrows from the decision node indicate the preferred course of action, which in this case shows both to be equivalent, causing the decision maker to be indifferent).

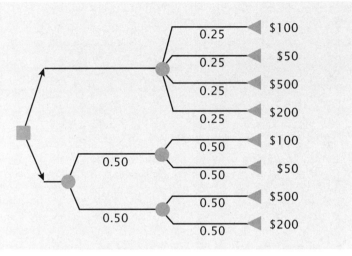

Figure 11.18 Probability Axiom

The order axiom is the most basic to understand and states that:

You can rank outcomes from best to worst and that this ordering is transitive.

Axiom 2. Order

This means that if you prefer $100 to $50, and $50 to $10, then you prefer $100 to $10 ($100 > $50 and $50 > $10, so $100 > $10).

The equivalence axiom states that:

If you are faced with two opportunities, of which one has a guaranteed outcome and the other has at least two possible outcomes, then there is some probability p at which the uncertain opportunity and the guaranteed opportunity are equivalent.

Axiom 3. Equivalence

In Figure 11.19 for example, you would be indifferent between the guaranteed sum of $50 and the uncertain opportunity to receive either $100 or $10, given some probability p.

Axiom four is sort of the "put your money where your mouth is" rule. Based on the equivalence axiom above:

You are willing to give up a guaranteed outcome of $50 for an uncertain outcome of either $100 or $10.

Axiom 4. Substitution

Figure 11.19
Equivalence
Axiom

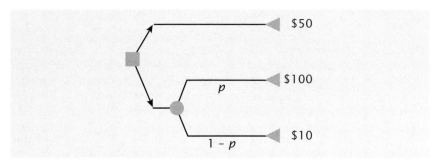

If you are unwilling to give up the guaranteed outcome for an uncertain outcome, then the probability of p you have given is not correct and should be changed.

The choice axiom simply states that:

If there are two or more opportunities with the same sets of outcomes, then you should choose the opportunity with the highest probability of the best outcome.

In Figure 11.20, you would choose the bottom path with a 60% probability of receiving the $100 over the top path with a 40% probability of $100.

Figure 11.20
Choice Axiom

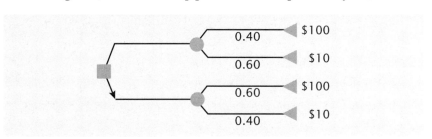

The ability to encode the decision maker's preferences into the decision problem and quantify the state of risk-taking preferred by the decision maker is a unique quality of decision analysis. Without the help of utility, we have to assume a risk neutral or expected value decision maker for all problems. While most people are expected value decision makers for some level of risk and financial gain, as the stakes increase, both people and organizations quickly become risk averse.

Exponential Utility Function

In the exponential utility function, as x increases, $u(x)$ approaches 1. The parameter R determines the degree of risk aversion and is commonly known as **risk tolerance**. As R increases, the curve flattens or approaches the expected value. This reflects the ability or willingness to accept a bad outcome. R can be assessed very easily by using a simple gamble. Using the decision tree in Figure 11.21, what is the largest value of R for which you would accept this gamble? This is your risk tolerance.

Figure 11.21
Risk Tolerance

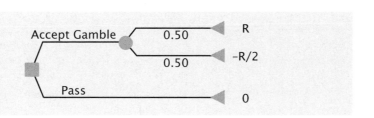

For example, if the most you would ever gamble given these probabilities is $1,000, then your risk tolerance or R is $1,000. This would then provide a utility function of:

$$u(x) = 1 - e^{-x/1000}$$

Using this function, you can then find the certain equivalents for any opportunity. However, there is an approximation method put forth by McNamee and Celona[1] which simplifies the process. If you can determine the expected value and the variance of the outcomes, then the certain equivalent can be approximated by:

$$CE \approx \mu - \frac{0.5\sigma^2}{R}$$

$$\mu = EMV$$

$$\sigma^2 = variance$$

or the certain equivalent is approximately

EMV – 0.5 [Variance/Risk Tolerance].

Risk Premium and the Certain Equivalent

Using the certain equivalent instead of EMV allows for a more complete appraisal of the alternatives. The certain equivalent adjusts the value of an opportunity by your degree of risk aversion, thereby creating a **risk premium** to equal expected value. Figure 11.22 shows the change in expected value versus the certain equivalent as risk increases.

Swanson case
continued

John Anderson is very impressed with the results of the analysis and is prepared to hear your final presentation to the decision board on the recommended course of action. You have conducted a sensitivity to risk attitude assessment using John's initial R value of $1,500,000. This analysis is shown in Figure 11.23. However, you have recently learned that the company's financial condition has deteriorated and John is now considerably more risk averse than previously, and his new R value is $100,000.

How does this change the decision? Figure 11.23 shows the change in project value when R is decreased to $100,000.

---

[1] McNamee and Celona, *Decision Analysis with Supertree, 2nd Edition*, The Scientific Press, 1990.

*Figure 11.22
Risk Premium*

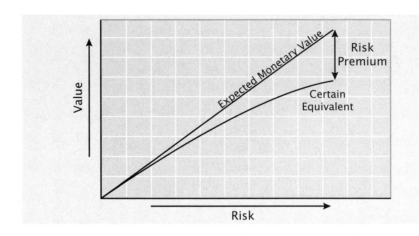

Using Risk Attitude to Make Better Decisions

We all want to make better decisions. Decision analysis provides the methodology and tools to help us improve our decision making abilities. It should be apparent by now that expected monetary value is not a satisfac-

Figure 11.23 Sensitivity to Risk Graph Showing $1,500,000 and $100,000 Risk Tolerance

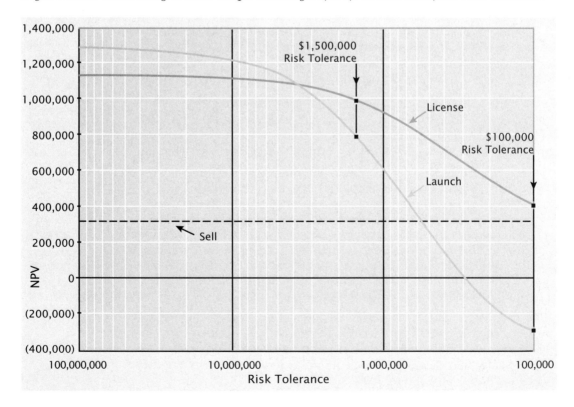

tory decision criteria for many decisions. We must be able to incorporate our risk tolerance or willingness to accept bad outcomes into the decision criteria to choose the appropriate course of action.

Swanson Case Study: conclusion

The decision board met with the project team on a Thursday morning for the final presentation. The consultant who was leading the project reviewed with the decision board the highlights of past meetings to ensure continuity of thought on the problem. He then began discussing the three alternatives in depth, including the rationale behind each and the method of evaluation.

He explained that the Sell alternative was the least valuable alternative to the company based on deterministic and probabilistic evaluations. He then explained that, based on expected value, the Launch alternative was the best decision. The consultant put the combined risk profiles of the three alternatives on the screen (Figure 11.4). The Launch and License decisions were close in value but the Launch alternative was slightly better. However, because of the company's deteriorating financial condition and the investment required to launch the new product, the board should carefully examine the License alternative. Using John's risk preference, the best course of action is to License the product.

The board asked several questions about the quality of the inputs and the methods of gathering and analyzing the information, but agreed the analysis was valid and reliable. John asked each board member if they would stand behind this analysis, and they all agreed. John then appointed Kristen Harper to be the project

Ford Mustang – Beating the Competition

In the mid to early 1960's, the first wave of post-war baby-boomers was set to enter the car buying market. Lee Iacocca, Ford Product Manager, reasoned that the market needed a youthful, affordable automobile that appealed to this growing market. Iacocca championed a new automobile that was introduced at the 1964 New York World's Fair – the Mustang. This began what has been heralded as the most successful product launch in automotive history. In the first two years of production, Ford sold over 1.5 million Mustangs.

Mustang's print ads declared: "Mustang has the look, the fire, the flavor of the great European road cars." Ford combined style with affordability into a car that was fun to drive and looked great parked in your driveway.

Chrysler and General Motors were caught off guard and rushed to compete. Chrysler considered its recently launched Plymouth Barracuda to be a competitor to the Mustang, but the sales figures never came close. GM installed bucket seats and a stick shift in the Corvair and re-dubbed it a Monza. While the Monza did fairly well, its sales were no where near the Mustang either. Ford and the Mustang "owned" this market. The Mustang customer wanted something new and unique. Chrysler and GM both presented re-tooled existing vehicles.

1. How else could Chrysler and General Motors have reacted to the competitive pressure of the Mustang?

2. In an industry with long product development time lines, what measures should a company take to prevent being caught off guard?

implementation leader and chartered the team to implement this decision as soon as possible. The meeting adjourned with all the participants feeling they had done a good job and had made a decision which was clear, compelling, and defensible.

11.5 Summary and Interpretation

To choose the best course of action, you must fully understand and appraise the problem. It is easy to quickly get an initial answer and rush to implementation. In the case of the Swanson Company, they could have decided to implement the Launch alternative after the determination of expected value. While we do not know what the outcome would have been if that course of action had been pursued, we do know that after completely understanding the situation and the risk tolerance of the Company, that would not have been the best course of action.

11.6 Key Concepts

deterministic model
probabilistic model
sensitivity to probability
Clairvoyant
risk premium
risk attitude - Seeking - Neutral - Averse
risk profiles - cumulative probability distributions
value of information (perfect or imperfect)

optimal decision
tornado diagram
utility function
certain equivalent

11.7 Study Questions

1. Explain how influence diagrams help to model the decision and provide insight not available from decision trees.

2. Why do we use deterministic sensitivity analysis?

3. What are the steps in performing deterministic sensitivity analysis?

4. Explain the concept of dominance.

5. What is a tornado diagram?

6. How do you construct a tornado diagram?

7. What role do spreadsheets play in decision analysis?

8. What is a risk profile?

9. What insights can be gained from tornado diagrams?

10. If one alternative is dominant over another alternative in the tornado diagram, should you make the decision or continue with the analysis?

11. What is an optimal decision?

12. How is sensitivity to probability different than deterministic sensitivity analysis?

13. Can we ever achieve perfect information? If so, how?

14. What insights can be gained from a risk profile?

15. How do risk profiles account for uncertainty?

16. If one risk profile is dominant over another, should you always choose the dominant profile?

17. Explain the basis for Bayes' Rule.

18. Why is Bayes' Rule important to decision analysis?

19. Why do we often place our personal risk attitudes on corporate decisions?

20. What does risk premium mean?

21. Explain the concept of risk aversion.

11.8 References and Further Reading

Bunn, D. *Applied Decision Analysis*. New York: McGraw Hill, 1984.

Clemen, Robert T. *Making Hard Decisions: An Introduction to Decision Analysis*. PWS-Kent, 1991.

Howard, R. A. and J. E. Matheson, ed. *The Principles and Applications of Decision Analysis*. Vol. 2. Palo Alto: Strategic Decisions Group, 1984.

McNamee, P. and J. Celona. *Decision Analysis with Supertree*. 2nd ed., San Francisco, CA: The Scientific Press, 1990.

von Winterfeldt, D. and W. Edwards. *Decision Analysis and Behavioral Research*. Cambridge: Cambridge University Press, 1986.

11.9 Exercises

1. Explain the concept of perfect information. How does this provide insight into the problem?

2. Using the following information, build a tornado diagram using Microsoft Excel. The values for each uncertainty below are 10-50-90's.

   Value function = Rev – Cost
   Rev = (Vol) (Price)
   Cost = (Sales + Mfg.)(Vol)

	100	500	1000
Vol	100	500	1000
Price	$2	$3	$4
Sales	$0.25	$0.30	$0.40
Mfg	$0.50	$0.75	$1.00

3. Draw a decision tree based on the previous information from Exercise 2 and include a decision to fund or not. The not-fund decision branch has a value of $0.

    a. Using the weights of 0.25–0.50–0.25, calculate the EMV of the problem.
    b. Calculate the value of information for the uncertainty Vol.
    c. Draw an influence diagram for this problem.
    d. Add a test node to the influence diagram from part c and calculate the value of imperfect information given the test is 70% accurate.

4. What is risk attitude?

5. Explain why for personal decisions you can have any risk attitude, but for most corporate decisions you should be risk neutral.

6. Why should you use a utility function to account for risk in a decision?

7. You have been given the opportunity below. Using the exponential utility function, what is your probability p, given a risk tolerance of $1,000.

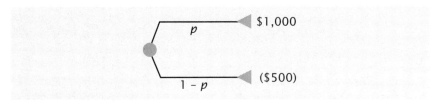

8. Explain the concept of certain equivalent and how it is better than using the discount rate to adjust for the riskiness of a project.

11.10 Guide to Action

1. Use the decision model to perform a deterministic sensitivity analysis to sort the important or critical variables from those which are less important.

2. Use Tornado Diagrams to record and illustrate the impact of each variable on strategy value. Tornado Diagrams are excellent communication tools and can also provide insight into dominance.

3. Review the strategies. Are there any that can be dropped from the analysis as either infeasible or dominated? Are there any strategies which need to be added?

4. Assess the probabilistic data for the critical variables for the credible strategies.

5. Decision trees are very useful for illustrating the sequence of decisions and variables. A skeleton decision tree can be used if the full tree becomes too complex.

6. Use the decision trees or a full probabilistic model to develop risk profiles, i.e. cumulative probability distributions. Graphing the strateg curves on the same chart is an excellent way to compare and contra__ the strategies' risk, reward, expected values, etc.

7. A sensitivity to probability analysis can lead to further insight. Search for circumstances where the strategy selection would change. Review and validate with the content experts as necessary.

8. A value of information exercise can highlight areas where further information might influence the decisions. Determine if other information is available and use the value of perfect information and the value of imperfect information analyses to determine what that information would be worth to the organization.

9. Assess the risk attitude of the organization/decision maker and apply the appropriate risk attitude to the strategy choices.

11.11 Case for Analysis: "Unexpected Results"

Jim is the team leader of a decision analysis team tasked with developing a new marketing strategy for a large portion of the products sold by Large ChemCo Inc. Jim feels like his team did an excellent job of working through the decision analysis process, but the results were unexpected.

As the team was developing strategies, one of the Leadership Team members insisted that a "Harvest and Get Out" strategy be included in the analysis, primarily for comparison purposes. When the analysis was complete, this strategy showed the best financial results, based on Net Present Value.

Jim and his team are now faced with presenting the data to the Leadership Team along with their recommendation. None of the team members wants to recommend the Harvest and Get Out strategy, but they are struggling with how to recommend a strategy that is less than the best financial option.

- What are Jim and his team forgetting? (This is common for teams after they spend weeks in the Evaluation Stage, building the financial models, assessing experts, and studying value of information, etc.)

- Besides the financial results, what should Jim include in his presentation to the Leadership Team?

- What can cause the best financial strategy to not be the recommended strategy? Name some non-financial measures that you have seen included in projects.

- What are the limitations of using NPV as the only financial value measure?

12

Getting to Agreement

I attribute the little I know to my not having been ashamed to ask for information, and to my rule of conversing with all descriptions of men on those topics that form their own peculiar professions and pursuits.

— *John Locke*

One of the greatest benefits of decision analysis is that it brings both improved communication and clarity to any situation. By using the common language of probability and tools like influence diagrams and decision trees, members of a project team are able to share knowledge and expand their collective insight. Greater understanding of a situation is beneficial in the framing and analysis phases of the decision analysis process, but it is even more important in the implementation phase.

12.1 Agreement and Implementation

Agreement is the framework of verifying and communicating the course of action proposed for the organization. I have seen analyses which had decision maker involvement and commitment produce dismal results because of poor implementation. It is easy for a project team to assume the work product and insights produced by the analysis will be sufficient for the implementation team – but all too often this is not the case.

Agreement provides the framework necessary for implementation to proceed without unnecessary disruption and in the manner designed by the project team. In the Agreement phase, the project team:

- develops a clear statement of the course of action,
- verifies that the chosen course of action is appropriate,
- ensures decision maker support for the course of action,
- develops a list of resources necessary for implementation,
- develops a communication plan for the organization,
- involves implementation personnel,
- shares knowledge with the organization.

Agreement phase deliverables

Developing an Action Statement

An action statement is a means of communicating the preferred course of action to the decision maker and the organization. The action statement should be a clear and concise statement of the chosen alternative and what goals are to be accomplished. Without a clear action statement, the organization can misinterpret the recommendation from the project team. The action statement should include the problem to be solved, the alternatives considered, the chosen alternative, the rationale for the alternative chosen, the goal or objective, and the expected value to the company (see Figure 12.1 for an example action statement).

Figure 12.1
Action
Statement

Action Statement

Problem: How to expand production capacity with minimal capital investment?

Alternatives:
- · Use a toll manufacturer
- · Hire second shift of workers
- · Purchase more efficient equipment

Chosen alternative: Use toll manufacturer

Rationale: Provides the ability to vary both cost and production. No fixed costs and minimal up-front costs with toll production costs similar to internal manufacturing costs.

Goal: Expand production capacity to meet growing demand without increasing overhead and fixed costs.

Expected Value: $1.5MM

Is the Course of Action Appropriate?

The chosen course of action must be appropriate for both the decision maker and the organization. It should not violate any rules or policies of the organization, and it should be within the decision maker's and the organization's risk tolerance. This is important if you expect the organization and the decision maker to support the course of action. There are no hard rules to determine if a course of action is appropriate, but if the decision would cause a third party to question it on the grounds of moral, ethical, or social considerations, then it may not be appropriate. Also, remember to use the decision hierarchy (Figure 12.2) to help set the perspective.

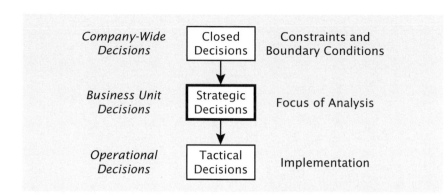

Figure 12.2 Decision Hierarchy

Ensuring Decision Maker Support

The easiest way to ensure decision maker support for the chosen course of action is to involve the decision maker in the process and to validate at each phase of the decision quality process. If the decision maker agrees with the problem definition, the alternatives generated, the data gathered, and the risk tolerance analysis applied, it will be difficult to disagree with the recommended course of action.

What Resources are Necessary for Implementation?

Determining the best course of action is only part of solving the problem. Without good implementation, the solution may never become reality. Good implementation is difficult (if not impossible) without the right level and kind of resources. I have found it beneficial to begin developing a resource list during the analysis. This list also helps to determine the appropriateness of an alternative – if the resources are not available, would the course of action be appropriate? When determining needed resources, you must include time, money, and personnel. Make sure not to underestimate the resources required, as this may cause you to choose an incorrect course of action. Two major causes of underestimation of resources are failure of management to listen to experienced technical personnel and inadequate initial framing of the problem to clearly define the scope.

Developing a Communication Plan

One of the biggest errors organizations make is neglecting to develop a communication plan. You need a communication plan to describe what the course of action is, why it was chosen, and what each employee's role is in implementing it. Without a communication plan, employees become discouraged and may not trust the analysis and the course of action. The plan should include all of the information that you think is relevant to allow an adequate level of understanding. The plan should not be ambiguous or laced with buzzwords or corporate jargon. Make the communication clear and to the point (short, sharp, and shiny!).

Figure 12.3
Sharing
Perspectives

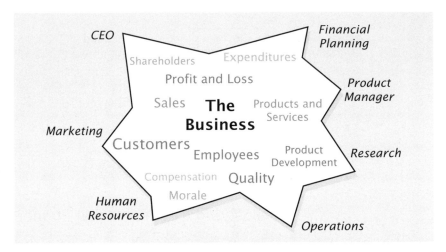

Involving the Implementation Personnel

Some project teams become the implementation team, but for many projects, implementation is given to another team, usually composed of operational personnel. It is important to involve some of the personnel who will be responsible for implementation early in the analysis. This allows them to become fully aware of the thought processes, the alternatives and resources required, and the reasoning for the chosen course of action. By involving these people, you eliminate much of the hand-off problems associated with different teams developing and implementing a course of action.

Sharing Knowledge

A main emphasis in the Agreement phase is to share and enlarge the organization's knowledge. Every organization can be considered an encyclopedia of sorts – most of the information about a problem and how to solve it may reside within the organization itself – the problem is that information is often not readily available or easy to find. The key to solving many of the organization's problems is finding the sources of the information and eliciting the information in a shared environment.

Decision analysis is a means of conducting high quality, logical discussions. These discussions or dialogs allow individuals to share their knowledge, thereby increasing the overall knowledge of all the participants. This knowledge is then captured using an influence diagram and communicated to the decision maker and others. Because everyone has a different perspective of the problem and may prefer different alternatives, it is imperative to share and communicate knowledge. Fig. 12.3 illustrates the difference in perspectives and why sharing knowledge is important if you are to see the entire view of the problem.

Figure 12.4 DQP Structuring Page

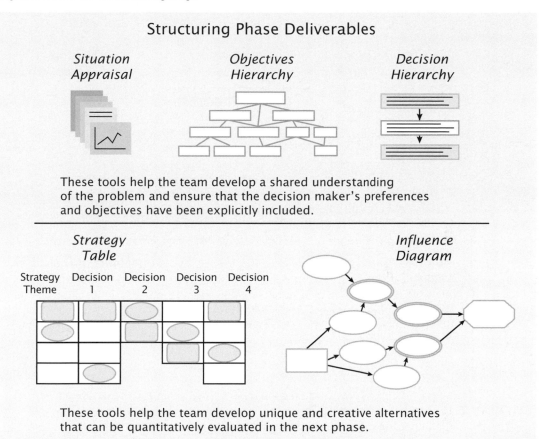

Structuring Phase Deliverables

Situation Appraisal   *Objectives Hierarchy*   *Decision Hierarchy*

These tools help the team develop a shared understanding of the problem and ensure that the decision maker's preferences and objectives have been explicitly included.

Strategy Table   *Influence Diagram*

These tools help the team develop unique and creative alternatives that can be quantitatively evaluated in the next phase.

12.2 Developing a Decision Quality Package

One way to help with implementation and improve organizational learning is to develop a ***Decision Quality Package*** (DQP). The DQP is a synopsis of the work products the team has developed.This package can be used for communicating to the whole organization, the implementation team, and any other parties affected by the decision. The document does not need to contain every piece of information the team developed, but it should summarize key insights.

Figure 12.4 is an example of the information that should be included from the Structuring phase. The information presented can be as simple as the examples on the next three pages or can become a more comprehensive document. Actually, it is a good idea to have two versions – one that is condensed for general communication of the team's work, and a more in-depth package for the implementation team.

Decision Quality Package considerations

Figure 12.5 DQP Evaluation Page

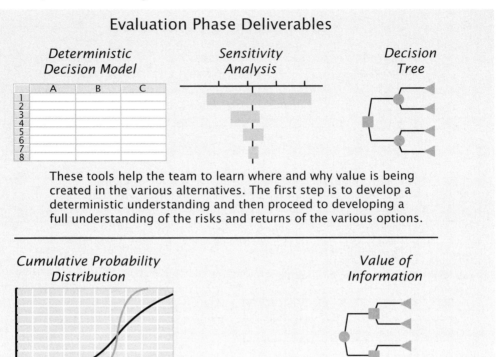

Figure 12.5 is an example of the Evaluation phase of the process in a DQP format. By providing the information in logical chunks on a single page, it is easier for people to comprehend large amounts of information and insight.

The Agreement phase of the DQP should clearly show why the chosen alternative is the best for meeting the decision maker's objectives and how the alternative will be integrated into the organization's culture and processes. Figure 12.6 is an example of the Agreement page of a DQP.

12.3 Preparing the Organization

Effective implementation of decision analysis requires more than just some new tools and processes – it may require a change in the organizational culture. This culture change often takes years to accomplish, but it yields substantial results.

Figure 12.6 DQP Agreement Page

Agreement Phase Deliverables

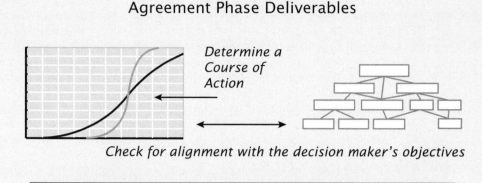

Determine a
Course of
Action

Check for alignment with the decision maker's objectives

In the agreement phase, we are reviewing the insights created from the previous states and we are deciding on an appropriate course of action.

Action Plan

Action Plan
* Problem:
* Alternatives:
* Recommendation:
* Rationale:
* Objective:
* Expected Value:

Integration Plan

Agreement phase documentation should provide a bridge between the project team and the implementation team. There should be a clear understanding of what resources will be required to be successful.

Usually the biggest change is in understanding and rewarding good decisions, not just good outcomes. This is often a challenge, as management systems usually recognize and reward good outcomes.

Another cultural change is using ranges and probabilities to communicate uncertainty rather than single point estimates or ambiguous terms such as probably or likely. Usually, once people have had some exposure to giving probabilities, they become comfortable with their use. People need to understand that knowing what you *don't* know is as important as what you *do* know.

Cultural change: ranges and probabilities

It is important that the organization is prepared for these changes. I recommend that the whole organization attend some level of training in decision analysis – usually one to three days. This will allow the project teams and management to better understand and interact with the process. However, most organizations begin by using decision analysis on some type of pilot project before committing to full implementation or training throughout the company.

12.4 Summary

The Agreement phase of the decision analysis process is important in communicating the courses of action and the uncertainties which affect them to the organization. Agreement also focuses on improving the hand-off from analysis to implementation by the project team. Without the Agreement phase, many analyses would never be implemented, or if implemented, would produce dismal results compared to the computed expectation.

Implementation is just as important as working on the right problem – both can waste your time and money if adequate attention and resources are not provided. This is why it is so important to involve the implementation personnel early in the process.

You also want to develop a comprehensive communication package for the organization. Communication has been an important factor in getting employee involvement and understanding for every project that I have worked on. Use the action statement as a means to easily and quickly inform the organization of the course of action.

12.5 Key Concepts

agreement   action statement
resource allocation   communication plan
Decision Quality Package (DQP)

12.6 Study Questions

1. What are the hurdles to implementing decision analysis in your personal or business life?

2. Describe an action statement.

3. Why is shared knowledge important?

4. Why is Agreement necessary?

5. How does the decision hierarchy help you to understand if the course of action is appropriate?

6. What aspects of implementation do you think are the most difficult?

7. Describe an implementation you have participated in. How effective was the implementation?

8. Describe a communication plan. Why is it important?

9. What should be included in the Decision Quality Package?

10. Why is it important to list and evaluate the resources necessary for each alternative?

12.7 References and Further Reading

Howard, R. A. and J. E. Matheson, ed. *The Principles and Applications of Decision Analysis*. Vol. 2. Palo Alto: Strategic Decisions Group, 1984.

Skinner, David C. "A Quest for Certainty." 1.1 ed., Vol. Oklahoma City, OK: SilverWare Software Co., 1991.

Skinner, David C. "Risk Based Decision Making: A Decision Analysis Viewpoint." In *American Petroleum Institute Safety and Fire Protection Conference in San Antonio, TX*, American Petroleum Institute, 47-57, 1994.

von Winterfeldt, D. and W. Edwards. *Decision Analysis and Behavioral Research*. Cambridge: Cambridge University Press, 1986.

12.8 Guide to Action

1. Agreement is the framework of verifying and communicating the course of action proposed for the organization.

2. The team needs to develop an Action Statement. This includes a description of the Problem, Alternatives Considered, Alternative Chosen, Rationale, Goals, and Expected Value.

3. The team should review whether or not the chosen alternative is appropriate for the decision maker and for the organization.

4. Remember to ensure the decision maker support of the final decision by including the decision maker(s) in the process from the beginning and having periodic reviews.

5. Identify the resources that are required for implementation.

6. Develop a communication plan that takes into account all the stakeholders.

7. The team needs to develop a Decision Quality Package (DQP). The DQP includes all the work done by the team. If the DQP is a large document, be sure to include a concise synopsis as an Executive Summary at the beginning of the document.

8. Remember that the main emphasis in the DQP and communication plan is to share knowledge with those outside the decision team.

12.9 Case for Analysis: "Rolling out the Plan"

Amy supervises the engineering department at a medium sized manufacturing company in the southeast. She has just completed working with the company's site manager and operations manager to prioritize the site's capital project spending for the next three years. Many projects which the organization wanted to see completed will not be done due to constraints on the total amount of money available for capital spending.

She is getting ready to inform the other site management of the decisions she and the two other managers have made. The site manager has asked her to take responsibility for this and to try to minimize conflict and disruption.

■   How should Amy communicate with the rest of the management at the site?

■   What potential pitfalls do you think she might face?

■   How will she know if her communication plan has been successful?

■   How will Amy know if her team has achieved an appropriate level of decision quality?

■   How can Amy use the decision hierarchy to help her communicate the new plan?

13

A Thirty-minute Guide to Better Decisions

Where there is no difference, there is only indifference.
—Louis Nizer

In a previous edition, I created a section called "Lecture Notes," which included overheads from my public course. Since that edition, I have had many interesting comments on how to make this book even more useful. This encouraged me to develop a chapter which would take the reader through a real case in a short period of time.

The intent of this chapter is to be a quick reference for analysts, a guide for decision teams, and a quick overview for decision makers. This thirty-minute guide is designed to give insight into facilitating the process and to give you a feel for the speed with which the process can be performed. This case study, while fictional, is based on two actual projects with similar results and timeframes.

13.1 Company Background

Cleanflow Corporation (see organization chart in Figure 13.1) is a leading producer of air and water filtration systems for consumer and industrial use. Their patented Puraflow filter is the number one home water filtration system. Over the past nine years, the company's growth has mirrored the growth in consumer health consciousness.

The company was founded by two brothers, George and Fred Murphy. They began the business in 1982 by converting an old automotive parts plant over to manufacturing HEPA air filters for industrial use. The company developed its first new product in 1984 – SmokeOut. This air filtration system was designed to be installed in public places like bars and restaurants to remove cigarette smoke. SmokeOut was a big hit with retail and industrial users. During this time the company grew rapidly, nearly doubling every two years during the 1980s. Since 1990, the firm's

Cleanflow
Case Study

Figure 13.1   Cleanflow Corporation Organization Chart

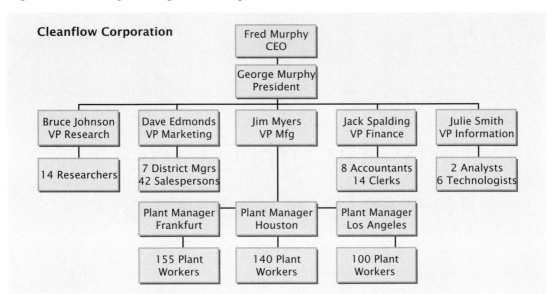

growth has leveled out at about 3-5% per year. However, due to changes in both consumers attitudes and legislation, most building and public places have gone to being smoke free. This has caused a dramatic decrease in sales for SmokeOut.

In 1986, the brothers began looking for other products that could be manufactured using similar techniques and equipment. During this same time consumers were becoming increasingly interested in health issues like water quality. The brothers decided to create a water filtration product for home consumers. Within five years after introduction, the Puraflow product was the market share leader with 12% of the market and it now accounts for $120 million in sales annually.

The company now operates two manufacturing plants in the United States and one in Europe, all of which are at or near capacity. To continue the company's growth, production capacity must be increased to meet future product demands. To meet this anticipated future demand, the brothers are trying to decide whether to build a new plant or to expand the current plants. Both brothers are concerned with the ability of the company to grow with their current product mix.

13.2 The Process

In response to this problem, the brothers have brought in a consulting firm to help them develop a strategy for continued growth. George and Fred Murphy recognize that their current strategic plans do not include a real understanding of the future market potential. They see that the company must develop more products and production

Figure 13.2 The Scalable Decision Process (SDP)

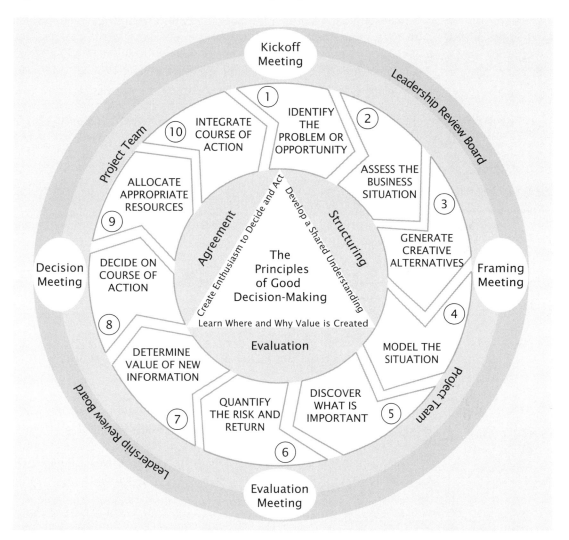

capacity if the company is to continue to grow. It is important to note that the brothers view this expansion project as an opportunity to improve, rather than as a problem to be solved.

The consulting firm hired by Cleanflow came in and met with the two brothers and the vice presidents of Manufacturing, Marketing, Finance, Information, and Research. The consultants discussed the process they were going to use to develop a new growth strategy for Cleanflow Corporation.

Figure 13.2, the Scalable Decision Process, illustrates the entire 10-step process starting with identifying the problem and proceeding all the way through to solution implementation.

13.3 Pre-Project Planning

Establishing a clear charter and direction for the project is important before beginning a project. During this pre-project work, the decision maker(s) and project leader should work together to understand the scope of the project and to identify potential resources and team members.

George agreed to be the project sponsor since he was the one who contacted the consulting firm. In addition, both George and Fred agreed that the team leader should be Sherry Winston. Sherry is a District Marketing Manager and has a good knowledge of and is well respected by the entire organization.

Planning the kick-off meeting

Meeting: Pre-kickoff
Attendees: George & Fred Murphy, Sherry Winston, Process Consultant
Purpose: Develop project scope and select team members

During this pre-kickoff meeting, the decision makers, the project leader, and the process consultant:

- discuss the initial project scope,
- select the team members for the leadership review board and the project team, and
- develop an objectives hierarchy that reflects the decision maker's objectives for the project.

Determining Leadership Review Board Members

Because of the overall importance of the project and the relatively small management team, George and Fred decided to include all functional vice presidents on the leadership review board. This team will include Finance, Marketing, Research, Manufacturing, and Information Systems.

The process consultant worked with George and Fred to help them understand that the leadership review board is responsible for:

Leadership review board responsibilities

- communicating the need for change and its urgency,
- providing adequate resources for the project,
- validating project findings and results,
- ensuring project quality and timeliness,
- communicating management concerns to the project team,
- actively participating and contributing to the project,
- being responsible for implementation of the strategy, and
- being an advocate of the team's effort.

The decision maker(s) and project leader need to develop a list of objectives which cover the leadership board's concerns and objectives.

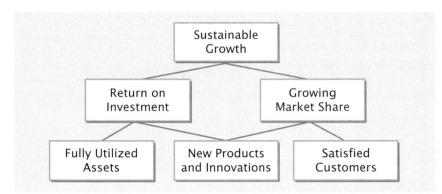

*Figure 13.3
Cleanflow
Objectives
Hierarchy*

Objectives Hierarchy

George Murphy and Sherry Winston met with the process consultant and developed an objectives hierarchy for the decision (Figure 13.3). They also determined that expected monetary value would be the main financial decision criteria for the project. Using this information, the project team will be able to develop a situation analysis for the project.

Building the project team is an important task and should not be considered trivial. This team must be composed of people who are knowledgeable about the organization, respected by the organization, and committed to finding the best alternative.

Building the Project Team

The process consultant, George, Fred, and Sherry met and began listing names of possible team members. In addition, they tried to determine the time commitments possible with each team member.

Up to this point in the process, all interactions have been between the process consultant, the leadership review board, the project sponsor, and the project leader. The previous steps are critical to having a good kickoff meeting and in setting the team up for success. The remaining tasks in step one will be completed during a kickoff workshop with the entire project team.

13.4 Kickoff Meeting

Meeting: Project kickoff
Attendees: Decision Makers, Process Consultant, Project Team
Purpose: Review and further define project scope and deliverables, set project timeline, and identify project resources

The meeting started with George describing why the project is important to the company and why each of the team members had been chosen. Then Sherry discussed with the team all of the pre-kickoff activities which had taken place. She outlined the objectives hierarchy that had been developed and asked Fred and George to discuss their thinking on the hierarchy.

Once the team was given time to discuss the pre-kickoff work, the process consultant led the team through an exercise to develop their roles, responsibilities, and project ground rules. From that activity, the team developed the following work products.

The Team Leader will coordinate all aspects of team activities and will be responsible for managing its work and supporting its members. The leader will be accountable for meeting project goals and key functions including:

Team leader responsibilities

- leading the team,
- communicating team vision and progress outside the team,
- seeking input from outside the team,
- providing individual feedback to team members,
- organizing meetings and reporting,
- providing resources for the team as needed,
- participating as a core team member, and
- advocacy of the team's effort.

Team members will be responsible for doing the work in each process step, developing a robust strategy, and working with the leadership review board to ensure proper implementation. This will involve attending all team meetings, actively participating in all team activities and being responsible for meeting project goals. Key functions include:

Team member responsibilities

- developing creative alternatives,
- taking responsibility for team assignments,
- making recommendations for most efficiently accomplishing team goals,
- articulating needs, issues, concerns and expectations of those outside the team,
- gathering data and information from content experts,
- evaluating and comparing alternatives,
- communicating its ideas and progress as well as seeking input from those outside the team,
- participating in the implementation of the strategy, and
- supporting the team's effort.

The process consultant will take responsibility for guiding the team in all aspects of its work and ensuring that a practical methodology based on the consultant's experience is available to the team. Principal functions include:

■ facilitate the work of the team,
■ organize team meetings and work with the team leader,
■ advise the team leader and team members,
■ provide the knowledge and methods necessary for successfully accomplishing the project objectives, and
■ educate Cleanflow participants in methodology and skills.

Consultant responsibilities

The team also developed a set of project ground rules, which include:

■ Don't cut each other off when talking.
■ Be on time.
■ Keep a balance of listening & talking.
■ Don't take things personally.
■ Clarifying is OK, but don't restate positions.
■ If you miss meetings, it is your responsibility to stay informed.
■ Minimize "backtracking," i.e. redefining scope.
■ Inform the team leader when you will miss a meeting.
■ Offenses to these rules will cost a dollar.
■ No hidden agendas.
■ Respect others' opinions.
■ Process facilitator will intervene when needed.
■ Air grievances in meeting, not off-line.
■ Have fun!

Example ground rules

At this point in the meeting, the process consultant gave a brief introduction to the decision analysis process that would be used for this project. He outlined each of the steps and described what the finished work product would look like and the insights that should be developed at each phase.

Figure 13.4 Cleanflow Project Timeline

Cleanflow Strategy Project Timeline

Process Step	1	2	3	4	5	6	7	8	9	10	11	12	13	14	15	16	17	18	19	20	21	22
Identify opportunity																						
Assess business situation																						
Generate creative alternatives																						
Model the opportunity																						
Discover what is important																						
Quantify risk and return																						
Determine value of new information																						
Decide on course of action																						
Allocate appropriate resources																						
Integrate the solution																						

Preparation time for process step ▨
Team time devoted to process step ▨

After this discussion, the team developed a timeline for completing the project (Figure 13.4). At the conclusion of this one-day meeting, the project team understood the project plan and had a brief description of the deliverables and how they would participate in the process.

13.5 Structuring Phase

Identify the Problem or Opportunity

George and Fred Murphy had originally thought that the problem was the need for more production capacity and had narrowed the scope to only include an expansion of the current plants or building a new plant. However, after discussing the situation with the project leader and the process consultant, they quickly realized that they must first decide on the product development strategy before deciding on the plant capacity decision. This was a real insight for the decision makers. If they would have proceeded with the original scope, the team could have developed the wrong set of alternatives.

Developing the Cleanflow decision hierarchy

In addition, George thought that the scope would be incorrect if the team did not address the customer relationship strategy, as that is how the company would capture the value from new products and plant capacity. From this input, the team developed a decision hierarchy for the project scope (Figure 13.5).

Assess the Business Situation

The project team began a business assessment to determine the internal strengths and weaknesses of the company in relationship to opportunities and competitive threats. The team developed a straw model of the eight areas where they would focus on gathering information. These key information areas are diagrammed in Figure 13.6. Using this straw model, the team developed the following set of insights for the project.

Figure 13.5   Cleanflow Decision Hierarchy

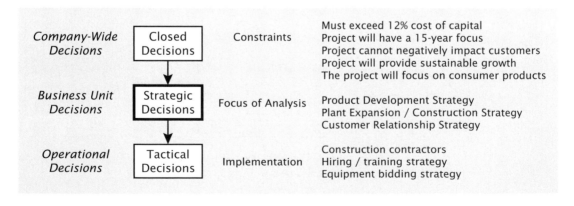

Company-Wide Decisions	Closed Decisions	Constraints	Must exceed 12% cost of capital Project will have a 15-year focus Project cannot negatively impact customers Project will provide sustainable growth The project will focus on consumer products
Business Unit Decisions	Strategic Decisions	Focus of Analysis	Product Development Strategy Plant Expansion / Construction Strategy Customer Relationship Strategy
Operational Decisions	Tactical Decisions	Implementation	Construction contractors Hiring / training strategy Equipment bidding strategy

*Figure 13.6
Cleanflow Case:
Situation
Appraisal*

Know the Market

The market for consumer water and air filtration products is growing at about 22% per year based on the last five years data and future projections. Cleanflow currently has about 12% of the water filtration and 2% of the air filtration market as shown in the two pie charts in Figure 13.7.

Understand the Customer

A market survey conducted by a research firm indicates that customers are interested in products that provide a high quality filtration system, have filters that are easy to change and inexpensive to purchase, and are easy to install in their homes.

Figure 13.7   Cleanflow's Water Filtration and Air Filtration Market Positions

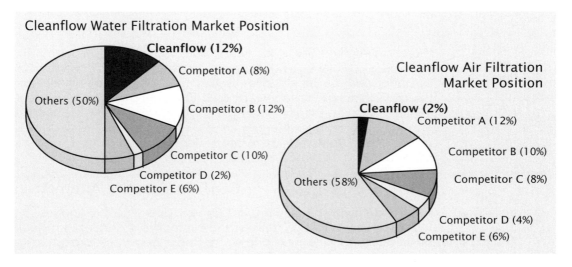

Understand the Competitors

The consumer water and air filtration market is dominated by six large manufacturers (of which Cleanflow is one) which compose about 50% of the market. The rest of the market is comprised of small companies or specialty manufacturers who supply niche market segments.

Know the Industry

The industry has undergone tremendous growth over the past five to seven years due in part to an increase in consumer awareness of health issues. Most analysts agree that this trend will continue and possibly even accelerate over the next few years. Most analysts are predicting a growth rate for the industry of 25 to 30%.

Understand the Cost Drivers

A manufacturer must have good cost controls to control a significant portion of market share in this industry. As there is usually not a high degree of differentiation in many of the products, the key differentiation is price. The main cost drivers for the industry are manufacturing and marketing costs. Most products have a 20 to 25% net margin.

Determine Core Competencies

Cleanflow has a core competency in technology development, specifically in high volume, low cost filters. This competency comes from the company's experience in dealing with industrial and commercial filtration customers.

Understand Competitive Advantages

Cleanflow has several competitive advantages which allow them to compete with much larger companies. These include a small and focused management team, a well trained and customer-focused sales force, and modern manufacturing facilities.

Understand Key Uncertainties

There are many issues and uncertainties that Cleanflow faces. The team used a brainstorming technique to elicit the issues and then categorized them as uncertainties, decisions, values or objectives. From this brainstorming, the team was able to develop a list of key uncertainties. The greatest key uncertainties facing Cleanflow are the size and rate of growth for the consumer filtration market, the number of new products and their associated success in the market, and the manufacturing efficiency of its plants.

Generate Creative Alternatives

After performing the business assessment and situation analysis, the team began working on defining the alternative strategies that would be evaluated in the next phase. The team began by brainstorming possible options for each of the strategic decisions. The team developed the strategy map shown in Figure 13.8. After developing this strategy map, the team developed an objective and rationale statement for each of the strategies:

"Embrace the Customer"

Objective: Develop incremental innovations with current product line and production facilities but develop a direct consumer marketing channel.

Rationale: This would require limited capital and would only be a small change for the organization. It would require developing additional sales and marketing personnel and infrastructure. Advertising would also become more of a factor for continued growth.

"License the Future"

Objective: This strategy provides a means of limiting the development and expansion capital requirements for the company. The strategy relies on the ability to purchase new products and innovations as a means for continued growth.

Rationale: The strategy provides a means to leverage the company's resources and limit the future capital exposure. The strategy also relies on developing an intimate distributor relationship which would limit the number of outlets for the company's products but could provide higher margins through exclusive distributor arrangements. However, because the strategy is so dependent upon being able to purchase new products and innovation, it has a high risk associated with it.

*Figure 13.8
Cleanflow
Strategy Map*

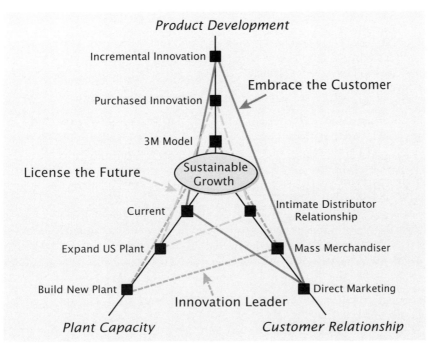

"Innovation Leader"

Objective: Become the innovation leader in the industry. Capitalize on the company's core competencies in product development.

Rationale: By creating the technology curve rather than following it, the company could extract higher margins and premiums from its distributors and customers. However, this strategy would require a significant increase in product development and would include building a new plant with flexible manufacturing technology.

Model the Alternatives

With the three alternative strategies defined, the team began to build a decision model for communication of the problem and for evaluating the alternatives. The first model the team built was an influence diagram. This diagram shows how the key uncertainties and the decisions interact to create value. Figure 13.9 shows the completed influence diagram.

The influence diagram uses ovals to indicate uncertainties, rectangles for decisions, and an octagon for the value node. After creating the influence diagram, the team's modeler will use it as a map for the financial spreadsheet model. The spreadsheet model will be used to calculate the base case value of each strategy and will be used in the next stage to understand where and why value is created.

Figure 13.9
Cleanflow
Influence
Diagram

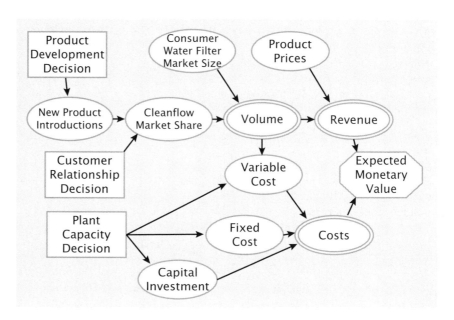

Alternative Meeting

Meeting: Alternative Review
Attendees: Leadership review board (LRB), Project Team, Process Consultant
Purpose: Validate insights developed from the business situation, review alternatives developed, select alternatives for evaluation, validate decision model and identify content experts.

The leadership review board (LRB) agreed with the insights developed during the business situation assessment and also added that they believe one of their major competitors is about to file for Chapter 11. If this information is correct, Cleanflow may be able to capture some market share from this competitor. The LRB also said this reinforced their belief that the company must develop a strategy that balances risk and return.

Cleanflow case leadership review board discussion

Using the influence diagram, the team reviewed the decision problem with the LRB and identified the content experts the team will use to gather information. During this meeting, the LRB decided not to evaluate the "License the Future" alternative because they do not believe purchasing technology is a viable means to sustain the company's growth rate.

13.6 Evaluation Phase

Discover What is Important

After identifying the content experts with the LRB, the team contacted the experts and began to gather the needed assessments. The process consultant worked with the team to develop interview templates and instructed the team on interviewing techniques. The team interviewed the experts and gathered a range of possible outcomes using the 10-50-90 tool (Figure 13.10).

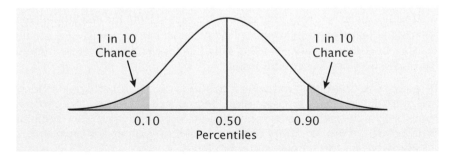

*Figure 13.10
10-50-90*

The team gathered the necessary information and created a base case financial comparison for the "Embrace the Customer" and "Innovation Leader" alternatives. Using the base case number, both alternatives met the policy decisions developed by the decision makers.

Figure 13.11
Cleanflow
Tornado Chart

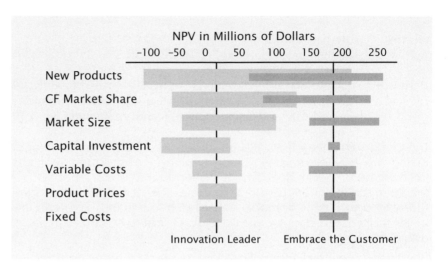

To gain further insight into the value and key uncertainties of each alternative, the team performed a sensitivity analysis. This information was then converted into the tornado chart (Figure 13.11).

Using this information, the team made an initial conclusion that the "Embrace the Customer" alternative is the best choice. However, tornado diagrams do not indicate the risk versus return for an alternative. The diagram only represents the change in value created by swinging a variable from its high to low value. What we can see from this diagram is that the two key uncertainties which would change the decision are the number of "New Products" and the Cleanflow "Market Share."

Quantify the Risk and Return

Now that we have a deterministic understanding of the changes in value due to variations in the key uncertainties, we need further insight that can only be gained by incorporating probability into the analysis. We will build a decision tree using the insight gained from the sensitivity analysis in the last step to incorporate the probabilities of occurrence for the various uncertain events. By using only the key variables we can simplify the analysis to provide greater insight.

The process consultant explained to the team the best way to begin this phase is to develop a skeleton decision tree to show the chronology of the decisions and uncertainties, create a simplified decision tree based on the sensitivity analysis, and then gather the probabilistic assessments for the simplified decision tree.

Figure 13.12   Cleanflow Skeleton Tree

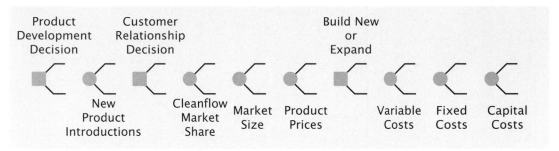

A skeleton tree is simply a chronological ordering of the decisions and uncertainties without connecting the branches.

Figure 13.12 is the skeleton tree for all of the decisions and uncertainties in this project. Creating this full decision tree would require many assessments and it would be quite large.

By simplifying the tree, we can keep all of the uncertainties which did not dramatically change the project value at their base case values. In doing so, we create a tree that is manageable and provides insight into the paths of greatest risk. Using the program TreeAge Pro® from TreeAge Software, we can build the decision tree below in less than a minute (Figure 13.13).

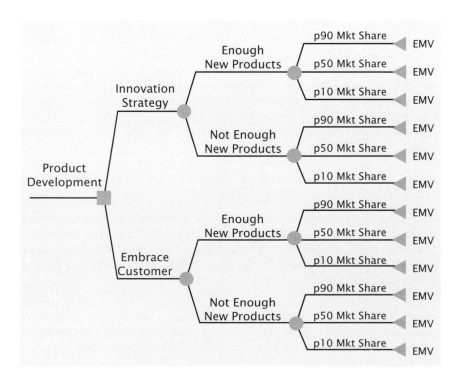

*Figure 13.13
Cleanflow
Decision Tree*

Figure 13.14
Cleanflow
Cumulative
Probability
Graph

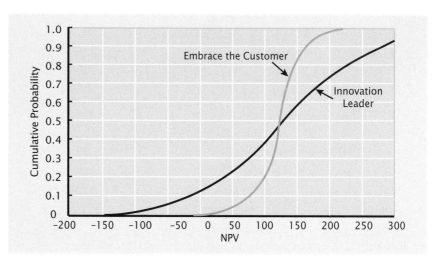

Using this decision tree, we can gather specific probabilistic assessments from the identified content experts. This is different information than we gathered earlier for the sensitivity analysis. For that analysis, we were only concerned with the possible range of outcomes, now we are concerned with the probability those outcomes will occur.

The project team leader (along with the process consultant) interviewed the experts and gathered the needed assessments. They took this information and generated a cumulative probability curve, or risk plot, for the two strategies. Figure 13.14 shows this graph.

From this graph we see that both strategies have similar EMV's but the risk associated with each strategy is very different. The "Embrace the Customer" strategy has little downside risk, but also the upside is limited. This would be considered a "conservative" strategy. It would be appropriate if the company could not afford the downside risk of the "Innovation Leader" strategy. Either strategy would be appropriate for the company, depending upon the corporate risk profile and the decision maker's preferences.

Determine the Value of New Information

The team has now finished the deterministic and probabilistic analyses for the two strategies. The last form of analysis is informational. What could the team do to mitigate the risk associated with the Innovation Leader strategy, while still maintaining the upside potential? Determining the value of new information is an important step and a form of analysis that is only available through decision analysis.

Given that two uncertainties created the greatest change in project value, the team decided to calculate the value of perfect information. Using this method, the uncertainty is known before the decision is made. The decision tree (Figure 13.15) illustrates the concept.

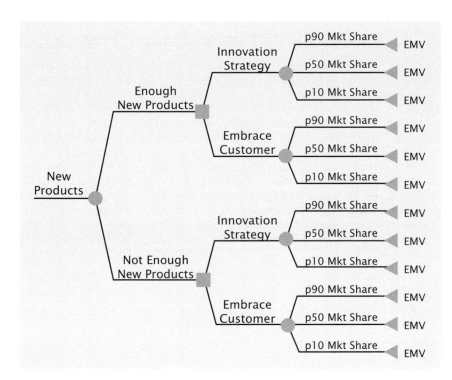

*Figure 13.15
Cleanflow Tree:
Value of Perfect
Information*

In this case, the team will know if enough new products will be developed before deciding on which strategy to pursue. The analysis also tells the team and the LRB how much they could spend to resolve this uncertainty if information were available. Understanding how much information is worth is a powerful tool in eliminating analysis paralysis and in creating new hybrid alternatives.

The team decided to hold a focus group meeting with the technology department to help gain a quick consensus of the probability of meeting the new product targets and to develop a quick list of products for use during the Leadership Review Board.

Evaluation Meeting

Meeting: Evaluation
Attendees: LRB, Process Consultant, Project Team
Purpose: Review and validate the team's evaluation findings and insights. Determine whether a decision can be made or if new information should be gathered.

13.7 Decide on a Course of Action

Because of the thoroughness of the team's analysis and the integration of the LRB's insights, the LRB was ready to make a decision at the evaluation meeting. The LRB decided to pursue the "Innovation Leader" strategy based on the focus group insights and the ability of

Rackspace – Risky Move for Rackspace Managed Hosting

Rackspace Managed Hosting of San Antonio, Texas was founded in 1998 as a website hosting company. While other providers have struggled to survive, Rackspace has been profitable and is one of the fastest growing hosting specialists in the world. How has Rackspace been successful?

"Our approach is simple – build extensive expertise in managed hosting and stay focused on our customer. This comes to life in our unique philosophy of Fanatical Support™."

Rackspace has recently introduced a new element into their own website – embedded interactive chat. After visiting their website for a short period of time, an interactive chat window appears asking if the Rackspace salesperson can assist the visitor. In a world where pop-up advertisements are considered visual pollution, installing a chat window into the website where customers are seeking website hosting service seems to be a risky maneuver. However, over 50% of the new customers of Rackspace are initiated through the interactive chat sales windows.

1. What risk/reward analysis do you think the managers of Rackspace considered prior to using this method?

2. What contingency plan do you think they had in place in the event of a bad outcome?

the company to accept the possible downside risk. The LRB also decided to pursue purchasing new technology if it became available. This was one of the insights from the value of information and the focus group. The technology development group said that they had seen several promising new products presented to the company, but they thought the company was not interested in purchasing technology. Usually these new products come from inventors looking for a company with resources to finish developing the products.

Using all of this information, the LRB felt confident in their decision and scheduled a meeting to announce the new strategy to the whole company.

13.8 Allocate the Appropriate Resources

Based on the strategy resource requirements, the LRB chartered the project team to develop a resource allocation plan and to present it to them within one month. The resources allocation plan should include nonfinancial as well as financial resources that will be required for successful implementation.

13.9 Integrate the Course of Action

Within two months, the LRB had communicated the new strategy to the company and had allocated the necessary resources for implementation.

14

Using the Scalable Decision Process on Large Projects

Concern without the ability to make decisions is simply "worry."
—Ronald A. Howard

In Chapter 5, I introduced the term Scalable Decision Process and gave a brief introduction to the process. That chapter focused on the macro level, because it was not appropriate at that time to go into more detail. However, this chapter will focus on explaining the actual Scalable Decision Process in step-by-step detail. By examining this process, you will begin to understand how to facilitate large projects. While the overall process is the same regardless of the size of the project, with smaller projects many of the sub-steps are not needed. I included this chapter after having many conversations with practitioners about needing a template for facilitating large projects. While this chapter will provide a step-by-step format for large projects, it will not substitute for a well-trained process facilitator. If this is your first project, I highly recommend seeking help.

Before documenting each step and sub-step in the process, it is important to understand the significance of the SDP diagram (Figure 14.1). This diagram represents both the art and the science of decision analysis in that it incorporates the psychological and subjective aspects of judgement with an analytical tool box.

Facilitating the process is the hardest part to learn, and it can only be accomplished through time and experience. Even if you are a good meeting facilitator, there are new techniques for gathering data and interviewing experts that take time to learn. The science of decision analysis is very straightforward and relatively easy. After reading this book, anyone with basic math skills should be able to perform the mechanics of decision analysis. Because of this, many new practitioners begin the process with-

Gaining facilitation experience

Figure 14.1 The Scalable Decision Process (SDP)

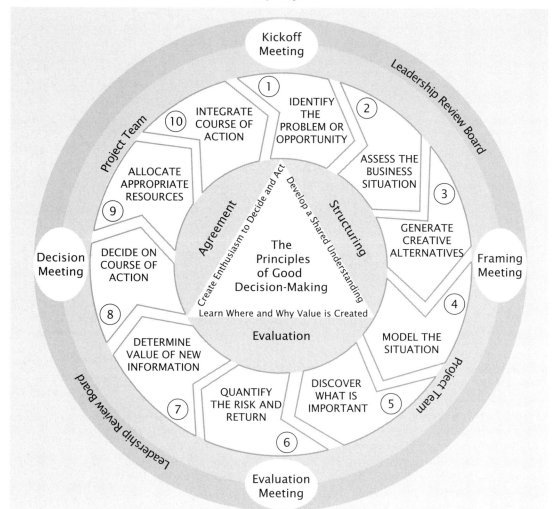

out understanding the facilitation skills involved and end up frustrated. I encourage you to use this chapter as a template for understanding the nuances of the process.

14.1 Understanding SDP

Before discussing the process in detail, I want to explain the significance of the diagram itself. The triangle in the center of the process represents the principles of good decision making. This is the philosophical foundation upon which the process is built. Outside of the triangle, there are three phases of the decision analysis process - structuring, evaluation, and agreement. These phases each have distinct process steps and products which lead to high-quality decisions.

Figure 14.2 The Scalable Decision Process (SDP)

Structuring

1.0 Identify the Problem / Opportunity

1.1	Recognize the need
1.2	Identify project sponsor and team leaders
1.3	Establish leadership review board and responsibilities
1.4	Develop project objectives
1.5	Create team incentive plan
1.6	Build project team(s) and commitment
1.7	Establish team roles, responsibilities, and ground rules
1.8	Develop project vision, scope, and charter
1.9	Generate initial set of project issues
1.10	Educate the team in methodology
1.11	Develop project plan and time line
1.12	Create a project resource list
1.13	Set the valuation criteria
1.14	Create a decision hierarchy
1.15	Establish a project information system
1.16	Develop a project communication plan

2.0 Assess the Business Situation

2.1	Perform stakeholder analysis
2.2	Identify and understand current momentum
2.3	Perform market and segment analysis
2.4	Develop key processes and organizational map
2.5	Develop core enabler assessment
2.6	Develop value creation template
2.7	Perform competitor analysis
2.8	Identify performance benchmarks
2.9	Discover best practices
2.10	Develop performance gap analysis
2.11	Document key learnings and communicate findings

3.0 Generate Creative Alternatives

3.1	Create future business history
3.2	Develop model of ideal competitor
3.3	Brainstorm ideas, issues, and alternatives
3.4	Create strategy table
3.5	Develop strategy write-ups
3.6	Test strategies for creativity and distinctiveness—alternative mapping
3.7	Create influence diagram(s)
3.8	Record assumptions and key uncertainties
3.9	Hold peer+1 focus groups
3.10	Develop alternative communication packet

Evaluation

4.0 Model the Opportunity

4.1	Develop a financial block diagram
4.2	Educate team on evaluation methodology
4.3	Identify content experts
4.4	Develop assessment templates
4.5	Assign assessment tasks
4.6	Assess uncertain variables
4.7	Create financial spreadsheet
4.8	Create decision model
4.9	Develop base case economics

5.0 Discover What is Important

5.1	Perform sensitivity analysis
5.2	Build tornado diagram
5.3	Determine key variables affecting value
5.4	Validate key inputs
5.5	Develop key inputs communication packet

6.0 Quantify Risk and Return

6.1	Build decision tree
6.2	Probabilistically evaluate key inputs
6.3	Create risk profile for each strategy
6.4	Test strategies with leadership team
6.5	Determine inputs causing negative valuation or risk
6.6	Develop strategy hybrid
6.7	Create resource needs assessment
6.8	Assess organizational change readiness

7.0 Determine Value of New Information

7.1	Determine key uncertainties to evaluate
7.2	Evaluate information value of uncertainties
7.3	Identify possible sources of new information
7.4	Estimate quality of new information
7.5	Evaluate value of imperfect information
7.6	Develop evaluation communication packet

Agreement

8.0 Decide on Course of Action

8.1	Compare and contrast strategies
8.2	Decide on acquiring new information
8.3	Make strategy decision
8.4	Understand organizational impact
8.5	Develop integration time line and milestones
8.6	Review decision quality matrix
8.7	Develop change/decision plan
8.8	Create strategy document

9.0 Allocate Appropriate Resources

9.1	Identify financial resource requirements
9.2	Identify human resources in affected organizations
9.3	Identify technical and systems resources
9.4	Allocate financial, human, and technical resources to meet strategy commitments

10.0 Integrate the Solution

10.1	Form integration team
10.2	Develop and define new policies
10.3	Define links with other organizations
10.4	Implement tools and training
10.5	Set up measurements and rewards
10.6	Create strategy communication plan and systems
10.7	Establish on-going review team
10.8	Establish processes to redesign
10.9	Redesign key processes
10.10	Implement redesigned processes
10.11	Monitor strategy results

There are three tenets which summarize and correspond to these phases of the process – develop a shared understanding, learn where and why value is created, and create enthusiasm to decide and act. These three tenets are the basis of the entire decision analysis process.

The ten process steps which encircle the inner circle each represent specific steps required to move from identification of the problem to integration of the solution. Each of these steps has a set of sub-steps which will help guide you through the development of a robust analysis and course of action. Use Figure 14.2 as a checklist to make sure that you have not overlooked a key aspect of decision quality.

Project Team and Leadership Review Board roles

Further encircling the process steps are two layers – the Project Team and the Leadership Review Board. The Project Team is responsible for performing the specific steps in the process, with the Leadership Review Board being accountable for the final product and providing guidance and resources to the project team. A key distinction with this process is the focus on choosing a course of action in the face of uncertainty and implementing it. This is why the Leadership Review Board must be involved with the entire process. There are four main interaction points in the process for review and validation of insights. These interaction points are critical for reviewing work products before proceeding with further steps. In a way these are like phase gates, with the Leadership Review Board being the gatekeeper.

Structuring phase

In the **Structuring** phase, you need to first develop a shared understanding of the problem or opportunity before you can begin to develop an appropriate course of action. At this point in the process, the team members are learning about each other's view of the problem and are beginning to develop a shared understanding. Using this shared understanding, the team is then able to generate creative alternatives which can be evaluated in the next phase. During this phase, the project team elicits the decision maker's preferences and objectives.

Structuring phase example

I once worked with a large manufacturing team which was working on a production line problem. The line was designed for 100% of capacity but would shut down when pushed over 70%. The team included people from research, marketing, senior management, and the plant. Each person came to the meeting with their specific ideas of how to solve the problem, and each person was sure they knew the right solution. There were ideas from de-bottlenecking the plant to building a second plant. As the team talked through the problems they were facing and began to discuss each other's opinions about the problems, they soon developed a mutual or shared understanding of what the final solution should encompass. By gaining this new understanding, the team was able to develop several very creative alternatives for eliminating the production problem which were all better than any of the initial ideas each person had contributed. The key to having a good Structuring phase is to encourage and develop a shared understanding of the problem or opportunity. Use this understanding to search for creative and feasible alternatives which can be evaluated and refined.

The **Evaluation** phase is characterized by the search for value, specifically where and why it is created. I have seen many situations where a team has prematurely decided on an alternative without fully understanding the value or risk implications, only to have either the leadership reject the proposed alternative or, worse yet, to accept it and then not understand why it did not perform as promised. Without an understanding of where and why value is created, it is easy to under or overestimate the value potential and risk of a certain alternative.

Specifically during this phase, the team will learn through sensitivity analysis which factors or uncertainties affect value the greatest and, given the probability of certain events occurring, the risk profile for each alternative. This will allow the team to begin formulating actions which enhance value and mitigate risk. Additionally, the team will investigate the value and use of new information, which might be made available at some cost.

The final phase, called **Agreement**, is where the rubber meets the road. This phase of the process examines the need for further analysis and refinement before integrating the solution into the organization. Deciding on a course of action is only part of this phase and is relatively easy if the team has involved the decision maker in the process. However, making the decision is a long way from integrating the solution into the organization. This is where I see most unsuccessful projects fail. It is a common tactic after deciding on a course of action to simply "roll-it-out" to the organization in a communication and assume that the organization understands and will follow the course of action. In my years of working on both large and small projects for companies, I have never seen this approach work. Strategies are usually complex and involve both near-term decisions and policies for future decisions. These decisions must be explained to the organization in a way that people can see a direct connection to their jobs. Failing to do this will either delay or completely stop the implementation.

This chapter is designed to give you a quick synopsis of the detailed process. Because there are ninety sub-steps I will not go into great detail on any item.

14.2 Structuring Phase

Identify the Problem / Opportunity (1.0)[1]

Many project teams fall into the trap of plunging into the analysis without fully understanding the problem. This will cause the team to do a lot of rework and can result in the analysis not being used at all. The identification step defines the problem or opportunity and what is to be accomplished, establishes who will work on the problem, who will make the decision, and defines the time and commitment required for a high-quality, compelling course of action.

---

[1] Numbers refer to steps noted in Figure 14.2, The Scalable Decision Process.

*Strategic
question*
Asking, "What is the strategic question?" often helps to clarify the problem. A strategic question is a concise statement of what the team is to work on.

Recognize the Need (1.1)

The key to any successful project is the ability of the organization's leadership to recognize the need. The easiest way to recognize a need is if you have a problem, especially when the problem is significant, and you do not see a clear solution. More difficult, but often even more valuable, is the ability to recognize the need to improve when things are going well. This is one of the essential keys of being a leader: to know that even while market share is growing, or employees are increasingly productive, there is still room to improve. While the need can be recognized at any level in the organization, it is important for the right level of management to be committed to the project.

Identify Project Sponsor and Team Leaders (1.2)

Every project needs a **project sponsor**. This person should be on the leadership team and usually is the decision maker or can act as the proxy for the decision maker. The project sponsor is responsible for establishing the guiding roles in the project which include the leadership team, project leaders, and process facilitators or coaches. If the project sponsor does not have the respect and influence needed to create the change necessary, then another project sponsor should be chosen.

*Project team
leader
characteristics*
The project team leader should be someone with respect and credibility in the organization. Do not appoint someone as a team leader who has nothing better to do. This is the kiss of death. The leader should be a person who can effectively lead the team, manage conflicts, and remove operational barriers.

Establish Leadership Review Board and Responsibilities (1.3)

*Leadership
responsibilities*
The reason many project solutions never get implemented is because teams fail to involve the decision makers until too late in the process for them to be comfortable with the project frame or evaluation. For this reason, we must involve the decision makers from start to finish and charge them with auditing the project for quality, consistency, and completeness. The leadership team should be comprised of those who will be responsible for allocating the resources to implement the chosen course of action. In addition, the leadership team is responsible for creating enthusiasm within their organizations for the project and the changes resulting from it.

*Who is the
decision
maker?*
Can this person or board sign the check? That is, does the person have the ability to allocate the resources necessary for implementation? If not, then you probably do not have the right decision maker or leadership board.

Develop Project Objectives (1.4)

After establishing the leadership team, the project team leader and process consultant need to have a rich dialog about the objectives of the project. The project leader should establish a comprehensive set of objectives the project is to achieve. An objectives hierarchy is a great tool for eliciting these objectives. The objectives should encompass both the financial and nonfinancial objectives the decision maker will use to judge the appropriateness of any alternative.

Create a Team Incentive Plan (1.5)

A project incentive plan is a good way for management to show support for the project and to reward the project team for taking the extra time and effort to work on the project. This plan should be a significant show of support by the leadership team. Giving the project team a big dinner or an award is nice, but those do not convey a sense of urgency and importance like a significant incentive plan. While an incentive plan does not guarantee project success, people are generally more focused, put the project first, and achieve the desired results more quickly if there is a good plan in place. Generally, incentive plans are developed for long-term projects that can last up to one year. Smaller quick projects that only last a month or so usually do not require this.

Examples of significant incentives are:

- giving each team member and their "significant others" an all expense paid vacation,
- large monetary rewards (10-20% of annual salary), or
- stock options.

Example team incentives

If the team is being asked to give up time with their families, work on the weekends, or travel a significantly higher fraction of their time, it is a good idea to develop a team incentive plan.

Build the Project Team(s) and Commitment (1.6)

The essential force behind any project is the project or work team. This group of individuals must perform the day-to-day work required to get the project completed. It is well worth investing a reasonable amount of time up front to get the "right people" on the project.

The team members should have a good skill set which reflects the diversity of the work force and draws out the creativity of the organization. In addition, the project team should include members that represent the various business units that the project will affect. Finally, all the **project team members** should:

- be open minded and willing to share ideas,
- have a total company view, not just their domain, and
- be focused on creating value.

Project team member characteristics

Establish Team Roles, Responsibilities, and Ground Rules (1.7)

The size of the leadership and project teams will depend upon the significance of the project and the number of business units affected. In general, the leadership team should be composed of 3 to 6 decision makers and the project team composed of 4 to 6 team members. If a project team needs to be larger, consider splitting the team into a core team which does the majority of the work, and an extended team which gathers data and interacts with the core team.

Project team roles and responsibilities

Establishing and documenting roles and responsibilities provides team members with clarity about what is expected and how they can contribute to the overall project. Documenting these roles and responsibilities ensures that each project activity has an owner responsible for its completion. A large project may involve the roles of a leadership team, a project team leader, a process facilitator, a modeler, team members, and a meeting assistant or scribe. In addition, the project team will require the assistance of content experts, technologists and analysts, and other people with skills and experience which will benefit the team.

The **Leadership Team** provides direction for the project team and will periodically validate key findings and decisions as well as develop management support. The leadership team's principal functions are as follows:

Leadership team responsibilities

- Communicate the need for change and urgency.
- Provide adequate resources for the project.
- Validate project findings and results.
- Ensure project quality and timeliness.
- Communicate management concerns to the project team.
- Actively participate and contribute to the project.
- Be responsible for implementation of the strategy.
- Be an advocate of the team's effort.

The **Team Leader(s)** will coordinate all aspects of team activities and be responsible for managing its work and supporting its members. This person(s) must have strong leadership capabilities and a good understanding of the organization's strengths, weaknesses, and culture. As the leader, this person will be accountable for meeting project goals. Team leader key functions are as follows:

Team leader responsibilities

- Lead the team through the process.
- Develop agendas and manage the work plan.
- Communicate the team's vision and progress outside the team, including dealing with political aspects of the work.
- Seek input from outside the team.
- Identify and implement support for team members.
- Provide individual feedback to team members.
- Organize meetings and reporting.
- Manage specific analyses.
- Act as "devil's advocate" at times to stimulate thinking.
- Coordinate consultants or facilitators.
- Provide resources for the team as needed.
- Participate as a team member.
- Be an advocate of the team's effort.
- Make things happen.

Team Members have the responsibility for most of the day-to-day work required to complete the project. This involves attending all team meetings, actively participating in all team activities and being responsible for meeting project goals. Key functions of the team members are as follows:

Team member responsibilities

- Participate in developing creative alternatives.
- Perform research, data collection and analysis, and assess content experts.
- Take responsibility for team assignments.
- Make recommendations for most efficiently accomplishing team goals.
- Be an advocate of the team's effort.
- Articulate needs, issues, concerns and expectations of those outside the team.
- Provide resources and content for the team.
- Accept responsibility for helping the team accomplish its project goals.

The Project **Modeler** is the person who takes the raw data, information, and assessments and synthesizes this information through the use of an elegant model into insights the team can use to make recommendations. The modeler position is the only position with an exclusive task, which is to build an analytical model. The modeler should be a person with exceptional analytical skills, good organization, extensive experience with spreadsheets and databases, and the ability to work under pressure and tight time constraints. The principal functions of the modeler are as follows:

Modeler characteristics

- Create a financial model block diagram.
- Develop and document all project models.
- Interface with team members to accurately incorporate content assessments.
- Articulate needs and issues which affect the model.
- Run sensitivity and probabilistic analyses.
- Be an advocate of the team's effort.
- Communicate insights and findings to the team.

Modeler responsibilities

The **Process Facilitator** takes responsibility for guiding the team through the decision methodology. He or she tailors this role according to the experience of the team members. The process facilitator's principal functions are as follows:

Facilitator responsibilities

- Facilitate the work of the team.
- Organize team meetings and work with the team leaders.
- Advise team leaders and team members.
- Be accountable for providing the knowledge and methods necessary for successfully accomplishing the project objectives.
- Support and interact with subteams to ensure consistency of methods.
- Educate team members in methodology and skills.

The **Project Assistant** or **Scribe** is responsible for maintaining the project memory. This person attends all team meetings and assists the team in their activities and meeting preparation. The project assistant's primary functions are to:

- Record the meeting notes.
- Help to prepare charts and presentations.
- Distribute documents to team members.
- Provide team administrative support.

RACI chart

After setting the roles of each team member, it is important to have each team member understand his or her responsibility. A good way to do this is with a Roles and Responsibility Matrix, also known as a RACI chart. This matrix outlines each person's role and helps make sure that every project task has an owner. This matrix utilizes four key activities–Accountability (this person is accountable for getting it done), Responsibility (this person performs the work), Consulting (this person provides information, assessments, or other resources), and Informing (these are people who should be informed about the task).

In addition to developing roles and responsibilities, the team should develop a list of team ground rules. These rules should be focused on helping the team to function more efficiently. An example of these rules is listed below:

Example ground rules

- Be on time.
- Don't cut each other off when talking.
- Keep a balance of listening & talking.
- Don't take things personally.
- Clarifying is OK, but don't restate positions.
- Inform "team leaders" when you will miss a meeting.
- If you miss meetings, it is your responsibility to stay informed.
- No hidden agendas.
- Respect other opinions.
- All topics within the scope are fair.
- Air grievances in meeting, not off-line.
- Have fun.

Develop Project Vision, Scope, and Charter (1.8)

To help in setting and maintaining the project frame, it is important to create a project vision, scope and charter.

- The vision describes what we are going to do, how we are going to do it, and what could happen to cause us to fail.
- The project scope is a document for defining the boundaries of the project.
- The charter is a unifying document designed to enhance communication of the project and how the teams are going to work together.

These documents should be developed based upon the objectives of the decision maker.

Figure 14.3 Example Project Timeline

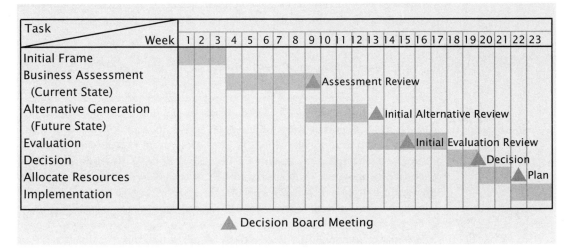

Generate an Initial Set of Project Issues (1.9)

During the project kickoff meeting, the project team and leadership team should have a rich discussion about the issues affecting the project. This set of issues should encompass decisions, uncertainties, information, or values. Refer to Chapter 6 on framing the problem for more information.

There are many ways to elicit an initial set of issues. Techniques like brainstorming, future business histories, and the Delphi method provide a means for teams to generate relevant issues.

Issue generation techniques

Educate the Team in the Methodology (1.10)

A common failure mode, for both external consultants and internal resources, is to not educate the teams about the decision analysis process. Both the project team and the leadership team need education in the methodology. However, the type of education is different for each team. The project team needs training on how to conduct the various analyses and information gathering tasks. The leadership team needs training on how to understand and ask hard questions about the information presented by the project team.

A best practice that I encourage all of my clients to do is to provide just-in-time process training for project teams. This is the best approach I have seen to reinforce training course learnings.

Training the team

Develop Project Plan and Timeline (1.11)

The combined team should develop a project plan and timeline during the kickoff meeting. The project plan should include resource requirements and deliverables along with an appropriate timeline with major milestones. Figure 14.3 is an example of a project timeline. Note that

Microsoft Project software is useful for developing critical path time-lines – there are even third party add-ins for MS Project which allow you to use probabilistic task timing assessments (e.g. @Risk).

Create a Project Resource List (1.12)

The combined team should develop a project resource list. This list should be broken into physical and intellectual resources. The physical resources could include meeting rooms, computer and telecommunication equipment, and other resources available to the team. Included on the list of resources should be a contact person and/or location of the equipment.

The team should also identify the intellectual resources or content experts both within and outside of the organization. Knowing who has the resources and where they are located greatly enhances project facilitation and planning further in the project.

Set the Valuation Criteria (1.13)

In order to evaluate one alternative against another, we must establish a common set of valuation criteria. The objectives hierarchy will provide insight into the valuation or decision criteria for the project. It is the leadership team's responsibility to determine the measure(s) and to articulate them to the project team. The valuation criteria should be clear, meaningful to the decision maker(s), and repeatable.

NPV: a key economic measure of value

While most consultants will tell you that the decision criteria should be expected net present value, I have not found many decision makers who will make a decision using NPV as the economic measure of value.

Create a Decision Hierarchy (1.14)

The issues raised during the kickoff meeting with the combined team usually contain a large number of issues which are decisions. These decisions are usually at all levels, ranging from policy decisions, to those that are givens, to tactical or operational decisions. The decision hierarchy (Figure 14.4) provides a template in which to categorize the various decisions so that the team can communicate which decisions are in and outside of the scope of the project.

Figure 14.4 Decision Hierarchy

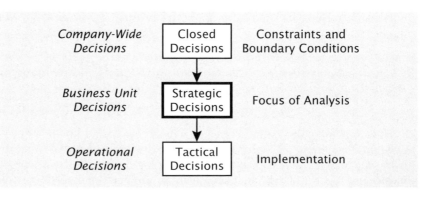

Establish a Project Information Plan (1.15)

Early in the project, the team needs to develop an information plan that describes how the team is going to create, store, and access information. This plan is vital to documenting the project and providing an information trail for the implementation team. Lotus Notes® or other types of groupware applications are well suited for this type of need.

Maintaining the project information system is often the responsibility of the project assistant. While database maintenance should be the responsibility of the organization's IT group, the project team must take responsibility for the quality of the information.

Information plan responsibility

Develop a Project Communication Plan (1.16)

A crucial piece of any project is how the team is going to communicate with the greater organization and receive feedback. This is often an overlooked and under appreciated task. However, it can be the difference between successful implementation and failure. Some organizations have communications specialists who can help you develop an appropriate plan. Otherwise, work with the team to determine what types of communication will be most effective with the organization.

Assess the Business Situation (2.0)

Perform Stakeholder Analysis (2.1)

The project team should understand the perspectives and objectives of the organization's various stakeholders. This is important when formulating alternatives to meet the decision maker's objectives. Many times the decision maker's objectives will include meeting some type of stakeholder criteria like return on investment.

Identify and Understand Current Momentum (2.2)

An important part to assessing the business situation is identifying and understanding what the organization is currently doing. The team needs to understand the current processes and strategies that the organization is following. Without this understanding, it is difficult (if not impossible) to develop and gain acceptance for a new strategy. Also, the team should try to build on processes or strategies that are in place, if possible. Don't just throw out the last strategy because you are developing a new one. There may be valuable pieces of the strategy that can be adapted to the new strategy, thereby saving the team time and the organization the strain of relearning.

Perform Market and Segment Analysis (2.3)

Depending upon the type of business the organization is engaged in, a market or segmentation analysis will likely provide insights and help in identifying value-creating propositions. This analysis also helps with understanding the intricacies of how the business functions.

Develop Key Processes and Organizational Map (2.4)

In developing a new strategy for an organization, it is important to understand the key processes the organization uses to create value, and to understand which and how business units and functional support interact with each other. Knowing how these processes work will lead to a better developed strategy with greater acceptance and ease of integration. Figure 14.5 is an schematic of a key process map.

Figure 14.5
Key Process
Map

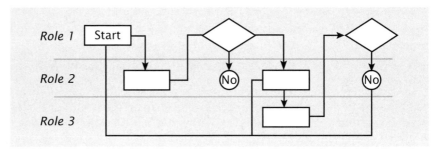

Develop Core Enabler Assessment (2.5)

The team needs to assess the core competencies or enablers (Figure 14.6) that provide unique value to the organization and provide a distinct advantage over competitors. This understanding will feed into the value creation template. "Parity" in Figure 14.6 refers to a comparison versus the competition.

Develop Value Creation Template (2.6)

An understanding of where and why value is created by the organization is very important when developing new strategies or creating project alternatives. There are different value creation templates available. One of the most widely used is Michael Porter's value chain template.

These templates help organizations and teams identify where value is being created and destroyed and provide key insights for the strategy table development.

Figure 14.6
Core Enablers

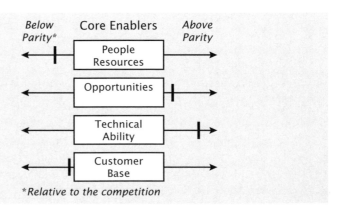

The template illustrated in Figure 14.7 is one that I developed several years ago to describe the relationship between an organization's intellectual and physical assets and how they transform into value.

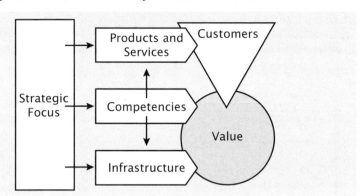

Figure 14.7 Value Creation Template

Perform Competitor Analysis (2.7)

Critical to any successful strategy is an understanding of competitors and their anticipated future moves. There are many different models that can be used such as Michael Porter's "Five Forces" model.

The main idea is to understand a competitor's competencies, strategies, weaknesses, and potential countermoves to your strategy. In addition, developing a competitor map of where a competitor is involved in your industry's value chain is also effective in understanding the competitor's possible future moves. Figure 14.8 is an example of such a map.

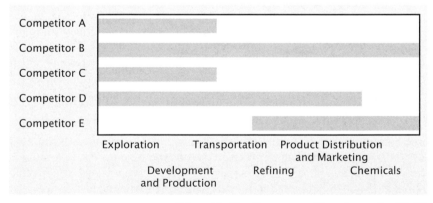

Figure 14.8 Example Competitive Map (Oil Industry)

Identify Performance Benchmarks (2.8)

Benchmarking between similar and dissimilar organizations can often provide new and useful insights into better ways of achieving your business goals. Using benchmarking data can provide the team with insights into value creating activities and provide a better understanding of competitors' business intents. However, you must understand the accuracy of benchmarks and have a means to validate the data before drawing conclusions (Figure 14.9).

Discover Best Practices (2.9)

From the benchmarking surveys, you will undoubtedly discover best practices. These best practices may be in your own organization or may come from others in the benchmarking study. Best practices often provide breakthrough thinking and results. The team should include best practice insights in its discussion with the organization and with decision makers. If a best practice provides a significant competitive advantage, this should be noted.

Figure 14.9
Example
Benchmarking
Assessments

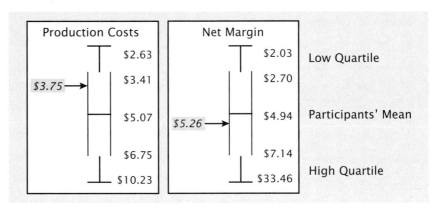

Note that it is easier to identify best practices than to successfully replicate those practices in your organization.

Develop Performance Gap Analysis (2.10)

The performance gap analysis is a way to compare your current processes and results to those of other competitors or benchmarking partners. Once you have compared your results to those of best-in-class, you can begin to formulate plans for closing the gap. A gap analysis is beneficial for creating unique alternatives and for developing stretch goals.

Document Key Learnings and Communicate Findings (2.11)

The last but maybe most important step in this phase is to document and communicate key findings. Without this documentation and communication, many projects fail to produce the desired results. The communication should focus on key insights developed during this phase. The insights should also be documented in the Decision Quality Package.

Generate Creative Alternatives (3.0)

This part of the methodology requires the team to really expand their boundaries and to think "out of the box." I have seen projects where the alternatives developed by the team were only incremental changes from the current strategy or alternative the company was pursuing. While this may occasionally be appropriate, often the "new" alternative is not compelling or the organization does not view it as a change from the current course of action.

Create Future Business History (3.1)

This exercise is designed to get the project team thinking about the future and how their strategies either "succeeded" or "failed." This type of exercise is especially helpful at the beginning of this phase to help breakdown biases, barriers, and preconceived solutions.

To create a future business history, pose a situation where the company had either a fantastic success or a huge failure at some time in the future, usually five or ten years from the present time. Have team members work in groups of two and develop a Wall Street Journal type of article. Then have the team discuss the insights from the exercise.

How to create a future business history

Develop Model of Ideal Competitor (3.2)

Another exercise that aids in expanding the collective mind of the project team is the concept of an ideal competitor. This exercise allows the project team to construct a competitor with only what the team feels are the best characteristics. After doing this exercise, I like to ask why their organization has not tried or implemented some of these qualities or abilities. This provides a good basis to start brainstorming possible alternatives.

Brainstorm Ideas, Issues, and Alternatives (3.3)

The brainstorming at this phase is to further stretch the team's thinking about alternatives. Brainstorming is a great tool to elicit ideas, issues, and possible alternatives. Brainstorming is not new, and most teams feel comfortable in doing this type of exercise. Be sure to allow adequate time for the team to brainstorm.

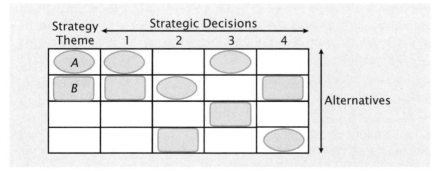

Figure 14.10 Strategy Table

Create Strategy Table (3.4)

Strategy tables (Figure 14.10) use the strategic or "focus" decisions from the decision hierarchy and connect the possible choices into a coherent set or theme. The alternatives for each decision can come from the previous exercises or from a new brainstorming session. The goal of the strategy table is to quickly develop a reasonable set of possible strategies. Strategy tables provide a means of thinking about all the possible combinations of decision alternatives, but only doable combinations are evaluated.

Figure 14.11
Strategy Map

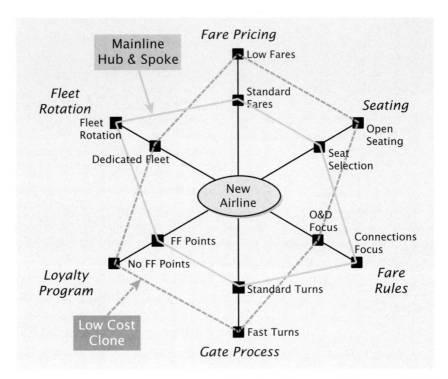

Develop Strategy Write-ups (3.5)

Developing strategy tables helps to link each of the decision alternatives together into a coherent set of decisions. However, these tables do not adequately tell a complete story. Each of the decisions (and, more importantly, the interactions and combinations of decisions) must be fully described in clear terms so the whole organization can understand the distinctions of each strategy.

Test Strategies for Creativity and Distinctiveness (3.6)

Once the team has developed a set of strategies which they believe will accomplish the decision maker's objectives, they need to test those strategies for both creativity and distinctiveness. *Creativity* has to do with how unique the strategy is to current momentum, while *distinctiveness* has to deal with how different each of the new strategies are from each other.

A good tool for testing both of these dimensions is the strategy map (see Figure 14.11; figure courtesy Gary Bush, Decision Strategies).

Create an Influence Diagram(s) (3.7)

At this point, the team now has a well defined set of possible strategies to pursue. With each strategy defined as to the decisions that must be made, we now need to understand the timing and interactions of those decisions and the uncertainties which will affect the value. An influence diagram provides the means to graphically communicate the nuances of each strategy. The influence diagram can also be used as a map for developing the deterministic decision model.

Record Assumptions and Key Uncertainties (3.8)

After creating an influence diagram, it is very useful to record in a table format the key uncertainties and assumptions that were made when the diagram was created. This information can then be used when assessing the content experts.

Hold Peer + 1 Focus Groups[2] (3.9)

After developing and testing the strategies internally with the project team, the group needs to test the strategies with the larger organization. A good way to do this is with focus groups composed of team member peers. These groups usually have a good dialogue and free flow of information, therefore, the larger organization has a chance to provide input to the strategy and becomes more comfortable with the alternatives the team will evaluate in the next step. In addition to peer interaction, it is good for the team to take the alternatives to the next level above the peer group. This interaction often provides valuable insights that would not be received without that discussion.

Develop an Alternative Communication Packet (3.10)

After holding the peer group discussions, the project team should develop a communication packet for greater distribution throughout the organization. This communication packet should contain the alternatives considered, the basis for the alternatives, and the assumptions and key uncertainties affecting the value.

14.3 Evaluation Phase

Model the Opportunity (4.0)

Once a comprehensive set of alternatives have been developed and validated by the decision maker, the team will need to evaluate the alternatives. The first step in evaluation requires building a decision model.

Develop a Financial Block Diagram (4.1)

A first step in building an evaluation or decision model is to diagram the model in simple terms. This block diagram provides a simple means of communication, both within the project team and with content experts, as to how the model will function and transform their inputs into value outputs. Figure 14.12 is an example of a simplified block diagram.

---

[2] By "Peer+1," we mean the peer group plus the next level of management higher up.

Block diagram purpose

The purpose of building a block diagram is to quickly explain to the decision maker and project team members how the evaluation model will convert the chosen alternatives into a quantitative value.

Figure 14.12 Block Diagram

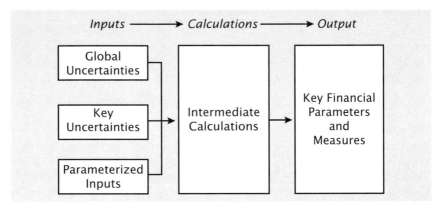

Educate Team on Evaluation Methodology (4.2)

In continuing with the use of just-in-time training, the project team and the leadership team need to have training on how the process of evaluating the various alternatives will work. The project team needs training in how to conduct a high-quality content assessment, how to build financial and decision models, and how to analyze these models to reveal insights. The leadership team needs training on how to interpret the insights from the project team and what questions to ask to ensure a high-quality analysis.

Identify Content Experts (4.3)

After diagraming the financial model and reviewing the resource list and key uncertainties table, it is time to identify who will provide the actual assessments for each of the uncertainties in the model. The influence diagram is a good tool for both identifying and communicating the various content experts who will provide the data for evaluation.

Identify the correct experts

The project team needs to review the identified content experts with the decision maker before gathering the data. Often decision makers will have a particular expert in mind, and without that person's input, the decision maker will not believe the results.

Develop Assessment Templates (4.4)

After identifying all of the content experts needed to complete the assessments for the model, the team needs to develop a common assessment template that will be used in assessing the experts. This common template should provide easy data compilation, common terms and understandings, and consistent data scaling.

Assign Assessment Tasks (4.5)

With the content experts identified and the templates developed, the project team must then decide who is going to do the assessments.

Gather Key Uncertainty Assessments (4.6)

The process for gathering the key assessments is somewhat simple and straight forward, but it often causes team member confusion and difficulty until it has been done a few times. The assessments should be gathered using the 10-50-90 tool. By gathering a range of data, the uncertainty can be adequately addressed and experts do not feel that they are being held accountable for a specific outcome. See Chapter 10 on how to perform expert assessments.

Create Financial Spreadsheet (4.7)

While the uncertainty assessments are in progress, the person designated as the team's modeler should be putting together the financial spreadsheet. This spreadsheet is based upon the financial block diagram

Gasoline Additives – What Do We Really Want?

It is well known that certain chemicals act as detergents when added to motor fuels. These chemicals clean deposits from intake values (IVD) and port fuel injectors (PFID) resulting in more complete combustion in the engine and lower emissions.

In July, 1997, the US Environmental Protection Agency (EPA) mandated that gasoline retailers "ensure that all gasoline sold or transferred to the ultimate consumer is properly additized with certified detergents". The EPA states on its website, "Implementation of the detergent certification program will realize the full expected environmental benefits of controlling IVD and PFID, namely, reductions in emissions of hydrocarbons (HC), carbon monoxide (CO), and oxides of nitrogen (NOx), and improvement of fuel economy."[*]

Prior to these requirements, gasoline sold in the United States may or may not have contained a detergent additive. Many gasoline retailers used additives as a means to differentiate their product on the market. The marketing claims they made were substantiated by laboratory or field testing by the gasoline retailer or by the additive supplier to the satisfaction of their internal controls (and lawyers).

In establishing the new regulations, the EPA created a "government approved" minimum standard test protocol that all detergent additives must pass in order to be called a "certified detergent". All gasoline retailers were required to put a certified detergent additive into their fuel.

While many gasoline retailers were forced to put detergents into their fuels where previously there was none, the creation of a minimum standard resulted in the total fuel detergent usage in the US market to decline. Since every gasoline had some minimum detergency by law, there was less room for differentiation in the market and many companies that were previously adding a significant dose of detergent defaulted to the minimum standard.

The program's goal was to increase detergent usage in gasoline sold in the US with the stated benefits, but the outcome was a reduction of detergent usage.

1. Can you think of other alternatives the EPA could have evaluated in selecting its strategy?

2. How could use of decision analysis framing tools affected the EPA's decision making?

3. What are other examples of policy implementation that result in outcomes inconsistent with the original policy objectives?

[*]http://www.epa.gov/oms/regs/fuels/additive/fact7gda.htm

and the influence diagrams. The objective of this spreadsheet should be to validate base case economics and provide the framework for deterministic analyses.

Keep the model as simple as possible

When building the project spreadsheet, keep in mind that the model should be kept as simple as possible and is not being built for accounting purposes but for generating insights into the best course of action.

Create the Decision Model (4.8)

The decision model is usually the second phase of the financial spreadsheet. In this phase, the decisions which affect the value proposition or outcome of the model are coded into the financial spreadsheet or developed in a specialized software package such as TreeAge Pro®.

Develop Base Case Economics (4.9)

At this phase in the process, the modeler should produce a financial package for the team members with the base case economics of each strategy and the key uncertainty assessments. The base case economics are the values for each strategy with all of the inputs set at their base or "50" values. These values are the first evaluation or quantitative insights developed by the team. However, these insights only provide a deterministic (non-probabilistic) look at the values of each strategy.

Discover What is Important (5.0)

The focus of the evaluation phase is to understand what is important in choosing a particular course of action. This involves developing insights into the various uncertainties which affect the strategic decisions and validating those insights with the decision maker and project team members. Without these quantitative insights, any strategy developed is left to ambiguity and advocacy.

Perform Sensitivity Analysis (5.1)

Sensitivity analysis is a means to identify what variables are important in creating the value of a strategy. A sensitivity analysis is easy to perform with any spreadsheet program and a simple macro. The basic idea of the analysis is to swing each variable from its low to its high input value and record the change in the output value. By doing this, you can quickly determine the impact each variable has on the overall strategy.

Build Tornado Diagram (5.2)

The tornado diagram is a means of displaying the sensitivity analysis previously performed. A tornado diagram displays the impact of each variable by establishing a baseline case (all inputs at their base case) and then plotting the swing in value of each variable as bars around the baseline case. The variable bars are then arranged from largest swing to smallest swing. This yields a bar graph on its side which looks like a tornado. It is important to remember that the tornado diagram is not probabilistically weighted and therefore only indicates the deterministic change in value.

Determine Key Inputs Affecting Values (5.3)

From the tornado diagram, it is easy to quickly identify variables which greatly impact the value of the strategy, both positively and negatively. When examining variables, it is important to not only look at independent variables but also dependent variables. If there are conditional uncertainties in the decision model, a purely independent tornado will not properly illustrate the swings in value.

Validate Key Inputs (5.4)

After determining the key variables which most impact the value of the strategy, we need to validate those variables with respect to the range and base values that were assessed. As with all models, garbage-in is garbage-out. This quality step is necessary before proceeding with further evaluation of the alternatives. The validation of these variables should be performed by content experts in a peer type validation exercise.

Develop Key Inputs Communication Packet (5.5)

After performing the deterministic analysis of the strategies, it is important to communicate the analysis to the greater organization. This information packet should include a brief discussion of the model (including a block diagram), a list of the key variables and content experts, the tornado diagram, and base case economics for each strategy.

Quantify Risk and Return (6.0)

After evaluating the key variables which affect value in a deterministic manner (all scenarios are equally likely), the team needs to probabilistically evaluate each strategy. Many times we see a switch in the decision that would be made once the probabilities are included.

Build Decision Tree (6.1)

The first step in quantifying each strategy from a probabilistic view is to create a decision tree. Decision trees provide a means of evaluating all the possible paths or scenarios that emanate from a decision or set of decisions and ultimately determine the possible outcomes. Decision tree packages such as TreeAge Pro® can link into the financial spreadsheet models and automatically run all of the analyses and create the risk profiles.

Evaluate Key Inputs Probabilistically (6.2)

After building the decision tree, we need to evaluate the key variables. Because decision trees expand in an exponential manner, we need to only include those variables which have the greatest impact on strategy value, leaving the other variables at their base values. Generally the top three to six variables in the tornado are what should be included in the probabilistic analysis.

Create Risk Profile for Each Strategy (6.3)

After evaluating the decision trees for each strategy, we need to create a risk profile for the strategies. This risk profile plots the value measure or decision criteria against the probability of achieving a given value. These plots are an important means of communicating the range of value and the probability of achieving any particular value to the decision makers.

Explain the risk profiles

Risk profiles are probably the best communication tool for describing the relative risk of one strategy to another.

Test Strategies with Leadership Team (6.4)

Once the full evaluation of each strategy has been completed, the leadership team should review and test the strategies for robustness and for meeting the goals and objectives set forth in phase 1. The leadership team should provide the project team with guidance on which strategies interest them the most and if there is a strategy they would like to see that is not currently defined.

Determine Inputs Causing Negative Valuation or Risk (6.5)

Most projects or strategies involve a downside risk of losing money. A key insight is to determine which variables are causing the negative valuation. Then brainstorm possible ways to either mitigate or eliminate the risk of loss.

Use the trees

Decision trees can provide valuable insight into the paths which create negative value and often help a team think of ways to mitigate the consequences

Develop Strategy Hybrid (6.6)

Using the input from the leadership team and an understanding of what causes negative valuation, we should look at creating a hybrid strategy. A hybrid strategy can be a combination of the best parts of several strategies or a completely new strategy from the team or the decision maker. Not all situations require a hybrid, and many times a hybrid is no better than the alternatives developed (incremental change). But it is important for the team to think carefully about the set of alternatives that have been developed to make sure a valuable alternative has not been left out.

Create Resource Needs Assessment (6.7)

Once we have a robust set of strategies, we need to develop a comprehensive set of resource needs for each strategy. These resources may include financial, marketing, personnel, technical, and research. This information will help the decision maker fully understand the impact and resource requirements for each strategy.

Resource assessment

A resource assessment can be as simple as a set of bullet points, or as complex as a full resource audit. However, at this phase bullet points are usually sufficient.

Develop Organizational Impact Assessment (6.8)

To implement any new strategy, or even a project, you will probably impact organizations other than your own. We need to develop an impact assessment and begin working with representatives from those organizations if they were not already included in the project team. The types of impacts that should be included are changes in resource levels, personnel, inter-unit charges, and effects on other business units.

Value of New Information (7.0)

Having evaluated each strategy from a deterministic and probabilistic manner, we now need to think about what would allow us to resolve some of the uncertain variables.

Determine Key Uncertainties to Evaluate (7.1)

The project team should now look at determining what uncertain variables could be or should be evaluated with respect to information. All variables that deal with the future are uncertain, however, some are more uncertain than others. If you can gather new information that would resolve the outcome of a variable, you can significantly reduce the risk or uncertainty of the whole strategy.

The key uncertainties which impact value the most will come from the top of the tornado diagram.

Use the tornado diagram

Evaluate Information Value of Uncertainties (7.2)

Before acquiring new information to resolve any uncertainty, you should be asking questions such as: "What uncertainty will the information resolve?" "How reliable is the information and what should I pay for the information?" We can determine the maximum amount you would ever pay for perfect information by addressing the uncertainty before making the decision.

The value of perfect information is the maximum value you would ever pay for perfect information. In nearly every situation, your information will not be perfect and you should pay less than this value.

Determining information's value

Identify Possible Sources of Information (7.3)

After determining the maximum value for attaining perfect information, the team should brainstorm possible information sources. Often during the kickoff meeting, teams will create an information wish list that identifies many of the sources of information.

Estimate Quality of New Information (7.4)

After determining the possible sources of information, the team must look at what sources might be the most relevant and reliable. The team needs to determine in a quantitative manner what they think the quality of the information is before purchasing the information. The team can estimate the quality of the information by using internal experts who have dealt with the information sources in the past, by asking for references, or by developing a relative scoring system for the information.

Evaluate Value of Imperfect Information (7.5)

After understanding the possible sources of new information and the associated quality of the information, we can determine the maximum we should pay for that imperfect information. The calculation for determining the value of imperfect information is in Chapter 11.

Develop Evaluation Communication Packet (7.6)

At the end of the evaluation process, the team needs to develop a communication packet for the general organization. This packet should include what strategies were evaluated and why; what the evaluation indicated in relation to value, risk, and resources needed; and the possible sources of new information and the value of obtaining that information.

14.4 Agreement Phase

Decide on Course of Action (8.0)

The focus of any decision analysis is the course of action which is chosen. However, this is where many organizations lose value if the decision is merely passed to someone to "make it happen."

Compare and Contrast Strategies (8.1)

Include both value and risks of each strategy

After evaluating all of the possible strategies and paring them down to a few significantly different and creative strategies, the team should present the remaining strategies to the leadership team. This presentation should focus on the value and risks of each strategy and the differentiation of the strategies.

Decide on Acquiring New Information (8.2)

The leadership team should be presented with the value of information calculations, and they should determine whether the new information should be gathered before making the strategy decision. The team should not use this as a means to delay making a decision if the decision maker is confident in the chosen alternative.

Test for value of more information

Information only has value if it could change the decision or provide insights with more value than the cost!

Make the Strategy Decision (8.3)

The leadership team has to either make the decision to go with one of the strategy recommendations or to ask for another iteration due to a lack of clarity or commitment. This iteration process is very rare if the team has engaged and integrated the leadership team and its thinking during the project.

Understand Organizational Impact (8.4)

After making the decision as to the strategy, the project team must examine and understand the organizational impacts of the specific strategy and begin working with the various affected organizations to develop commitment to action.

Many strategies fall apart because other parts of the organization are not on board with the recommendation.

Consider all stakeholders

Develop Integration Timeline and Milestones (8.5)

The project team needs to develop an integration timeline, which details how the strategy will go from a thought process and decision model to action and value creation. This integration timeline is where many organizations integrate with project planners and other project management resources.

In addition to the timeline, the project team needs to develop and set milestones for the strategy integration. Milestones should be specific with the required action, desired results, and rewards.

Review Decision Quality Matrix (8.6)

A decision quality matrix is a good way for teams to review the work they have done and to provide insights into future projects. It should be part of the decision quality package and include any key team learnings. Key questions include: "Did the project team achieve the quality of strategy and commitment they had envisioned?" "If not, what could be improved in future projects, and what should still be improved in this project?"

Develop Change/Decision Plan (8.7)

The change plan is a written document outlining what should be accomplished during the integration and how it will be accomplished. This document is critical if the implementation team is different from the project team. It is also useful as a communication packet for the organization.

Create Strategy Communication Document (8.8)

The strategy communication document should be designed to concisely illustrate the strategy from concept to action and should relate how the strategy will affect the organization and its employees on a day-to-day basis.

Allocate Appropriate Resources (9.0)

An often overlooked part of strategy development is allocating the appropriate resources once a decision has been made. Without this allocation of resources, a strategy project is no more effective than a paper study which sits on a shelf in someone's office.

Identify Financial Resource Requirements (9.1)

The project team should identify the needed financial resources, when they are needed, and who needs to be involved to allocate the resources. The best way to do this is to keep a resource requirement journal during the project.

Identify Human Resources in Affected Organizations (9.2)

The project team also needs to identify the human resources and skills needed for the strategy to be implemented and how it will affect the various organizations.

Identify Technical and Systems Resources (9.3)

In addition to financial and human resources, the project team must address technical and systems resources. In most large strategy projects, the existing organizations have processes which will impede the full value creation of the strategy. These processes must be identified and changed, or if no change is to occur, the decision maker must make a conscious choice recognizing potential consequences.

Allocate Financial, Human, and Technical Resources to Meet Strategy Commitments (9.4)

The final step in this phase is actually allocating the needed resources. Allocation of resources usually requires more time than most teams anticipate. For this reason, it is often a good idea to have a team member follow the allocation of resources to ensure that time is not wasted.

Integrate the Solution (Implement Course of Action) (10.0)

Form Integration Team (10.1)

The project and leadership team need to work together to establish an integration team to implement the strategy. Often many of the people who were on the project team are also on the integration team. However, the integration team will need a different set of skills than the strategy team. For this reason, it is good to bring on team members with project management experience.

Develop and Define New Policies (10.2)

The integration team needs to develop and define new policies as to how future decisions which affect how the strategy will be implemented should be made. These new policies should only provide guidance so that future decisions will not be in conflict with the accepted strategy.

Define Links with Other Organizations (10.3)

The team must define the on-going and future links to other organizations. These links provide the information flows needed to keep the strategy on track and to know when changes need to be made. All organizations that are affected by the new strategy should have some means of effective communication so that key issues are discussed during and after implementation of the strategy.

Implement Tools and Training (10.4)

In general, implementing a new strategy often requires training and educating the general organization on new tools. These tools and processes are often a part of the organizational assessment or other needs identified by the project team.

Set up Measurements and Rewards (10.5)

The integration team should set measurements and rewards which promote the strategy integration and provide valuable feedback. It is important to carefully select the measurements as you usually get what you measure. Also, the organization should reward individuals and groups for implementing in a way that is consistent with what was designed – arbitrary changes without a sound business purpose consistent with the preceding work should not be rewarded.

Create On-going Communication Plan and Systems (10.6)

The integration team must set up an on-going communication plan and a system of disseminating and receiving information. Communication is most often the stumbling block in strategy implementation. I have yet to find an organization which claims to need less communication.

Establish On-going Review Team (10.7)

There often needs to be an on-going review team which will preside over the strategy implementation. This team should be charged with the responsibility for ensuring the quality of the implementation.

Examine Processes to Redesign (10.8)

The integration must also examine processes identified during the strategy as potential candidates for redesign. If a current process will impede the implementation or value creation of a strategy, the process is a candidate for redesign.

Redesign Key Processes (10.9)

With the key processes for redesign identified, the integration team can either work on the redesign or charter a redesign team which would include key implementation personnel.

Implement Redesigned Processes (10.10)

As with the rest of implementation with a new strategy, the implementation of redesigned processes typically requires a direct and concerted effort by the team. It is not enough to do the paper redesign and assume the organization will accept the implementation.

Monitor Strategy Results (10.11)

As we learned in Chapter 1, a "good decision" does not necessitate a good outcome. Even if your team completes all phases of decision analysis and implementation with excellence, there are always uncertainties involved and the outcome can be less favorable than desired. Having an effective means of monitoring the results can provide the organization with an opportunity to take advantage of a favorable situation or to enact any pre-planned risk mitigation plans that might be needed. Additionally, the organization can learn from the results and these learnings in the next decision analysis issue.

14.5 Summary

Use the process outlined in this chapter as your guide as you implement decision analysis projects. This will allow you to scale the process appropriately for each project and will allow you to bring the appropriate quality of thinking to your projects. Do not neglect any of the three phases of a project: structuring, evaluation, or agreement. Be flexible yet complete in your thinking. Use good judgment and teach your teams how to use the tools which have been presented here.

15

Portfolio Analysis and Management

It is only in our decisions that we are important.
—Jean-Paul Sartre

So far, this book has examined decision making as it relates to single projects. This chapter discusses a broader topic – Portfolio Management – and how the same concepts that assist in making good decisions in single projects can help when faced with difficult decisions concerning multiple opportunities.

15.1 Introduction to Portfolio Analysis and Management

A ***Portfolio*** *is a collection of projects, investments or opportunities that compete for the same resources.*

Portfolio defined

Examples include a research and development portfolio of projects or a financial portfolio of investments. Even a sports team can be considered a portfolio of athletic talent.

Resources are anything that must be allocated to a project or investment for it to be completed. This includes money, time, people, raw materials or equipment. An example of a monetary constraint would be a department budget. Time resources can be available man-hours to work on a project or time on a piece of specialized equipment. Additionally, people resources are typically not fungible. The skill set of each person should also be considered when allocating resources based on the needs of the projects.

Portfolio analysis and management are useful when one or more of the resources are limited and not all the projects can be funded. The portfolio manager is faced with a series of decisions concerning which projects should be funded and which ones need to be placed on hold. In the unlikely, but enviable, event that none of the resources are in short supply and all projects have sufficient time, money, people, and equipment to proceed, portfolio management is not necessary. In that case, the project manager can simply direct the projects individually to best effect. The number of projects or investments might be sufficient, but the manager should ask whether or not the portfolio has been considered broadly enough to meet the company's objectives.

Portfolio management is not about the individual assessment of projects. Usually, but not always, the projects for consideration are worthy of funding outside the portfolio consideration. If a project has a negative net present value, the portfolio management process is not going to improve that value unless there is some synergistic effect with another project such as reduction of cost or improvement of benefits. This can occur when the projects are not independent and completing one project has an impact on another. The combination effects of the projects should be considered in the portfolio analysis.

Strategic interest   Additionally, if there is some overriding non-financial attribute of the project that makes it worthy of consideration that should also be included in the analysis. An example would be a loss-leader type project that paves the path forward in the Far East. Such a project might be considered strategic and included in the portfolio regardless of the economic evaluation. Frequently, projects might be identified as essential to the continued business. If the portfolio manager believes that to be true, these projects should probably be included in the portfolio as a baseline or as givens regardless of their expected financial results.

Just as the "givens" are confirmed with upper management in the decision analysis process, the givens in the portfolio analysis should be justified and reviewed with management.

15.2 Portfolio Management System Objective

Simply stated, the objective of the portfolio management system is to add clarity to a complex set of decisions. The result should be an optimized set of investments or projects that maximizes the return on available resources, aligns with corporate objectives, and meets the short and long term needs of the company.

A portfolio management system should answer questions such as:

Questions a portfolio management system should address

- Which projects should receive funding?
- What is the priority of the projects?
- Do the funded projects align with the strategic goals and objectives of the company?
- Does the portfolio have the right risk balance?
- Is the company spending enough in short and long term projects?
- Are all the products being supported?
- How much spending is appropriate between updating old products and developing new ones?
- Are all the company's resources utilized for maximum benefit?

- Where is the "low hanging fruit"?
- Will the portfolio provide for the company's needs into the future?

Unfortunately, there is no one portfolio analysis and management system that has universal applicability to all business environments. Specifics of the analysis need to be tailored to the needs of each company. The portfolio manager can use these guiding principles and examples to construct a system that fits within their unique situation.

Most companies rely heavily on their own set of heuristics to decide how much to spend in which area of the business. Also, successful systems involve several iterations through the process with periodic updates.

Gillette – The Beginning of an Empire

Our story begins with a middle-aged salesman who was also a part-time inventor. At the age of 40, he had accumulated four patents, but none of his inventions managed to attract much interest. He seemed destined to spend the rest of his life traveling from town to town in swaying trains selling other people's products.

One morning in 1895, as he was preparing to begin another long day on the road, his frustration hit the boiling point. His straight razor wasn't working. As he tried to sharpen it, he realized that the blade was so worn that it wouldn't hold an edge. If this random scribble were done as a cartoon, this would be the moment when you'd see a light bulb appear above the salesman's head.

Wouldn't it be great, he thought, to own a razor that never needed sharpening? Perhaps one that worked with disposable blades that could be thrown away when they were dull? Imagine how wonderful it would be to create a razor you could actually use on a train without risking a severe flesh wound.

He immediately grabbed a pen and paper and scribbled a quick note to his wife. "I've got it!" the note read. "Our fortune is made!"

Although it would take several years of hard work and sacrifice for his dream to become reality, King Camp Gillette had taken the first steps on the road to inventing the safety razor. In 1901, with the help of William Emery Nickerson, Gillette perfected the double-edged safety razor blade, which fit into a specially designed holder with a handle and an adjustable head.

Then, he had one more stroke of genius.

He began giving his razors away for free. Of course, once you owned a free razor, you needed to own the blades to have a functional unit. By the time 1910 dawned, Gillette was 55 years old and he had become both rich and famous. His company dominated the razor business and, since his face was on every package of razor blades, his became one of the most recognized faces in America.

Disposable razor blades turned King Gillette into a millionaire.

1. What risks and uncertainties did Gillette face as he started up his new company?

2. If Gillette had been working for you and brought you the idea of giving the razors away for free, what would you have thought? How would you have reacted?

3. As Gillette planned to expand his company, what criteria do you think he used as he considered additions to his portfolio?

Some characteristics of an effective portfolio management system are as follows:

*Characteristics
of an effective
portfolio system*

- Uses a common set of agreed upon measures to evaluate projects and contains a methodology to gather that information
- Provides for an accurate assessment of available resources
- Does not overburden the process with unnecessary analysis
- Provides a method to evaluate risk and uncertainty
- Helps balance the risk and uncertainty versus the potential value of the project
- Provides a means to assess projects for strategic alignment and value
- Provides a multi-faceted analysis approach to the data
- Periodic updates and reviews to modify the portfolio as needed

15.3 Strategy and Portfolio Management

Should the company strategy come from the portfolio of projects or should the portfolio of projects be developed from the company strategy? While the answer may seem obvious, that the company strategy should determine which projects are selected, many companies struggle with this concept.

For example, since many business managers are unsure what is technically feasible for the research departments, they might say to the R&D Manager, "Tell us what products you can develop and when they will be available and the company strategy will be developed around those factors." Obviously the strategies of the company should not be based on impossible expectations, but limiting the overall goals of the company on the sometimes arbitrary constraints of one department can be a serious mistake.

As mentioned, an effective portfolio management system will circulate the portfolio among the stakeholders within the company to ensure alignment. If the business strategies are based on unreal expectations, iteration through the business units will shed light on the situation. If the resource constraints of one department are blocking the company from achieving its objectives, maybe further resources can be made available. Maybe outside expertise can be secured to bolster the internal resources. Maybe the entire business segment needs to be reevaluated.

*Beyond
addition*

Merely summing the individual projects with the highest net present values within the constraints of the resources is not difficult, but creating a set of projects that not only provides excellent financial results but also aligns with the company's objectives and goals can be a complex task. Balancing the projects with the future needs of the company can cause a different set of projects to become important. Allowing for flexibility within the portfolio and for freedom to stretch and explore new areas should also be considered when developing a portfolio.

Sometimes portfolio managers select projects based on their intuition or allow project managers free reign to work on what they desire. While this approach may produce a workable portfolio, it is very unlikely to result in the most effective combinations of projects, and the company will likely have performance and efficiency below that of a competitor who uses an effective system. An effective portfolio analysis and management system reduces the risk that the right combination of projects eludes the intuition of even the most experienced managers.

15.4 Effective Portfolio Analysis and Management

The first step toward effective portfolio analysis is the development of an agreed upon set of common parameters to evaluate each project in the collection. As discussed in other chapters, using a probabilistic technique to gather and model the data is an excellent way to capture and provide insights concerning the inherent risk and reward for the individual projects.

A list of direct financial parameters is the easiest place to begin to gather data. Some examples of typical values used for portfolio analysis include:

- NPV – net present value
- ROI – return on investment
- ROR – rate of return
- IRR – internal rate of return
- CPI – capital productivity index (NPV divided by capital investment)
- Capital Investment
- Revenues
- Personnel costs
- Raw Material Costs
- Any Other Limited Resource Costs

Portfolio analysis measures of value

While critically important, the financial parameters are only one dimension used by the portfolio analysis. For example, a maximized financial return portfolio might be short sighted in providing for the next strategic business move planned by the company or in supporting an existing, yet vital, product line. Another danger of using a single financial metric can be ignoring the timing of the cash flows. If all the projects are long term, the company's pipeline of new products might run dry causing a cash flow deficit in the short term.

In order to develop a portfolio that provides balance as well as alignment to the goals of the company, factors such as probability of success (commercial as well as technical), alignment to vision or strategy, type of products, type of projects, time to completion, percent complete, etc. will need to be included in the analysis.

The non-financial parameters can be difficult to assess, as most are subjective and consolidating a variety of opinions can be complex. It is important to maintain consistency within the assessments so the projects can be compared effectively. One useful method in achieving a common understanding and agreement is to bring a diverse group together to jointly develop the data. If that is not feasible, circulate the data among various business units for comment.

Portfolio analysis: compare the projects

The second step in the portfolio analysis system is to use the collected data to compare and contrast the projects. Different types of visual charts and various permutations of the data can add clarity to the analysis. The data should be plotted in different formats to allow for comparison of the projects along as many dimensions as necessary.

Bar charts, pie charts, and histograms are also very good tools to present the various aspects of the project data. Other types of charts can provide further information on the same graph. As examples, the points on the chart can be colored to represent different product groups, varying sized bubbles can be used instead of points to reflect capital investment required, error bars can be added to provide an indication of the risk inherent in each project, etc.

The simplest charts are two dimensional plots of one parameter such as project value compared to another like probability of technical success. Two dimensional plots can be divided neatly into four quadrants of the grid to provide groupings of the projects.

For example, high value and high risk (low probability of success) projects can be grouped as "Long Shots" (Figure 15.1 shows an example of this type of plot for an example portfolio). Obviously, the company does not want a majority of the portfolio tied up in Long Shots projects. As you can see, this type of chart can assist in creating balance in the portfolio.

The danger of presenting too much data on one chart or creating too many charts is information overload. The portfolio manager can quickly become overwhelmed, confused and "analysis paralysis" may result.

Figure 15.1 Probability of Success versus NPV for an Example Portfolio

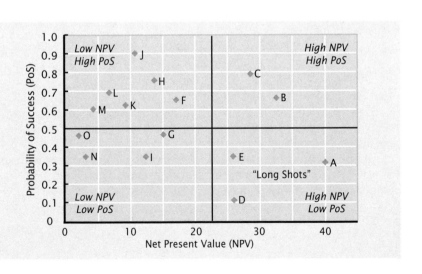

Deciding which charts are important and useful and which to ignore is a critical component of establishing an effective portfolio management system.

Remember, the charts should be used to provide clarity to the analysis. They are not decision making tools per se, but they are tools to help the manager distinguish between projects and to develop the best set of projects that fit within the strategic objectives, provide the highest potential financial gain, optimize available resources, and balance the short and long term needs of the company.

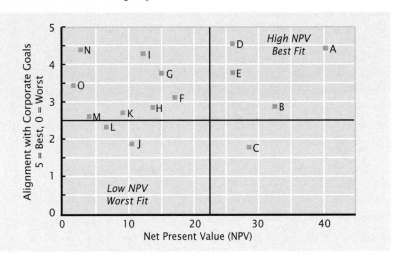

*Figure 15.2
Corporate
Alignment
versus NPV*

Other dimensions of the projects should be fully explored. Examples of charts that might be useful include:

- Strategic importance versus NPV
- Alignment with goals, vision or objectives versus NPV (Figure 15.2 shows this graph for the same example portfolio as is shown in Figure 15.1).
- Probability of technical success versus CPI
- Probability of commercial success versus NPV
- NPV or expected NPV versus investment
- NPV or expected NPV versus manpower (Figure 15.3)
- Investment versus product line categories
- Investment versus type of project (short, long term, etc.)
- Investment versus type of product (upgrade to existing, new, etc.)

*Potentially
useful portfolio
charts*

Figure 15.3
Manpower
versus NPV

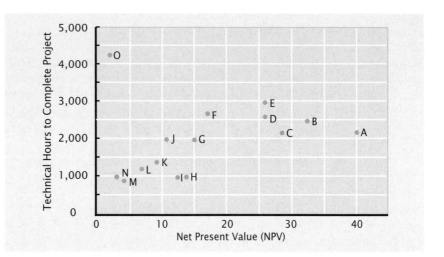

Many other permutations of ways to present the data are possible. Remember, the objective is to add insight for the decision maker(s).

15.5 Creating and Testing Balance Within the Portfolio

Unfortunately, there are no set of common rules or guidelines for achieving balance within a portfolio. The type of balance the portfolio manager should strive to achieve depends upon factors within the company itself. The manager should first understand the needs of the company and translate those into the requirements for the portfolio. For example, if a company is young and has only a few strong products, that company might need a flexible portfolio that is heavy in developing new products quickly as opportunities arise. If a company is mature and already has a stable product slate, the portfolio might include more projects to upgrade or support existing products to defend the current business base. A business that is searching for new markets might include a large investment in high risk – high reward projects to explore new areas of potential business.

Here are a few examples of the types of balance that may need to be achieved in the portfolio:

Portfolio
trade-offs

■ Risk versus value
■ Number of total projects in each business area or product
■ Number of early developments versus later
■ Number of risky projects versus projects with high probabilities of success
■ Number of new products versus upgrades to existing
■ Number of fast projects versus long term
■ Number of projects in various market segments

Whatever the needs of the company, the portfolio should try to match those needs. In order to include as many viewpoints as possible within the time constraints, the portfolio manager should cycle the recommended portfolio and the justification for each project through as many other managers as feasible.

15.6 Selecting the Right Portfolio Management Tools

Deciding what information is important and which graphs to use can be a daunting task the first time a portfolio analysis and management system is put into place. Each new piece of information adds to the permutations of charts and graphs that can be constructed and the portfolio manager can quickly become inundated in lines and curves. With each layer of information, the portfolio manager should ask:

- Does this add clarity to the decision making process?
- Is this information important enough to include in the analysis?
- Does this information present a differentiation between the projects?
- Can I decide between projects using this information?

Deciding what to present

The portfolio analysis should begin with the simple charts and graphs such as:

- Rank order of projects by Net Present Value
- Rank order of projects by Investment
- Rank order of projects by requirements for other resources

Using this type of information, the portfolio manager can hopefully begin to sort the projects into those which obviously need to be included and those which should be considered first for being placed on hold. The portfolio analysis process should narrow the choices to a smaller subset of projects where difficult decisions need to be made.

Once the initial analysis is complete, the portfolio manager can move forward to the more complex data presentations and begin to include the balance items and the non-financial considerations. Be careful not to present too much information on the same graph as that only leads to confusion.

Some examples of more complex graphs include:

- Probability of success versus Net Present Value
- Grouping by project type, product type, geographic location, etc.
- Number of total projects in each business area or product
- Number of new products versus upgrades to existing
- Number of fast projects versus long term
- Net Present Value versus risk
- Net Present Value versus Capital Performance Index
- Capital Efficiency Curves

More example portfolio analysis graphs

Table 15.1
Example
Portfolio Data

	NPV $MM	Technical Hours	Slope	Cumulative NPV	Cumulative Technical Hours
Project A	40.3	2,200	0.0183	40.3	2,200
Project H	13.6	1,000	0.0136	53.9	3,200
Project C	28.6	2,200	0.0130	82.5	5,400
Project B	32.5	2,500	0.0130	115.0	7,900
Project I	12.2	1,000	0.0122	127.2	8,900
Project D	26.0	2,600	0.0100	153.2	11,500
Project E	26.0	3,000	0.0087	179.2	14,500
Project G	15.0	2,000	0.0075	194.2	16,500
Project K	9.0	1,400	0.0064	203.2	17,900
Project F	17.0	2,700	0.0063	220.2	20,600
Project L	6.5	1,200	0.0054	226.7	21,800
Project J	10.5	2,000	0.0053	237.2	23,800
Project M	3.9	900	0.0043	241.1	24,700
Project N	2.6	1,000	0.0026	243.7	25,700
Project O	1.5	4,300	0.0003	245.2	30,000

Efficiency
curves

Efficiency Curves are very useful tools to compare projects. The efficiency curves can be created with almost any set of financial or numerical information, such as investment or professional-hours. The x and y axis show the cumulative data starting from zero and ending at the sum of all the values. The data is sorted such that the highest slope (y value / x value) for the projects runs from left to right – highest to lowest.

To create an efficiency curve using the number of technical-hours needed to complete a project and the net present value, first create a table of all the values (See Table 15.1).

Since the NPV will be plotted on the Y-Axis and the technical-hours will be shown on the X-Axis, the slope calculation is the NPV divided by the Technical Hours. The units for the slope are million dollars of NPV for one technical hour. This is a measure of the resulting NPV for every technical hour invested. Next, sort the table from highest to lowest slope and add cumulative NPV and Technical-Hour columns as shown in the following table. The resulting efficiency curve is shown in Figure 15.4.

The higher NPV per Technical-Hour projects are toward the left with the less efficient projects to the right on the curve. The vertical line shows the Total Technical-Hours available. The projects to the left of that line should be considered for the portfolio while those to the right should be placed on hold, based on this one dimension. The same type of efficiency curve can be created for other combinations of data. These curves are particularly useful when optimizing the portfolio for the constrained resources.

The portfolio manager also has the responsibility to ensure that the portfolio is balanced and aligned with the corporate goals and objectives. To accomplish these tasks, each project should be assessed for how well it matches the overall corporate strategies and individually where it fits within the business. Plots or graphs of number of projects in each business area or product group can aid in creating a balanced portfolio. For example, if the business objectives for the next five years are based on increased sales of one product class, the portfolio should include enough projects in that area to prepare for that growth.

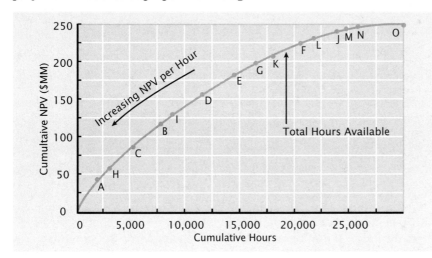

Figure 15.4
Efficiency
Curve:
Cumulative
NPV versus
Cumulative
Hours

15.7 Efficient Frontiers

At a constant investment, such as the budget, there exists a set of all possible project combinations or portfolios that sum to that investment. Each portfolio in the set has its own value and risk profile. A graph of the value versus the risk for each portfolio on a scatter plot defines the decision space for the portfolio manager. The standard deviation of the expected value NPV for each portfolio is a good surrogate for the risk of the portfolio.

As shown in Figure 15.5, a curve connecting the highest value portfolios (the uppermost points on the chart) defines what Harry Markowitz, a Nobel Prize winning economist, described as the Efficient Frontier or Markowitz Frontier. The points on the efficient frontier curve represent the best combination of projects or investments or the highest value portfolios. The points below the curve are considered sub-optimal, or alternatively stated, the portfolio points that make up the efficient frontier are considered to be dominant to the points below the curve. These charts can be created for any of the limited resources - time, money, people, or equipment - to show the sets of portfolios that optimize that resource.

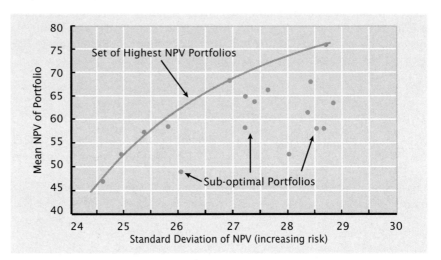

If a project is included in the portfolio due to some non-financial attribute such as it helps the company achieve a critical strategic objective, the entire portfolio might fall below the efficient frontier curve. The delta between the curve and the value of the portfolio is an estimate of the cost for selecting a less than optimized set of projects. The cost might be in money, time, equipment or people.

If the budget or total investment is not fixed, a useful chart comparing all the combinations of portfolios at various levels of investment can be constructed such as Figure 15.6.[1]

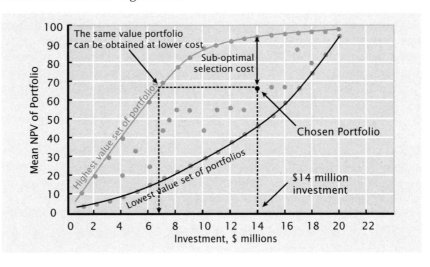

[1] After Klimack, William K., Gregory Lamm, Gregory Parnell, and Brian Stokes. "Army Budget Prioritization," INFORMS Annual Conference, Denver, Colorado, October 26, 2004.

The gray line represents the set of highest value portfolios. The black line is the set of lowest value portfolios, and the space between the lines is the decision space of possible value – investment combinations. If the lines are close together, there is little danger in selecting a sub-optimal portfolio. If there is a large decision space, as shown in the figure, the selection of a sub-optimal portfolio can be expensive in terms of un-realized value and high investment costs.

15.8 The End Result of a Portfolio Analysis and Management System

As mentioned earlier, the goals of a portfolio analysis and management system are:

- Provide clarity in selecting the right mix of projects or investments
- Optimize the portfolio for maximum financial return within the resource constraints
- Develop a rationale and justification that can be supported
- Align the portfolio with the business objectives and provide for both the long term and the short term business needs

Most successful portfolio management systems involve iteration through the various business units or stakeholders within the company. Ensuring that as many points of view within the company are consider and included in the analysis will help guarantee an effective portfolio.

15.9 Summary

Portfolio Analysis and Management are necessary when the following are true:

- A collection of projects or investments are competing for the same resources.
- The resources are limited in some way such that all the projects or investments can not be made simultaneously.

The objective of the portfolio management system is to add clarity to a complex set of decisions. The result should be an optimized set of investments or projects that maximizes the resources available, aligns with corporate objectives, and meets the short and long term needs of the company.

The portfolio analysis is done using a common set of criteria for each project. Visual charts and graphs are used to provide clarity to the sets of decisions to be made. The portfolio manager should narrow the projects/investments to a smaller subset by eliminating the less resource efficient projects and including the high value – high efficiency projects.

The remaining projects can then be reviewed in much greater detail. The portfolio also should be tested for balance and alignment with the corporate goals. Circulating the final portfolio along with the rationale and justification to the various stakeholders within the company will ensure that all points of view are considered.

15.10 Key Concepts

portfolio analysis
resources
constraints
efficiency curves

efficient frontier
portfolio balance
alignment with corporate goals

15.11 Study Questions

1. When are portfolio analysis and management necessary?

2. What is the first step in portfolio analysis?

3. What is common among all projects or investments to be considered for a portfolio?

4. How can you ensure that a portfolio includes all the viewpoints of the relevant stakeholders?

5. What is an efficiency curve? And what is it used for?

6. Name three permutations (x-axis and y-axis) of visual charts that can be used for portfolio analysis.

7. Name two important ways that risk or probability of success should be used in portfolio analysis.

8. Why should the portfolio manager progress from simple charts and graphs to the more complex ones in the analysis?

9. What caveats should the portfolio manager be aware of in creating the portfolio?

10. Should negative NPV projects be included in the portfolio?

15.12 References and Further Reading

Cooper, Edgett, and Kleinschmidt. "Portfolio Management for New Products." Reading, Massachusetts: Perseus Books, 1998.

Klimack, William K., Gregory Lamm, Gregory Parnell, and Brian Stokes. "Army Budget Prioritization," INFORMS Annual Conference, Denver, Colorado, October 26, 2004.

Allen, Michael S., "Business Portfolio Management, Wiley, 1999.

William Haskett, Marco Better, and Jay April, "Practical Optimization: Working with the Realities of Decision Management," SPE Paper number 90497, SPE Annual Technical Conference, September 2004.

15.13 Guide to Action

1. Create a set of agreed upon common parameters with which to evaluate each project.

2. Gather data on each project – financial – technical – probability of success – type of project – type of product – etc.

3. Gather information on the corporate goals and objectives.

4. Assess each project with regard to alignment with the corporate goals.

5. Start with simple visuals to develop a baseline of projects to include and ones to consider for being placed on hold.

6. Progress to the more complex visuals to add clarity to the decisions on the remaining projects.

7. Test the portfolio for balance and alignment with corporate goals.

8. Circulate to stakeholders with rationale.

9. Iterate and test as needed until the portfolio is optimized.

15.14 Case for Analysis: "Portfolio Analysis"

Mike is the Director of the Marketing Department for Big Products, Inc. His budget for the upcoming year has been significantly reduced and the programs Mike had planned need to be reviewed. This is the first time since Mike took over as Director that all the programs did not have adequate funding.

As Mike considered which programs to fund and which ones to cancel, he realized that he needed more information.

- What financial information does Mike need?

- What non-financial information should Mike use?

- What types of graphs would be helpful to Mike in deciding which programs to fund?

- How can Mike ensure that his viewpoint on which programs are important and which can be postponed or canceled agrees with the other stakeholders within the company?

16

Implementing the Decision Analysis Process

Nothing is a waste of time if you use the experience wisely.

– Rodin

Decision analysis is currently being applied to many different types of problems in many different industries.

- Oil and gas companies are using it to analyze investment portfolios and to determine the value of additional information before making drilling decisions.

- Pharmaceutical companies are using it to help determine which drugs to commercialize and to better understand the probabilities of commercial success.

- Utilities and large manufacturers are using it for customer demand forecasts and new product launches and acquisitions.

- Even the motion picture industry is beginning to use it to analyze their portfolio of projects.

There has probably never been more activity in decision analysis than there is right now.

I wrote the preceding paragraph over ten years ago, and I am still amazed at how fast decision analysis is being adopted. Even then, I did not imagine the response that I have seen in the past few years. There is now a practitioner focused group called the Decision Analysis Affinity Group or DAAG (www.DAAG.net), which promotes sharing of ideas, best practices, and pitfalls at an annual conference. Each year this group has grown significantly; it now has over 65 member companies which are using decision

Decision Analysis Affinity Group

analysis. However, all of these companies have experienced implementation difficulties or as James Mitchell of DSI puts it, "crossing the chasm." Because very few companies have integrated decision analysis into their organizations, implementation issues and ideas are a constant topic at these meetings.

Pascal's Wager – What do You Believe?

One of the more famous decision analysis problems was presented by Blaise Pascal (1623-1662), a French mathematician and religious scholar. What has become known as "Pascal's Wager" deals with the existence of God and mankind's decision whether or not to believe in that existence and to live a pious life here on Earth.

The decision tree for Pascal's Wager is as follows:

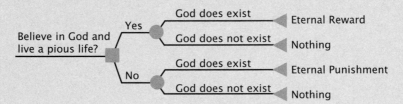

The decision to believe in God has two branches – YES, believe in the existence of God and live a pious life (or however a life pleasing to God would be defined) and NO, do not believe in God and live however one desires. The uncertainty is whether or not God exists. Pascal postulated that if God does exist, He rewards belief and punishes those who did not believe. If He does not exist, nothing happens either positively or negatively.

It was Pascal's thinking that since belief in God cost the decision maker only the sinful pleasures of this world they would forgo to lead a pious existence and the consequences of being right or wrong were so dramatic (infinite), it was only logical that everyone should believe in God.

Pascal's supposition is based on there being a non-zero probability that God does exist. Since the reward or punishment is infinite, even a minute probability that God does exist makes the decision a choice between eternal punishment and eternal reward.

There have been many criticisms of Pascal's Wager and his underlying assumptions. For example, there have been challenges to the premise that God rewards belief and punishes non-belief. If the reader is interested, further information is readily available (for example, see http://plato.stanford.edu/entries/pascal-wager/).

We are interested in Pascal's Wager from a decision analysis point of view because decision makers can find themselves dealing with a "Pascal's Wager" situation. How would you use decision analysis to deal with these examples of "Pascal's Wager" situations?

1. How much should a company spend on safety to prevent the potential loss of life?

2. What speed limit on US highways should be mandated as every mile per hour increase represents more accidents?

3. How much should businesses spend on reducing greenhouse gas production since global warming could be disastrous to the environment?

4. How far should the government legislate to protect potentially endangered species?

16.1 Implementing Decision Analysis

When people talk about implementing decision analysis in their organizations, this can mean several different things. In some organizations, implementing means hiring a consultant and using them as a contractor, usually only for large projects. This may be appropriate given the organization's desire and immediate ability to change its culture.

Other organizations have adopted a centralized approach and have set up internal consulting groups. Often these groups engage external consulting firms to help with training, coaching, project facilitation, and work load balancing.

Several approaches to implementing decision analysis

Some organizations use a decentralized approach, which involves training people throughout the organization to perform analyses in their own business units. This approach is useful when there are many important projects in diverse parts of the organization, and a centralized group could not handle the project diversity or work load.

Finally, there is a combination of all three approaches. Each approach has certain benefits and pitfalls for both the decision maker and the organization. In this chapter, I will discuss experiences that I and others have had with these various approaches and hopefully give you some insight into what approach may work best for your organization.

Why is Implementation Difficult?

Implementing decision analysis using any of the approaches above is a challenging undertaking for most organizations, regardless of size, but even more so for large corporations with multiple layers of management. Often, the more layers of management in an organization, the more the organization functions in an advocacy mode. Using decision analysis requires us to change the way we think about the world and incorporate new information. It also changes the context within which we process this information.

Because decision analysis is radically different from the traditional business decision process, implementing decision analysis is more difficult and challenging than most organizations imagine. I will discuss what I consider the five biggest reasons implementations have difficulties or fail and some possible approaches to overcome them.

Decision Maker Support

Probably the biggest difficulty most organizations have is getting the initial decision maker support and understanding of the process. Most decision analysis implementation efforts start at a staff or mid-management level in the organization. There are very few organizations where decision analysis is initially championed by the top executives. This is because many executives (and analysts alike) view this as another tool for evaluating projects, not as a culture change for the organization. So ask yourself this question, "Why should a senior executive spend time thinking about implementing a new evaluation tool?" The answer is they should not.

Changing culture versus a new analytical tool

So what does this mean for you in trying to get decision analysis implemented in your organization? You must educate the decision makers as to how decision analysis can help them in making decisions and how it can change the overall decision making culture of the company. Because decision analysis is focused on insight development, creative alternatives, and uncovering of biases, it is a radically different and new approach that executives may find frustrating. Without education, executives may feel an initial loss of control due to the change in how decisions are made – from optimistically biased reports which hide the inherent uncertainty – to analyses which bring the uncertainty to light. This feeling of losing control can be overcome through internal or external courses focused on the decision maker's role in the process.

However, in most implementation efforts I have seen, decision makers either never attend a course or are the last people to attend. The following quote came from a 1969 survey of decision analysis users in industry: "Decision analysts have indeed been pioneers and missionaries on behalf of decision analysis...their impact has been seriously limited, however, by the absence of appropriate educational efforts aimed at the decision makers...we have very few key decision makers who are *alive* to its possibilities and comfortable in its use."[1]

For successful implementation, the decision makers should be the first to attend a course, and the course should provide an understanding of what to expect from the process and how they can participate. For example, when Conoco initially implemented decision analysis, they required all of its executives, including senior vice presidents, to attend the same three day course as the rest of the company. By doing so, the executives were able to experience the entire process and quickly gained an understanding of how it could help them. Without this education, it is difficult for decision makers to understand how the decision analysis process differs from the traditional business decision process and how their role has changed from authoritarian to participatory. This education is also important in providing insight into the types of resources necessary to perform this process.

Process Resources

Regardless of the implementation approach used, the organization must make a commitment to provide adequate resources and to act on the recommendations generated by those resources. When I talk about resources, I mean the internal and external people who will be performing the decision analysis process. This includes subject matter experts, project leaders, facilitators, process consultants, analysts, and decision makers. Because decision analysis is focused on developing the best

---

[1] J.T. Axon, Manager, Management Science Division, DuPont.

Table 16.1 Decision Analysis Process Roles

	Participant	Executive	Practitioner	Consultant
Abilities	Understands DA process and tools	Understands DA language and outputs	Able to lead process with coaching	Understands nuances and people issues
Specific Skills	Issues and ideas	Effective DA utilization for insight and action	Framing, expert interviews and analysis	Practitioner skills plus related process consulting
Process Roles	Content contribution	Alignment and quality assurance	Facilitate parts of the process and team work	Internal consultants to lead projects and coach practitioners

course of action, more people are usually involved than in the traditional business decision process. Each person has a specific role in the process, and each role requires a different levels of training. Table 16.1 illustrates the different roles and levels of knowledge or training needed for each resource.

As you can see from the table, each process role requires different skills and competencies. This fact is sometimes overlooked when implementing decision analysis. Often organizations believe everyone should have the same level of training and understanding. Typically these organizations offer a single decision analysis course, usually three days, for the whole organization. However, this is not always appropriate and may actually be a waste of time and money for the organization. This is because there is a bell curve effect (Figure 16.1) which impacts the acceptance and use of any new process. Usually 10-20% of the organization are energized about the process and want to learn more and begin applying it immediately.

Then there is the other tail of the curve, with a corresponding number of people who do not believe in the process and resist using it. These people may vigorously fight the process when working on project teams.

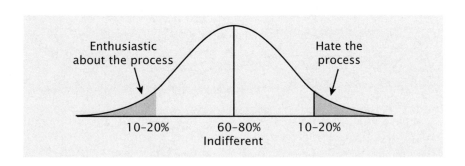

Figure 16.1 Process Acceptance Bell Curve

The majority (60-80%) of the people attend a course and find the process useful. They will use it for their work if required to do so but seldom try to apply it on their own. This usually happens because the course was not at the right level of detail or it did not make a personal connection with the participant.

Training

The organization needs to understand and determine what level of training is appropriate, given different process roles and how the organization wants to implement decision analysis. In general, for organizations that want either a decentralized or a centralized approach, I recommend the following training curriculum:

Example
training
curriculum

Participants – a one-day introductory course
Decision makers – a one or two-day decision maker course
Facilitators – a three or five-day advanced course in addition to the introductory course
Consultants – all the courses for the facilitator plus a ten-day consulting course

Decision analysis is like any other discipline – if you don't practice the discipline, you will lose or forget some of the skills. So, in addition to the initial training, the organization should develop a training curriculum for maintaining and enhancing skills. These courses should provide additional hands-on exercises for people to further develop their skills.

Becoming skilled in decision analysis is not a trivial task and cannot be accomplished through a few courses. I have taken many courses offered by universities and consultants on decision analysis. While most of the instructors will tell you it takes more than a quick course (I always tell my students a short course does not make you competent in decision analysis) to become proficient in decision analysis, some will not.

Figure 16.2
Training Model

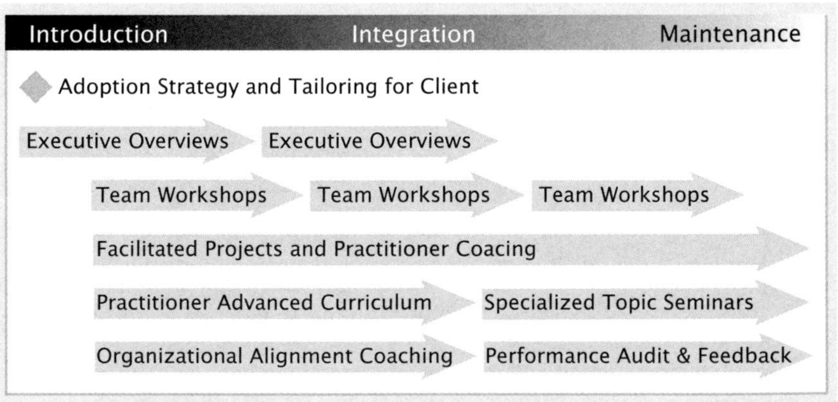

| Introduction | Integration | Maintenance |

Adoption Strategy and Tailoring for Client

Executive Overviews   Executive Overviews

Team Workshops   Team Workshops   Team Workshops

Facilitated Projects and Practitioner Coaching

Practitioner Advanced Curriculum   Specialized Topic Seminars

Organizational Alignment Coaching   Performance Audit & Feedback

I have found that it usually takes about 600 hours of in-depth training and project time for a person to become proficient in the process. Using 600 hours per person as a rule of thumb often discourages executives and analysts alike, but I always reply with this question – would you hire an engineer with only a few days of training to design a new product or a building? The answer is always No! But because of the clarity and simplicity of decision analysis, many people believe it is as simple as attending a few training courses. In my work as a consultant, I have developed training curriculums for many clients. I have developed (in conjunction with Decision Strategies, Inc.) a training model (Figure 16.2) which is useful for corporate clients

Time Commitment

Any consultant, researcher, or instructor will tell you that it takes time to learn a new technology or process. While some people may trivialize the learning curve, it is real. There are two parts to the decision analysis learning curve – process mechanics and process facilitation (See Figure 16.3). Learning the mechanics of decision analysis is by far the fastest. I define mechanics as knowing how to build decision trees, spreadsheet models, influence diagrams, strategy tables, etc. Most of these tools can be learned in a short amount of time. The slow part of the learning curve is the facilitation of the process; this is also somewhat of an art. While anyone can learn the mechanics, some people do not have the desire or personality for facilitation.

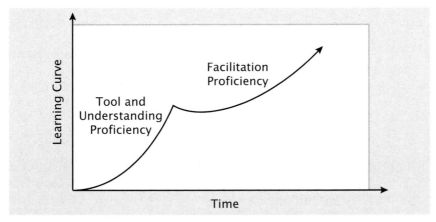

Figure 16.3
Learning Curve

The effects of this learning curve have a definite impact on how fast an organization can implement decision analysis. As I mentioned earlier, it usually takes about 600 hours (approximately 6 months) for a person to become semi-proficient with the process. As you can see, this is a significant time commitment for both the individual and the organization. Many organizations like General Motors, ExxonMobil, and Chevron have been working on implementation for more than five years. So you may be asking the question, "Is it worth it?" In my opinion, yes!

Decision analysis provides a framework for developing options and acting upon them in a way that promotes a shared understanding of the problem and possible solutions. In doing so, the organization will spend less time refining trivial issues and forecasts, and spend more time focused on issues which most greatly impact the bottom line of the organization. By eliminating the rework and analysis paralysis of the traditional business decision making process, the organization will actually make better decisions faster and with more confidence than in the past. Decision analysis can also provide much more insight and creativity than the traditional process.

In addition to having appropriate resources, decision maker support, proper training, and an adequate time frame, the organization must choose the right test project.

Choosing the Right Test Project

Regardless of how much training a person has, the only way to really learn the process is by doing. This is also the only way the organization will realize the benefits of the process. But it is important to choose the right test or pilot project(s). The first few projects that apply decision analysis should be chosen carefully, as they will set the tone for the implementation. The organization will closely watch how these projects impact the decision making culture of the organization.

There are a few guidelines that can help in choosing the right pilot project. These include having a project which:

Test project selection guidelines

- is important to the organization,

- is not too difficult to solve,

- has a high degree of uncertainty and / or ambiguity,

- is not merely validation of an already-made decision, and

- can be communicated to the whole organization.

16.2 What is Right for Your Organization?

As I previously explained, there are several different approaches to implementing decision analysis. Each approach may be valid, depending upon the company, its culture, and how it intends to apply the process. There are several key questions that an organization should answer before it decides what approach to use. These few questions drive to the heart of why and how an organization should implement decision analysis:

Questions to consider

- What is the nature of the business and its decisions?

- How large is the organization?

- How dispersed is decision making and accountability?

- How willing is the culture to change?

The nature of the business and the decisions that it makes are important in deciding an appropriate implementation approach. Many companies try using a decentralized or network model. This allows for many users across the company to act as process champions and can help speed up the implementation process. If the business has many high-stake decisions with a high degree of uncertainty and/or ambiguity, then this approach may be very beneficial. By using the decentralized approach, the organization can spread the use and more importantly the understanding of decision analysis more efficiently throughout the organization. Typical industries with these types of projects include the oil and gas and pharmaceutical industries. Also, industries with many routine decisions may want to consider a decentralized approach due to the possible number of applications.

While the decentralized approach is preferred by many organizations, it takes the longest to implement and also encounters the most analysis quality problems. Another major drawback of this approach is finding and training enough people who can devote a major portion of their time to this effort. An important distinction in the decentralized approach is whether there will be process champions in each business unit or whether everyone in the organization is expected to use the process. In the latter case, I have yet to see this approach become truly effective, as only a small portion of the people trained will use the methodology or become proficient enough to use it (see Figure 16.1 again).

Decentralized decision analysis implementation

When I was with DuPont/Conoco, we started with a centralized approach in the "Downstream" or products section of the company. I spent a little over five years building an internal consulting team that could handle projects across the company. At that time, the company did not want to pursue a decentralized approach. The central group had several advantages including project quality control, internal consultant expertise, and process network development. A centralized approach may be appropriate for an organization that makes a few very high-stake decisions per year, such as large manufacturing, biotech, or product development companies. In these situations, it is paramount that the decision analysis be of the highest quality, since only a few decisions per year will be analyzed in this way.

Usually these centralized functions work closely with the senior management of the organization and provide analyses, advice, and support. The centralized approach may also be appropriate for other organizations which plan to keep the process internal, that is, not using external consultants. In this case, the central group can develop a functional excellence in the process and act as an internal consultant to the organization. Also, the group can be the point of contact for all internal clients of the organization. Typically, most organizations gravitate to this approach in the early years of implementation as a way to maintain control on quality, provide a critical mass of educated and experienced people, and minimize process confusion.

Centralized decision analysis implementation

The downside to this approach is the limited number of projects which can be handled, as very few organizations will build a large centralized group.

*Table 16.2
Implementa-
tion Styles*

Implementation Style	Benefits	Concerns
External Consultants Only	• Fast response • High-quality analysis • External perspective	• Limited client capability development • Very expensive
Internal Consultants Only	• Less expensive • More flexibility • Client capability development	• Limited external perspective • Quality can be inconsistent
External Consultants as Coaches	• Faster client capability development than internal • Consistent quality	• Limited consultant accountability
External Consultants Working Side-By-Side	• Best client learning experience and capability development • Cost effective	• Can take longer than external only

*Using external
consultants*

Another approach is to only use external consultants. While you may not consider this a means of implementing decision analysis, it actually is the easiest implementation for an organization. If an organization decides that it does not have the time, resources, or commitment to internalize the process, this approach may provide the most benefit to the organization. This is also how most organizations start using decision analysis, as they are usually sold the process by a consulting firm. The only problem with this approach is that you may never internalize the process, and therefore miss many opportunities to add value. This approach is also costly as most consultants charge between $2,000 and $5,000 per day. In Table 16.2, I have described some of the benefits and concerns of the different approaches.

*Hybrid
implementa-
tion approach*

Finally, the approach that I have found most useful with clients in various industries is to use a little of each. In the beginning, every organization is going to need help from a consultant to develop training programs, work on projects, and help to educate the decision makers. A core team or centralized group will usually form either out of necessity or by executive charter. This group should act as the internal quality monitor and the contract manager of the external consultants. In this role, the central group can learn from the consultants and at the same time have more flexibility in project manpower. As the understanding and use of decision analysis grows, the organization will move to a more decentralized approach where each business unit will have its own resources. At this point, the central group can provide additional support through partnering with the business unit people on projects and in promoting the benefits of the process to the business unit leaders. The organization should be able to maximize its value for the process by leveraging the different process people. In addition, the consultant should be in a coaching more than a consulting role for the organization to internalize the process.

16.3 Implementation Issues

There are several major implementation issues that have surfaced in the past few years with organizations that have been trying to integrate decision analysis and change the organization's culture. These issues include:

- maintaining the initial enthusiasm,

- creating and maintaining technical competence, and

- developing an advancement ladder.

Typical implementation issues

Maintaining the Enthusiasm

There are about ten large companies which have been pursuing an implementation strategy for more than five years. All of these companies have experienced some difficulty in maintaining the enthusiasm of the initial pilot projects. This is not to say that implementation is not progressing, but the rate has slowed. While there are probably many reasons for this, I often think that it is due to a lack of continued training and development and lack of appropriate rewards. I have still not seen companies actively rewarding teams for making good decisions; we are still stuck on the outcomes. I hope in the future this will change, but for now we must think of ways to maintain that initial thrust and enthusiasm.

Maintaining the Technical Competence

As important as maintaining the enthusiasm for the process is maintaining the expertise and technical competence of the internal process champions and facilitators. In the decentralized approach, it is more difficult to maintain technical competence in the various business units as people internally change jobs or leave the organization. Without a plan to maintain the business unit competence, the business unit may find itself without the appropriate resources to staff projects. The same can be said for the individual. If the organization does not have a training program or plan in place, the process champions and facilitators will not further develop their skill sets.

Developing an Advancement Ladder

An issue that is always a hot topic at the DAAG conference is the development of an advancement ladder for dedicated resources. In most organizations, you remain on an engineering or finance track regardless of whether you are doing decision analysis 100% of the time or 10% of the time. For the full time resources, this is becoming a problem as there is no promotional ladder for this discipline. This is also a problem for the organization when they promote a full time resource into a position where they no longer use their decision analysis skills. At this time, several companies are discussing the creation of a decision analysis discipline ladder, but I have yet to see it implemented.

16.4 Real World Problems

While the examples and case studies presented in this book have been simplified and are rather straight forward, most corporate decisions are full of complexity and competing objectives.

Remember to look deeper

As an analyst you will encounter politics, hidden agendas, personal biases, deep convictions, and a wide array of emotions when working on a project.

This is not to say that your project teams will not be professional. As a whole, most of the people you will work with have the company's best interests in mind and are motivated by doing a good job and finding the best solution. But a large percentage of your time will be spent on organizational and interpersonal issues rather than the techniques illustrated in this book. I recommend that anyone leading a team invest some time in organizational training. Being able to deal with the many complexities and interpersonal issues will usually be the difference between a successful project and a failure.

If you are reading this book as a decision maker, you should understand that while the methodology is very clear and powerful, it can overwhelm a novice project team. You *must* be willing to provide the appropriate resources, either consultants or internal training, and you must allow an appropriate amount of time for solving the problem. With almost every project I have worked on, time has been a major factor influencing the success of the project. I am not saying projects should not be done in a timely manner, but if a decision has to be made in a short period of time which does not allow for a full in-depth analysis, the decision maker must understand the level of analysis that can be performed.

Allocate enough time to do the work

I once had a unique opportunity to teach a class to a group of supervisors and their subordinates. The class lasted three days, and we worked a rather detailed case study in an industry with which they were not familiar. I separated the supervisors and subordinates into two separate teams to solve the case study. At the end of the class, I asked each group how long they thought this project would take in real time. The supervisors thought the project could be completed in sixty days, while the subordinates believed it would take six months. This illustrates the difference in perspectives between the decision makers and the analysts. Make sure you understand what can be accomplished in a reasonable amount of time.

Strategic Decisions

I have applied the decision analysis techniques discussed in this book on several hundred corporate decisions, many of which were strategic decisions. Strategic decisions usually involve multiple decision makers and many uncertainties. It is hard to say how many uncertainties you will have in a strategic project, but my personal experience has been anywhere from 15 to over 70. These projects require a skilled analyst to lead the project and build a quality model. Without this level of skilled support, you may end up choosing a path that is inferior at best and devastating at worst.

It is critical for strategic projects that you have a good project team and the appropriate amount of time to solve the problem. A common pitfall that many teams face when working on a strategic decision is not having a high enough perspective. Most project team members are mid-level managers and often view the problem from their perspective and not from the CEO's view. This can lead to a shortsighted solution or one that is not acceptable or which the decision board does not understand.

Operational Decisions

I always recommend starting with simple problems that are not too convoluted or confrontational – usually operational problems. Operational problems tend to be routine, and if you make a mistake, they are not going to devastate the organization. Also I find that most organizations want to start with a simple problem so they can evaluate decision analysis' effectiveness before committing the resources of a strategic project. Look for projects where you can add value by taking a different approach to the problem.

Routine decisions offer a perfect training ground for internal corporate staff. By their nature, there usually are many of these decisions in every organization, regardless of size, and they offer a means of auditing the effectiveness of the team since these decisions are usually implemented quickly. As I said in the Preface, if you really want to learn how to make decision analysis an integral part of your decision making – start with simple problems.

16.5 Implications and Reactions

Decision analysis has many implications at all levels in the corporate hierarchy. At the operational level of the organization, there can be a tendency to "bias" the inputs to produce the desired output. However, the clarity of decision analysis now makes it easier to inspect the input, and close scrutiny tends to bring an end to such biasing.

In mid-level management, decision analysis can quickly bring to light hidden agendas and other obstacles which were never before seen or at least not officially discussed. The impact to the organization is usually positive but can cause disturbances depending upon the management involved. However, I have usually seen the greatest improvements in the level of commitment to decision analysis at this level of the organization.

At the highest levels of the organization, decision analysis has the ability to generate the most impact of all. Depending upon how the decision maker reacts (which is dependent upon the level of training and knowledge of the methodology), the decision maker can view decision analysis as a loss of control or as a source of greater control. Most executives become comfortable after one or two projects which produce insights previously not available by other types of analyses.

Overall, the organization will experience a change in thinking style from the traditional single-point estimates to a probability-based vision. This change in thinking takes time and can be somewhat traumatic to those reluctant to give up old habits and old thinking.

16.6 Summary

Implementing decision analysis in any organization can be a challenge. The key is to understand what implementation approach is most appropriate for the organization. In this chapter, I discussed four approaches, from using external consultants to developing an in-house consulting group. Each approach has certain benefits and concerns, but all are viable depending upon the organization's desire and ability to change its culture.

Once an organization has started down the road of implementing decision analysis, many issues will surface. After nearly a decade of applications, we are just now discovering some of these issues, like developing an advancement ladder for practitioners and maintaining technical competence. The best forum for discussing these issues is the annual Decision Analysis Affinity Group meeting.

16.7 Key Concepts

implementation challenges	decision maker support
process resources	process roles
training model	DA learning curve
choosing a pilot project	decentralized approach
centralized approach	consultant approach
combined approach	maintaining enthusiasm
technical competence	advancement ladder

16.8 Study Questions

1. Name five of the biggest reasons why implementation of a decision analysis process within an organization might be difficult or might even fail.

2. Some decision makers feel threatened by implementation of a decision analysis process. How can you show them that the process actually provides more control of the decision making process?

3. How can using outside decision analysis consultants aid in the implementation of the decision analysis process within the organization?

4. Beyond the understanding of the decision analysis tools and process, what other elements of the process must be mastered for the internal personnel who assume the role of decision analyst?

5. What are five characteristics you should look for when selecting the "right" first test project to use the decision analysis process on?

6. Describe the four implementation styles and the pros and cons of each style.

7. What is the Decision Analysis Affinity Group (DAAG)?

8. Name three major issues that could surface as you try to implement the decision analysis process within your organization.

9. As mentioned, the examples in this book are simplified. Real world problems can be full of complexity, politics, hidden agendas, and emotional biases. What can you do as a decision analyst to effectively deal with these further complications?

16.9 References and Further Reading

Brown, Rex V., Andrew S. Kahr, and Cameron Peterson. *Decision Analysis for the Manager*. New York: Holt, Rinehart & Winston, 1974.

Krumm, Fred V. and C. F. Rolle. "Management and Application of Decision and Risk Analysis in DuPont." *Interfaces 22* (6 1992): 84-93.

Skinner, David C. "Decision Analysis: Implementation and Implications for a Large Corporation." In *Decision Analysis for Utility Planning and Management in New Orleans*, EPRI 1994.

16.10 Guide to Action

Keep these guidelines in mind when implementing decision analysis:

1. Investigate the different approaches to implementation and choose the approach that is most appropriate for the current organization. You can always modify the implementation strategy later, but choosing a strategy that will not be accepted or implemented today will not yield the desired results in the future.

2. Find a consulting firm that is truly focused on developing your capabilities and has experience in integrating this process within organizations.

3. Talk to other organizations in your industry and others to get a different perspective on implementation hurdles and solutions.

4. Find a high-level champion in your organization that will take the time to learn about the process and provide the necessary support to make the implementation happen.

5. Don't underestimate the time and resources required to make decision analysis part of your organization's culture.

16.11 Case for Analysis: "Go For It"

Bill recently led the first decision analysis team within his company. An outside consultant provided just-in-time training and facilitated the meetings. While the project that was selected was small and fairly straightforward, it did offer enough complexity to allow the team to use the process and to present results to the organization. The CEO was impressed and he tasked Bill with leading an effort to put a decision analysis process in place over the next year for all major decisions.

■   What should Bill do first?

■   How will time constraints affect which implementation style Bill uses?

■   What options are realistically available to Bill?

■   What are his major obstacles?

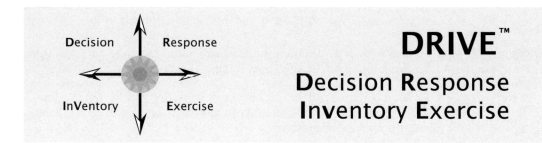

DRIVE™
Decision Response
Inventory Exercise

Instructions for Self Assessment

This exercise is designed to provide you with feedback on your risk-taking and analytical preferences.

In Section 1, there are thirteen sets of four words each. Think of a recent or particularly difficult situation where you made a decision. Keeping this in mind, *rank order* each of the four words across the page with 4 being the word which *best* describes how you evaluated the decision, and 1 being the *worst* word to describe how you evaluated the decision. You may find it hard to differentiate some words from others, but make sure to assign a different number to each word.

In Section 2, read each case and then apply the same scoring technique to the answers provided—4 for the *closest* answer to your own, and 1 for the *least closest* answer.

Section 1

1.	Intuitive		Shrewd		Questioning		Risk-taker
2.	Doing		Observing		Thinking		Active
3.	Acceptance		Reservation		Evaluation		Venturesome
4.	Impartial		Reasonable		Circumspect		Excessive
5.	Thoughtful		Inquisitive		Enlightened		Incoherent
6.	Emotional		Receptive		Analytical		Productive
7.	Slight		Rational		Discerning		Daring
8.	Reactive		Reflective		Conceptual		Inspective
9.	Involved		Careful		Stewardly		Bold
10.	Feeling		Cautious		Pondering		Prodigal
11.	Inconsistent		Sensible		Pragmatic		Casual
12.	Reserved		Speculative		Responsible		Irrational
13.	Ignorant		Wise		Conservative		Intense

Section 2

Question 1

You are in Las Vegas and have just won $1,000 at the blackjack table. You now have an opportunity to double your money or quit and take your winnings. If you take the opportunity the odds of winning are 55%.

a._____ Definitely quit and take the money

b._____ Maybe take the bet (some hesitation)

c._____ Maybe quit (some hesitation)

d._____ Definitely take the bet

Question 2

You have just paid $10 for one of these opportunities. Which deal do you prefer?

a._____ 50% chance of making $40, 50% chance of making $0

b._____ 50% chance of making $100, 50% chance of losing $60

c._____ 20% chance of losing $100, 80% chance of making $50

d._____ 10% chance of making $110, 90% chance of making $10

Question 3

You have $10,000 to invest. You can invest in a certificate of deposit (CD) at a bank for a guaranteed 5% return, or a mutual fund with a 5 year average of 15% (range –10% to +35%), or in a common stock with a 3 year average of 30% (range –30% to +75%). The investment is only for 1 year and is not needed for daily maintenance.

a._____ Not invest-all are to risky

b._____ Invest in mutual funds

c._____ Invest in CD

d._____ Invest in common stock

Question 4

You are the product manager for an innovative new product your company has just finished market testing. You have a choice of going after market leadership or average sales. If you go after market leadership, sales have a 60% chance of being $5,000,000 and a 40% chance of being $1,000,000. If you choose average sales, you are certain to make $2,500,000. What do you do?

a._____ Commission a market study

b._____ Go after market leadership

c._____ Go after average sales

d._____ Toss a coin

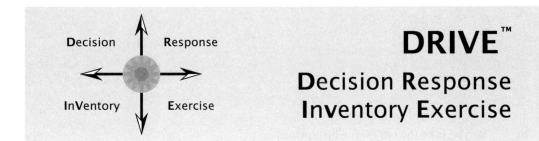

Instructions for Scoring

In Section 1 add the scores from each column according to the key below. Then multiply each score by two and record in the box below. Record each score from Section 2 on the appropriate line labeled A to D.

Add the total score from Section 1 to the total score from Section 2 and record in the box labeled Section 1 + 2. Then subtract column A from column B, and column C from column D.

Plot the intersection of the two numbers on the graph on the next page using B – A as the horizontal axis, and D – C as the vertical axis.

Section 1

1.____Intuitive	1.____Shrewd	2.____Thinking	1.____Risk-taker
3.____Acceptance	5.____Inquisitive	4.____Circumspect	3.____Venturesome
4.____Impartial	7.____Rational	6.____Analytical	4.____Excessive
6.____Emotional	9.____Careful	7.____Discerning	7.____Daring
8.____Reactive	11.____Sensible	9.____Stewardly	9.____Bold
10.____Feeling	12.____Speculative	11.____Pragmatic	10.____Prodigal
11.____Inconsistent	13.____Wise	13.____Conservative	11.____Casual
____Total A	____Total B	____Total C	____Total D
☐ Total A X 2	☐ Total B X 2	☐ Total C X 2	☐ Total D X 2

Section 2

1.____A	____B	____C	____D
2.____A	____B	____C	____D
3.____A	____B	____C	____D
4.____A	____B	____C	____D
☐ Total A	☐ Total B	☐ Total C	☐ Total D
☐ Section 1 + 2	☐ Section 1 + 2	☐ Section 1 + 2	☐ Section 1 + 2
	☐ B – A	☐ D – C	

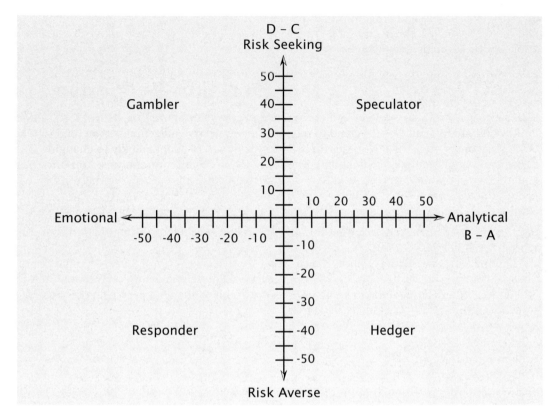

About your Score

Speculator

You are willing to take calculated risks, but insist on analyzing the problem before committing to a course of action. You excel in the ability to investigate all the possibilities and to see them from several perspectives rather than a single perspective. You tend to incorporate other people's views which are relevant to the decision or problem and excel in building an integrated, logical analysis from disparate information. You use analytical tools which are comfortable to you, but also are willing to try new techniques which may offer additional insight. You perform well in situations which call for creativity and quick thinking. You also tend to express your feelings and beliefs in a logical manner and are often frustrated when others do not see the solution to a problem as quickly or clearly as you do.

Hedger

You prefer low risk alternatives and are willing to take opportunities which have a lower downside potential or a more certain outcome over large payoff or less certain opportunity. You tend to be analytical when analyzing a problem but sometimes get trapped in "analysis paralysis." You excel in having the patience to analyze a situation and are not rushed by others. You often listen to other people's views, but are not always sure whether or how to incorporate them into your analysis of the situation. You tend to investigate all of the possibilities and are very good at gathering information. You do best with problems that are well defined and often only have a single correct answer or solution. You tend to be objective about a situation and prefer to deal with facts rather than emotions.

Gambler

You enjoy taking opportunistic risks and making decisions quickly and without much formal analysis. You trust your gut instincts over other people's opinions or analyses. You excel in the ability to take quick action and to rely on your subjective judgements. You tend to take more risks on average than the other three styles. You tend to adapt quickly to changing situations and can assimilate information without much intervention or analysis. You often discount other people's views, especially if they are at odds with your own, preferring to use your own judgement. You are willing to solve problems by trial-and-error and believe in luck and that you can often beat-the-odds. You tend to be more emotional than analytical when solving a problem, and often fall into the "gamblers fallacy" of believing the odds must come back in your favor.

Responder

You make decisions which are usually guided by emotion rather than analysis. You almost always prefer a low risk alternative over a higher risk/payoff alternative. You listen to other people's views and ideas, but often become more confused about the best course of action. You tend to believe in destiny and sometimes solve problems by letting nature choose your course of action. You regret hasty decisions but feel paralyzed by formal analysis, so you tend to solve problems by trial-and-error. Your strength lies in the ability to learn from your mistakes and those of others, and to challenge assumptions.

Neutral or Balanced

If you scored at or near zero (± 5), then you are tend to place an equal emphasis on both ends of the dimension. This usually indicates that you are risk neutral or well balanced use the appropriate style based on the situation and no one particular style is dominant. Or this may be a sign of internal conflict, in which case you are drawn equally to both sides of the dimension. This can cause great confusion and you may show signs of two or more styles.

Facilitation and Analysis Summary: Eliciting Issues

Why Elicit Issues?

Developing a good problem frame requires getting at the issues that the team believes to be important. This is also usually the first time the team has functioned as a team and provides valuable insight into each other's perspectives.

Step-by Step

Eliciting issues can be tedious, boring, and time consuming if the exercise is not well planned. Good planning involves making sure that an adequate amount of materials are available, including sticky notes, flip charts, and colored pens. Also the meeting should be planned to give ample time for team participation and discussion. Do not end an issue raising session too soon; rather, continue as necessary. Above all, try to make the sessions fun for the team. Bring in pizza and cookies or ice cream for breaks.

Step 1   Explain why the team is eliciting issues and how they will be used to frame the problem.

Step 2   Ask each team member to write down one issue on a sticky note and continue until they have elicited all their issues. Remind them to use only one per note as they will group the issues later.

Step 3   Collect the issues by going around the room and asking each team member for their top issue. Have the team member read their issue aloud and then place the issue on a wall or flip chart. Usually after several rounds most of the issues will be collected, but do not stop until the team feels comfortable with the issues elicited. During this time make sure that the team is not in a critiquing mode and that questions asked are for clarification only.

Step 4   After collecting the issues, have the team work on grouping the issues. The grouping should focus around a common theme such as market share, price, volume, etc. After grouping the issues look at removing redundant issues from a group. Make sure before removing an issue that the issue's owner agrees with removing it from the list.

Step 5   Categorize each issue as a decision, uncertainty, value, fact, or objective. Decisions are things we can control. Uncertainties are things out of our control, but which we can gain information about. Values are what we want. And objectives are what we would like to achieve.

Step 6   After categorizing the issues it is a good idea to prioritize them if there are over 25-30 issues. A common voting method is the N/3 rule wherein you take the number of issues and divide that number by 3. Each member then gets that many votes to cast. You can use Avery dots or colored pens to mark on the issue's sticky notes.

Step 7   Record the issues elicited during the day. Include in the list both the top priority and lower priority issues. This recorded list will then be used to develop a decision hierarchy and/or decision matrix. A good method for recording issues is to use the outlining view in Microsoft Word®.

Facilitation and Analysis Summary: Decision Hierarchy

Why Develop a Decision Hierarchy?

The decision hierarchy is a tool for helping teams to frame a problem correctly. It forces a meaningful discussion about what decisions should be in the analysis, what decisions have already been made, and what decisions should be made after the analysis. By carefully categorizing the set of decisions identified in the issue raising session, the team can confirm the project scope and frame with the decision maker(s). When completed, the decision hierarchy provides a starting point for developing a strategy table by placing the "Focus" decisions in the column headings on the strategy table.

Step-by-Step

Step 1   Explain the three different categories of decisions:

Givens (also known as policy decisions) are constraints that influence the flexibility and range of options to be considered in the analysis. Common policy decisions include:

- staying within corporate guidelines,
- meeting financial hurdles, and
- not violating government regulations.

Focus decisions, also known as strategy decisions, are the focus of the analysis. These decisions should include the key decisions that must be made now.

Deferrable or tactical decisions are those that will be made once the strategy has been determined.

Step 2   Display the decisions from the issue-raising list. A projector works well for displaying the decision list. Or you can rewrite the decisions on sticky notes. Either way, have the project team determine the category for each decision.

Step 3   After categorizing the decisions, write them in the appropriate space in the decision hierarchy graphic.

Step 4   Test the Givens or Policy decisions with the decision-maker(s) for realistic constraints on the focus decisions.

Facilitation and Analysis Summary: Influence Diagrams

Why Use an Influence Diagram?

Influence diagrams provide the ability to capture and communicate the essence of a problem in a logical and easy to understand manner. In doing so they:

- Help to structure the problem discussion.
- Identify influences and dependencies between decisions and uncertainties.
- Show how value is created in this situation.
- Provide a means to identify information sources and assign tasks.
- Develop the logic and structure for the decision model.

Step-by-Step

Influence diagrams are as much an art as a science. When facilitating teams, focus on developing a clear and meaningful diagram. Ask probing questions and make sure to not develop a flow diagram. Influence diagrams do not have feedback loops and influence diagrams are not flow diagrams.

Step 1   Explain to the team why they are doing this activity and how it will be used in the future.

Step 2   Begin by considering the essence of the problem. Is it business development, marketing, R&D, exploration, etc.? This understanding will help in guiding the development of the diagram.

Step 3   Put a value node with the decision criteria written in the center at the middle of the right side of the whiteboard or flip chart. Most diagrams begin with NPV as the value node being influenced by Revenue, Costs, and Capital.

Step 4   Begin development by asking what piece(s) of information would most help in resolving the uncertainty or deterministic value.

Step 5   Choose one uncertainty emanating from the value node and develop it completely before beginning with the other nodes. Make sure nodes are clearly defined and specific.

Step 6   Review the uncertainties from the issue-raising list developed earlier. If there are uncertainties which are not in the influence diagram, determine which should and should not be included and why.

Step 7   Identify calculation nodes. Designate these nodes by using a double oval. Can you write the formula that would calculate the value in the oval? If not, list the information that is missing and needed to complete the calculation.

Step 8   Identify information sources and write the source's name by the node they can resolve.

Step 9   Review the diagram for completeness and problem description accuracy.

Step 10 Develop an information gathering task list.

Facilitation and Analysis Summary: Strategy Table

Why Develop Strategy Tables?

Developing creative and coherent strategies that involve many decisions often confuse teams. Strategy tables provide a means to brainstorm decision alternatives and then visualize the set of decisions for each strategy. Strategy tables are also useful for presenting information to the decision makers. Limit the strategies to four to avoid overloading a table.

Step-by-Step

Step 1   Explain why the team is performing this activity.

Step 2   Prepare templates or wall materials. You can use a PowerPoint or Excel template to make changes on-line using a computer. Or you can create a paper template using paper on a wall or a large white board. As the leader, determine which method the team is more comfortable with using.

Step 3   Transfer the focus decisions from the decision hierarchy to the strategy table. Place one decision in each column heading and arrange the decisions by grouping similar functions or putting them in sequence. If decisions are combined, break them into two or more separate and distinct decisions.

Step 4   Have the team discuss the meaning of each decision in the column headings and validate that the decision should be listed and has a clear and specific meaning. If a decision is tactical or contingent, list it on a separate sheet and remove it from the strategy table.

Step 5   Give each team member a pad of sticky notes and ask them to brainstorm possible alternatives for each decision heading. It is a good idea to have team members work in groups of two to four depending upon the size of the team. Alternatives should be written one per note.

Step 6   Place the alternatives in the columns under the appropriate decision headings. Alternatives should be significantly different and range from incremental to radical in nature. The alternatives should also be mutually exclusive and collectively exhaustive. That is, you should not be able to choose more than one alternative for a strategy, and the alternatives listed should encompass all possible choices within the constraints of the problem.

Step 7   Develop strategy themes. A theme is a short phrase or set of words which communicates the essence of the strategy. The theme should convey the path developed through the strategy table. Brainstorming is a very useful process for developing these themes. Have team members work in groups or pairs to develop several themes.

Step 8   Develop initial strategy write-ups. Once the team has developed its set of themes, each member group should develop a write-up or rationale for each theme. The write-ups should be no more than two paragraphs and convey why the company would want to pursue this strategy.

Step 9   Review and prioritize strategy themes. Using the write-ups, each group should describe to the team their rationale for each theme. The team should then choose the compelling strategy themes for mapping through the table.

Step 10 Map out each strategy theme in the strategy table. Examine the strategy table for other compelling strategy hybrids that may have been missed earlier.

Facilitation and Analysis Summary: Assessment

Why Assess Data Ranges?

A fundamental aspect of decision analysis is the use of ranges and probabilities to effectively deal with uncertainty. We all know from experience that it is impossible to exactly predict the outcome of some future event. However, it is possible to develop ranges of data which can reliably encompass the fluctuations of future events. By assessing these ranges and incorporating them into the decision model, we are able to have better insight into the potential risk and value of a problem.

Step-by-Step

Initial data can be assessed from individuals or from project teams. Do not begin assessing data until you have an influence diagram developed and can explain conditional situations and uncertainties. Be sure to search for biases or other conflicts that may affect the expert's assessment.

Step 1   Review the influence diagram or decision model structure with the project team.

Step 2   Develop an assessment task list and assign project team members to collect the data.

Step 3   Develop assessment templates and a timeline for completing the assignments.

Step 4   Collect the data ranges.

     a. Explain the reason for collecting the data and how the information will be used. Emphasize that you are not trying to extract a promise from the expert, but are trying to assess that person's state of information.

     b. Review the influence diagram or decision model with the person or team being assessed. The logic of the model should be well understood, and may require some changes for reliable assessments from the content expert(s).

     c. Explain the 10-50-90 concept. Use the diagram below for explaining the percentage distinctions.

     d. Collect the data and test for reliability. Ask the expert if he or she is comfortable with these ranges and if they would invest money on a project based on the validity of this information.

Step 5   Review the data ranges with the project team for completeness and reliability.

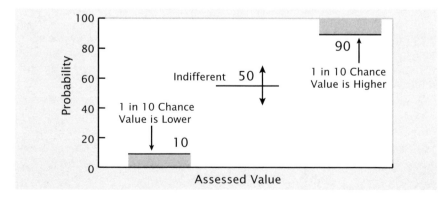

Facilitation and Analysis Summary: Decision Trees

Why Use Decision Trees?

Decision trees provide a structured approach to incorporating uncertainty into decision problems. Decision trees should be:

- built after conducting sensitivity analysis on the decision model,
- concise and limited to three to six uncertainties,
- composed of the most important uncertainties identified in the sensitivity analysis, and
- built using the chronological sequence of decisions and uncertainties.

Step-by-Step

Decision trees are straightforward and logical in design. If there are more than eight uncertainties, consider combining several of them into a "scenario" or build sub-trees which can then be evaluated. Remove decisions from the tree if the decision has no effect on the strategy to be evaluated.

Step 1   Identify key uncertainties from the sensitivity analysis.

Step 2   Construct a skeleton decision tree. Determine the chronological order of decisions and key uncertainties.

Step 3   Build the full tree by propagating the tree and connecting the branches.

Step 4   Add probabilities and outcomes to the tree diagram.

Step 5   Roll back the tree to calculate expected value.

Facilitation and Analysis Summary: Decision Quality Radar Chart

Why Use the Decision Quality Radar Chart?

The Decision Quality Radar Chart helps teams perform a self-assessment concerning the decision quality associated with their work. It should be:

- included as a part of the Decision Support Package,
- used to obtain insight about which parts of the Scalable Decision Process went well and which parts could be improved, and
- validated with the Decision Review Board.

Step-by-Step

Step 1   Give each team member a blank chart (see example below).

Step 2   Allow each team member five to ten minutes to complete their own assessment of the Team's work.

Step 3   Using Excel or a white board, chart each team member's assessment.

Step 4   Discuss and record key insights, especially where individual assessments differ.

Step 5   Plot the p10, p50, and p90 from each distribution of quality attribute scores on the Decision Quality Radar Chart (hint: use the percentile function in Excel).

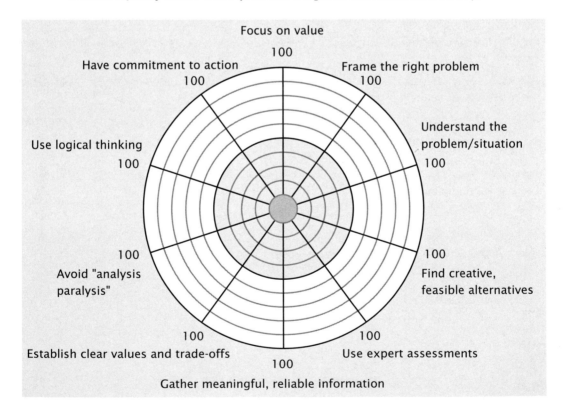

Glossary

ALTERNATIVE—What you can do—a feasible allocation of resources which are available now or can become available to the decision maker.

ALTERNATIVE BRANCH—A branch emanating from a decision node representing one available alternative.

ASSESSMENT—Obtaining a range of outcomes (usually over an 80% range of uncertainty: "10-50-90") for a particular uncertainty from an informed expert acceptable to the decision maker or decision board.

CERTAIN EQUIVALENT—The lowest cash value where the decision maker would be indifferent between accepting that cash amount in exchange for the rights to a venture with an uncertain outcome. For risk-averse decision makers, it is always less than the expected monetary value.

CLAIRVOYANT—A conceptual being having the ability to see the future with perfect clarity. Useful for structuring uncertainties and assessing the value of information.

CUMULATIVE PROBABILITY DISTRIBUTION—A chart with probability on the y-axis and value on the x-axis, which describes the entire range of probable outcomes resulting from a course of action. The chart is always read from right to left, stating the probability Y resulting in the value of X or less.

DECISION—A conscious, irrevocable allocation of resources with the purpose of achieving a desired objective.

DECISION ANALYSIS CYCLE—A systematic approach to solving problems; STRUCTURING a problem to capture the essentials, EVALUATION to gain insight and AGREEMENT with the world to make something happen.

DECISION BOARD—A group of persons with the responsibility and authority to allocate resources and implement decisions.

DECISION HIERARCHY—A method to organize decisions into those that are policy or constraints, those which are the focus of the analysis, and others which are required for implementation.

DECISION MAKER—Person or team with the responsibility and authority to allocate resources and implement the decision.

DECISION NODE— A point in a decision tree where a decision must be made.

DECISION POLICY—A rule for the selection of alternatives. Decision policy designates which alternative to take at each and every decision node in a decision tree.

DECISION THEORY—The mathematical theory of decision making under uncertainty.

DECISION TREE—A sequential graphical representation of decisions and uncertainties which represent all paths the decision maker might follow through time. There are four basic elements from which a decision tree is constructed: decision nodes, alternative branches, probability nodes, and outcome branches.

Glossary (Continued)

ENCODING UNCERTAINTY—The process by which individual judgments about an uncertain variable are characterized by a probability distribution.

EXPECTED MONETARY VALUE—The weighted average of all possible outcomes multiplied by their respective probabilities.

EVALUATION PHASE—Compares opportunity versus risk for each alternative.

HISTOGRAM—A probability distribution in bar graph form where the height of any bar represents the probability of obtaining a value within the corresponding interval.

INDIFFERENCE—Indifference between two opportunities means they are equally desirable or indistinguishable in terms of value to the decision maker.

INFLUENCE DIAGRAM—A graphical representation of decisions and uncertainties which shows what is known and uncertain at the time of each decision and the dependence and independence of each uncertainty on all other decision and uncertainties.

INFORMATION—PERFECT information is that which completely eliminates uncertainty about a particular variable. IMPERFECT information decreases uncertainty but does not eliminate it.

ISSUE—Anything of concern, e.g., a decision, uncertainty, value or objective.

LOTTERY—A set of outcomes together with their probabilities of occurrence.

MODEL—an explicit approximation of reality, typically expressed as a series of mathematical relationships.

NET PRESENT VALUE (NPV)—The sum of future annual cash flows discounted at the cost of capital.

OBJECTIVE—The desired level of performance against a value.

OUTCOME—The subsequent events that determine the ultimate desirability of pursuing a particular alternative.

OUTCOME BRANCH—A branch emanating from a probability node representing the possible outcome and its probability of occurrence.

PORTFOLIO—A collection of projects, investments or opportunities that compete for the same resources.

POSSIBILITY TREE—A graphical representation of possible opportunities and outcomes.

PREFERENCE—The decision maker's attitude toward the value, timing, and uncertainty of outcomes.

PROBABILITY—A number between zero and one (inclusively) representing the degree of belief a person attaches to the occurrence of an event.

PROBABILITY DENSITY—A function (curve) describing the relative likelihood of the occurrence of the possible values of an uncertain quantity.

Glossary (Continued)

PROBABILITY NODE—A point in a decision tree where an uncertainty will be resolved; often called chance node.

RELEVANCE—The extent to which one uncertain event depends on another uncertainty or on a decision, i.e., "X is relevant to Y".

SENSITIVITY ANALYSIS—Measuring the impact of each uncertainty on the value of an alternative to determine which are critical, i.e., would change the order of preference for the alternatives.

SENSITIVITY CHART—Also known as a tornado diagram shows the results of a sensitivity analysis graphically.

STRATEGY—In the context of decision analysis, is a coordinated set of decisions.

STRATEGY TABLE—Used to develop alternative strategies to evaluate. Columns represent areas of decision, and items within each column represent the range of choices within each area of decision. A strategy is represented by selecting choices in each column.

STRUCTURING PHASE—Raises important issues, creates wide range of alternative and provides framework for analysis.

UNCERTAINTY—Any event for which the outcome is not known at the time a decision is made.

UTILITY—A mathematical function (curve) which represents the decision maker's risk attitude.

VALUE—An outcome measure, e.g., NPV, ATOI, IRR.

VALUE OF INFORMATION—The maximum price one should pay for knowing the actual value of an uncertainty prior to making the decision.

Answers to Selected Questions

Chapter 1

1 - Explain the difference between normative and descriptive decision analysis.
Normative decision analysis describes how decisions should be made while descriptive decision analysis tries to explain how people actually do make decisions. (Section 1.3)

3 - Why should you use decision analysis?
Decision analysis should be used to consistently make good decisions. (Section 1.5)

5 - Where can decision analysis be applied?
Decision analysis can be applied to every decision problem both professional and personal. It will yield the greatest benefit in problems where there is a high degree of complexity and where the outcome or consequences are significant. (Section 1.6)

7 - Explain how you can have a good outcome from a bad decision.
Decision analysis can help clarify the problem, incorporate uncertainty into the analysis, and ascertain the state of knowledge, but the outcome of any complex decision will still involve some degree of unknown or uncertainty that may cause an unexpected result - good or bad. (Section 1.8)

9 - An effective decision making process should be able to provide what seven abilities to the decision maker?
An effective decision making process will provide the decision maker with the ability to:

- Identify the real problem,
- Clearly understand the goals and objectives,
- Develop unique and compelling alternatives,
- Discover what is important,
- Adequately deal with uncertainty and ambiguity,
- Make appropriate trade-offs of risk and value, and
- Provide the clarity to act with confidence. (Section 1.2)

11- What issues can complexity bring to the problem solving process?
Complexity creates different problems than uncertainty as it can cloud immediate decisions with future decisions. Complexity can cause the decision maker to focus on the wrong problem or decision. Decision analysis helps to structure the complexity in a way that brings clarity to the problem. (Section 1.2)

Chapter 2

1 - Think about some decisions you have made recently. What type of decision making approach did you take to solve them? Did you use the same approach each time or did you use different approaches depending upon the complexity of each problem?
You should use different approaches to decision making based on the complexity of the problems and also on the ambiguity of the goals and objectives.

3 - What makes decision making difficult for you? What would you want in a decision making process to minimize these difficulties?

Answers could include: uncertainty, defining clear objectives, identifying the decision maker, unknowns, working with probabilities, unknown consequences, non-financial impacts of decisions, etc. A good decision making process would be one that acknowledged these difficulties and provided direction on how best to handle them. (Section 2.1)

5 - Are good outcomes the direct result of good decisions? What are the differences between a good decision and a good outcome?
While you would hope for a good outcome from every good decision, there will always be some uncertainty involved with every complex decision that might influence the outcome. A good decision does not guarantee a good outcome, but a quality decision will provide the best chance for a good outcome. A good decision is the best alternative given the state of knowledge, the defined problem and objectives, the decision maker's preferences and criteria, the probabilistic estimates, etc., while a good outcome is a positive result. (Section 2.2)

7 - Give an example of a recent decision you made which involved a significant amount of uncertainty. Was the outcome lucky or unlucky?
A lucky outcome would be one where the unknowns and uncertainties fell to favor your decision.

9 - Can decision analysis be useful for making routine or programmed decisions?
Decision analysis can be useful for making routine decisions, but it would be particularly beneficial when used to initially establish the programs, procedures, or systems used in the decision making process. (Section 2.3)

11 - Under what conditions of ambiguity and uncertainty would full decision analysis become the most appropriate course of action?
Full process decision analysis is recommended for those situations where a high level of uncertainty is combined with a high level of ambiguity. (Section 2.3)

13 - What change is occurring in organizations today with decision makers that adds complexity to the decision making process?
Organizations are moving away from the hierarchical and dictatorial structures to more decentralized and empowered organizations. The single decision makers have disappeared and have been replaced by decision boards, committees, management review teams, etc. Having multiple decision makers means that decisions must be made based on consensus rather than by a single person. (Section 2.1)

Chapter 3

1 - Give some examples of distinctions that you would use to describe yourself.
Some examples may be: married, employed, engineer, scientist, father, son, daughter, mother, sister, brother, healthy, sick, etc. (Section 3.7)

3 - Give your definition of the clarity test.
The clarity test is a method by which terms, assessments about uncertainty, and analysis results can be checked for ambiguous terms or possibly misleading information. The clarity test can be used to ensure effective communication and clear understanding between decision team members and decision makers. (Section 3.7)

5 - Explain the fallacy of sunk cost.
Sunk cost is a term used to describe money already spent on a project. Since it has already been spent, it is not relevant to the decision to be made about further spending. Including sunk cost in the analysis is a common mistake made by decision teams and decision makers. (Section 3.6)

7 - What characteristic should a measure of merit have and why?
A measure of merit should:

- Be able to provide a comparison of alternatives in a clear and unbiased manner,
- This will allow a clear and accurate comparison of all the alternative decisions
- Incorporate the firm's cost of capital and risk,
- This will allow the decision to be made within the company's guidelines
- Provide an indication of whether a given alternative exceeds an economic hurdle and by how much,
- This provides an accurate measurement for evaluating the alternatives by their differences - the important feature
- Indicate the size of the value proposition.
- Overall and total value of an alternative should be used in the decision making process. (Section 3.2)

9 - Describe what an appropriate discount factor is and how it should be determined.
The discount factor should represent the rate at which an organization can reinvest future revenues. It should be representative of the true cost of capital for the company and should reflect the internal cost for funds. This should be determined based on the company's tax rate, cost of borrowing, proportion of equity financing, and stockholders' expected return on investment. Risk should not be used in this determination. (Section 3.3)

11 - When is the net present value a significant measure for determining the acceptance or rejection of a project?
Net Present Value uses a discount rate to determine the single value today for a stream of cash flows in the future. It can be used to compare projects and determine which provides the most value to the organization. It can be used as a significant measure in those situations where the outcome is certain. Since NPV does not take risk or uncertainty into account, it should not be used exclusively in those situations where the risk is a factor. (Sections 3.3 & 3.4)

13 - Organizations make decisions in different ways. Name three and evaluate how your company fits into these categories.
An organization with a strong team culture will make decisions by group methods such as consensus or majority vote. The leader or executive will make decisions in an authoritarian company with little to no input from the employees. In hierarchal companies, the decisions will be delegated within authority limits. (Section 3.1)

Chapter 4

1 - Describe decision quality in your own words.
A high-quality, rational decision will integrate the basic elements of any decision: what you want, what you know, and what you can do, into a logical, defensible, and compelling course of action. (Section 4.1)

3 - Do you have difficulty making quality decisions? If so, why?
Section 3.2 describes seven quality traps that can prevent us from making quality decisions:

- Lack of creative and significantly different alternatives
- Refinement of unimportant details
- Inability to deal with competing objectives
- Solving the wrong problem
- Not involving the real decision makers
- Wrong level of detail in the analysis
- Lack of credibility in the information content.

5 - Describe a RACI chart.
The RACI chart is a tool used to set expectations and responsibilities when going through the decision quality process. RACI stands for Responsibility, Accountability, Consultation, and Information. The chart should clearly detail the involvement of each party in the process as well as help to define the time commitments and the roles of each person. Each activity that the team needs to keep track of is listed and the responsible parties are noted for RACI. (Section 4.3)

7 - Explain how a radar chart can be used to communicate decision quality.
The radar chart is a useful tool for use in discussing multiple objectives. It can be used to show graphically the trade-offs between alternatives and can be used to quasi-qualitatively weigh the various alternatives against the decision maker's preferences and values. (Section 4.4 and Section 2.4)

9 - Give an example of analysis paralysis.
Analysis paralysis occurs when a team becomes locked in data analysis and does not progress to the next phase of the decision analysis process. This can occur when the decision maker lacks faith in the reliability of the data or is concerned about the uncertainty or risk and requests seemingly endless scenario evaluations. It can also happen if the team/decision maker feels that they can eliminate uncertainty from the decision through continued data analysis. (Section 4.2)

11 - Explain why the decision quality process is important.
It is critical for an organization to have a decision quality process in place to help make the best decisions on a day-to-day basis, but it is especially important in strategic decisions where there is a long time horizon and the direction of the company is set. The traditional "inspection of the outcome" method of determining decision quality could devastate the company. Having a quality process in place will mold the thinking of the organization. (Section 4.1)

13 - If your decision analysis team becomes overwhelmed with the shear volume of data collected, what can you do to still move the process forward?
Check the problem for scope creep or for poor problem framing. Determine if the level of analysis is appropriate and necessary to achieve clarity of action. (Section 4.2)

15 - Why is it important to consider the effects of time and/or delay on the decision?
One alternative that often escapes our thinking is time. By delaying the decision for a period of time, if appropriate, the team can gather more data or develop more alternatives. The decision situations might change as well. (Section 4.1)

Chapter 5

1 - Why is the 10-step decision process outlined in this chapter referred to as the scalable decision process?

The decision analysis process outlined in this chapter is called scalable because it can be fitted to the problem under consideration. It also describes a scope that is beyond what is typically considered in traditional decision analysis. SDP focuses on the facilitation of the process and the implementation of the eventual decision as well as the evaluation techniques. (Chapter Introduction)

3 - What causes perceptual problems (in the context of problem or opportunity identification)?

Perceptual problems can occur when an individual is trying to protect you from the negative information concerning a decision or situation or when they are trying to defend a position. They might distort or ignore the negative information that makes it difficult to define the true problem. (Section 5.2)

5 - What is likely to happen if the business assessment is not completed or is completed poorly?

A good business assessment will help to orient the team as to the validity of the internal information assessments and the sources of external corroborative information. Without a good business assessment, many teams find themselves in endless iterations and rework before the decision maker will decide on a course of action. (Section 5.2)

7 - What do we mean by value of imperfect information?

In the decision process, specific new information about key uncertainties will often change the decision. The new information has a value that can be calculated prior to making the decision. This value is the value of the information. Perfect information is 100% correct, but most times we cannot obtain perfect information. Imperfect information is still high quality but not 100% certain. The imperfect information has a value that can be calculated. (Section 5.3)

9 - What should you do when the answer becomes clear and compelling?

When performing a decision analysis, if the answer becomes clear and compelling at any point in the process, you should stop and make the decision. Be wary of short-circuiting the process. (Section 5.4)

11 - Name three broad categories of problems you will encounter and the SDP methods that are necessary for each category.

Routine - easily solved using intuition, established procedures, previous experience, or a structured decision process depending on the level of uncertainty and ambiguity involved.

Non-Routine - should be handled using a structured and logical decision analysis process like SDP.

Opportunities - these are typically hidden problems or issues that arise. We should be on the look out for these situations and use a structured/logical process like decision analysis to determine how best to take advantage of the opportunities. (Section 5.2)

Chapter 6

1 - Why can't a good analysis compensate for a poor problem frame?
Without the proper problem frame, the project team will find themselves in a continual re-examination mode. The real problem might be completely different from the one the team is analyzing, however good and thorough that analysis might be. (Section 6.1) Additionally, without a clearly defined problem, the decision maker will likely not accept the recommendation or possibly implement a poor solution due to time constraints. (Section 6.2)

3 - What are the distinctions between policy and strategy decisions?
Policy decisions are typically givens and are provided to the project team as constraints on the strategic level decisions. The project team will be focusing on the strategic decisions and making their analysis and recommendation within the boundaries established by the policy decisions. (Section 6.3)

5 - What is a strategy theme?
Strategy themes are short phrases or sets of words that communicate the essence of the strategy. The theme should convey and describe the path developed through the strategy table where the alternatives have been organized into strategies. (Section 6.4)

7 - What are the distinctions between project team members and content experts?
Project team members are actively involved on the project team and assist throughout each phase of the analysis. Content experts are outside sources that provide input to the team within their area of expertise. Team members may also be content experts if they happened to be experts in a particular discipline and also on the team. (Section 6.2)

9 - When should the project team meet with the leadership review board?
The project team should first meet with the leadership review board and the decision maker to frame and validate the problem itself. After the initial meeting, the team should work to develop a complete set of alternatives. Once that has been completed, the team should again meet with the leadership review board for feedback and input. As the team progresses, the leadership review board and the decision maker should be consulted whenever the team reaches a key point in the analysis and requires feedback, course direction, or validation of their efforts. (Section 6.5)

Chapter 7

1 - How do you start building an influence diagram?
You begin building an influence diagram with the value measure and then decompose the diagram from that point. The influence diagram is constructed from right to left by working through everything that has an influence on the node before it. (Section 7.1)

3 - Why do we say that no influence diagram is "absolutely correct"?
No influence diagram is absolutely correct because they are similar to subjective probabilities, and there are many ways to show the various relationships of decisions, uncertainties, and values. If the diagram accurately communicates the decision problem, then it can be considered complete and correct. (Section 7.1)

5 - What advantages do influence diagrams have over decision trees?

Influence diagrams provide a very concise graphical means to communicate the essence of the problem, even very complex problems. It is also an excellent tool to use to communicate between the team and the leadership review board/decision maker. While decision trees link the decisions to be made and identify and quantify the uncertainties involved, they tend to be very complicated as opposed to the influence diagram that can represent the entire problem on a single sheet of paper. Influence diagrams can also simplify or provide an indication of the underlying influences on each of the variables and decisions in a problem. (Section 7.2)

7 - How do you evaluate a decision tree?
In order to evaluate a decision tree, the probabilities of each branch of the tree need to be input into the model. From those probabilities and the values associated with the outcomes, the expected values for each branch can be calculated. The value of the path would be the expected value multiplied by the probability for the entire path. This expected value allows for the comparison of the different paths through the model. (Section 7.2)

9 - Name the three rules for constructing influence diagrams.
1. No feedback loops; 2. Start from the right and work to the left; 3. Keep in mind the rule of thumb that the diagram should fit comfortably on one sheet of 8 1/2" x 11" paper with reasonable fonts. (Section 7.1)

11 - What are three rules for constructing decision trees?
1. Start with decision node; 2. Uncertain nodes should contain branches that correspond to a set of mutually exclusive and collectively exhaustive outcomes; 3. Decision trees must contain all possible paths available to the decision maker. (Section 7.2)

Chapter 8

1 - What is probability?
Probability is a state of knowledge about the likelihood of an event based on your beliefs, data, knowledge, and experiences. It is the only clear way to state your beliefs about a future event. (Section 8.1)

3 - What is the correct probability of an event?
There is no one correct probability, but a good probability assessment incorporates all relevant information into the state of knowledge. (Section 8.1)

5 - What is meant by the term decomposition?
Decomposition refers to the process of taking uncertainties and breaking them into other influencing uncertainties to provide a better understanding of the problem. By decomposing the uncertainty into smaller and more specific pieces, the problem can become clearer and input from different experts can be added. (Section 8.2)

7 - What do we mean by marginal probabilities?
Marginal probabilities are calculated by summing the probabilities across and down the probability table. The marginal probability of event E is the sum of all the probabilities of mutually exclusive and collectively exhaustive events X_i and E. (Section 8.5)

9 - What is conditional probability?
Conditional probability refers to the modifying of the probability of an event conditioned upon the outcome of another event that precedes it. (Section 8.5)

11 - What is a cumulative distribution graph and how is one prepared?

The cumulative distribution graph is built from the probability table of values and shows the probability that the actual value of a problem is less than or equal to the value shown on the horizontal axis. The horizontal axis represents the values, and the vertical axis is the cumulative probability. To build the graph, start by sorting the values from lowest to highest. Begin the plot at the lowest value and draw a line from that value vertically until it intersects the probability associated with that value. Then draw a horizontal line from that point to the intersection of the next value. Again draw a vertical line until it meets the intersection of the sum of the first value probability and the second value probability. Continue until the probabilities have summed to 1. (Section 8.7)

13 - What are Probability Trees and how do they differ from Venn Diagrams?
Probability trees are graphical representations of events with their associated probabilities. These trees use nodes to represent uncertainty and can be used for the calculation of the probabilities of each branch of the tree once the probabilities for the distinctions have been assessed. The probability trees are typically much easier to use and understand than Venn Diagrams that tend to become very complex in all but the most simple of problems. (Sections 8.3 & 8.7)

Chapter 9

1 - What is a Monte Carlo simulation?
A Monte Carlo simulation is a process that generates random number inputs for uncertain values, which are then processed by a mathematical model, so that many scenarios can be evaluated. (Section 9.1)

3 - What is a random number?
A random number can be any number (x) from a group of uniformly distributed numbers that falls within an established boundary, usually 0 and 1. Uniformity is important, in that it means every number within the boundaries is possible and has an equal chance of being chosen. (Section 9.3)

5 - What is a discrete distribution?
A discrete distribution is a group of numbers with specific values in the range being examined. For an uncertainty, a discrete distribution would return specific numbers for the variables within the boundaries of the uncertainty. (Section 9.3)

7 - Describe how to construct a histogram chart.
A histogram chart shows the relative frequency of the outcomes. Sort the outcomes from smallest to largest. Calculate the probabilities for each value as the weighted average of the number of occurrences of that value with regard to the total number of trials. Plot the probability of each value using a bar chart. (Section 9.4)

9 - Why is Monte Carlo analysis not a substitute for decision analysis?
While Monte Carlo analysis is a valuable and informative tool to use in the decision analysis process, it should not be substituted for decision analysis. The model construction, the thought process, and the various inputs should still receive appropriate attention and rigor. Understanding the simulation and the distributions are also critical to using Monte Carlo analysis as a proper part of the decision analysis process.(Section 9.6)

11 - If the results of a Monte Carlo simulation are plotted on a cumulative distribution, what information can be interpreted from that graph?

The cumulative distribution shows the risk profile of the outcomes and allows the decision maker to better understand the range of possible outcomes and how likely they are to occur. (Section 9.4)

Chapter 10

1 - Why do we need to use limited information?
Because almost all decisions, especially those involving the future, are based on limited information we must be able to use limited information to make decisions. Otherwise, we fall into the trap of asking for more and more information - analysis paralysis. More information will never resolve the unknowns in the process. (Section 10.1)

3 - What does uncertainty mean to you, and how do you typically deal with it?
Uncertainty in decision analysis represents an event for which the outcome or value is unknown at the time the decision is made. To deal with it effectively, one must use the probabilistic assessments of experts to quantify the range of possibilities.

5 - What is a bias and how many kinds are there?
A bias is a conscious or subconscious discrepancy between the expert's response and an accurate description of his or her underlying knowledge. There are two main types of biases: motivational and cognitive. (Section 10.3)

7 - What are the six cognitive biases?
Cognitive biases are introduced by the way the expert processes information. The six cognitive biases are: anchoring, availability, coherence, overconfidence, representativeness, and sampling. (Section 10.3)

9 - In your own words, describe the overconfidence bias.
The overconfidence bias occurs when the expert believes that he or she knows everything there is to know about the subject. (Section 10.3)

11 - Why is it important to understand the expert's assumptions?
An understanding of the expert's assumptions will help you to uncover biases and also ensure that the expert has the proper perspective going into the assessment process. (Section 10.4)

13 - When discretizing a curve, how many points are needed to accurately describe it?
The curve should be discretized into as few points as possible to adequately describe it. Typically, the 10-50-90 values are adequate since these values also refer to the areas above and below the curve. These values can be used to describe the entire curve and simplify the calculations. (Section 10.6)

15 - How do you know if you are an expert?
An expert is a person who should be able to provide multiple layers of information from the obvious and simple to the detailed and difficult. In providing this information, the expert should be able to provide powerful distinctions in knowledge that separate the level of their ability from those with lesser knowledge. (Section 10.2)

17 - What weights should be applied to a 10-15-90 distribution and why?
The 10-50-90 values are not just points on the curve; they also refer to the areas above and below the curve. Since these values refer to the areas, the weights used should either be 25-50-25 respectively for a normal distribution or 30-40-30 for a distribution containing a lot of skewness. (Section 10.6)

Chapter 11

1 - Explain how influence diagrams help to model the decision and provide insight not available from decision trees.

Influence diagrams are graphical representations of the problem and can provide insight not available from decision trees. The influence diagram lists the relevance of all uncertainties on other nodes in the problem. The decision tree separates the uncertainties into pathways, but it does not show relevance or dependence of one node to another. (Section 11.1)

3 - What are the steps in performing deterministic sensitivity analysis?

There are four steps to building a deterministic sensitivity analysis:
1. Build the deterministic value model using the variables identified in the influence diagram
2. Choose a low, base, and high value for each variable in the model.
3. Setting all variables to their base value, calculate a nominal value for each alternative.
4. Calculate the swing of each variable by changing the value of one variable at a time from its high to its low while holding all the other variables at their base values. Record those changes in value.

The recorded changes in value are the sensitivities of the analysis to each variable. (Section 11.1)

5 - What is a tornado diagram?

A tornado diagram is a graphical tool designed to show the change in value created by swinging each variable from its low to high value. This tool can show graphically which variables are most important to the final value of the project. (Section 11.1)

7 - What role do spreadsheets play in decision analysis?

Spreadsheets are very important tools in decision analysis. They can be used to build and test deterministic models. They provide a method of modeling that does not have the "black box" stigma of some other computerized modeling programs. (Section 11.1)

9 - What insights can be gained from tornado diagrams?

Tornado diagrams are graphical representations of the swing in value of the project with the change in each variable from its highest to its lowest predicted values. The diagrams can show which variables are most important to the value of the project and also which variables can be disregarded in the analysis as unimportant. (Section 11.1)

11 - What is an optimal decision?

An optimal decision is the preferred and compelling course of action given a full understanding of the problem and the sensitivity to probability and to the variables. The optimal decision will also incorporate the decision maker's preferences for risk tolerance. (Section 11.2)

13 - Can we ever achieve perfect information? If so, how?

Perfect information is rarely available. If it is available for the problem, it typically requires additional research to clear up an ambiguity or time to clarify an unknown. Both of these processes require more resources. (Section 11.3)

15 - How do risk profiles account for uncertainty?

Risk profiles or cumulative probability distributions show the entire range of values and the associated probabilities for each alternative. This allows the decision maker or team to evaluate the upside and the downside of each alternative and decide whether or not the reward is worth the risk. The uncertainty is accounted for by the probabilities. (Section 11.4)

17 - Explain the basis for Bayes' Rule.
Simply stated: Bayes' Rule states that the joint probabilities through the branches of a decision tree containing mutually exclusive and collectively exhaustive alternatives remain the same even if the internal nodes of the tree are reversed. Using the law of addition and the law of multiplication of probabilities, the intervening probabilities of the branches can be calculated. (Section 11.3 & Chapter 8)

19 - Why do we often place our personal risk attitudes on corporate decisions?
It is natural to impose our own personal risk attitudes on the corporate decisions and we should guard against this happening. When an employee is a "gambler", s/he will ascribe added value to a riskier decision. A risk averse person will subtract value from an alternative that involves risk. Most corporate decisions should be risk neutral. An employee's performance metrics might play a role in how they view decisions as well. (Section 11.4)

21 - Explain the concept of risk aversion.
As the stakes and risk of a decision increase, most corporations and individuals become risk averse. This means they discount the expected value of the alternative in proportion to the risk involved. The risk aversion of the decision maker can be ascertained and incorporated into the decision analysis through the use of a utility function. The utility function helps to quantify the risk aversion of the decision maker and combine it with the probability of the alternatives to provide a risk preference adjusted expected utility. (Section 11.4)

Chapter 12

1 - What are the hurdles to implementing decision analysis in your personal or business life?
Answers could include - reliance on intuition, reluctance to use probabilities or risk assessments - lack of focus on the real problems - education - multi-functional teams need to be formed, etc.

3 - Why is shared knowledge important?
Shared knowledge is important so that everyone on the team and the decision maker have a complete view and understanding of the problem. It is also important to share knowledge so that multiple perspectives and influences might be considered. The organization likely has all the knowledge necessary to solve the problem contained somewhere within it. By sharing knowledge, the team members and the decision maker can develop better alternatives to solve the problem. (Section 12.1)

5 - How does the decision hierarchy help you to understand if the course of action is appropriate?
The decision hierarchy is a good place to start when considering the appropriateness of an alternative. At the top are the policy decisions and constraints issued by the company. The alternative must be in alignment with those issues. Next are the strategic decisions and business unit strategies. If the alternative contradicts one of these strategic decisions, it might not be appropriate. Lastly, the decision hierarchy shows the operational decisions. If an alternative cannot be practically implemented or there are not sufficient resources to implement an alternative, that alternative might not be appropriate. (Section 12.1)

8 - Describe a communication plan. Why is it important?

The communication plan should describe the course of action, why it was chosen, and what the employee's role is in implementing it. Without a proper communication plan, the employees become discouraged and may not trust the analysis or the recommended course of action. (Section 12.1)

9 - What should be included in the Decision Quality Package?
The DQP is a synopsis of the work products the team has developed. The DQP should include sufficient information for the audience from each of the phases of the team's work. From the Structuring phase, a summary of the tools used to develop a shared understanding of the problem and the creative alternatives should be included. From the Evaluation phase, the analysis should be summarized and the analyses of the alternatives should be presented. The Agreement phase should clearly indicate the chosen course of action and the Action Plan. (Section 12.2)

Chapter 15

1 - When are Portfolio Analysis and Management necessary?
Portfolio analysis and management techniques are necessary when a manager has a collection of projects or investments and one or more of the resources that are critical to success for the projects or investments are limited and not all the projects can be funded. (Section 15.1)

3 - What is common among all projects or investments to be considered for a portfolio?
They must all be individually project worthy of funding and they must all compete for the same resource pool. The projects can be worthy of funding due to their financial strength, their strategic value, or their synergistic impact on other projects. (Section 15.1)

5 - What is an efficiency curve? And what is it used for?
An efficiency curve is a cumulative plot of two variables. The X-axis shows one of the variables (typically the resource to be allocated) and the Y-axis is the contrasting variable (typically the result - like NPV). An example would be the cumulative NPV versus cumulative capital investment. To create the efficiency curve, the projects are plotted in order from the highest ratio of the Y-axis variable to the X-axis variable from the left to the right, e.g. highest "bang for the buck" from the left to the right. (Section 15.6)

7 - Name two important ways that risk or probability of success should be used in portfolio analysis.
The financial analysis of each individual project is typically calculated based on technical and commercial success. These numbers can be multiplied times the probabilities of success to create "risked" financials for comparison. Additionally, the overall risk of the entire portfolio can be reviewed and compared to other possible portfolios. (Sections 15.4 & 15.7)

9 - What caveats should the portfolio manager be aware of in creating the portfolio?
Not enough information becomes too much information rather quickly. Being inundated in charts and graphs is a real danger. The portfolio needs to have a wide circulation in the company to include as many viewpoints and inputs as possible. The portfolio manager must also consider all dimensions of scarce resources; neglecting the impact of the portfolio on one scarce resource could lead to problems. The portfolio manager must keep in mind the company's long and short term objectives and balance the portfolio accordingly. (Chapter 15)

Chapter 16

1 - Name five of the biggest reasons why implementation of a decision analysis process within an organization might be difficult or even fail.

- Lack of decision maker support
- Lack of process resources or under-estimating the resources required
- Lack of training
- Lack of time commitment
- Selecting the wrong test project (Section 16.1)

3 - How can using outside decision analysis consultants aid in the implementation of the decision analysis process within the organization?

- By training and coaching of the internal decision analysis personnel
- By providing decision analysis process expertise
- By facilitating the first project
- By training the decision makers
- By providing further recommendation for training or other resources that might be useful. (Section 16.1)

5 - What are five characteristics you should look for when selecting the "right" first test project to use the decision analysis process on?

- The project is important to the organization,
- is not too difficult to solve,
- has a high degree of uncertainty and / or ambiguity,
- is not merely validation of an already-made decision, and
- can be communicated to the whole organization. (Section 16.1)

7 - What is the Decision Analysis Affinity Group (DAAG)?
The Decision Analysis Affinity Group (DAAG) is a multi-industry group of decision analysis practitioners who get together once a year to share ideas, successes, and failures. Industries represented include oil and gas, pharmaceutical, utilities, heavy manufacturing, automotive, and chemical. (Chapter Introduction)

9 - As mentioned, the examples in this book are simplified. Real world problems can be full of complexity, politics, hidden agendas, and emotional biases. What can you do as a decision analyst to effectively deal with these further complications?

- Allocate enough time to solve the problems
- Keep the decision maker and leadership team apprised as the process unfolds
- Use peer reviews and third parties to review the decision analysis
- Seek external consultant assistance
- Set up training for those who might not be as familiar with the process or train them yourself. (Chapter 16)

About the Author

David Skinner is the Chief Executive Officer of Decision Strategies, Inc. (DSI) and an original founder of the company. He works with senior executives and Boards to address decision-making processes, organizational change management, and development of game-changing business strategies. David Skinner is frequently an invited guest speaker at international conferences, contributes to numerous books and papers, and is on the faculty of Rice University where he teaches decision analysis in the EMBA program. David has taught over 7,500 people at universities, major corporations, and governments around the world.

Prior to founding and then merging The Institute for Organizational Effectiveness with DSI in 1999, Mr. Skinner was the Group Leader for Decision and Risk Analysis at Conoco, at that time the petroleum subsidiary of the DuPont Company. At Conoco, he led and participated in the economic evaluation of Upstream, Downstream, and Midstream projects and helped several business units develop long-term strategies. He played a major role in implementing decision analysis methodology across the company.

David has a Bachelor of Science in finance, a Bachelor of Science in administration, and an M.B.A. Additionally, he has done post-graduate work at Harvard University's School of Public Health.

Mr. Skinner is listed in the Who's Who of Executives and Professionals. He is a member of The Institute for Operations Research and the Management Sciences, The Society for Risk Analysis, The Decision Sciences Institute, and the Society of Judgment and Decision Making. Mr. Skinner has served as Chairman of the Decision Analysis Affinity Group, and as a Session Chairman for The Institute for Operations Research and the Management Sciences.

David, his wife Kristen, and daughter Mackenzie live in League City (near Houston), Texas.

Index